Globalization and Economic Development

Globalization and Economic Development

Essays in Honour of J. George Waardenburg

Edited by

Servaas Storm

Erasmus University Rotterdam and Delft University of Technology, The Netherlands

C.W.M. Naastepad

Delft University of Technology and Utrecht University, The Netherlands

Edward Elgar

Cheltenham, UK • Northampton, MA, USA

Published by
Edward Elgar Publishing Limited
Glensanda House
Montpellier Parade
Cheltenham
Glos GL50 1UA
UK

Edward Elgar Publishing, Inc.
136 West Street
Suite 202
Northampton
Massachusetts 01060
USA

A catalogue record for this book is available from the British Library

Library of Congress Cataloguing in Publication Data

Globalization and economic development : essays in Honour of J. George Waardenburg / edited by Servaas Storm, C.W.M. Naastepad.
   p. cm.
Includes bibliographical references and index.
   1. International economic relations.   2. Globalization.   3. Economic development.   4. Waardenburg, J. George.   I. Storm, Servaas.
II. Naastepad, C.W.M., 1961–

HF1359.G58177   2001
338.9—dc21   2001023595

ISBN 1 84064 693 4

Printed and bound in Great Britain by MPG Books Ltd, Bodmin, Cornwall

Contents

v

Figures

Boxes

Tables

Contributors

Irma Adelman is Emeritus Professor of Economics, University of California, Berkeley, USA.

Amit Bhaduri is Professor of Economics, Centre for Economic Studies and Planning, School of Social Sciences, Jawaharlal Nehru University, New Delhi, India.

Lalita Chakravarty is former Fellow of the Nehru Memorial Museum and Library, New Delhi, India.

Sukhamoy Chakravarty (1934–1990) was Professor of Economics, Delhi School of Economics, India.

John H. Dunning is Professor of International Business, Rutgers University, Newark, USA.

Roger van Hoesel is a Consultant at Rijnconsult, Velp, The Netherlands.

Gopal K. Kadekodi is Professor of Economics, Centre for Multi-Disciplinary Research, Dharwar, India.

Hans Linnemann is Emeritus Professor of Agricultural and Development Economics, Free University of Amsterdam, The Netherlands.

C.W.M. (Ro) Naastepad is Associate Professor of Economics at Delft University of Technology and Utrecht University, The Netherlands.

Song Byung Nak is the Vice Chancellor of Seoul National University, Seoul, Korea.

Mihir K. Rakshit is Emeritus Professor of Economics, Indian Statistical Institute, Calcutta, and Director of the ICRA Project on Money and Finance, ICRA, Calcutta, India.

J. Mohan Rao is Professor of Economics, University of Massachusetts at Amherst, USA.

Jørn Rattsø is Professor of Economics, Norwegian University of Science and Technology, Trondheim, Norway.

xi

Ashwani Saith is Professor of Rural Development, The Institute of Social Studies, Den Haag, The Netherlands, and Professor of Development Studies, London School of Economics, UK.

Frances Stewart is the Director of the International Development Centre and Professor of Development Economics, Oxford University, UK.

Servaas Storm is Research Fellow, Erasmus University Rotterdam and Delft University of Technology, The Netherlands.

Lance Taylor is Arnhold Professor of Economics, New School for Social Research, New York, USA.

831
(J.G. Waardenburg)

BK Title:

Foreword

In 1954 the then Queen of The Netherlands gave, in the city of Leyden, an address to an audience of young citizens urging them to consider the world's future development as a common responsibility of us all. Queen Juliana was deeply convinced of the need to improve the socio-economic conditions in the countries of what came to be known as the Third World. A freshman of the University of Leyden, by the name of J. George Waardenburg, had just started his study in the department of mathematics and physics. He may or may not have been present in the Queen's audience, but her message must have reached him anyhow.

Rumour has it that in preparing her address the Queen consulted Prof. Jan Tinbergen, who had started at the Netherlands Economic Institute in Rotterdam in the same year, 1954, a new research unit focusing on the development problem: the Division of Balanced International Growth (BIG). When George graduated in mathematics at Leyden University in 1961, to whom could he better turn for advice on future work on the development issue than Jan Tinbergen – himself, too, a graduate in mathematics and physics of the same university. After his compulsory military service, George Waardenburg was appointed as Research Associate at BIG, and for further study seconded to MIT and Stanford University in the US. Upon return, he worked at BIG, and was appointed in 1967 as Assistant Professor at the Centre for Development Planning of The Netherlands School of Economics (now incorporated in the Erasmus University Rotterdam).

In his teaching and research, Waardenburg focused initially on topics such as mathematics for development planning and regional and interregional planning (Waardenburg, 1975). These subjects also constitute the hard core of a volume that he co-authored with Mennes and Tinbergen: *The Element of Space in Development Planning* (1969). His activities were not limited to these academic duties, however; right from the start, Waardenburg took an active interest in broader issues of development policy. To mention one example: he was one of the principal authors of a report prepared for the largest protestant church in The Netherlands, in which a strong plea was made for enhanced support and commitment to the national effort in development assistance.

xiii

In the course of the 1970s, George Waardenburg widened the scope of his research and teaching – on the one hand by delving more deeply into the particulars of individual socio-economic sectors (such as small industry, housing and health), and on the other by paying in applied research special attention to the Asian context: India, China and South Korea. Waardenburg's earlier work on regional planning stimulated his interest in the rural–urban dimension of the economic development process, with a particular concern for employment. He became convinced that the *urban* industrial sectors of developing countries would never be able to productively absorb the large and growing *rural* labour surplus, however rapid the urban industrial sector would grow. This explains his interest in the scope for rural non-agricultural employment generation (Waardenburg, 1988a, 1988b). He supervised a number of PhD theses in this area, including Wickramanayake (1988), Tambunan (1994) and Eapen (1999). It also explains his interest in matters of technology choice (Waardenburg, 1988b, 1993; and PhD theses by Piek, 1998; and Lal, 2000) and in international research cooperation as a means to further economic development (Lavakare and Waardenburg, 1989; Waardenburg, 1989, 1988c).

The late 1970s and the 1980s brought new tasks and responsibilities. George Waardenburg was appointed to a full professorship in development planning at Erasmus University and played a major role in the newly established research body focusing on economic and social development in India, to which he gave its name: the Indo-Dutch Programme on Alternatives in Development (IDPAD). Regular contacts with his eminent Indian colleague and close personal friend, the late Professor Sukhamoy Chakravarty, no doubt provided a further stimulus in this direction. Waardenburg became actively involved in Dutch development policy. For five years, until 1984, he chaired the (national) Advisory Council on Development Research. Two years later, he was to become chairman again, now of the Commission for Consultation of Sector Councils. A number of articles and papers from his hand appeared in this period, some on topics mentioned earlier and some on his new field of activity: R&D and research policy. He co-edited two volumes, *Science Policy in International Perspective* (1989) and *A Dual World Economy: Forty Years of Development Experience* (1992).

In the early 1990s, George accepted the offer to become the Chief Scientist for Development Cooperation at the Ministry of Foreign Affairs in The Hague, a new position created by the then Minister of Development Cooperation, Jan Pronk. While continuing his association with Erasmus University, at the Ministry George took it as his task to bridge the world of academia and policy as well as between 'the North' and 'the South' by actively involving scientists, in particular from developing countries, in the design and implementation of development cooperation. An important reason for him to accept this position must have been the stimulating personality of the Minister for Development Cooperation himself, Jan Pronk, an old friend and colleague at the Division BIG and the Centre for Development Planning. In 1993, Waardenburg was elected Vice-Chairman of the United Nations Commission on Science and Technology for Development and in 1995 became its Chairman. Thanks to his intimate knowledge of the social and economic structure of India, he became actively involved in a collaboration project with the Indian Planning Commission, which aimed to develop new models to support policy formulation in the more liberal environment of the 1990s.

Ties with the Erasmus University were maintained throughout, and Waardenburg remained actively involved in some of the tasks of the Centre for Development Planning. For one thing, he continued his role as thesis supervisor of the Centre's research associates, some of them coming from developing countries (for example, Weixin, 1992; Lal, 2000), some from The Netherlands (for example, Terhal, 1988; van Hoesel, 1999). Two of the latter should be mentioned here explicitly: Servaas Storm (1993) and Ro Naastepad (1999). Together with two other former PhD students, Hannah Piek and Roger van Hoesel, these two former students of his, took the laudable initiative to invite a number of George's colleagues from all over the world to contribute to a *Festschrift* in his honour on the occasion of his retirement. The result of this endeavour is the present volume.

In his research and teaching, and as a policy-maker, George has always deliberately articulated the developing country perspective, rather than (as is common practice) reiterating the dominating views of donor governments and/or the international financial institutions. He has always regarded his own role as one of building bridges between (social science) researchers and policy-makers in the North and the South, keeping to Chakravarty's dictum that 'either we unite or we explode'. The papers in this volume testify to George's important role in furthering North–South understanding.

Retirement? Yes! Dutch law is very strict regarding the retirement age of civil servants, and of those treated likewise such as academic staff. So, when George on 10 July 1999 reached the age of 65 he legally passed a threshold – marking both an end and a beginning. Experience teaches us that in academic life the crossing of the age line does not change one's life overnight. The pressure on the daily schedule is only gradually reduced, and it takes some time before the backlog of unfinished jobs melts away. But then, new opportunities for fruitful activity arise, within one's profession or in other areas. Far from being a tragic event, retirement opens up a new phase in life with formerly unexpected possibilities. After a very busy life, filled to overflowing with all sorts of tasks and obligations to which he attended with utmost devotion and care, one wishes George Waardenburg wholeheartedly many gratifying years in good health in his new status of Professor Emeritus!

Hans Linnemann

REFERENCES

Adriaansen, W.L.M. and J.G. Waardenburg (eds) (1992), *A Dual World Economy: Forty Years of Development Experience*, Delhi: Oxford University Press.

Eapen, Mridul (1999), *Rural Industrialisation in Kerala. Its Dynamics and Local Linkages*, PhD Dissertation, Rotterdam: Erasmus University Rotterdam.

Hoesel, Roger van (1999), *New Multinational Enterprises from Korea and Taiwan: Beyond Export-Led Growth*, London: Routledge.

Lal, Kaushalesh (2000), *Adoption of Information Technology and Its Consequences in a Development Context*, Amsterdam: Thela Publishers.

Lavakare, P.J. and J.G. Waardenburg (eds) (1989), *Science Policy in International Perspective: The Experience of India and the Netherlands*, London: Pinter.

Mennes, L.B.M., J. Tinbergen and J.G. Waardenburg (1969), *The Element of Space in Development Planning*, Amsterdam: North-Holland.

Naastepad, C.W.M. (1999), *The Budget Deficit and Macroeconomic Performance. A Real-Financial Computable General Equilibrium Model for India*, Oxford: Oxford University Press.

Piek, Hannah (1998), *Technology Development in Rural Industries: A Study of China's Collectives*, London: IT Publishers.

Storm, Servaas (1993), *Macroeconomic Considerations in the Choice of an Agricultural Policy. A Study into Sectoral Interdependence with Reference to India*, Aldershot: Avebury.

Tambunan, Tulus (1994), *The Role of Small-Scale Industries in Rural Economic Development: The Case of Ciomas Subdistrict, Bogor District, West Java, Indonesia*, Rotterdam: Erasmus University Rotterdam.

Terhal, Piet (1988), *World Inequality and Evolutionary Convergence*, Delft: Eburon.

Waardenburg, J. George (1975), 'Regional disaggregation of national development planning: A framework' in A. Kuklinski (ed), *Regional Disaggregation of National Policies and Plans*, Paris: Mouton, pp. 159–212.

Waardenburg, J. George (1976), 'De rol van de gezondheidszorg in een proces van economische ontwikkeling' (Healthcare and economic development: A simulation model), in H.A. Becker (ed), *Simulatie in de Sociale Wetenschappen*, Alphen a/d Rijn: Samson.

Waardenburg, J. George (1988a), 'Small-scale leather shoemaking in Agra: a case study in small-scale industry in India's development', in K.B. Suri (ed), *Small-Scale Enterprises in Industrial Development: The Indian Experience*, New Delhi: Sage.

Waardenburg, J. George (1988b), *De Rurale Industrieen van India en China als*

Elementen van Ontwikkeling (*The Rural Industries of India and China as Elements of Development*), inaugural address, Rotterdam: Erasmus University Rotterdam.

Waardenburg, J. George (1988c), 'Cooperation in social research: Alternatives in development', in P. de Waart and E. Denters (eds), *International Law and Development*, Dordrecht: Martinus Nijhoff.

Waardenburg, J. George (1989), 'International R&D cooperation in a North–South perspective: Some theoretical and practical issues', in P.J. Lavakare and J.G. Waardenburg (eds) (1989), *Science Policy in International Perspective*.

Waardenburg, J. George (1993), 'Small-scale units in the Agra leather footwear industry', in I.S.A. Baud and G.A. de Bruijne (eds), *Gender, Small-Scale Industry and Development Policy*, London: IT Publications.

Weixin, Huang (1992), *Economic Integration as a Development Device: The Case of the EC and China*, Saarbruecken: Breitenbach.

Wickramanayake, B.W.E. (1988), *Rural Industries in Transition: A Case Study of Southern Sri Lanka*, PhD Thesis, Rotterdam: Erasmus University Rotterdam.

Acknowledgements

One of the pleasures of editing this *Festschrift* for J. George Waardenburg has been the warmth of the response – from so many people, in so many parts of the world – to all our requests for contributions, advice and assistance. We thank Roger van Hoesel and Hannah Piek for their input during the preparatory stage of the project, Hans Linnemann for writing the foreword, and Lalita Chakravarty for permission to publish the (hitherto unpublished) lecture on dynamic methods in economics by Sukhamoy Chakravarty, given at Erasmus University in April 1990.

The editors
Rotterdam, October 2000

1. Development: Not by globalization alone

Servaas Storm and C.W.M. Naastepad

1. INTRODUCTION

The process of global economic integration has sharply altered the context in which most governments are thinking about policies for economic development. Indeed, in many developing economies, traditional developmental concerns relating to industrialization, employment generation and poverty have lost priority relative to the pursuit of international competitiveness (Rodrik, 1999). In response, mainstream economic theorizing, as usual following in the footsteps of (the changed) political reality, has formulated an intellectual rationale for globalization that is almost prescriptive. Thus, globalization is perceived as a means of ensuring not only efficiency and growth, but also equity and development for countries that join the global system, while bringing economic deprivation to countries that do not (Sachs and Warner, 1995; World Bank, 1999). However, the chapters contributed to this book argue that this view of globalization as the road to development has lost its lustre, as the development experience during the 1990s belied expectations of the gains from external integration in terms of faster growth, greater employment opportunities and reduced levels of poverty. Moreover, the downside risks of globalization have proved to be far greater than was generally expected, as was demonstrated by the Asian and Latin American crises. Against the background of this experience, this introductory chapter analyses the implications of globalization for strategies of development. Section 2 discusses the distinguishing features of the recent wave of globalization for the developing world. Section 3 briefly outlines the mainstream view of liberalization and globalization as a means to achieve both growth and equity. Focusing on developing countries and offering a range of perspectives, the contributing authors in this book provide a thorough review of the theoretical arguments underlying and the empirical evidence in support of the mainstream view of globalization. Section 4 outlines the structure of the book and takes

1

a tour through the chapters to identify their main substantive findings as well as the most important issues of continuing debate. Taken together, as Section 5 concludes, the chapters argue that, given the reality of globalization, it is necessary to think of correctives and interventions in national development strategies that would make for a more egalitarian development.

2. CONTOURS OF GLOBALIZATION IN THE DEVELOPING WORLD

What is globalization? Following Baker, Epstein and Pollin (1998), globalization entails a significant step-up in the level of economic interaction between different countries, leading to a qualitative shift in the relationship between nation-states and (national and international) markets. This increased economic interaction is the result of the increased pressure on firms – by consumers and competitors alike – to continually innovate, as the escalating costs of research and development, coupled with ever shortening product life cycles, compel firms to search for wider markets (Dunning, Chapter 10 this book). It has been made possible by a decline in the barriers that inhibit international trade, investment and finance on two accounts. First, the technological revolution in transport, communications and information technology has significantly reduced the costs of international transactions (UNDP, 1999). Second, globalization has been made possible by the liberalization of trade, Foreign Direct Investment (FDI) and foreign capital flows (UNCTAD, 1999a; Nayyar, 2000; Rao, Chapter 3 this book). Empirical evidence for developing countries indicates that there has indeed been a marked acceleration in economic interaction during the last quarter of the twentieth century, which is manifested in a sizeable increase in the importance of international trade, investment and finance. It is worth highlighting the characteristics of these changes.

Trade data show that an increasing proportion of developing country output is being channelled into world trade. Gross trade flows (that is, the sum of exports and imports), which are a better measure of trade integration than net flows (that is, the trade deficit) because they show the total value of transactions during a given period, increased from 24 per cent of gross domestic product (GDP) of all low-income countries in 1980 to 37 per cent in 1998. Excluding China and India, the ratio increased from 48 per cent in 1980 to 57 per cent in 1998 (World Bank, 2000). The increased trade integration reflects both rapid export and import growth. For all low-income countries, the ratio of exports (imports) to GDP increased from 12 (12) per cent in 1980 to 19 (18) per cent in 1998, implying only a small (one percentage point) rise in the trade deficit. However, excluding China and India, the developing country trade deficit in 1998 was higher than in 1980 by almost 5 percentage points of GDP (see UNCTAD, 1999a). Net trade flows to developing countries other than China and India have therefore also significantly increased, which is a euphemism for the fact that their payments disorders remain as acute as ever.[1] In addition to these quantitative changes in trade flows, the nature of trade integration has also changed, as the share of intra-firm trade in world trade, which was one-fifth in the early 1970s, rose to one-third in the early 1990s (UNCTAD, 1999a; Dunning, this book). Multinational enterprises (MNEs) are often conduits for this intra-industry trade (UNCTAD, 1999b). At the same time, however, a larger share of developing country exports is being produced by the small-scale industrial sector (see Saith, Chapter 15 this book). In sum, indicators based on international flows of goods point to increased trade integration. In contrast, price indicators show that markets are not converging toward a single world price for a given product; in particular, the law of one price does not hold as between rich and poor countries (Baker et al., 1998; Rao, this book). This is due to the great unevenness in trade integration (due to MNEs' monopoly power), the presence of tariff and non-tariff barriers to trade and the existence of regional trading blocs (Rao, this book; Nayyar, 2000).

The closing decades of the twentieth century also witnessed a significant upturn in economic interaction between countries in terms of FDI flows. Between 1980 and 1997, the stock of (inward) FDI in the developing countries as a proportion of their GDP rose from less than 5.9 per cent to 16.6 per cent (UNCTAD, 1999b). Inward FDI flows as proportion of developing country gross fixed capital formation rose from 3.9 per cent during 1987–92 to 10.3 per cent in 1997. Developing countries, particularly from Asia (see Dunning, this book; van Hoesel, Chapter 11 this book), are also increasingly engaging in outward FDI: outward direct investment as a proportion of gross fixed capital formation in developing countries increased from 1.4 per cent during 1987–92 to 3.9 per cent in 1997. But such global integration in terms of FDI flows is a highly selective process. During 1990–97, 10 developing countries accounted for more than three-quarters of total FDI inflows of developing countries; China, Brazil and Mexico alone accounted for almost half of the total inflow; and per capita FDI inflows in sub-Saharan Africa were under US$5 a year compared with US$62 in Latin America and US$31 in Asean (UNCTAD, 1999a). Africa's low share in global FDI flows reinforces the foreign exchange constraint on its development (Rattsø, Chapter 4 this book). It is further worthy of note that, during 1990–97, only 30 per cent of FDI inflows to developing countries (excluding China) consisted of additions to a country's real capital stock, while the remaining 70 per cent was resources utilized for mergers and acquisitions, largely in non-tradeable services (UNCTAD, 1999a). MNEs are responsible for a large and increasing proportion of the FDI inflows to developing countries (UNCTAD, 1999b; Dunning, this book).

To many, the defining characteristic of present-day globalization is the increased integration of many developing countries into the global financial system (IMF, 1999). To clarify matters, it is necessary to distinguish between gross capital flows and net flows. In terms of net financial resource transfers between countries, the evidence of financial globalization is surprisingly weak. As shown by the United Nations Conference on Trade and Development (UNCTAD, 1999a) data, the upsurge in net private capital flows in the 1990s represents no more than a return to trend after the depression years of the 1980s. The annual net capital inflow in the 1990s was around 5 per cent of GNP, which was about the level in 1975–82. While the average level of net capital inflows in the 1990s did not change as compared to the late 1970s, the composition of these inflows changed dramatically. First, official development assistance has steadily declined, falling in real terms in 1998 to its lowest level for many years (see Stewart, Chapter 9 this book). Consequently, the share of official financing in total capital inflows of developing countries fell from over 50 per cent in the 1980s to 20 per cent in the 1990s, implying a rapid expansion of *private* capital flows into developing countries. But it should be noted that these private capital flows have increasingly become concentrated in a select group of developing countries, prominently featuring China, Brazil, Mexico and Indonesia (more on this below). Second, unlike in the earlier period, when private inflows represented long-term bank lending, the largest capital inflows in the 1990s have been short-term loans and portfolio equity. Such short-term flows are driven by international arbitrage opportunities arising from large international interest-rate differentials and by prospects of short-term capital gains. However, while net financial flows have not grown substantially, gross capital flows have grown spectacularly (IMF, 1999). There has been a great expansion of international lending and an explosion of secondary market trading in stock, bond, foreign exchange and derivative markets since the emergence of deregulated domestic financial markets. Global foreign exchange transactions have soared, from $60 billion per day in 1983 to $1500 billion per day in 1997. By comparison, in 1997 world GDP was $82 billion per day and world exports $16 billion per day, while the foreign exchange reserves of all central banks put together amounted to $1550 billion (Nayyar, 2000). The growth in international finance has been explosive, so much so that, in terms of magnitude, trade and investment are now dwarfed by finance (Michie and Grieve-Smith, 1999). But, again, financial integration has been highly selective: over 90 per cent of net private capital inflows was received by only 20 countries during the 1990s, as compared with 50 per cent during the 1970s and 1980s (UNCTAD, 1999a).[2]

Considering the empirical evidence, there certainly has been an acceleration of integration according to a range of measures. Trade flows, FDI flows and gross capital flows to developing countries have all grown substantially. But – as yet – the spread of globalization is very uneven and selective, both among people and across countries (UNDP, 1999; Stewart and Berry, 2000). The changes in international trade, investment and finance have further moved new players to centre-stage, in particular the MNEs, which dominate investment, production and trade in the global economy, and international banks or financial intermediaries, which control world finance (UNCTAD, 1999a,b; Nayyar, 2000). These new players are changing the rules of the game, enabling them to manage the risks associated with globalization. In their attempt to achieve this, they receive much-needed support from the governments of the industrialized world (UNCTAD, 1999a). The multilateral framework of the World Trade Organization (WTO), the International Monetary Fund (IMF) and the World Bank is – as argued by Stewart (this book), Pieper and Taylor (1998), and Nayyar (2000) – the most important medium.

The rules of the game for the international trading system are being progressively set in the WTO. Adherence to WTO rules, which are much stricter in terms of law and its implementation than the earlier General Agreement on Tariffs and Trade (GATT) rules, implies the loss of most instruments of commercial trade policy (Adelman and Yeldan, 2000; Storm, Chapter 13 this book). Developing countries that are late-comers to industrialization can no longer strategically use tariffs and quotas or sector-specific subsidies to climb the ladder of comparative advantage. They can no longer increase the effective exchange rate for exports through subsidized allocation of scarce resources (such as credit or foreign exchange) because the effective exchange rate must be the same for exports and imports and must be uniform across sectors. WTO members can also not grant exporters virtual monopoly in the domestic market (for fear of being accused of dumping) and cannot impose export targets on firms (for the same reason). The WTO's tight system for the protection of intellectual property rights might stifle the development of domestic technological capabilities (UNDP, 1999; UNCTAD, 1999a). And the proposed multilateral agreement on investment (MAI) would almost certainly reduce the possibilities of strategic bargaining with MNEs. Thus, by virtue of GATT/WTO, the major instruments that developing countries retain are the macro-economic ones, of exchange rate devaluation, setting economy-wide interest rates and wage repression. It is true that, under GATT/WTO, countries can carry out direct government investment in specific sectors and/or court certain foreign investments. They can also continue to generate externalities by investing in public education, research and infrastructure. But despite these options the ability of developing countries to induce a structural transformation of their economies into higher-productivity activities has become severely curtailed – even without free short-term capital movements (Adelman and Yeldan, 2000).

The IMF and the World Bank set the rules for borrowing countries in the developing world and in the transitional economies (Rakshit, Chapter 8 this book). The loan conditionality is meant, in principle, to ensure repayment, but in practice it imposes conditions to serve the interest of international banks which lend to these countries (Pieper and Taylor, 1998). In doing so, the IMF's programmes of stabilization and the World Bank's programmes of structural adjustment impose conditions stipulating the structural reform of policy regimes. Commitments to structural reform inevitably require industrial deregulation, privatization, and trade and financial liberalization. Their objective is to raise growth and efficiency by increasing the degree of openness and reducing the role of the state in these economies. From our perspective, the essential reforms include the liberalization of trade and foreign investment, the deregulation of the domestic financial sector and the introduction of capital account covertibility on the balance-of-payments capital account. Due to the liberalization of foreign capital flows, traditional macro-economic policy instruments (interest rates, government expenditure and tax rates, and exchange rates) have lost much – if not all – of their effectiveness. Thus, raising interest rates above world market levels – as in South Korea during the early 1990s (see Adelman and Nak, Chapter 5 this book) – triggers a large foreign capital inflow. This often contributes to an exchange rate appreciation, a consequent loss of international competitiveness and a rise in the trade deficit, which, at some stage, undermines foreign confidence in the strength of the currency and hence results in capital outflows. The end result may be – as is argued by Bhaduri (Chapter 7 this book), Rakshit (this book) and Taylor (Chapter 12 this book) – a financial crisis, once the exchange rate tumbles, capital flight escalates, real estate prices and stock markets crash, the corporate sector becomes illiquid and a depression develops. Conversely, setting interest rates below world markets immediately triggers a large capital outflow, precipitating the start of the crisis. Likewise, running a fiscal deficit to stimulate growth (see Naastepad, Chapter 6 this book) or to provide social protection to the poor in times of distress (see Chakravarty, Chapter 14 this book), causes capital flight, as domestic actors fear inflation and international actors fear devaluation. This may again set the stage for a subsequent financial crisis. Finally, setting the exchange rate below its perceived equilibrium level will induce capital flight abroad, eventually producing a financial crisis. Setting the exchange rate too high (overvaluation), on the other hand, leads to a current account deficit which may undermine confidence in the country's currency and start the process described above (Grabel, 1999). It follows that developing countries with open and unregulated capital markets are severely constrained in the extent to which their governments can further development. Developing-country governments are left with economic responsibilities without proper instruments they can control (Taylor, this book).

3. GLOBALIZATION AS THE ROAD TO DEVELOPMENT

Many developing countries were prompted to globalize their economies by the fiscal and balance-of-payments crises of the early 1980s, caused by the dramatic rise in real interest rates and the sharp adverse movement in the external terms of trade (Rao, this book). For many, the crisis was final proof that indigenous inward-oriented growth strategies and interventionist (trade) policies were not effective in helping developing countries to escape from poverty and underdevelopment. Thus, in the second half of the 1980s and early 1990s, a powerful consensus was forged around an alternative, liberal policy agenda, centred on a fast and close integration into the world economy through rapid liberalization of trade, investment and finance (Pieper and Taylor, 1998; UNCTAD, 1999a). This policy agenda, reflecting the so-called Washington Consensus, rests on two arguments (see Rao, this book). First, governments are incapable of intervening efficiently, because they lack adequate information and/or are liable to be captured by special interest groups. Political discipline is best secured by integrating the domestic market completely with global markets (see Rakshit, this book). Second, free markets optimize national welfare, assuming that: (1) markets can fully coordinate individual decisions (for example, produce full employment); (2) distributional problems can be resolved, if they must be, without 'distorting' the market; (3) complementarities between public and private investment are absent; and (4) the unhindered import of technology can provide an adequate basis for developing competitiveness. Based on these assumptions, it is argued (World Bank, 1999) that the lowering of tariffs and the consequent relative price changes will ensure the best allocation of resources according to comparative advantage, securing the export revenues needed to import key ingredients of faster growth.[3] Trade liberalization will further discipline domestic firms (reducing the distortions created by monopoly power) and raise firm productivity by providing access to up-to-date technology. A bigger inflow of FDI would accelerate growth not only by supplementing domestic resources for capital accumulation, but also through transfer of technology and organizational skills. Financial liberalization would attract foreign capital seeking high returns in these capital-scarce countries of the South, allowing them to invest more than they save without running into a balance-of-payments deficit (IMF, 1999).

While governments and international institutions promoting globalization justified liberalization in terms of the visible increases in economic efficiency and growth that it was supposed to bring, they were less explicit about its distributional and poverty consequences. This is noted in a recent external review of IMF programmes (Collier and Gunning, 1999), which argues that adjustment programmes have often been seriously flawed by a lack of distributional analysis. Notwithstanding this lack of attention, the predominant view is that globalization is good for the poor. The reasoning is that: (1) globalization leads to higher income growth, at least in the medium to long run (World Bank, 1999; Frankel and Romer, 1999); (2) in per capita terms, the real income gains due to the consequent employment growth more than outweigh the income losses due to real wage erosion and reduced social expenditures (Winters, 1999; Collier and Gunning, 1999); and (3) the poor benefit from the per capita income growth to the same extent as the whole economy (Dollar and Kraay, 2000). However, even if there are adverse transitional effects on poverty and distribution, these can be cushioned by social policies; and in any case, after some time they will be outweighed by more rapid income growth, triggered by the external liberalization.

Market-led, close integration into the world economy thus seemed to promise an alternative to government-led development planning, discredited by the 1980s debt crisis, and it provided the inspiration for widespread policy reform – often with the help of the Bretton Woods institutions. The growth of world trade and, perhaps even more decisively, the recovery of financial flows to developing countries in the 1990s were taken as confirmation that a new era of economic prosperity was beginning to unfold and that it would include a growing number of developing countries (UNCTAD, 1999a). Indeed, in this view, to induce economic development, developing countries only had to jump on the global bandwagon by eliminating all impediments in the way of integrating their domestic economies with global trade and financial flows (Sachs and Warner, 1995; Rao, this book). However, of late the Washington Consensus view of globalization as the road to development has lost its lustre as the development experience during the 1990s has belied its expectations. Its prescriptions are now subject to questions; and the questions have not come from the critics alone (Stiglitz, 1998; Rodrik, 1999).

4. OUTLINE OF THIS BOOK

We have tried to make clear that globalization exists as a process, however selective, of increasing international resource and goods flows, resulting from changes in technology and in policy regimes. These policy shifts have been justified in neo-liberal (Washington Consensus) terms as providing the best means to development. Focusing on developing countries and offering a broad spectrum of perspectives, the chapters contributed to this book challenge this mainstream view of globalization.

Part I, Globalization, Instability and Path Dependence, sets the stage – analysing the effects on growth and stability of developing countries of the Washington Consensus policies. It opens with a (hitherto unpublished) lecture on dynamic methods in economics (given in 1990) by the late Professor Sukhamoy Chakravarty. Although the lecture is not concerned with globalization, Chakravarty – in his re-interpretation of the Frisch–Tinbergen revolution in economic dynamics – discusses theoretical concepts which, in our view, are fundamental to the study of contemporary global capitalism. First, Chakravarty evaluates the concepts of 'equilibrium' and 'structural stability'. In Frisch's dynamical systems theoretic approach, equilibrium presupposes that adjustment processes are heavily dampened, that is, once perturbed, the (economic) system reaches a new equilibrium so quickly that, in describing the adjustment, any explicit reference to time can be eliminated. But like Frisch, Chakravarty does not think that this realistically represents the workings of contemporary capitalism. In his view, while real-life economic processes do only very rarely show anti-dampened behaviour (for example, explosive and/or exponential growth), they generally tend to be *slowly* dampened, often generating sustained oscillations (for example, business cycles) in response to exogenous shocks. A system is called structurally stable if small perturbations of its coefficients do not shift the system in a dampened or anti-dampened direction, but result in sustained oscillations. It follows that structural stability rather than equilibrium is the relevant concept in analysing the behaviour of the capitalist system. The second fundamental concept highlighted by Chakravarty is that of structural change (or mutations within capitalism). The importance of structural change lies in the fact that, in response to exogenous impulses, the capitalist system neither settles down at some equilibrium position, nor does it break down, but rather it survives by transforming its structure over time. Hence, the explanation of the evolution of a capitalist system over time cannot be separated from the analysis of the accompanying changes in its structure. Insights from evolutionary economics as well as chaotic dynamics indicate that the nature and pace of this structural change of a given system is extremely sensitive to initial conditions, that is, it is strongly *path-dependent*. This, in conjunction with the possible structural instability of the economic system, has important consequences for economic policy, because it is no longer possible to identify precise and universally 'optimal' government interventions, effective in realizing given policy goals. Rather, in Chakravarty's view, the attempt should be to identify possible corridors of action which are effective – given (initial) circumstances.

The notions of structural stability and path dependence are important for the understanding of contemporary globalization. This becomes clear from reading Chapter 3 by J. Mohan Rao, who subjects to scrutiny the proposition that increased global economic integration leads to a convergence in national living standards. This proposition follows from neoclassical theory which predicts that increased trade will result in the equalization of prices of both goods and factors across countries. Based on a sample of 123 countries, Rao's statistical analysis rejects the proposition that there was (absolute) convergence of per capita incomes across countries during 1960–92, but cannot reject the hypothesis that there was growth divergence. This divergence suggests that, in Chakravarty's terms, the process of globalization is structurally unstable. Likewise, contrary to the trend toward apparent global integration, Rao finds that the law of one price seems to have grown progressively less valid. While several theories, including convergence club theory, contingent convergence theory and new growth theory, try to rationalize this lack of income and price convergence, none of these offers developing countries a way out of the malaise of continuously lagging behind. The only ones who offer the developing countries a handle to reverse the process are the protagonists of globalization, who argue that the failure of convergence of living standards is due to the failure of nations to join the global system. But Rao shows that their claim is not robust. First, he argues that the protagonists of globalization have their causality wrong: income convergence produces external market integration (automatically and by inducing policy change), not the other way around. Second, old, new and new-political-economy trade theories can explain only modest gains from trade liberalization and – conversely – do not therefore provide much support for the claim that illiberal trade regimes explain the failure of living standards to converge. What then can explain nonconvergence? Rao puts forward two hypotheses, each one of which underscores the importance of *initial conditions* in explaining historical processes. First, international economic integration is constrained by (MNE) monopoly power in commodity and technology markets and the imperfect mobility of capital; the result is global market fragmentation. Second, the potential for international arbitrage gains is small, because productivity differentials across economies cannot be bridged by trade, technology or capital flows, but require local learning and skill development. Whichever one of the two applies (or combination of the two), the implication is that national economic development within less developed countries (LDCs) must preceed external integration.

That globalization affects an economy's growth and income distribution differently according to initial conditions, is also emphasized by Jørn Rattsø in Chapter 4. Rattsø evaluates the distribution and growth effects of trade liberalization as well as protectionism in the context of sub-Saharan Africa in general and Zimbabwe in particular. In a model assuming underemployment and distinguishing between agriculture/exportables and industry/importables, Rattsø argues that the removal of quota protection to the (final goods) industrial sector does not necessarily shift the economy to a higher-level equilibrium, but brings with it a non-negligible risk of de-industrialization and consequent distributional conflict. De-industrialization may occur if exportables output reacts more slowly to the changed incentive structure than importables production – as happened in Zimbabwe in the 1990s. If so, labour demand in the exportables sector does not increase enough to absorb the excess labour from the importables sector, and hence wages and domestic final demand fall, reducing domestic industrial output. The de-industrializing effect of the quota removal may be augmented further if the new availability of importables reduces private savings, raises demand and hence increases both inflation and the trade deficit – which also happened in Zimbabwe. Rattsø emphasizes that, though the costs of trade liberalization in sub-Saharan Africa cannot be neglected, this should not be taken as an argument to maintain trade protection. In fact, adding productivity dynamics to his model, Rattsø shows that the discrimination of agricultural exports implicit in the industrial/importables protection lowers agricultural output and reduces the economy's foreign exchange generating capacity. This, in turn, compresses import-dependent industrialization from the side of supply and may prevent a growth process based on learning-by-doing in industry from taking off, keeping the economy in a low-level equilibrium. Rattsø's analysis suggests that sub-Saharan African countries are walking an economic tightrope in which they cannot afford to continue their trade protection, but run the risk that too rapid and too comprehensive a liberalization of their trade is contractionary.

The threat to economic development posed by the fundamental instability of global financial markets is illustrated by the recent currency crisis in Asia. The most startling development in this crisis was the collapse of the region's prototypical 'miracle economy', South Korea. The conventional wisdom on the collapse is that the regional crisis exposed the failure of an economy whose strength was based on the corrupt and opaque business practices of family-owned financial-industrial conglomerates (*chaebols*).

But a more careful analysis by Irma Adelman and Song Byung Nak (Chapter 5) reveals that several elements have combined to generate the crisis: Korea's vulnerability to external shocks, both inherent and development strategy-induced; domestic institutional inadequacies, including the highly leveraged private corporate sector and a poorly regulated financial system; the unstable, speculative and excessively liquid nature of the international financial system; domestic policy mistakes, including a high real interest rate policy and premature capital account liberalization; and exogenous external shocks (for example, the loss of export competitiveness *vis-à-vis* Japan in the 1990s and the contagion from the financial crises in Thailand, Indonesia and Malaysia in 1997). Adelman and Nak view Korea's crisis as the result of a fundamental incompatibility between an independent exchange and interest rate policy, which the country tried to pursue, with smoothly functioning, unregulated and unstable global capital markets. Korea's attempt to set the domestic interest rate above world market encouraged (short-term) foreign borrowing, mainly by private banks. Because the foreign loans were dollar-denominated and mostly short term, the solvency of banks and, indirectly, *chaebols*, became very sensitive to foreign confidence in Korea's economic prospects. Its attempt to maintain an overvalued exchange rate, in the absence of restrictions on currency outflows, forced Korea to use foreign exchange reserves to buy foreign currency to prevent a devaluation. But a country's reserves can only be small relative to the volume of global capital flows, and hence, when the massive currency attack on the won started, Korea's attempt to defend its overvalued exchange rate turned out to be futile. According to Adelman and Nak, Korea has been misdiagnosed by the IMF as suffering from over-expansionary fiscal and monetary policies. Consequently, the standard conditionalities imposed (tightening domestic credit further and reducing domestic absorption) seriously misfired, deepening the crisis and delaying the economy's recovery. Unfortunately, Koreans are paying the brunt of the cost of these mistakes, while international banks are getting off more or less scot-free.

Chakravarty's emphasis on the importance of initial conditions and path dependence is again underscored in Chapter 6. C.W.M. (Ro) Naastepad evaluates the rationale of a key element of the Washington Consensus, namely the need to reduce (and eventually remove) government budget deficits in the interest of sustained low-inflationary growth. Naastepad analyses the linkages between the public deficit and the real and the financial sectors of the Indian economy with the help of a multi-period computable general equilibrium (CGE) model. Focusing on credit rather than money, and explicitly analysing the relation between the budget and the credit creation process, the model recognizes the dual role of credit for working

capital and investment, incorporates credit rationing, and allows for endogenous switches between credit-constrained, capacity-constrained and
demand-constrained regimes. Naastepad's analysis shows that, when initial
conditions in credit markets are tight, monetized deficit reductions – the
norm of the Washington Consensus policies – may involve a monetary
squeeze which results in credit rationing. Because credit is used to finance
working capital as well as investment, credit shortages reduce the supply of
goods and services in both the short and medium term. In addition,
because in certain sectors public investment is complementary to private
investment, deficit reductions achieved through a reduced public investment restrict the economy's capacity growth and hence lower supply. When
supply is reduced more than demand, the budget deficit reduction may be
inflationary. Moreover, Naastepad's results indicate that, in a situation of
credit shortage, increased public investment financed by monetization is
expansionary as well as deflationary. Taken together, her analysis shows
that, contrary to the Washington Consensus' claim, public deficit reduction
is *not* universally optimal, and under certain real-financial conditions can
even be harmful to growth, inflation and income distribution. Naastepad's
conclusions support Chakravarty's view that the attempt should be to identify possible corridors of action, which are effective given (initial) circumstances in real and financial markets.

Part II, International Capital Flows, presents analyses of developments
in international capital flows, both private and public, and their implications for economic policy and policy autonomy. How the impact of international capital flows is transmitted to aggregate demand in the domestic
economy of a developing country is analysed by Amit Bhaduri in Chapter
7. Extending Keynes' and Kalecki's closed-economy analysis of aggregate
demand to the context of an open, foreign-exchange-constrained economy,
Bhaduri distinguishes two polar regimes: pure quantity adjustment and
pure price adjustment. In the first regime, and assuming that neither
investment nor savings respond to capital inflows, a higher capital inflow,
by permitting a higher trade deficit, has a contractionary impact on income
– which according to Bhaduri resembles the experience of many African
countries. The impact of a higher capital inflow will be expansionary,
however, when it raises domestic investment more than domestic savings –
as happened in East Asia. Moving next to the other regime of pure price
adjustment, Bhaduri introduces debt-servicing costs in the model, which
enables him to extend the analysis beyond the short term. Higher capital
inflows during the previous period imply higher debt-servicing costs and
hence a larger current account deficit in this period, which is likely to,
directly or indirectly, lead to exchange rate appreciation. If this induces
further capital inflows and currency appreciations, the economy may get

trapped in a process of perverse price adjustment, eventually resulting in a crisis. However, this need not occur if the capital inflow stimulates domestic investment, which mainly depends on its impact on the domestic rate of interest. Both through the domestic money market and through the secondary market for financial assets, the capital inflow will reduce the interest rate – and hence raise investment. But, in Bhaduri's view, it is not likely that the resulting bank debt financed or equity-financed investment boom can be sustained for a long period by foreign capital inflows with their bias in favour of 'finance' rather than 'industry'.

Mihir Rakshit, in Chapter 8, addresses crucial analytical and policy issues in the context of the globalization of capital markets. Rakshit points out the following benefits of unrestricted capital mobility: static gains in allocative efficiency; gains due to the inter-temporal smoothing of consumption; benefits due to the reduction of risks through cross-holding of assets; and dynamic gains due to the transfer of knowledge inherent in cross-border capital flows. These benefits are argued to become even larger, because of the policy discipline imposed by unrestricted capital mobility, forcing governments to pursue fiscal and monetary policies congruent with the expectations of global capital markets. But if capital mobility is so beneficial, why are countries extremely reluctant to permit the free flow of funds across their borders? This reluctance – in Rakshit's view – is due to the costs associated with free capital movements. First, unrestricted capital mobility makes it difficult for national governments to maintain full employment or effect macro stabilization by making the domestic economy vulnerable to external shocks and by seriously reducing the effectiveness of fiscal and monetary policy. Second, capital mobility tends to increase the inequality in income distribution both within and between countries. Third, given the lenders' lack of adequate information and given the higher expected yield from riskier investment on equity capital than on that on total funds employed, increased reliance on (foreign) loans for financing investment causes serious moral hazard problems by way of diverting investment to high-risk projects. The consequent distortions in the pattern of investment in turn raise the probability of default or bankruptcy and hence of a more general financial crisis. Finally, given the extraordinarily large volume of global foreign exchange transactions, the increased financial interdependence between economies, and the predominance of herd behaviour among investors, unrestricted capital mobility increases a country's proneness to currency crisis. Rakshit concludes that to contain these costs some control over capital movements, especially short-term ones, will be necessary.

We have seen that, while the volume of private capital flows to developing countries has grown dramatically during the last two decades, public capital flows, for example, aid flows, have dropped as a percentage of donor country GDP, particularly so during the 1990s. The reason lies, as is argued by Frances Stewart (Chapter 9), in the fundamental changes in the international economic order following the collapse of the Soviet model and the ascent of the Washington Consensus on economic policy (at the expense of Keynesian interventionism). While in the 1980s multilateral aid was used systematically – under the policy conditionality of the IMF and World Bank – to open up developing countries to MNEs from the industrialized countries, this programme is now carried forward by the WTO and by planned new rules on intellectual property and multinational investment, rather than by aid. Aid (as a proportion of donor country GDP) is not only likely to decline further in the future, but it will also increasingly serve as emergency aid (in times of humanitarian and/or financial crisis). Stewart argues that this decline in aid is not a tragedy since the record of aid over the past 40 years has not been good, especially in reaching the poor. Rather than focusing on the quantity of aid, efforts should be made to improve its quality. The approach emphasized by Stewart is to put aid in a human rights framework, redirecting it towards countries which are constrained in realizing human rights by their poverty and lack of access to foreign exchange. At the same time, aid should be complemented by reforms of the international trade, finance, investment and technology policies in the interest of developing countries.

Due to the decline in official development assistance, developing countries are increasingly financing their rising external payments deficits by means of private capital inflows including FDI. In Chapter 10, John Dunning analyses recent trends in FDI flows to and from Asia. Dunning provides comparative data to show that Asian developing countries are at the forefront of the globalization process. Asian firms share in the export growth of dynamic products, engage in outward FDI (not only elsewhere in Asia but also in the Organization for Economic Cooperation and Development (OECD), make good use of international communications facilities, and increasingly become involved in cross-border strategic alliances, mergers and acquisitions. And most strikingly, Asian countries (China in particular) have generally recorded higher levels of FDI inflows than those of other developing countries, which reflects the rising locational advantages of Asian compared with other developing countries and a greater interest by foreign MNEs to internalize Asia's markets. One key factor responsible for the fact that Asian economies are more deeply integrated into the global economy than other developing countries is – in Dunning's view – the forceful yet market-friendly development strategies pursued by their governments.

Chapter 11, by Roger van Hoesel, analyses one of the distinctive features of Asia's globalization discussed by Dunning in more detail: the recent growth of outward FDI from Asia. Korean and Taiwanese MNEs are among the most prominent outward investors from the South. On the basis of a Tobit analysis of recent firm-level data for the Korean and Taiwanese electronics industry, van Hoesel investigates the firm-level determinants of outward investment. His results show that, apart from variables such as firm size and export orientation that are well-known determinants of FDI by firms located in the OECD countries as well, FDI by Korean and Taiwanese firms is affected by variables typical of the so-called late-indus-trializing countries. Two important examples of the latter determinants of FDI behaviour are the presence of trade barriers (which leads to tariff-jumping FDI) and the high productivity growth of these late-coming firms (which makes them less sensitive to domestic wage increases and thereby reduces the motivation for outward investment). Van Hoesel's results thus show that firms in late-industrializing countries face qualitatively different constraints on their FDI behaviour from those experienced by their counterparts in the early-industrialized countries.

Part III, Equality, Employment and Environment, explores the effects of globalization on income distribution, employment and important social indicators within developing countries and on the environment. Chapter 12, by Lance Taylor, provides a wide-ranging investigation of the macro-economic and social implications of external liberalization on the basis of the recent experiences of 21 developing and transition countries. According to the mainstream view, liberalization is likely to have positive effects on income, productivity and employment growth. It acknowledges the pos-sibility of adverse transitional effects, but argues that these can in principle be smoothed over by social policies, and in any case after some time they will be outweighed by more rapid income growth. In contrast, Taylor's analysis of country experiences points to the much more disquieting pos-sibility that liberalization can unleash dynamic forces, leading not only to an unimpressive macro-economic performance but also to long-term slow employment growth and rising inequality. Using a model allowing for unemployment, factor immobility and product market imperfections, Taylor argues that rising capital inflows following external liberalization tend to lead to exchange rate appreciation, which offsets liberalization's incentives for traded goods production and forces greater reductions in real wage costs. This appreciation in turn may be linked to high real interest rates, which augment production costs and penalize capital formation and growth. Higher interest rates may also draw in more external capital, setting off a high interest rate/strong exchange rate spiral. In Taylor's sample of countries, external liberalization was generally associated with foreign capital inflows, increases in reserves, domestic credit expansion, real exchange rate appreciation, and higher interest rates. Capital inflows, credit creation, and real appreciation together stimulated aggregate demand to increase more than GDP, with a consequent widening of the current account deficit. Distributionally, the effects of liberalization turned out to be adverse. Inequality (of primary incomes) increased in two-thirds of the countries, wage differentials between skilled and unskilled workers rose with liberalization, and unemployment often increased. The social costs of the external liberalization are large, because the loss of wage income and employment in the non-traded sectors is not offset (neither in the short nor in the longer run) by a rise in wages and employment in traded production. One reason for this is the contraction of domestic demand for non-traded goods caused by the real wage fall and loss of jobs by workers with high consumption propensities. Country evidence further suggests no significant aggregate productivity increases and employment growth following liberalization. Some countries (notably Colombia, Cuba and Korea) introduced social programmes to offset some of the negative consequences of liberalization. Other countries, for example, Russia, Turkey and Zimbabwe, facing fiscal resource constraints had to cut back on social spending. Hence, while governments can in principle put countervailing social policies into place, in practice they generally lack the capacity to do so. Taylor concludes that, to date, the social costs of liberalization in many countries have outweighed its benefits, and this situation may persist for an extended period of time.

Taylor's argument is complemented by an analysis of the distributional effects of globalization in the context of Indian agriculture in Chapter 13. Using a multiperiod Computable General Equilibrium (CGE) model, Servaas Storm assesses the growth and distributional effects of a strategy of close integration of India's agriculture with world markets. Such close integration implies the removal of trade protection and the withdrawal of domestic subsidization in Indian agriculture. He finds that, because structural rigidities in agriculture inhibit its supply response and consumption demand for foodgrains is price-inelastic, close integration of Indian agriculture with world markets has a larger impact on domestic (relative) agricultural prices than on output. This agriculture-induced inflation is augmented and sustained by a large currency depreciation, required to maintain balance-of-payments equilibrium. Although the relative price improvement for agriculture raises investment and agricultural growth, it also erodes nominal wages and non-agricultural profits, thereby depressing non-agricultural growth. The net effect is GDP contraction in conjunction with a significant deterioration of India's income distribution. In particular, landless rural labourers and small farmers, who are net buyers of food, suffer dramatic real income declines, implying a rise in poverty as well. The substantial and unevenly distributed costs of such close integration argue for a more selective engagement of Indian agriculture with the world economy. Storm operationalizes two alternative policies of strategic integration, the medium-term results of which are superior to the close integration strategy in terms of growth as well as income distribution. Hence, the simulation outcomes show that, even in times of globalization, there still exists considerable room for strategic government intervention to improve upon market outcomes.

The impact of globalization on the welfare of the poorest in India is analysed by Lalita Chakravarty (in Chapter 14). Focusing on the poorest of India's poor, who face a disproportionately higher risk than the other income groups of falling sick and – worse – of premature death, her argument is that biological stress signals (that is, the simultaneous occurrence of heightened mortality and lowered fertility rates) can be relevant for the study of poverty and deprivation. Using (de-trended) national and state-wise time-series data on mortality and fertility for India (1970–95), Chakravarty is able to identify years of significant biological stress, which she next tries to align with historical trends in the extent and the depth of poverty. What strikes the reader is that, whereas there is a relatively close alignment between years of biological stress and years of increased poverty during the 1970s, this is no longer the case in the 1980s, when biological stress signals were largely absent but (the depth of) poverty increased. Underlying the simultaneous occurrence of physical stress and increased economic poverty in the 1970s were droughts, due to which the poorest lost employment and real income and suffered severe biological stress. In the 1980s, in contrast, droughts did not produce significant biological stress, though deepening poverty did. This, as Chakravarty argues, is likely due to effective public intervention, which succeeded in providing a *de facto* floor to the consumption of the poorest. Importantly, her analysis shows that biological stress signals reappear (in conjunction with increased poverty) in the 1990s in the absence of droughts. If not droughts, what does explain this biological stress? Chakravarty conjectures that it may reflect a boom famine (rather than the traditional slump famine), caused by two factors related to the globalization of the Indian economy since 1991. The first factor is the decline in the domestic availability of millets (the staple food of the poorest), caused by a decline in acreage under millets and a rise in millet exports. The second is the increased physical stress for casualized workers, due to a decrease in local employment opportunities brought about by the economic restructuring induced by the reforms.

The inequality in death, stressed by Chakravarty, reflects the greater vulnerability of the poorest income groups to market shocks during India's transition towards a more market-based economy. The only sustainable way to reduce this vulnerability is to provide these groups with adequate and gainful employment opportunities. India has a long tradition of trying to create employment by means of special programmes for (rural) small-scale industries. In Chapter 15, Ashwani Saith offers a comparative assessment of the performance of small-scale industries in India and China. In both countries, (rural) small-scale industrialization was supposed to take the burden of employment generation and the production of mass consumer goods off the shoulders of the modern capital-intensive industrial sector. Within its rural collectivist framework, China converted (rural) small-scale industries into cooperatives, which laid the basis for their subsequent modernization. In India, the small-scale industry, while remaining private-property based, was initially made the beneficiary of market reservation on the demand side, and of priority access to credit, technical support and marketing on the supply side. While the modern Chinese small-scale sector has experienced explosive growth (especially since the early 1980s), the performance of the Indian small-scale industry has been lagging. The differential growth performance is partly due to the larger inflow of FDI into China and the more active involvement of the Chinese overseas community in the Chinese economy. But it is also partly attributable to India's policy approach, which – in Saith's view – is overly bureaucratic, excessively protective (to the extent of stifling private initiative) and not well coordinated. Hence, he welcomes two recent potentially significant policy changes in India's small-scale industrialization policy. First, coinciding with the trend toward globalization, policy has shifted toward de-reservation and removal of quota, exposing the sector to competition from domestic and external sources. As a result, the small-scale sector has become more dynamic and much more export oriented. Second, policy thinking is now encouraging clustering as a desirable, prototypical organizational form for small-scale industrial development. Clustering has the potential to improve the sector's performance because of reasons of collective efficiency, flexible specialization, agglomeration economies, cooperation, and vertical integration. Saith discusses the scope for cluster development in the Indian context, highlighting two important negative externalities associated with rapid output and export growth: the environmental damage and the exploitation of labour. But, in Saith's view, clusters make such effects concentrated and this in turn could induce countervailing action.

The environmental and resource constraints on growth are – in the view of Gopal Kadekodi in Chapter 16 – the major challenge for development economics in the new century. According to Kadekodi, in almost all the thinking on economic development, natural and environmental resources have been treated either as an externality or as a free gift of nature (and hence valueless and non-exhaustible) or as having man-made substitutes.

As a result, although growth is acknowledged to have environmental effects, any feedback effect of the environment on growth and development is – by assumption – neglected. Kadekodi points out that the (policy) conclusions derived from conventional theories will drastically change, once environmental and natural resources are included in the analysis as a factor of production with an intrinsic valuation. For instance, free trade or globalization will lead to the immiserization of natural resource-rich countries as soon as the (conventionally unvalued) costs of the depletion and degradation of natural and environmental resources are taken into account. Therefore, in his view, it is high time that traditional development theory is replaced by a theory of sustainable development, which is concerned with improving living conditions of present and future generations alike. This paradigm shift has – at least – three distinctive features. First, it recognizes the fact that natural capital and man-made capital often are complementary, not substitutes. Second, it takes account of irreversibilities in production and consumption, for example irreversible waste generation in the process of using a natural resource, and of the associated entropy. Due to such irreversibilities, economic development is highly path-dependent, as was stressed by S. Chakravarty in Chapter 2. Third, Kadekodi argues that sustainable development is fundamentally a *global* problem, because the welfare of countries is interdependent due to the scarcity of natural resources at the global level and due to the cross-border nature of major environmental problems (acid rain, ozone depletion and global warming). Sustainable development is not served by market-based globalization, because markets inherently fail to internalize environmental externalities. Accordingly, sustainable development demands new institutional approaches, based on cooperation rather than competition.

5.   CONCLUSIONS AND IMPLICATIONS FOR DEVELOPMENT POLICY

The chapters that follow challenge the mainstream view of globalization by demonstrating that the opening of national borders to trade, investment, and capital (most of which occurs beyond the control of national governments) does not automatically result in higher growth, increased employment, and reduced poverty. Indeed, if anything, many chapters suggest that there exists a trade-off between globalization and development, at least in the short and medium run. At the analytical level, many chapters dispute the validity of the assumptions underlying the mainstream view (listed in section 3 of this chapter). In particular, it is argued that free markets do not optimize national welfare, because of the following reasons:

- Markets fail to fully coordinate individual decisions and, hence, do not produce full employment due to the fragmentation of global markets (emphasized by Rao), moral hazard and adverse selection related imperfections in global capital markets (analysed by Rakshit) and in domestic capital markets (stressed by Naastepad), and structural rigidities in commodity and labour markets (see Rattsø, Taylor and Storm). Once the assumption that the economy always operates at full employment is given up, questions of macro-economic adjustment and instability arising in the context of developing-country globalization can be analysed. It can then be shown that trade liberalization can be contractionary and distributionally regressive (Rattsø, Taylor and Storm) and that external financial liberalization can be contractionary (Bhaduri) as well as destabilizing (Rakshit).
- Global financial markets are fundamentally unstable, which is underscored by the frequency and intensity of crises in global financial markets in the 1990s. The collapse of South Korea illustrates – as explained by Adelman and Nak – that the structural causes of financial crisis are not so much related to country-specific factors (economic mismanagement, political instability and corruption), but rather the result of systemic factors concerning the interaction between global markets and domestic economies. Moreover, due to the increased interdependence, a financial crisis may now spread from one economy to other economies with apparently limited trade or financial links with the original crisis economy and in the absence of a change in the latters' macro-economic fundamentals (see Rakshit). Hence, globalization may have made the global financial system – in S. Chakravarty's terminology – structurally unstable (see also Vercelli, 2000).
- Global markets are operating in a highly selective manner. Developed countries, whether as sources or destinations, account for a disproportionately large share of global flows of trade, FDI and capital relative to their share in income (Rao). Within the South, FDI and net capital inflows are concentrated in only a handful of developing countries (Dunning), while official flows tend to favour the group of poorer developing countries (Stewart). And only a few, mostly Asian, developing countries, have become able to engage in outward FDI (van Hoesel). The global market rules are increasingly made and invoked by the MNEs and international banks and financial institutions, while they are implemented within the multilateral framework of the WTO, the IMF and the World Bank (see Stewart; Adelman and Yeldan, 2000; Nayyar, 2000). In the WTO, for instance, major trading countries resort to a unilateral exercise of power, ignoring the rules,

because small countries do not have the strength, even if they have the right, to retaliate. On the other hand, developing countries are obliged to open up their agriculture to international trade and compromise the food security of their populations (as shown by Storm), while major trading blocs such as the EU are in a position to continue their protectionist agricultural trade regime.

*   The distributional effects of globalization are large and generally adverse, both between and within nations (as is demonstrated by Rao, Rattsø, Taylor and Storm). The ensuing distributional conflicts cannot be resolved – by taxing those who gain and compensating those who lose – in case the aggregate (GDP) impact of globalization is negative, as is true for many countries in Taylor's sample. But even in the absence of aggregate contraction, the distributional shifts are so large that it will be difficult, if not impossible, to tax the gainers and compensate the losers without 'distorting' the market. Finally, the concept of compensation becomes irrelevant, once we acknowledge that some of the distributional consequences of globalization are irreversible, as in the case of a rise in mortality of the poor (found by L. Chakravarty) or of irreparable degradation of the environment (stressed by Kadekodi and observed by Saith).
*   Complementarities between public and private investment are important, particularly in the development of physical infrastructure for agriculture (as is shown by Naastepad and Storm) and clusters of rural industries (Saith).
*   Technological spillovers from FDI, which can be used as a basis for developing competitiveness, do not arise spontaneously but are the result of bargaining with MNEs to improve the terms of trade, obtain market access for exports, and facilitate the transfer of technology – as was the practice in East Asia (see Dunning and van Hoesel).

The unstable, selective and asymmetric nature of present-day globalization is bound to have major adverse consequences for economic development. The chapters identify the following threats to economic development due to globalization:

*   The costs and benefits of globalization spread unequally and inequitably, concentrating power and wealth in a select group of people, nations and (trans-national) corporations, marginalizing the others. The marginalization of nations is implied by the divergence of per capita incomes across countries found by Rao (see also UNDP, 1999). Market-driven globalization will also immiserize natural resource-rich countries – as argued by Kadekodi. The marginalization of

people due to globalization follows from the evidence by Taylor of a rise in the wage gap between unskilled and skilled workers and a rise in both economic inequality and poverty (occurring after trade and investment liberalization). It is also brought out clearly by the analyses of trade liberalization of Rattsø and Storm. That the distress caused by the economic restructuring, induced by globalization, shows up not only in monetary indicators of poverty and inequality, but also in indicators of physical distress, is shown by L. Chakravarty. Globalization is finally likely to raise inter-generational inequality, because it induces the over-consumption and hence the degradation and depletion of (under-valued) natural and environmental resources in developing countries (Kadekodi). The environmental costs caused by the high export growth of Indian small-scale industries, analysed by Saith, are a case in point.

- Due to the liberalization of foreign capital flows, the policy autonomy of developing countries has been seriously compromised. First, as is argued by Bhaduri and Rakshit, it is no longer possible for developing countries to pursue an interest and exchange rate policy which deviates from world market norms, without the risk of inducing a financial crisis. That this risk is non-negligible even for the strongest developing countries is made clear by Adelman and Nak. Second, globalization also seriously constrains fiscal policy choice, because governments run the risk of triggering capital flight when they increase the deficit to stimulate growth. As a result, the scope to put social policies into place to countervail the adverse social effects of liberalization is severely restricted (see Taylor). The loss of the fiscal policy instruments is even more dramatic because it is based – as shown by Naastepad – on fundamental misperceptions regarding real-monetary linkages. Her analysis shows that, depending on initial conditions in real and financial markets, a fiscal deficit increase need not be inflationary, and hence need not give rise to capital flight.

- The growth of (short-term) capital flows to developing countries is somewhat of a mixed blessing. As Bhaduri argues, under certain conditions, increased capital inflows can encourage excessive imports, which can depress domestic production. His argument is supported by the findings of Rattsø and Taylor. From Rakshit's assessment, it follows that private capital flows constitute an unreliable source of development finance, because they can be highly volatile and susceptible to large swings in a relatively short period, causing gyrations in exchange rates (see also Adelman and Nak).

What are developing-country governments to do in response to these threats posed by globalization? We closely follow Adelman and Nak (this book) who argue that, fundamentally, governments have four types of options (see also Adelman and Yeldan, 2000; Nayyar, 2000; UNCTAD, 1999a).

The first option is that developing countries globalize, that is, closely and passively integrate into the world economy, relinquishing their economic autonomy and renouncing their responsibilities for macro-economic management, economic development and social policy. This option would have been desirable, were globalization the best way to achieve economic development. But in view of the large social and developmental costs of globalization stressed by the authors in this book, it is hardly an appealing, or indeed responsible, option. Passive integration with world markets implies renouncing all developmental concerns. It is also in conflict with the development experience of contemporary industrialized countries. Historical evidence for OECD countries shows that long-term economic development entails a state-led process of systematic institutional, technological and structural change contributing to widespread improvement in the human condition. In the earlier stages of economic development, this means creating a physical infrastructure through government investment, investing in the development of human resources through education and medical care, catalysing institutional change, for example, through agrarian reform. In the later stages, it means using strategic industrial policy for the development of technological capabilities and establishing institutions facilitating, regulating and governing markets. It must be emphasized that the benefits of globalization will accrue only to those countries that have laid the requisite domestic foundations – as emphasized by Rao. Wherever these foundations were lacking, the effects of liberalization on income distribution and poverty have been dismal – as is evidenced by Taylor, Rattsø, Storm and L. Chakravarty. To enable governments to play their fundamental developmental roles successfully, some degree of economic policy autonomy is required.

The second option (distinguished by Adelman and Nak) is that governments limit themselves to the instruments they retain. These instruments include disguised subsidies to industry through education, infrastructure investment and low-wage, anti-union policies; targeted subsidies in the form of tax rebates and/or monopoly privileges of specific industries, regions and firms; the creation of generalized externalities via education investment, state-supported research, tax concessions to FDI and a stable well-functioning legal infrastructure; and selective tariffs to climb the ladder of comparative advantage. But the pace of development achieved through the combination of these instruments will be slow, because it will be severely constrained by a balanced-budget and relatively restricted monetary and fiscal policy stance – as is clearly indicated by Naastepad's analysis of India's fiscal policy. It is also doubtful whether the developing-country state will have enough (fiscal) power left to implement effective policies minimizing the negative externalities associated with globalization. The necessity for such intervention is greater in a developing country where poverty is widespread, environmental concerns are minimal and the rights of citizens are not assured (see Kadekodi; Stewart).

Third, developing countries can try to convince the international community that the current global economic system needs reform. As far as the global trading system is concerned, there is a clear need for greater symmetry in the rules of the multilateral trading system embodied in the WTO (Nayyar, 2000). If developing countries provide access to their markets, it should be matched by some corresponding access to technology (Rao), all the more so in view of the current 'aid fatigue' (Stewart) and the failure of private financial markets to provide adequate development finance (Rakshit). With respect to the global financial system, some mix of supranational regulation, disincentives or other impediments to short-term capital mobility is required to generate a global environment that is robust and friendly to economic development – as argued by Rakshit and Adelman and Nak. Finally, many environmental problems (acid rain, global warming and ozone depletion) have transboundary consequences, particularly for poor people and poor nations (UNDP, 1999). As stressed by Kadekodi, such emergencies demand global action.

Fourth, developing countries could unilaterally delink from global markets to preserve their economic independence, enabling the pursuit of development objectives and macro-economic stability. Many chapters propose some form of – in Chakravarty and Singh's (1988) words – strategic integration into world markets, that is, integrating up to the point that it is in the developing country's interest to do so as to promote economic development. 'Openness' is seen as a multi-dimensional concept involving trade, FDI, finance, technology, migration, education, science and culture. There exists no 'optimum' form and degree of openness of a developing economy, which holds true at all times. Rather, in line with S. Chakravarty's emphasis on path dependency, it depends on initial conditions including the world configuration, the past history of the economy, and its state of development. To further development, and in view of its initial conditions, a country can choose to be open in some directions, but not so open in others. For example, as explained by Adelman and Nak for Korea prior to 1991, a country can be export-oriented, but not closely integrated with the international economy in terms of imports, FDI or capital flows. Likewise, countries can restrict FDI flows to activities which are conducive to development and bargain with MNEs to improve the terms of trade, obtain market access for exports, and facilitate the transfer of technology – as was the practice in East Asia (see Dunning and van Hoesel). Countries can also restrict the exports of foodgrains to stabilize food prices in the interest of development – as is shown for India by Storm.

But because the loss of policy autonomy due to globalization is largely due to the rapid and close integration of developing countries into international financial markets (as is explained by Bhaduri and Rakshit), the question of strategic integration is most urgent in the context of the global financial markets. In view of the frequency, intensity and easy communicability of financial crises, the question becomes even more pressing. No exchange rate and/or interest rate policy can ensure the stability and autonomy needed for successful growth performance unless destabilizing capital flows are brought under control (Taylor; Rakshit). What options of strategic integration with the global financial system do developing countries have? They could either, like Malaysia and Russia, eliminate convertibility of their currencies on the capital account entirely or, alternatively, like India and China, they could delay the convertibility of their capital accounts until their economic and financial systems are sufficiently mature. Or, as in Chile, they could unilaterally introduce differential taxes and higher reserve requirements on short-term capital inflows and foreign deposits, and impose controls on foreign borrowing. These measures would make it more expensive to engage in short-term foreign borrowing and exchange rate speculation, and thereby provide the greater policy autonomy required for the pursuit of development.

In light of the above, development thinking and policy need a radical review if developing countries are to be assured of better growth prospects, narrow the persistent and growing income gap with the industrialized countries, and reduce their widespread poverty. The essential point made in the chapters that follow is that passively and closely integrating into the world economy brings with it substantial costs in terms of economic development. Instead, developing countries will need to actively manage their integration into the global economy if they are to overcome the imbalances and instabilities associated with international flows of goods and capital and be able to pursue broad-based and equitable economic development.

NOTES

1. While the reasons for this trade deficit increase are complex, empirical evidence shows that it is due mainly to a combination of a long-term decline in the terms of trade for and the 'big bang' liberalization of trade and capital accounts in the developing countries (UNCTAD, 1999a).

2. While these countries account for as much as 69 per cent of developing countries' population, in per capita terms the foreign capital they received was nevertheless around 4.5 times that of the other countries.
3. There exists a large empirical (cross-country) literature on trade openness and growth, including Dollar (1992), Sachs and Warner (1995), and Edwards (1998). The cumulative evidence emerging from this literature is that openness is growth enhancing. However, a more careful analysis of this literature reveals that the empirical research strategies employed are conceptually flawed and the econometric findings are non-robust, when relevant country characteristics are controlled for (see Rodriguez and Rodrik, 1999).

REFERENCES

Adelman, Irma and Erinc Yeldan (2000), 'Is this the end of economic development?', *Structural Change and Economic Dynamics*, **11** (1), 95–109.

Baker, Dean, Gerald Epstein and Robert Pollin (1998), *Globalization and Progressive Economic Policy*, Cambridge: Cambridge University Press.

Chakravarty, Sukhamoy and Ajit Singh (1988), 'The desirable forms of economic openness in the South', *mimeo*, Helsinki: WIDER.

Collier, Paul and Jan Willem Gunning (1999), 'The IMF's role in structural adjustment', *The Economic Journal*, **109** (459), F634–F651.

Dollar, David (1992), 'Outward-oriented developing economies really do grow more rapidly: Evidence from 95 LDCs, 1976–1985', *Economic Development and Cultural Change*, **40** (3), 523–44.

Dollar, David and Aart Kraay (2000), 'Growth is good for the poor', *Working Paper*, March, Washington, DC: World Bank (downloadable from: www.worldbank.org/research).

Edwards, Sebastian (1998), 'Openness, productivity and growth: What do we really know?', *The Economic Journal*, **108** (447), 383–98.

Frankel, Jeffrey A. and David Romer (1999), 'Does trade cause growth?', *The American Economic Review*, **89** (3), 379–99.

Grabel, Ilene (1999), 'Rejecting exceptionalism: Reinterpreting the Asian financial crisis', in Michie and Grieve Smith (eds).

IMF (1999), *World Economic Outlook*, October, Washington, DC: International Monetary Fund.

Michie, Jonathan and John Grieve Smith (eds) (1999), *Global Instability: The Political Economy of World Economic Governance*, London: Routledge.

Nayyar, Deepak (2000), 'Globalization and development strategies', Paper prepared for the High-Level Round Table on Trade and Development, UNCTAD X, Bangkok.

Pieper, Ute and Lance Taylor (1998), 'The revival of the liberal creed: The IMF, the World Bank, and inequality in a globalized economy', in Baker et al. (eds).

Rodriguez, Francisco and Dani Rodrik (1999), 'Trade policy and economic growth: A skeptic's guide to the cross-national evidence', *mimeo*, Department of Economics, University of Maryland.

Rodrik, Dani (1999), *The New Global Economy and Developing Countries: Making Openness Work*, Policy Essay Nr. 24, Washington, DC: Overseas Development Council.

Sachs, Jeffrey and Andrew Warner (1995), 'Economic reform and the process of global integration', *Brookings Papers on Economic Activity*, No. 1, pp. 1–118.

Stewart, Frances and Albert Berry (2000), 'Globalization, liberalization, and inequality: Real causes', *Challenge*, **43** (1), 44–92.
Stiglitz, Joseph E. (1998), 'More instruments and broader goals: Moving toward the post-Washington Consensus', *WIDER Annual Lectures 2*, Helsinki: WIDER.
UNCTAD (1999a), *Trade and Development Report 1999*, New York: United Nations.
UNCTAD (1999b), *World Investment Report 1999*, New York: United Nations.
UNDP (1999), *Human Development Report 1999*, Oxford: Oxford University Press.
Vercelli, Alessandro (2000), 'Structural financial instability and cyclical fluctuations', *Structural Change and Economic Dynamics*, **11** (1), 139–56.
Winters, L. Alan (1999), 'Trade liberalization and poverty', *mimeo*, University of Sussex, Brighton.
World Bank (1999), *World Development Report 1999*, Washington, DC.
World Bank (2000), *World Development Indicators*, Washington, DC.

PART I

Globalization, instability and path
dependence

2. Dynamic methods in economics*

Sukhamoy Chakravarty

24 April 1990

I thought of taking this particular subject as a possible topic for an infor-
mal talk after reading an article by the Swiss institutional economist Kurt
Dopfer [1988]. He wrote an article in the *Journal of Economic Issues* called
'Classical Mechanics with an Ethical Dimension: Prof. Tinbergen's
Economics', to which Prof. Tinbergen has given two replies: one in the
Journal of Economic Issues, the very first place where this article by Dopfer
appeared, and more recently another one which has been published, 'The
Functioning of Economic Research' [Tinbergen, 1988, 1989].

I must say that after reading the article as well as these two replies, I felt
that they were talking past each other completely, in the sense that one was
not listening to the other. I think they both had points to make, but that
their points are not meeting on the same plane. I think that this might be
an occasion in the Tinbergen Institute to say something about Tinbergen's
work, as we see it, from the vantage point of nearly 60 years after it was first
initiated. It was after all Tinbergen's first important paper, on the shipbuilding cycle, that was published in 1931 in the *Weltwirtschaftliches Archiv*
[which introduced for the first time in economics a mixed difference – differential equation, which subsequently played an important role in Frisch's
well-known paper on cycles (Frisch, 1933) and, more importantly, in
Kalecki's macrodynamic model (Kalecki, 1935)]. So I think that it was not
such a bad idea after all that younger people, many of whom were born
after the war, would have an opportunity to see how things looked to people
in the 1930s. So I shall not be initially referring to Dopfer and Tinbergen
and this controversy but I shall come to it towards the end of my discussion, because I think one or two of the points which Dopfer makes are of

* Lecture given at the Erasmus University Rotterdam at the Workshop *The Structure of Long-
Term Development* (jointly organized by the Centre for Development Planning and the
Tinbergen Institute, Erasmus University Rotterdam) at which Prof. Luigi Pasinetti was also
present as one of the main speakers. Apart from some minor editorial changes, this text is the
literal spoken text by Sukhamoy Chakravarty, who, as a very dear friend of many members of
the Centre for Development Planning, is very sadly missed. Additions to the text by the editors
are between square brackets and a list of references has been added by the editors. The editors
of this book are grateful to Prof. Amit Bhaduri for his help in editing the spoken text.

some interest and therefore will have to be thought about. A great deal of it is based on what I would call, in the absence of better words, some mis-understanding, but there are a few points towards the end which are of some interest and which do need to be discussed. I don't know how much formal exposure to economic dynamics people have here and more particu-larly if they know how economic dynamics evolved as a subject. I don't know whether these things are being discussed anymore or whether they are taken for granted or whether they straightaway move towards solving difference equations or differential equations, because a bit of history might not be a bad thing in this particular context and then one can really move on to the substantive issues.

I begin with an important and substantive observation made by a math-ematician called René Thom who wrote a very important book called *Structural Stability and Morphogenesis* [Thom, 1975], which some of you possibly have heard about and some of you may have read. In that partic-ular book, Thom makes an important observation where he says that:

> All models divide naturally in this way into two a priori distinct parts: one *kin-ematic*, whose aim is to parameterize the forms or the states of the process under consideration, and the other *dynamic*, describing the evolution in time of these forms. [Thom, 1975, page 3; emphasis in original.]

This is an interesting distinction and an important one, as you know, to physics, or in classical mechanics, which is the ostensible subject of attack by Prof. Dopfer, who doesn't make a distinction between kinematics and dynamics. I think kinematical considerations, which, as I said, is a problem of parameterizing the forms or the states of the process, are very impor-tant, as people know who have had an occasion to look at some elementary or in fact advanced physics, for example the theory of relativity. Now, if you use this distinction, you really would say that what went by the name of eco-nomic dynamics is often nothing more than kinematics in the sense that it is a way of trying to describe economic processes in time without necessar-ily providing it with a corresponding theory of how these processes evolve over time, and its problem is basically to capture the motion in a suitable space rather than the changes in structure. The structural dynamics that has been talked about by Prof. Pasinetti [1981] would fall under dynamics in the proper sense of the term, but it is not generally treated in this particular manner. I will come to this problem at a later stage.

In Newtonian dynamics, the really dynamic element in this sense would be provided by Newton's notions of gravitation, for example, whereas his three laws of motion are basically kinematical unless you include in it an idea of the gravitational force, which has a special characteristic of the inverse square law. And as you know, Einstein's special theory of relativity was a development of Newtonian mechanics in a purely kinematical sense of the term, by bringing in the restrictions or incompatibility of these laws with laws of electromagnetism. But dynamics, I think, is a substantive concept which has to deal with the gravitational Newtonian inverse square law and Newtonian potential, and which gives rise to the planetary orbits and the forms which they take and so on, while kinematics deals with the principles of locomotion.

Now, if you look at the literature of economic dynamics, how it evolved in economics, a very important place has to be given to the work of Ragnar Frisch [1933] who, I think doubtless, gave us the language for describing many of the problems that became important and significant. The pre-Frischian discussion on problems of economic dynamics in fact was extremely imprecise. Frisch's great contribution was in fact to bring in a clarity in a confused discussion by saying that expressions like static and stationary state are quite different in character. He used the word 'static' to describe the method of analysis and 'stationary' to describe a certain state of affairs, and 'dynamic', again he thought, was a method of analysis. He came up with this classificatory scheme: stationary equilibria, moving equilibria and various other kinds of things which are all well known to people of my generation because they had to read through this kind of material possibly more carefully than people do now. Looking at the distinction that Thom raised, one could say that Frisch's contribution was more important from the kinematical point of view rather than from the point of view of dynamics, because he, I think, really made a fundamental point (which was followed by everybody else) that in order to qualify for a dynamic method of analysis, the treatment must involve the use of functional equations involving time in an essential manner.

In other words, he talked about using differential equations, difference equations and mixed forms of equations and more complicated forms of integral differential equations and so forth. But in each case, the important point is that it should not be possible by simple transformation of variables to eliminate any explicit reference to time, and variables pertaining to different points of time must figure in the equation system. But I think that still leaves open what drives the system forward. That does not really say anything about what is the compelling reason of movements forward and movements backwards. And as Prof. Pasinetti mentioned yesterday in his presentation, if you look at it from the purely formal point of view, then differential equations which give rise to steady state solutions which are known to be stable (transient motions are very heavily dampened) could indeed be operating in a manner in which no changes are reflected. In other words, mutual proportions are preserved as invariant with respect to time, and it is quite doubtful whether this could be regarded as dynamic in the sense of evolution of forms which he had in mind when he criticized von Neumann's [1945] work as being a powerful mathematical piece of work, but not throwing much light on economic dynamics if I have understood him correctly. What I am therefore saying is that the kinematical approach has to be substantiated by dynamical considerations in the true sense of the term, which implies an ability to decipher the inner mechanism of the system which drives it forward and gives rise to oscillations.

Now, in the 1930s people were very much concerned with finding an explanation for oscillations, business cycles and so forth. In that particular context it was necessary for them to look into, what you might say, some economic principles which could give rise to oscillations, and not a purely mechanical notion which could really be regarded as a first step in this direction. Frisch in his famous paper 'Propagation and Impulse Problems in Economic Dynamics', written in the Cassel volume [1933], gives first a theory and then he really comes to another theory which shifts it down; he starts with a formulation which in some sense is a formulation given by Wicksell of the famous 'rocking horse', where a boy gives a push to a rocking horse and the horse comes to acquire a motion independent of the initial push, which means that what they are really thinking of is that there is an internal dynamics which is in the nature of a propagational process, and there is an impulse which comes from outside and he then says that these impulses could be regarded as random shocks to the system. What we really have to look at is to make this distinction between impulse and propagation. The propagation mechanism must be such as to give rise to oscillatory phenomena. The question of how this oscillation is sustained will have to be explained by economic argumentation.

Tinbergen applied these ideas in an empirical context. In other words, he took Frischian dynamics and ideas of his own, because he had studied physics. [However,] none of them (and this is Dopfer's basic misconception) tried to find out correlates with classical mechanical concepts such as energy, friction and so on, with well-specified economic categories. In this respect, Frisch's work was fundamentally very different from the earlier work of Frank Knight, who wrote an article called 'Statics and Dynamics in Economic Analysis' [Knight, 1956] which is based on an attempt to find a close analogical reasoning between classical mechanics on the one hand and economics on the other hand. In contrast to that kind of analogical reasoning, Frisch's argument was much more robust and much more powerful. In fact, he was really saying, taking a systems-theoretic point of view, for use of contemporary language, that if there is a system of equations which involves time in an essential way and that defines the possible trajectory of motion, and if that particular trajectory of motion is heavily dampened, then we might in fact talk about equilibrium as a reasonable concept as a first approximation in economics; but if it is anti-dampened, then in that case it does not describe an economic process; and if it has a slow damping then there is a possibility of sustained oscillations if exogenous shocks are allowed to be introduced as they are in economic phenomena. I think that in that way he gave a more robust way of modelling processes involving time in economics, whereas in classical equilibrium theory the things were so structured as to imply that processes were heavily dampened, so that it really did not matter; motions were so fast and reached a new equilibrium in such a short time, that you could possibly treat equilibrium as a state of affairs and then think of parametric variations, and that gives rise to what you call comparative statics, or what the physicists call adiabatic motions. Frisch's idea was that this need not be so, so that there could very well be [other] possibilities within the system. He thought that explosive systems cannot operate so as to lead to a breakdown of the state of affairs, and therefore they are not suitable as epistemic devices in terms of trying to model real life economic phenomena in time. At the same time, exponential processes going on for infinity make no sense. It is known that most processes saturate after a particular point of time, which again is one of the limitations of the steady state growth models where the underlying assumption is that scale-extensive magnitudes could grow exponentially over time. That, we know, is not correct.

But Frisch was not interested in problems of growth. At that particular time, he was concerned with the problem of oscillation. Now, de-trending therefore became important, and that is why Tinbergen's empirical work [for the League of Nations, see Tinbergen, 1939] took out the trend from the time series data and tried to look at the residual, and leaving out some irregularities and so on, he tried to find out an explanatory phenomenon of the residual movement. He was interested in finding out whether it was empirically dampened or anti-dampened. Here, I think, his famous business cycles work gave him the final autoregressive scheme and the second-law-order in which he showed that the roots would normally be in the inner circle of the complex plane, and therefore it is perfectly consistent with Frisch's hypothesis about systems if we assume shocks to be randomly distributed. This is where the discussion stood around that particular time.

In between, there was an interesting attempt made by Kalecki [1935, 1945], with the first model that he had on business cycles, where he used an earlier formulation of Tinbergen [1931], which Tinbergen had used in the shipbuilding cycle, in relation to macro-economics – a macro-dynamic model of the cycle as it was called. Now in that model, which some of you have possibly seen, mixed-difference and differential equations do in fact have problems that are not so simple to solve; you have transcendental polynomials, and if you really solve it you could have two possible paths. One could be a path which is a growth path – a steady growth path embedded already in Kalecki's first work [1935] – which he thought was uninteresting because we are no longer in the pre-war period thinking of steady growth as a serious possibility for the capitalist system, which again was in sharp contrast to what happened after the Second World War and in the so-called Golden Age when the whole focus was shifted. He concentrated on the other root and then he really made a funny suggestion: he said the parameters must be so chosen as to give a situation which is the precise borderline case between damping and anti-damping. And there is only one such case, namely when you have unit roots or when you have pure imaginaries as in the case of differential equations, which gives you a special movement [of closed trajectories around a centre]. He tampered with the data. In other words, his model was so structured as to give rise to only such possibilities. Frisch objected to it very seriously and said that this was not permissible. In that way, he anticipated [that] what we can say is a very important concept, the concept of structural stability or instability of the dynamical processes.

Structural stability of dynamical processes basically means that the system must be such that small perturbations will not disturb the phase-portrait of the system. In other words, it would mean that if you take an 'epsilon' perturbation in the coefficients, it should not be the case that this very special case where the roots are purely imaginary roots or lie on the unit circle of the complex plane on the disk is shifted either in a damped direction or an anti-damped direction. In other words, the movement should not be allowed to change. The phase-portrait should remain more or less [qualitatively] unchanged. [Otherwise it is] a structurally unstable system.

Frisch thought that a structurally unstable system is in fact not a serious possibility in real life. In other words, modelling of systems should not include structural instability. In fact, the word was not invented at that time. The word was invented a little later by two engineers in Russia, Andronov and Pontryagin, the mathematician [1937]. And they came up with the concept of structural stability. Now, from a design engineer point of view, a system which is structurally unstable obviously has much less sense, as it is not robust enough. But a question has been recently raised by a countryman of Prof. Luigi Pasinetti, Prof. Vercelli, who has written several articles on this particular question to which we shall come at a later stage, strongly supporting the case that we cannot really be wedded to the dogma of structural stability [Vercelli, 1984]. We should in fact allow the possibility of structural instability in economic dynamics [because] it is by allowing for structural instability that one should really be able to get possible changes and mutations in the economic system.

I think he overstates his case, because while I think structural stability may be too strong an assumption, one would like certain aspects of the mathematical system to remain reasonably robust. I think that becomes more important than structural instability. Some of the important physical systems, in fact, are structurally unstable, like the Hamiltonian systems, where there are no frictions and things like that. Or for that matter, [the] Lotka Volterra system of [predatory prey] model which Goodwin [1967] used in the context of the growth cycles, which is again an example of a structurally unstable system which Kolmogorov had redefined to give rise to possibilities of business cycles.

Thus Frisch's discussion of the 1930s was way ahead. So was the implementation of Frisch's programme in the hands of Prof. Tinbergen. The reason that I am mentioning these things is that these were very major steps forward in the context of the discussion, which was not done analogically. It was not done by just imitating classical mechanics, in the sense that they were looking for precise analogues of concepts, but you are looking more at the mathematical structure. And the underlying thing was basically the problem of what you should say of dynamical systems. It is a dynamical system's theoretic concept which was introduced by Frisch and which then became, I think, implemented in an empirical manner by Prof. Tinbergen.

I think the debate in the 1930s, after Frisch's intervention, took the form of straight-jacketing the discussion and clarifying it simultaneously. Clarifying it because it was so much more precise, although what Frisch was talking about was not really new. And straight-jacketing the discussion because it in fact became a part of linear systems analysis. And as you know very well, linear systems are capable of very limited kinds of behaviour. There is nothing very much unexpected that can appear here. And also it made the very fundamental distinction between trend movements and deviations from the trend.

This again is a problem of difference between Prof. Tinbergen and Prof. Dopfer. Tinbergen has always maintained the position that in the neighbourhood of an equilibrium, a smooth curve could always be represented by a tangent line. So you could always replace a non-linear system by a linear system of differential equations on which most analyses proceed. His justification is in fact that this should be true for any smooth differentiable function, and therefore there is no harm in taking the tangent line, [Tinbergen, 1959] – or the linear approximation as he calls it – as a first approximation. Whereas Prof. Dopfer says that much of the important information in the system may in fact be missed by taking such a linear approximation. To which Tinbergen could have easily replied (which he doesn't do here) that we could seek second order terms, third order terms, fourth order terms and so on, which in fact people did do in classical mechanics (I mean: mathematical theories). In those areas, they rely on the principle of analytical continuation, and you can have as good an approximation as you like by taking sufficiently important terms in this power series. So it would seem the problem of non-linearity is not fundamentally so very important as the problem of linearity plus the ability to take sufficient approximations. This is how I interpret Tinbergen's argument, although he does not spell it out here, but I am sure this is the sort of argument that he has in mind.

But in fact it is not true, unfortunately. And the particular fact that is not true makes life so much more complicated than earlier generations of theorists who really believed in this way. It is not true, as was pointed out by Poincaré a long time ago, that you could get formal power-series expansion but that they would not converge. In fact in many cases they diverge, in which case this sort of thing does not work out. That means that this idea that linear approximation (plus perturbations) could take care of possible difficulties is not an answer. Now, it is true that there are some exceptional voices which were heard. One of these exceptional voices, which did not have a good economics but did have a fairly good mathematics, was a Dutchman who unfortunately was killed during the war: Mr L. Hamburger. He wrote one or two papers during the 1930s including a short report in *Econometrica*, which is easily available [Hamburger, 1934], following some work of a compatriot of his, B. van der Pol. He tried to apply non-linear equations to economic problems. And that really gave the possibility of sustained oscillations, in a very different way. And that idea in fact was followed up by practically nobody, until Richard Goodwin appeared on the scene. He was the first one to make use of non-linearities which I think was a work of great imagination and depth for the time at which it was done [Goodwin, 1946; Goodwin, 1967].

But the Frisch–Tinbergen position was so generally acceptable and non-linearities were so much more complicated to handle (although Tinbergen himself had played around a little bit with non-linearities in one of his relatively less known papers in a Danish journal [Tinbergen, 1944]), that it really did not figure until Hicks [1950] came into the picture and gave a piecewise linear approximation which could be understood by most people. And I think Prof. Pasinetti also dealt with some such systems later on, in the 1950s if I recall, in a paper which I read a long time ago in *Oxford Economic Papers* [Pasinetti, 1960].

So, the sum and substance of what I am saying is that Frisch was a great innovator, and Tinbergen, along with Frisch, changed the terms of discourse as well as the implementation of what could be regarded as an empirical programme of economic dynamics. That was a great advance forward. But certain incipient and interesting ideas which were there as I said by Hamburger [1934] and also by a mathematician called le Corbeiller [1933], were lost sight of, as well as the very important work by Goodwin [1946], because everybody accepted it [the Frisch–Tinbergen position] until very recently. And that is where a really very major change in point of view is in fact taking place.

And that is where I will go to the next step of my discussion, which is connected with the change in focus of what exactly you are trying to do. And the change in focus is whether you are thinking in terms of quantitative dynamics, à la predictive models (like the predictions relating to the movements of planets and so on), or whether you are thinking of a broader qualitative dynamics.

Now if you are thinking in terms of qualitative dynamics, then in that particular case I think you are not interested so much in prediction as in understanding possibilities of movement and the evolution of forms. It is quite possible that this evolution of forms in a linear system is extremely restricted. The system either reaches equilibrium or breaks down, both of which are rather extreme possibilities. The question of different types of movements and motions is an important question, and Schumpeter was always very unhappy with this kind of approach because he felt that the dynamics of capitalism must be able to throw light on the problems of mutations in capitalism. Now, the capitalism of the 1850s is not the same as the capitalism of the 1950s, which means there has to be some possibility of endogenizing the notion of structural change. If you do not bring in the notion of structural change, then you are not in fact explaining the behaviour of the capitalist system. You are really dealing with a purely mathematical exercise. In fact that was his criticism. He was a great admirer of Frisch and Tinbergen, in fact he says great things about both of them, but he felt that they had not really elucidated the concept of business cycles as it appears in capitalist reality. It may well be an important methodological innovation. But he was not in a position, of course, to formalize these notions, and also the subject was not sufficiently developed, in particular in the way it has developed in very recent years. I think in recent years some of Poincaré's ideas have become much more generalized, taken up by many more people, which you can go into in a little more detail.

But there is another mode of thinking [about economic dynamics] which is really coming, and which has some relationship to Tinbergen's theory of economic policy, which I would like to mention here. If you think in terms of linear systems – and this was a question which in fact, in a different context, was raised by Haavelmo [1945] – then you make a clear distinction between the initial conditions and the parameters of the system; these are distinct categories. In this context the intrinsic fluctuations [. . .] are dependent only on the parametric configurations, and the initial conditions, in some sense, are unimportant. In other words, what you could get in this particular case would be a time shift. It makes no essential difference whether the process starts today or starts tomorrow or the day after tomorrow (we know this very interesting property called 'translation synthesis'). But he [Haavelmo] said this could not be the case, and the initial conditions are as important as the parameters. In other words, depending on the initial conditions you remain confined in a particular sub-space of the appropriate phase space, and you are not in a position to move out of it altogether; there are areas that you cannot possibly cross. And he sought for an explanation of evolutionary dissimilarities in his book, *A Study in the Theory of Economic Evolution*, along these lines [Haavelmo, 1954]. A linear system certainly cannot handle that kind of question. That is why non-linearities become very critical to the problem. Even aggregative non-linear models can throw up possibilities which linear models would not do – [this is] apart from questions we have talked about structural change – because in a non-linear system the phase space could in fact be broken up into several sub-spaces, and movements could be contained in different parts [or regions] of that [phase space.] [Trajectories] cannot really cross from one zone to another without violating the continuity assumption of the Lefschetz conditions and so forth, [causing] significant ruptures in the system. So you make all real changes exogenous, which is only one way of looking at the problem – not a very satisfactory way. That is why I feel the problem of economic dynamics centring on structural change is a very important research area, to which the earlier discussion was not adequately directed.

The second point, as I say, relates to economic policy questions. Tinbergen's approach, the targets-instruments approach, if you dynamize it – put it into a dynamic rather than a static context – would suggest that if you vary the initial conditions, the essentially intrinsic movements of the system are not changed. So you could think of varying the instrument variables, or varying the initial conditions if they take the form of change in structure of the initial variables, and still get into the same target state. In that context, the recent work in chaotic dynamics has shown that certain systems could have tremendous sensitiveness with respect to initial conditions, and that could be measured by the use of what are known as Liapunov exponents. And they really could get very far, as a result of deviations. In other words, small deviations in certain systems could be so much magnified that the system could in fact be completely different, end up in a very different area altogether, or fluctuate widely. If that is in fact the case, then possibly the classical theory of economic policy has to be somewhat re-examined. Instead of looking for simple solutions, or finding out the precise values of the instrument variables to reach the target variables, we may have to think much more carefully about possible corridors of action.

And this I think has a very important implication for the theory of planning.

I think the theory of planning in classical terms was based really on finding out exact numerical values of the instruments, like investment levels by sector, exchange rate, wage rate and so on, and you could find out, hopefully, the precise objectives, reach the precise objectives of the planner, in a suitable time-phased manner depending on how you classified it. But [this changes] as soon as you move into non-linearities, and some of the non-linear systems could in fact be so sensitive to the initial conditions, the extent of the sensitivity could be so serious, measured by the Liapunov exponents. And so the problem becomes to find out these measures, and on that a certain amount of work is in fact happening. And that is why I believe that it is important for us to shift attention to concepts from precise policies to finding out possible corridors of action, so that solutions can hopefully be bounded within a certain desired sub-space of the phase space, so that in that sense the system should have possibilities of showing robust behaviour in a precise mathematical sense, even though they are not structurally stable in the sense of Andronov and Pontryagin, [that is] that they show the same behaviour for all possible perturbations. I think this is one important issue.

The other issue that really has become very important (which I think is a part of solving the problem of structural change) is the problem of reformulation of economic policy, and [related] problems [such as] the fundamental problem [of whether] business cycles, with which much of the discussion should have started, are generated by a deterministic non-linear process or by a Frischian kind of mechanism. This once again becomes a very important question. And to the extent that non-linearities play an important role, it would be implied that the Lucas–Sargent approach also has to be rejected, and we really have to read more along the lines initially chalked out by Goodwin and others, on which some work is going on currently by quite a few people in Europe. For that purpose it is necessary for us to look at the time series, and find out suitable tests as to whether this time series data could have been generated, its irregularities could have been generated basically by a deterministic process, suitable parametric values, or tuning parameters as they are called, or are in fact conformable to the Frischian pattern. So I think a large class of researchable areas have recently opened up, and it is a very active area of research, and I think it is necessary to give it some thought.

Coming back to the problem of Dopfer and Tinbergen, it seems that Prof. Dopfer was possibly trying to get at something like that, but I think his analysis in many ways is pretty confused, so it is not very easy to always understand exactly what he is driving at, but here and there it is clear that he is relying on (and he states explicitly that there has been) a great deal of recent work on non-linear dynamics. He may not have been the best person to talk about it, but he has a point, to which Tinbergen's answer seems to me to be fairly inadequate, even though he may be basically right that they are not really imitating classical mechanics. They're in fact inventing what you might say is a dynamical systems approach with respect to understanding real life problems as they occur in economics, whether it is in the area of growth or in the area of fluctuations. Because after all, when he came to the theory of trend movements, Tinbergen gave non-linear theory, as he calls it in 'Zur Theorie der langfristigen Wirtschaftsentwicklung' [Tinbergen, 1942], but it is not connected to the business cycle theory. So these have not been integrated, which is Schumpeter's persistent question. And maybe now with all the developments just taking place we will have a slightly better theory, although one cannot say that very major results have yet been achieved. But Goodwin's work, beginning with a structurally unstable model, is moving in a direction which certainly has promise, which I found personally quite interesting and which I believe ought to be discussed. So that was the reason for taking the opportunity to say a few words on this fairly complex subject.

REFERENCES

Andronov, A. and Pontryagin, L. (1937), 'Systèmes grossiers', *C.R. (Dokl.) Acad. Sci. USSR*, **14**, 247–51.

'Cassel volume', ed. (1933), *Economic Essays in Honour of Gustav Cassel*, London: George Allen & Unwin.

Dopfer, K. (1988), 'Classical mechanics with an ethical dimension: Prof. Tinbergen's economics', *Journal of Economic Issues*, **22**(3), 675–706.

Feinstein, C.H., ed. (1967), *Socialism, Capitalism and Economic Growth*, London: Macmillan.

Frisch, R. (1933), *Propagation problems and impulse problems in dynamic economics*, in 'Cassel volume' (1933), pp. 171–205.

Goodwin, R.M. (1946), 'Innovations and irregularity of economic cycles', *Review of Economic Studies*, **28**, 95–104.

Goodwin, R.M. (1967), *A growth cycle*, in Feinstein (1967), pp. 54–8.

Goodwin, R.M., Kruger, M. and Vercelli, A., eds (1984), *Non-linear Models of Fluctuating Growth: An International Symposium*, New York: Springer.

Haavelmo, T. (1954), *A Study in the Theory of Economic Evolution*, Amsterdam: North-Holland.

Hamburger, L. (1934), 'Note on economic cycles and relaxation-oscillations', *Econometrica*, **2**(1), 112.

Hicks, J.R. (1950), *Contribution to a Theory of the Trade Cycle*, Oxford: Clarendon Press.

Kalecki, M. (1935), 'A macrodynamic theory of business cycles', *Econometrica*, **3**, 327–44.

Kalecki, M. (1945), *Theory of Economic Dynamics*, London: George Allen & Unwin.

Klaassen, L., Koyck, L. and Witteveen, H., eds (1959), *Jan Tinbergen: Selected Papers*, Amsterdam: North-Holland.

Knight, F.H. (1956), *On the History and Method of Economics: Selected Essays*, Chicago: University of Chicago Press. Chapter 8: 'Statics and dynamics: Some queries regarding the mechanical analogy in economics', pp. 179–201.

le Corbeiller, P. (1933), 'Les systèmes autoentretenus et les oscillations de relaxation', *Econometrica*, 1, 328–32.

Lotka, A.J. (1956), *Elements of Mathematical Biology*, New York: Dover.

Pasinetti, L.L. (1960), 'Cyclical fluctuations and economic growth', *Oxford Economic Papers (new series)*, 12(2), 215–41.

Pasinetti, L.L. (1981), *Structural Change and Economic Growth. A Theoretical Essay on the Dynamics of the Wealth of Nations*, Cambridge: Cambridge University Press.

Thom, R. (1975), *Structural Stability and Morphogenesis: An Outline of a General Theory of Models*, London: W.A. Benjamin.

Tinbergen, J. (1931), 'Ein Schiffbauzyklus', *Weltwirtschaftliches Archiv*, 34(2), 152–64.

Tinbergen, J. (1939), *Statistical Testing of Business-Cycle Theories*, New York: Agathon Press.

Tinbergen, J. (1942), 'Zur Theorie der langfristigen Wirtschaftsentwicklung', *Weltwirtschaft-liches Archiv*, 55, 511–49.

Tinbergen, J. (1944), 'Ligevægtstyper og konjunkturbevægelse', *Nordisk Tidsskrift for Teknisk Økonomi*, pp. 45–63. Reprinted as Tinbergen (1959).

Tinbergen, J. (1959), *Types of equilibrium and business cycle movements*, in Klaassen, Koyck and Witteveen (1959), pp. 15–36.

Tinbergen, J. (1988), 'Prof. Tinbergen's economics: A comment on Dopfer', *Journal of Economic Issues*, 22(4), 851–4.

Tinbergen, J. (1989), The functioning of economic research, *mimeo*, Rotterdam: Erasmus University Rotterdam.

Vercelli, A. (1984), *Fluctuations and growth: Keynes, Schumpeter, Marx and the structural instability of capitalism*, in Goodwin, Kruger and Vercelli (1984), pp. 209–31.

von Neumann, J. (1945), 'A model of general economic equilibrium', *The Review of Economic Studies*, 13, 1–9.

3. Cart before the horse: National versus international integration

J. Mohan Rao

1. INTRODUCTION

International flows of goods and of finance capital have doubtless increased sharply over the last few decades. Non-traditional manufacturing exports from the newly industrializing countries (NICs) of Asia to the developed world have scaled new heights. Some have heralded a new era of globalization marked by rapidly growing world trade and capital movements. Others argue, however, that the world economy is actually less integrated today than it was in the late nineteenth century (see for example Rodrik, 1998). But such comparisons invite further scrutiny. It is true that labour movements, in the form of mass migrations from the old world to the new, were substantially higher during the nineteenth century than they are today. Similarly, net capital outflow relative to gross national product was much higher in the UK prior to World War I than at any time since. But a large share of these labour and capital flows was restricted to the same group of countries which today account for the lion's share of goods flows. The significance of capital and labour movements in such a comparison cannot be considered apart from trade flows. Economies may be 'integrated' by goods flows even in the absence of any factor movements. Turning to trade volumes relative to national incomes, measured openness in the US and in Europe peaked before World War I, fell sharply between the wars and trended upward after World War II. By this measure, the advanced economies of the world are not any more open in 1997 than they were in 1897. But per capita incomes in these advanced economies are many times larger today and, as a result, the share of services, which tend to be far less traded than goods, is considerably higher. Hence even constant trade ratios represent a significant increase in openness.

A rather more compelling argument against the liberal use of the term 'globalization' is that the movement of goods, capital and enterprises across national boundaries is marked by great unevenness. First, developed

44

nations, whether as sources or as destinations, account for a disproportionate share of these flows relative to their share in global income. Second, even as tariff barriers have declined, old forms of non-tariff restraints on trade persist while new ones are coming into vogue. Third, the formal and informal creation of regional blocks for trading and investment may be seen as a threat to the forces of integration across these blocks and, even more, as a factor further isolating the numerous countries and regions in the south that do not enjoy political or economic proximity with Japan, the US or the EU. Finally, there remain great asymmetries in the stability and composition of exports as between the developed nations and NICs on the one hand and the less developed countries (LDCs) on the other.

On the whole, the balance of forces seems to point in the direction of globalization at least in the descriptive sense of a process increasing international resource and goods flows. Apart from the information and communication revolutions that have reduced the costs of international transactions, the impetus for these flows has come from changing policy regimes in both rich and poor countries. Formal processes of market integration have been initiated in North America and are reaching their culmination in western Europe. The GATT/WTO framework phases out important areas of managed trade and protectionist policy. Many among the less developed countries of the third world and the second have shifted policies, in some cases radically, towards opening up their economies to global markets.[1]

To some extent, the nature of policy changes has been conditioned by changing economic circumstances and institutions. All the same, the role of national and international policy deliberation (together with the powerful influence of politics and ideology that that implies) should not be underestimated whether in rich or poor nations. Consider the advanced countries first. Though the unravelling of the monetary arrangements of the post-War era in 1971, the productivity growth deceleration starting in the late 1960s and the oil price increase of 1973 had a definite impact on the shape of international economic relations during the succeeding decades; these are themselves best seen as following from the crumbling of the particular political-economic regime (termed 'Fordism') that maintained stable national and international regimes of rapid growth (the Golden Age).[2] The convergence of productivity and income levels in Europe and Japan to those prevalent in the US accelerated the growth of intra-industry trade and investments among these regions. Protectionist barriers to trade also came down in successive rounds. In other words, converging incomes produced market integration, not only the other way around.

By the same token, however, the maintenance of export competitiveness began to emerge as a new imperative rivalling the Fordist concerns about maintaining real wage growth and the welfare state. The new imperative arose at the same time that the internal growth potential of Fordism was petering out. Attempts at fine-tuning the economy led to structural inflation and external imbalance and, in response, businesses demanded fiscal and labour discipline (Cox, 1994). Inflation control on the macro side and all-around 'flexibility', including deregulation, on the supply side became the hallmarks of new conservative policy regimes. Assaults on the welfare state, more or less extensive, have followed in their wake. But the very diversity of policy responses across countries underscores the role of politics.

The LDCs, as a group and individually, enjoyed respectable rates of economic growth during the Golden Age which surpassed their dismal performance during the colonial era. This difference was not simply due to the global economic environment of the Golden Age alone; rather, a large if variable share of the difference must be accounted for by the transition from colonialism to sovereignty and the developmental role of the state. The growth momentum was maintained even through the 1970s, in part because of better export prices for many raw material exports and the recycling of petro-dollars. But the eventual crash in the early 1980s, brought on by the crushing rise in interest rates and the sharp adverse movement in the terms of trade, turned out to be far more costly in the South, particularly in Sub-Saharan Africa and Latin America, than the earlier one had been in the North. Straitened fiscs (reflecting the internal transfer problem arising from the debt crisis) undermined state capacities to pursue indigenous models of modernization or to sustain and expand anti-poverty programmes, prompting or necessitating a shift in regimes.

Conditionalities imposed by international creditors, in the form of orthodox stabilization and structural adjustment programmes, have been a major instrument for opening up these economies to the winds of global competition. Over the decade and a half since the Reagan–Volcker recession and the Mexican debt crisis that followed, the developing world has witnessed a remarkable convergence in official economic policy thinking and in policy regimes. The hard core of these widely espoused policies, the so-called Washington Consensus, may be accurately described as the neo-liberal nostrum of the *laissez-faire* market. Neo-liberalism augments the traditional liberal belief in conservative macroeconomic policy and unregulated markets with the dictum that the state can do little right if only because it is liable to be captured by special interests. Conversely, the market can do no wrong so long as the political process can be reined in. Political discipline is best secured by integrating the domestic market completely with global markets.[3] An economy significantly sheltered from world markets always affords a measure of policy autonomy. But then, like nature's abhorrence of a vacuum, economic subversion through political means must ensue. Hence, the neo-liberal prescription coupling internal liberalization and external market integration.[4]

But apart from this purely negative argument of the need to discipline the state (with the market providing the means), the neo-liberal view is equally founded on the old argument that free markets optimize national welfare. This central tenet is anchored in five basic assumptions:

1. that a politically unconstrained market regime is feasible (distributional problems can be resolved, if they must be, without 'distorting' the market);
2. that the market can fully coordinate individual decisions, for example produce full employment (the state can only get in the way);
3. that public investment is an inefficient substitute for private investment in the growth process (complementarities are negligible);
4. that the unhindered import of technology can provide an adequate basis for developing competitiveness (a level playing field imposes no handicaps in building up dynamic competitive advantage); and
5. that the free movement of finance and enterprises across the national border will produce internal and external balance (globalization is good for the South).[5]

In fact, the neo-liberal diagnosis and prescription have a timeless and spaceless character to them: they are supposed to apply with equal force to both rich and poor countries, North and South, early and late industrializers. Liberal policies and openness are predicted to be a guarantee of global economic integration and of convergence in national living standards – the creation of a global economic system. Existing inequalities among or within nations pose no impediments to any of them deriving these benefits; nor do such inequalities justify anything other than the neo-liberal prescriptions.

2.   ALTERNATIVE VIEWS ON ECONOMIC INTEGRATION

Despite the air of ineluctability that the term 'Washington Consensus' applied to this agenda conveys, alternative viewpoints or second and third opinions are scarcely lacking. Some predate the neo-liberal ascent, others are direct responses to the current phase of globalization. While some offer alternative means to development, others also question the very ends of development accepted in the mainstream.

First, there is 'traditional' development economics, the main thrust of which has been the analysis of the structural determinants of low incomes and productivity and the means by which they might be overcome. Capital market failures, the indivisibility of infrastructural investments and problems of investment coordination have been especially emphasized. Many of the structural determinants (such as low saving rates and low agricultural productivity) are themselves related to low incomes or to institutional impediments and asset inequalities. Hence, their self-perpetuating tendencies are seen to require proactive public interventions and policies. Confronted with two centuries of increasing inequalities among nations (which included significant periods of wide-open national economic borders), both early development economists and theorists of dependency and underdevelopment argued that the inherited international division of labour is part of the problem, not part of the solution (Prebisch, 1959 and Frank, 1966). The policy approach emphasizes accumulation, industrialization and mobilization of labour resources and presupposes a key strategic and coordinating role of the state. Although this approach has of course been refined in the light of experience and refashioned for a changing world, its basic insights remain undiminished in importance.

Second, one direction in which development theory has been reformulated is to incorporate what may be described as the influence of world time. This follows the lead of Gerschenkron (1962) who argued that in an unequal world, international demonstration effects tend to produce successive paths of development different from earlier ones. Gerschenkron did not deny the relevance of structural 'preconditions' for modern economic growth, but showed historically that late developers had sought institutional substitutions to meet these requirements. It seems clear that late-industrializing countries can secure the advantage of lateness (consisting in not having to reinvent the technological wheel) only by creating an appropriate infrastructural, informational and incentive base for local learning and development (Amsden, Kochanowicz and Taylor, 1994).[6] The contrast between the experience of the East Asian countries and much of the rest of the third world demonstrates little if not this basic lesson. While it is equally clear that such a course requires delicate management and a strong state, it makes no sense to take a mechanistic view of either markets or politics which forecloses (or renders inevitable) such an adaptive response.[7]

Third, another 'new' direction in development theory goes further than the pioneers of development economics in emphasizing the role of increasing returns in economic activity. Rosenstein-Rodan had emphasized the role of investment indivisibilities and externalities in producing market failures in backward economies. Following Smith and Young, Myrdal and Kaldor had similarly made increasing returns an important part of their theories of economic growth. The 'new' growth theory (Romer, 1986 and

Lucas, 1988) pursues this idea within a neoclassical methodological framework that emphasizes the role of learning based on human capital accumulation and knowledge spillovers across firms and sectors. Whereas early development theories spoke in terms of a low-level poverty equilibrium and ways of getting out of it, the new growth theory describes a moving equilibrium of rising relative poverty. Viewed purely mechanistically, increasing returns imply unbounded divergence and capital movements in the 'wrong' direction: high productivity nations enjoy faster rates of productivity increase and accumulation. The bare facts of divergent growth have been used to support the applicability of these theories.

Fourth, there is an emerging view that globalization poses a trade-off between the flexibility of resource allocation that it ensures and the uncertainty of incomes, occupations and ways of life it generates.[8] The uncertainty entails increasing state expenditures on the welfare state and social insurance. But these interventions can neither be entirely efficacious nor fiscally sustainable in a globalized world. If not adequately pre-empted, the argument goes, a reaction is likely to set in which may undermine the basis of a globalized economy. It is probably fair to say that this view, unlike the preceding alternatives, accepts the neo-liberal proposition that globalization increases resource efficiency and growth for all countries. Rather, it is troubled by the clipping of national autonomy that neo-liberals take to be a central virtue of globalization.

Finally, the preceding view finds a deeper and more extended statement in cultural theories of economic development and of politics.[9] For the most part, economists have been content with seeing technology and unchanging preferences as the bedrock on which economic growth rests. Pushed to their logical conclusions, both structural and neoclassical economic theories arrive at mechanistic cul-de-sacs. For one, economistic theories ignore the specific political and cultural histories of diverse regions and the ways in which they may shape economic possibilities. For another, the same histories may also define a heterogeneity of beliefs and values not only across but also within individual societies. Not all societies can be presumed to be playing the same 'game' and with the same expectations. But for the same reasons, there is a danger of ignoring the role of human creativity in producing new possibilities (whether for better or for worse).

Our aim in this paper is to explore the grounds on which a 'second opinion' to the Washington Consensus may be constructed. Several of the themes outlined above are pursued further with preliminary and partial empirical investigations covering the period from 1960 to 1995 and a large sample of 123 rich and poor nations. The historical record makes abundantly clear that international inequality has increased not only over the long haul of the past two centuries but also in recent decades. The self-reinforcing power of unequal development derives mainly from economic and political-economic forces internal to nations. Unregulated global market forces mostly follow this process rather than countering it chiefly because they reinforce inherited resource endowments and the inherited division of labour. At the same time, the fragile internal development process is vulnerable to the disruptive forces of unrestricted openness. To be sure, access to global markets can be a powerful factor in development. But development success in the post-War era has hinged on selective and phased integration with world markets.

This understanding clearly goes against the prevailing view that the economic growth benefits from globalization far outweigh the costs, and that the main task for developing countries is to jump on the global bandwagon by eliminating all impediments in the way of integrating their domestic economies with global trade and financial flows. But it is not only economic growth as it relates to globalization that is at issue. The historical record also shows that the wealth of nations alone fails to account for variations in the levels of national poverty and inequality. Hence, we must also be concerned about whether increasing globalization restructures incentives in a direction that is conducive to reducing inequality and poverty. Apart from the purely economic mechanisms, this concern must extend also to the capacities for public action that globalization might weaken. The paper is animated by the belief that given the continuing primacy of the nation state, a modicum of national policy autonomy is vital to a politically sustainable economy, particularly in redressing endemic problems of poverty and inequality.

3. DIVERGENCE RATHER THAN CONVERGENCE

Massive increases in inequalities among nations during the era of modern economic growth do not inspire confidence in the liberal prediction or prescription. Living standards over much of the old world were proximately similar around 1600. Even as late as 1800, per capita income in Europe and North America was roughly the same as that prevalent in Asia (Schwartz, 1994). But by 1900, incomes in the centre were around 10 times as large as in the periphery and the gap had doubled again by 1960. Yet markets in the periphery were largely open to world commerce (and to investments financed by the richer nations) for the century preceding World War II. Notably, however, most peripheral states lacked sovereignty and were subjected to colonial exploitation. India's per capita income, for example, precisely stagnated under the Crown-imposed policy of *laissez-faire* and virtual free trade. By contrast, a strongly regulated import-substitution regime after independence served to more than double India's per capita income. Moreover, there were significant episodes of industrialization in countries like Brazil, Mexico and India during the Great Depression and World War II when the world economy had virtually ceased to be global.

More recent evidence also provides broad support for this picture of divergent economic growth, notwithstanding the exceptional performance of the East Asian and (lately) South-east Asian countries. The convergence of per capita incomes across nations may be statistically tested by regressing period growth rates of income on start-of-period incomes. A negative (positive) coefficient on initial per capita income implies convergence (divergence). The exercise we report here is based on national income data for 123 countries, adjusted for nominal exchange rate deviations from purchasing power parity. The period covered by the PennTable data source is 1960–92. We examine convergence for the whole period and also separately for the sub-periods 1960–78 (which was part of the Golden Age of high growth) and 1979–92 (which includes the decade lost to development in much of the third world).[10]

Per capita income growth rates were calculated by fitting exponential trend equations for each country and period.[11] Table 3.1 classifies the countries for each period by both income growth (low, middle and high) and income level (low, middle and high), with countries arranged in ascending order of income growth in each group.[12] The Table shows that the number in the low-growth group greatly increased at the expense of the high-growth group between the two periods. Though the loss of growth momentum affected all income groups, it was particularly pronounced among the low-income and middle-income countries (especially in Africa and Latin America).

Table 3.2 presents the period-wise results of the convergence regressions for each country group taken separately and for the whole sample. Taking all countries together, the results show statistically significant growth divergence over the whole period and over each of the sub-periods, with the forces of divergence being stronger during 1979–92 than during 1960–78. Taking each income group separately, we find that there was income convergence within the high-income and middle-income groups over both periods (with a higher speed of convergence in the second period than the first). While the low-income group also converged 'within' during the first period, it showed no such tendency during the second (actually the coefficient of initial income is positive though not statistically significant).

The bald facts of world-wide income divergence reported above confirm, for the two periods (and income groups) taken separately, similar results found in other samples.[13] But the facts of divergence have met with varied responses in terms of a theory of convergence – a sort of convergence

Table 3.1 Countries ranked by level and growth rate of per capita income (constant international prices)

1960–78

Low growth (<1% pa)	Medium growth (1–3% pa)	High growth (>3% pa)
Low income Somalia Angola Chad Madagascar Burundi Bangladesh Benin Mali Haiti Burkina Faso Mozambique Senegal Uganda Zambia Ghana Niger Comoros Cen. Afr. Rep. India Sri Lanka Zaire Ethiopia *Mid income* Uruguay Chile *High income* —	*Low income* Sierra Leone Mauritania Myanmar Guinea Nepal Malawi Zimbabwe Honduras Liberia Cameroon Pakistan Sudan Guinea-Bissau Nicaragua Guyana Kenya Rwanda *Mid income* Venezuela Mauritius Cape Verde Papua New Guinea Argentina Peru El Salvador Guatemala Philippines Paraguay Trinidad Colombia South Africa *High income* New Zealand Switzerland UK Luxembourg USA Sweden Australia Denmark	*Low income* China Tanzania Congo Gambia Togo Yemen Nigeria *Mid income* Egypt Jamaica Algeria Indonesia Morocco Bolivia Costa Rica Fiji Dominican Rep. Seychelles Mexico Panama Turkey Swaziland Puerto Rico Thailand Ecuador *High income* Netherlands Canada Finland Norway Austria Belgium France Ireland Italy Iceland Cyprus Reunion Israel Spain Portugal Hong Kong Japan Germany Korea Singapore

1979–92

Low growth (<1% pa)				Medium growth (1–3% pa)		High growth
Low income	Honduras	Argentina	Hungary	*Low income*	Malaysia	*Low income*
Guyana	Zimbabwe	Namibia	Uruguay	Congo	*High income*	India
Niger	Ethiopia	Bolivia	Jamaica	Tanzania	Switzerland	China
Nigeria	Cameroon	Guatemala	*High income*	Burundi	Australia	Yemen
Madagascar	Rwanda	Ecuador	Germany	Guinea-Bissau	Iceland	*Mid income*
Zambia	Malawi	*High income*	New Zealand	Pakistan	Netherlands	Seychelles
Nicaragua	Nepal	Papua New Guinea		Sri Lanka	Sweden	Indonesia
Liberia	Guinea	Syria		Bangladesh	USA	Mauritius
Sierra Leone	Senegal	Venezuela		*Mid income*	France	Malta
Uganda	Mali	Jordan		Colombia	Canada	Romania
Mozambique	Ghana	Panama		Egypt	Israel	Thailand
Cen. Afr. Rep.	Kenya	Philippines		Greece	Belgium	*High income*
Gambia	Angola	Paraguay		Morocco	Finland	Portugal
Haiti	Burkina Faso	South Africa		Tunisia	Austria	Luxembourg
Benin	Myanmar	El Salvador		Barbados	Denmark	Japan
Comoros	*Mid income*	Poland		Chile	Italy	Cyprus
Sudan	Surinam	Lesotho		Cape Verde	Norway	Singapore
Chad	Swaziland	Algeria		Oman	UK	Hong Kong
Mauritania	Trinidad	Mexico		Puerto Rico	Spain	Korea
Somalia	Gabon	Fiji		Turkey	Ireland	
Togo	Peru	Costa Rica		Botswana		
Zaire		Dominican Rep.				
		Brazil				

Table 3.2 The relationship between income growth and initial income (1960–92) (trend growth rate of Y_{IP-85} regressed on the log of initial Y_{IP-85})

	1960–78			1979–92			1960–92		
	Constant	Initial y_{IP-85}	Adj. R^2	Constant	Initial y_{IP-85}	Adj. R^2	Constant	Initial y_{IP-85}	Adj. R^2
Low income	8.478** [4.092]	-1.098**** [0.622]	0.045	-0.752 [4.649]	6.6E-02 [0.683]	-0.023	9.562* [3.398]	-1.370** [0.516]	0.118
Middle income	9.304* [3.158]	-0.742*** [0.423]	0.064	9.616** [4.605]	-1.141** [0.569]	0.062	12.777* [2.228]	-1.389* [0.299]	0.310
High income	21.717* [3.123]	-2.078* [0.370]	0.549	22.116* [5.284]	-2.146* [0.577]	0.322	20.155* [2.141]	-2.001* [0.253]	0.694
All countries	-1.104 [1.600]	0.556* [0.217]	0.084	-4.514* [1.494]	0.649* [0.189]	0.081	-0.362 [1.393]	0.315*** [0.189]	0.014

Notes:
1. Standard errors in parentheses.
2. See appendix for variable definitions and data sources.
3. * denotes significant at 1% level
   ** significant at 5% level
   *** significant at 10% level.
Source: Author's estimates.

54

cacophony. In the conventional (Solow) model of economic growth with diminishing returns to labour and capital, growth and initial income are supposed to be negatively related for the following reason. Around a long-run steady state, a low initial capital–labour ratio (which is associated with a low level of per capita income) implies high returns to capital. A rise in saving follows, leading to a transitory rise in the capital-labour ratio, that is, as the economy moves to the steady state, accumulation and income growth will be at a higher rate than their long-run level.[14]

So on the face of it, the divergence results contradict the neoclassical Solow model of growth. This prompted a search for alternative theories that could explain the seeming anomaly. According to Baumol, Nelson and Wolff (1994), convergence is indeed not universal: there may be a convergence club. Members of the club are those who have high enough initial human capital endowments to take advantage of modern technologies. Apart from the high-income countries, these tend to be countries of middle rather than low incomes. Convergence is to be expected in restricted samples only, not in the world at large.

Another alternative was the so-called 'new' theories of growth based on diverse sources of increasing returns (Romer, 1986). Increasing returns to the scale of inputs may be due to such factors as knowledge spillovers across enterprises and sectors, learning by doing (related to the scale of output or its rate of growth), R&D activity and related human capital, various agglomeration economies and so on. High initial incomes, in this view, proxy for high levels of accumulated skill or human capital and, therefore, high future growth. Low-income countries cannot get high returns to human capital because they cannot take advantage of knowledge spillovers and so on, and will therefore grow more slowly. In short, divergence is a natural corollary of increasing returns. One difficulty with this argument, of course, is that divergence is *not* a fact of life among the advanced capitalist countries.[15]

Others, however, soon argued that the facts of divergence contradicted the Solow model only if the fundamentals of the economies being compared are indeed the same. The Solow model does not predict absolute convergence – a simple negative relation between growth and initial income as countries converge to identical long-run incomes. Its prediction is conditional upon the fundamentals, which include consumption preferences of the population, technology levels and long-run population growth rates. Countries may differ in their long-run per capita income levels (governed by the fundamentals). However, each country is predicted to grow more rapidly the larger is the gap between its initial income level and its own long-run per capita income level. In other words, the model predicts relative or contingent convergence (Barro and Sala-i-Martin, 1992). Long-run income levels may well be different, that is, absolute divergence may hold but the Solow model is not disproved if contingent convergence holds.

But how is one to test for 'long-run' differences in income levels? Barro, Mankiw and others found support for contingent convergence by introducing current values of variables that, they believe, could predict countries' future incomes. In their view, this vindicated the Solow model and diminishing returns. These results also seem to halt the new growth theory in its tracks. If economies differ in their exogenously given fundamentals, this is sufficient to explain divergent long-run incomes. Absolute divergence is not then due to a process of increasing returns working on nondiverging fundamentals (Pritchett, 1996, p. 42). Growth differentials are exogenous, not endogenous. Pritchett suggests the following analogy:

> Suppose we tried to explain people's weight gain with a model in which weight gains or losses are predicted based on one's weight last year and one's height. If an individual's weight fluctuates around a more or less stable level that depends on height, then one will find convergence of weight, conditional on height. People who are thinner than their long-term average will, on average, gain weight and those heavier will, on average lose weight. This does not imply that over time everyone will weigh the same. The distribution of weight across individuals will remain exactly the same, irrespective of the speed of 'conditional weight convergence'. (1996 p. 43)

This analogy works if we know people's heights (analogously countries' long-run income levels). But have we any more means to know the future possibilities of developing nations than the heights at maturity of growing babies? Besides, the predictor variables used in the contingent convergence equation – saving rate, the rate of growth of population, human capital stocks – are all known to be highly correlated with per capita incomes. Poor economies tend to have high rates of fertility, low human capital stocks, low rates of saving and investment. Indeed, traditional development theory starting from Kuznets used these relationships as the stylized facts of development without presuming anything about convergence/divergence across nations. But in terms of the contingent convergence hypothesis, this must imply systematically changing fundamentals. In short, the hypothesis of contingent convergence 'explains' the low growth rates of poor nations in terms of the very features that characterize their poverty, which is nothing but unalloyed divergence by another route.

The implications of the contingent convergence, convergence club and increasing returns hypotheses seem rather pessimistic from the viewpoint of the developing countries. The first two of these interpret divergence in terms of 'permanent' differences across nations using a 'closed' model of the economy. If one is prepared to entertain such an interpretation, then the statistical tests used to support it seem quite redundant. The tests transparently fail to address the real content of the hypothesis which remains buried in the black box of so-called 'fundamentals'. The increasing returns hypothesis is not any less 'closed' or pessimistic than the other two. But it relies on the accidents of history to tell a story of divergence that is at least amenable to deeper historical treatment, which some may find more satisfying. None of these hypotheses seems to call for any amendments to the neo-liberal policy position. But that may be so only because they are not directly concerned with international relations, the subject of the next two sections.

4. CAN THE FAILURE OF CONVERGENCE BE RESOLVED BY OPENING UP?

In many ways, international relations are at the heart of neo-liberal doctrine. Its predictions and prescriptions for economic development derive directly from orthodox trade theory. It understands globalization not merely as a process but as an end state: the creation of a market system in which national economies are integrated with each other through international markets. Integration is identified with the establishment of the Law of One Price (or LOOP), the equalization of prices of both goods and factors. The achievement of allocative efficiency and the diffusion of technology are the bases for both absolute benefits and the equalization of productive powers across nations. Inequalities among nations pose no barriers to any of them deriving these benefits. On the contrary, LOOP under full integration (the integration of product and capital markets even without global labour mobility) implies *equalization* of factor prices and living standards across the globe. LOOP must hold in a self-regulating global market system in essentially the same way as it is supposed to hold within nations. In sum, globalization plus liberalization equals absolute convergence.[16] As Sachs and Warner (1995) put it:

> The world economy at the end of the twentieth century looks much like the world economy at the end of the nineteenth century. A global capitalist system is taking shape, drawing almost all regions of the world into arrangements of open trade and harmonized economic institutions. As in the nineteenth century, this new round of globalization promises to lead to economic convergence for the countries that join the system. (pp. 62–3)

By implication, the failure of convergence whether in the recent or distant past is to be accounted for by the failure of nations 'to join the system'. This prompts two related questions: What are the mechanisms by which trade promotes development and are these weighty enough to warrant the neo-liberal position?; and, Is the recalcitrance of nations to join the system adequate to explain the failure of convergence?

First, consider the role of international relations in the case of the high-income countries. These nations enjoy practically identical living standards today, and a great deal of this is due to rapid convergence during the past four or five decades. However, this was not just a result of technological diffusion and related gains from trade. Not only were there important local deviations and adaptations in the diffusion process itself, but also high growth was led and sustained by rising wages which enlarged home markets in these countries. The coincident growth of home demands, together with US hegemony and the Bretton Woods institutions, also ensured the rapid growth of international trade without threatening conflicts between external and internal balance.

The convergence of productivity and income levels in Europe and Japan to those prevalent in the US accelerated the growth of intra-industry trade and investments among these regions as firms took advantage of new market opportunities and exploited the economies of scale that came with inter-penetration of each other's markets. Indeed, world trade is dominated by trade among the high-income countries and the great bulk of it is of the intra-industry type, that is, presupposing similar economic structures and levels of living. Moreover, as these countries prospered, protectionist barriers to trade also came down in successive rounds. In short, income convergence produced external market integration both 'automatically' and by inducing policy change, not only the other way around.

For the LDCs, it is useful to begin with an empirical assessment of LOOP. The major finding of the International Comparisons Project is that countries' overall commodity price levels, for any given year and when expressed in a single currency, are positively related to their real income per capita (see Summers and Heston, 1991). Thus, the price level in the US tends to be 2.5 to 5 times the price level (converted at nominal exchange rates) in most poor countries. Underlying the price level differences are also price structure differences affecting both tradables and non-tradables that the ICP has documented. Among the major structural differences are a much higher relative price of services in richer countries[17] and a much higher relative price of food in poorer countries (Summers and Heston, 1991). Hence the failure of LOOP to hold as between rich and poor countries is massive indeed.

Turning next to time trends in price levels, Table 3.3 presents data on the distribution of world incomes for 1960–89. The first two columns show the Gini coefficient of inequality for per capita GDP at international prices (purchasing power parities or PPPs) and at national prices. The rise in these

Table 3.3   The distribution of world income (1960–89)

Year	Gini coefficients		Ratio of top 20% to bottom 20%		P-level in top 20% to P-level in bottom 20%
	$y_{\text{IP-curr}}$ [1]	$y_{\text{NP-curr}}$ [2]	$y_{\text{IP-curr}}$ [3]	$y_{\text{NP-curr}}$ [4]	[5] = [4] / [3]
1960	0.44	n/a	11.10	n/a	–
1970	0.50	0.71	13.90	31.90	2.30
1980	0.53	0.79	16.00	44.70	2.79
1988–89	0.55	0.85	17.10	54.50	3.19

Source: Based on UNDP, cited in Griffin and Khan (1992).

inequality coefficients is consistent with our findings about growth divergence. This is indicated also in the next two columns which show the range of per capita incomes in the world measured as the ratio of the share of world income received by the top 20 per cent of the world population to that of the bottom 20 per cent of the population, once again in nominal and PPP terms. Column [5] shows the ratio of the two ratios (respectively at nominal and PPP terms) and represents the price level facing the top quintile of the population relative to that facing the bottom quintile. This ratio is, of course, greater than 1 in all years and, more remarkably, rose sharply from 1970 until 1989. In other words, the price structures of poor countries have been deviating further over the past 20 years from those of the rich countries. Contrary to the trend toward apparent global integration, the Law of One Price seems to have grown progressively less valid. This is the 'price dual' of the divergence in growth rates replicating the relationship between price levels and income levels over time.

Table 3.4 provides further evidence of price level variations over time and across country groups based on World Bank data. The Exchange Rate Deviation Index or ERD is measured as the ratio of GDP at international prices relative to GDP at national prices.[18] Since both are measured in terms of the US$ as numeraire, the ratio is the (weighted average) international price level relative to the respective country's national price level (P^{IP}/P_i^{NP}). Following the ICP results, this ratio is greater than 1 for LDCs and negatively related to income levels. Table 3.4 shows that the (unweighted) ERD rose 18 per cent for the low-income countries between the two periods, fell 18 per cent for the high-income countries and rose marginally (3 per cent) for the middle-income countries. Thus, price levels have risen faster than world price levels for the rich countries while the reverse has been the case for poor countries.

Table 3.4   Exchange rate deviation index (1960–95)

	1960–78	1979–95
Low income	2.29	2.70
	[1.36]	[3.95]
Middle income	1.92	1.97
	[1.50]	[2.03]
High income	1.26	1.03
	[1.00]	[0.88]

Notes:
1. The ERD Index is the nominal/PPP exchange ratio (which equals the ratio of GDP at international prices to GDP at national prices).
2. Figures in parentheses are GDP-weighted means; all other figures are unweighted country means.
Source: Author's estimates.

Table 3.5 shows the results of regressing the ERD on the (log of) per capita incomes in the pooled sample for 1960–95. We know from the ICP that the pure cross-section relation between ERD and income is negative. However, in a pooled sample, ERD variations reflect not merely the changing denominator of ERD (each country's own price level) which is related to income but also a changing numerator insofar as the weights of different countries in determining the international price level are changing. The latter source of variation arises if countries (or country groups) do not all enjoy identical growth rates which we know to be true in the present sample. This explains the mixed signs and statistical significance of coefficients in Table 3.5. The ERD is inversely related to incomes for each sub-period and for the whole period only in the case of the high-income countries. For the whole sample, the inverse relation holds only in the second period; it is actually positive (though not statistically significant) in the first period and the whole period. This finding also applies for the middle-income countries while for the low-income countries the inverse relation holds for each period but not for the whole period.

Evidence over several decades thus fails to sustain the expectation of growing price convergence from growing globalization; the general conclusion must be that both incomes and price structures differed much to begin with and have continued to diverge. These findings call for a reassessment of the theoretical basis for favouring liberal, free trade policies, that is, the mechanisms that are routinely adduced to assert a connection between free trade and growth.

Table 3.5 The relationship between the exchange rate deviation index and income (1960–95) (ERD index regressed on the log of y_{NP-87} pooled sample)

	1960–78			1979–95			1960–95		
	Constant	y_{NP-87}	Adj. R^2	Constant	y_{NP-87}	Adj. R^2	Constant	y_{NP-87}	Adj. R^2
Low income	5.651* [0.460]	−0.574* [0.079]	0.126	9.658* [0.602]	−1.186* [0.103]	0.197	−4.8E-06** [0.000]	1.0E-06** [0.000]	0.009
Middle income	−55.610 [46.911]	9.841 [6.698]	0.002	6.191* [0.263]	−0.577* [0.036]	0.307	−20.565 [26.989]	3.996 [3.771]	0.000
High income	4.515* [0.154]	−0.366* [0.017]	0.479	4.894* [0.176]	−0.410* [0.019]	0.572	4.697* [0.110]	−0.387* [0.012]	0.549
All countries	0.859 [10.402]	0.733 [1.449]	0.000	5.837* [0.123]	−0.523* [0.017]	0.392	4.009 [5.729]	0.032 [0.786]	0.000

Notes:
1. Standard errors in parentheses.
2. See appendix for variable definitions and data sources.
3. * denotes significant at 1% level
   ** significant at 5% level.
Source: Author's estimates.

5.   STRUCTURAL CONSTRAINTS ON GAINS FROM GLOBALIZATION

In conventional trade theory, countries gain from trading with each other.[19] But empirical estimates of the gains from trade liberalization rarely amount to more than one or two per cent of the liberalizing country's income. A graphic example is provided by the GATT reforms involving virtually the whole world. Despite the vaunted benefits from free trade, the latest round of GATT is estimated to produce no more than $250 billion in gains (about 1 per cent of GDP in the year 2000) for the world economy of which the lion's share accrues to the OECD nations, especially the US, Japan and Germany. These small one-shot gains are dwarfed by the cumulative growth rate differences that liberal enthusiasts attribute to differences in trade regimes. The defence of openness, therefore, has shifted by invoking several other mechanisms.

One response has been to elaborate a new political economy of the state which claims that state interventionism (not necessarily confined to trade) which generally creates rents breeds competition among rational market participants for those rents, but the competition in turn dissipates real resources equal in value to the rents themselves. Although the rents created by interventions are captured by competing agents, the competition itself entails costs that are equal to the rents (so there are no net gainers of the rent). The resource cost of such necessarily unproductive rent-seeking can be many times as large as the inefficiency loss of the interventions themselves. For trade interventions alone, typical 'estimates' of rent seeking waste are in the region of 10–20 per cent of national income.[20] However, neoclassical political economy mis-interprets the nature of competition for state influence by mis-specifying the behaviour of private agents and state functionaries alike. When respecified so as to be consistent with the neoclassical premise of rational action, rents created by interventions will be conserved[21] rather than unproductively dissipated (see Rao, 1995).

A second line of defence links openness with superior productivity, product quality and product variety. There are several aspects to this link:

1.   Trade generates knowledge spillovers which, through reverse engineering for example, are beneficial to productivity and quality. However, such spillovers are indirect, incidental and uncertain. Profit-maximizing firms will seek out profitable knowledge wherever it might be; free trade is neither necessary nor sufficient (much less is it efficient) in conveying new knowledge to producers.
2.   Import competition has a disciplining effect on producers who are obliged to exploit cost and quality economies, that is, reduce 'x-

inefficiencies'. If competition has such an effect, this argument does not provide any reason why it must originate in international trade; presumably, domestic competition can serve the purpose just as well. More fundamentally, such an effect is inconsistent with the basic neo-classical premise that firms maximize profits. For if they do, then they will minimize unit cost (or the cost–quality ratio) regardless of the degree of competition.

3. Import liberalization increases consumer welfare by enhancing choice in the varieties they consume. While this is true particularly in poor economies with small home markets, this link is tenuously relevant, if at all, to explaining visible measures of economic performance such as growth and export competitiveness as opposed to the invisible consumer gains from variety.[22]

If the old trade theory is too feeble to support the weight of the neo-liberal position regarding free trade, the new trade theories may appear to vindicate that position on new foundations. How far is this the case from the viewpoint of the South? The new theories are based on decreasing cost due to scale economies, product differentiation among firms and associated market structures of oligopoly or monopolistic competition.[23] As domestic and international firms producing similar products compete in each other's markets, the resulting intra-industry trade may yield gains in the form of increased product diversity or promotion of competition, the latter arising from the curtailment of monopoly power which serves to increase output. It is this last type of gain that matters for present purposes: as markets are integrated, market shares of monopolistically competitive firms, for example, are reduced, outputs rise and, given scale economies, costs fall. However, intra-industry trade does not necessarily produce net gains for the trading countries.[24] But the more central issue is the relevance of intra-industry trade for the South. Factor proportions remain crucial for the new theories as much as for the traditional theory. Inter-industry trade based on comparative or complementary advantage takes place between dissimilar economies while intra-industry trade based on absolute or competitive advantage characterizes similar (high-income) economies. The bulk of North–South trade is of the former type.[25] Even much manufactured export from the South is of standard products based on established technologies. Whereas equalized incomes drive the pattern of trade within the North, the pattern of specialization and trade supports if not induces non-equalization of factor prices between North and South. In fact, the absolute difference between average wages in the North and the South has been growing ever larger for close to two centuries.[26] Hence, North–South inequality (in the sense of absolute differences) must be understood in terms of uneven development, that is, dynamic factors making for persistently or even progressively different (physical and human capital) endowments.

Taken together, these observations deriving from established trade theories imply that the mechanisms for trade gains that are actually applicable to LDCs yield gains from trade liberalization that are empirically rather slight. They are far from the magnitudes required to sustain the orthodox view that illiberal trade explains the failure of living standards to converge. To be sure, LOOP need not hold even in orthodox theory. There are two standard arguments, both of which serve to explain why neither factor prices nor commodity prices may be equalized. The first is the differential productivity argument (see Balassa, 1964), according to which poor countries have a roughly similar level of productivity in services (or non-tradables such as services) but a lower level in tradables. (Even) if free trade equalizes tradables' prices, factor prices (basically wages) will be lower in the poor countries and so will the relative price of services.

The second argument is that free trade in technologies and products does not logically guarantee factor price equalization. If factor endowment ratios are sufficiently far apart (as is evidently the case between the North and the South), then specialization without factor price equalization will hold.[27] With their high relative endowment of labour, LDCs will specialize in labour-intensive goods and have low wages. The low wages, in turn, help explain the low relative price of services which are taken to be both non-tradable and relatively labour-intensive (Bhagwati, 1984). Thus, factor mobility has an independent significance in assuring full assimilation unless the economies are already similar to start with.

However, these 'explanations' of non-convergence amount to merely reformulating the question at hand. Why are there productivity differentials at all (let alone in the hypothesized directions)? Similarly, why is capital not sufficiently mobile across countries? If we leave out persistent, economy-wide increasing returns so that convergence is not ruled out right at the outset, then we are left with two broad hypotheses. First, we may suppose 1) that there does indeed exist a large unexploited potential for arbitrage gains through international economic relations, but 2) that there are barriers to its exploitation due to inherent market failures. Typically, these barriers include monopoly power in commodity and, especially, technology markets as well as the imperfect mobility of capital. We may call this hypothesis global market fragmentation. Second, we may suppose that the potential for arbitrage gains is in fact small because productivity differentials across economies cannot be bridged by trade, technology or capital flows. Rather, productivity differentials narrow only as a process of local learning, skill development and knowledge spillovers advances. We may call this hypothesis 'localization of development'. Fragmentation implies that tradable factors important to growth are not much traded; localization implies that important factors are not tradable.[28] But whichever explanation one may choose (actually, the two are not unrelated and there are sound reasons to combine the two), this cannot be any consolation for the neo-liberal viewpoint. National economic integration within developing countries must take precedence over international integration.

NOTES

1. Some use the term 'globalization' to denote policy changes intended to bring about increased global integration. Past experience shows that there is no necessary or one-to-one connection between such policy changes and the actual extent of integration. It is therefore best to restrict the term 'globalization' to indicators of actual integration while liberal policy moves on the external front may be denoted by 'external liberalization'.
2. Recent accounts of the constituents of the Fordist Golden Age and of the paths out of that regime of accumulation are given in Boyer (1995) and Lipietz (1995).
3. Srinivasan (1985) provides a lucid overview though debatable defence of what has come to be called 'neoclassical political economy'.
4. This line of thinking implies that an existing regime of protection will be difficult to dislodge: shelters provide policy autonomy which will be obligingly used to perpetuate the shelters. For the same reason, however, a neo-liberal regime, once instituted, will go on unmolested.
5. Characteristically, these benefits are supposed to diffuse widely among the population while the benefits of illiberal policies are supposed to be highly concentrated. But if diffuse beneficiaries are apt to be 'rationally' apathetic to politics, as this literature typically maintains, it is hard to see how a neo-liberal regime might ever get going.
6. Indeed, the very distinction between active technical invention and passive diffusion has had to be modified in the light of historical experience showing that the mere transfer or imitation of technologies does not realize the potential gains.
7. This admonition applies as well to the neo-liberal position. See notes 3 and 4.
8. See Rodrik (1998) for an elaboration of this viewpoint.
9. See, for example, the report of the World Commission on Culture and Development (1995), Greider (1993), Barber (1997) and Rao (1998).
10. See Summers and Heston (1991) for a description of the methodology of the International Comparisons Project (ICP) on which the PennTable is based. A possible objection to the use of ICP-based incomes is that since the method obtains weighted average international prices from national prices using the Stone-Geary weighting procedure, the use of these average prices risks incurring a cross-national Gerschenkron Effect, that is, overestimating income growth in the rich compared to the poor countries if quantities and prices are generally inversely related in the cross-section (see Nuxoll, 1994). In fact, however, Nuxoll found that growth rates at international prices were actually less than those at national prices for the poor, not rich, countries (though this relationship was not statistically significant).
11. We used the PennTable income variable RGDPCH rather than RGDP. The latter, with base prices in 1985, suffers from the Laspeyres fixed-base problem (as relative prices change, base year weights become less appropriate). RGDPCH, based on a chain index, has the merit that its growth rate for any period is based upon international prices most closely allied with the period.
12. The computed growth rates are not reported in the Table. The country groups are defined as follows: (1) by growth rates the ranges are <1 per cent (low growth), 1–3 per cent

(medium growth) and >3 per cent (high growth); and (2) by level of 1995 per capita incomes at national prices, the ranges being $\leq\$765$ (low income), $\$765-9386$ (middle income) and $\geq\$9386$ (high income). The latter classification is based on World Bank (1997).

13.   See for example Baumol (1986), Barro and Sala-i-Martin (1992) and Mankiw, Romer and Weil (1992).

14.   The argument may be reinforced through extension to an open economy. Free trade in goods and technologies and the international mobility of capital will hasten the speed of convergence.

15.   More generally, increasing returns may not hold without bound. One reason may be the transformation of economic structure (from agriculture to industry and then to services) which changes the scope of increasing returns. Another might be the slowing down of accumulation when wages rise and eat into profits. Technological leaders do sometimes lose their lead in particular industries. Entire economies may similarly change their relative positions. Moreover, changes in the system and organization of knowledge may change its tradability across enterprises or national frontiers. Laggard economies may also find wholly new ways of generating knowledge which produce a burst of convergent growth.

16.   Proponents of this world view generally do not allow their vision to be clouded by ideas about possibly divergent 'fundamentals' across nations. Although factor price equalization does not amount to absolute convergence, it does imply convergence of 'full incomes'.

17.   As these authors point out, though this is the prime stylized fact of the ICP, it is also the most open to question on account of the difficulties of allowing for quality differences in the case of services.

18.   These are both taken at current prices for each year and therefore free from the influence of inflation.

19.   The discussion here is confined to the case for openness to commodity and technology trade; capital mobility will be considered separately below.

20.   These estimates of waste are derived by simply equating them to the estimated value of rents created by state interventions.

21.   Private coalitions that succeed in creating rents for themselves through state interventions will also successfully capture the rents: rival coalitions will have no incentive to contest this capture so that no resource-using rent-seeking activity will be realized. Rents will then constitute purely redistributive transfers and therefore will be conserved.

22.   The argument also supposes that domestic producers have no interest in making the productivity or quality improvements in the first place.

23.   Smith (1994) provides a lucid survey of the main lines of inquiry in this mould.

24.   In the product diversity case, if goods with high fixed costs displace others with low fixed costs, the net gains from diversity may turn out negative. More to the point, intra-industry trade may also incur additional transport, advertising and selling costs while promoting competition. Once again, trade may produce net losses. These ambiguities arise from the fact that intra-industry trade adds its own distortion while reducing an initial distortion. In the European Community, estimates of gains from trade integration (including competition promotion and scale economies) amount to about 5 per cent (Hine, 1994: p. 258). But even there, the home market retains its importance 'with the largest part of virtually every market being taken by domestic firms' (Smith, 1994: p. 57). Similar preferences prevail even more strongly in Japan and in South Korea. In effect, these endogenous barriers allow monopolistic firms to retain substantial discretion in pricing.

25.   According to Hamilton and Winters (1992), 70 per cent of the variation in trade flows among a sample of 76 countries was explained by variables measuring national 'proximity' such as incomes rather than variables measuring national differences, a reflection of the large share of North–North trade. The bulk of exports from the South goes to the dissimilar North.

26. What matters for the factor price equalization theorem are wage levels and not their long-term relative convergence (if any) so the 'convergence debate' is beside the point here.
27. Factor intensity reversals within the available technologies must also be assumed away.
28. It is indeed true that labour is non-traded only due to artificial restrictions. But in a neo-classical two-factor world, factor price equalization requires mobility of one factor at best, not of both.

REFERENCES

Amsden, Alice, Jacek Kochanowicz and Lance Taylor (1994), *The Market Meets its Match: Restructuring the Economies of Eastern Europe*, Cambridge: Harvard University Press.

Balassa, Bela (1964), 'The Purchasing Power Parity Doctrine: A Reappraisal', *Journal of Political Economy*, **72**:584–96.

Barber, Benjamin (1997), 'Global Markets: Spur to Competition or the End of Diversity?', unpublished, Paris: UNESCO.

Barro, Robert J. and Xavier Sala-i-Martin (1992), 'Convergence', *Journal of Political Economy*, **100** (2), 223–51.

Baumol, William J. (1986), 'Productivity Growth, Convergence and Welfare', *American Economic Review*, **76** (5), 1072–85.

Baumol, William J., Richard R. Nelson and Edward N. Wolff (eds) (1994), *Convergence of Productivity: Cross-National Studies and Historical Evidence*, New York: Oxford University Press.

Bhagwati, J. (1984), 'Why are Services Cheaper in the Poor Countries?', *Economic Journal*, **94** (374), 279–86.

Boyer, Robert (1995), 'Capital–Labour Relations in OECD Countries: From the Fordist Golden Age to Contrasted National Trajectories', in Juliet Schor and Jong-Il You (eds), *Capital, the State and Labour: A Global Perspective*, Aldershot: Edward Elgar and United Nations University Press.

Cox, Robert W. (1994), 'Global Restructuring: Making Sense of the Changing International Political Economy', in R. Stubbs and G.R.D. Underhill (eds), *Political Economy and the Changing Global Order*, New York: St. Martin's Press.

Frank, André Gunder (1966), 'The Development of Underdevelopment', *Monthly Review*, **18**.

Gerschenkron, Alexander (1962), *Economic Backwardness in Historical Perspective*, Cambridge, MA: Harvard University Press.

Greider, William (1993), 'The Global Marketplace: A Closet Dictator', in D.N. Balaam and M. Veseth (eds), *Readings in International Political Economy*, Upper Saddle River: Prentice Hall.

Griffin, Keith and Azizur R. Khan (1992), *Globalization and the Developing World: An Essay on the International Dimensions of Development in the Post-Cold War Era*, New York: United Nations Development Programme, Human Development Report Occasional Papers No. 2.

Hamilton, Carl and L. Alan Winters (1992), 'Opening up International Trade with Eastern Europe', *Economic Policy*, **14**, 77–116.

Hine, Robert C. (1994), 'International Economic Integration', in David Greenaway and L. Alan Winters (eds), *Surveys in International Trade*, Oxford: Blackwell.

Lipietz, Alain (1995), 'Capital–Labour Relations at the Dawn of the Twenty-First Century', in Juliet Schor and Jong-Il You (eds), *Capital, the State and Labour: A Global Perspective*, Aldershot: Edward Elgar and United Nations University Press.

Lucas, Robert E. (1988), 'On the Mechanics of Economic Development', *Journal of Monetary Economics*, **22**, 3–42.

Mankiw, N. Gregory, David Romer and David N. Weil (1992), 'A Contribution to the Empirics of Growth', *Quarterly Journal of Economics*, **107** (2), 407–37.

Nuxoll, Daniel A. (1994), 'Differences in Relative Prices and International Differences in Growth Rates', *American Economic Review*, **84** (5), 1423–36.

Prebisch, Raul (1959), 'Commercial Policy in the Underdeveloped Countries', *American Economic Review*, **49** (2), 251–73.

Pritchett, Lant (1996), 'Forget Convergence: Divergence Past, Present, and Future', *Finance and Development*, **33** (2), 40–43.

Rao, J. Mohan (1995), 'The Market for the State: Rules, Discretion, Rent-Seeking and Corruption', *Department of Economics Working Paper No. 1995–3*. Amherst: University of Massachusetts.

Rao, J. Mohan (1998), 'Culture and Economic Development', in *World Culture Report, 1998: Culture, Creativity and Markets*, Paris: UNESCO, pp. 25–48.

Rodrik, Dani (1998), *Has International Integration Gone Too Far?*, Princeton: Princeton University Press.

Romer, Paul M. (1986), 'Increasing Returns and Long-Run Growth', *Journal of Political Economy*, **98**, S71–102.

Sachs, Jeffrey and Andrew Warner (1995), 'Economic Reform and the Process of Global Integration', *Brookings Papers in Economic Activity*, pp. 1–118.

Schwartz, Hermann M. (1994), *States versus Markets: History, Geography and the Development of the International Political Economy*, New York: St. Martin's Press.

Smith, Alasdair (1994), 'Imperfect Competition and International Trade', in David Greenaway and L. Alan Winters (eds), *Surveys in International Trade*, Oxford: Blackwell.

Srinivasan, T.N. (1985), 'Neoclassical Political Economy, the State and Economic Development', *Asian Development Review*, **3** (2), 38–58.

Summers, R. and A. Heston (1991), 'The Penn World Table (Mark 5): An Expanded Set of International Comparisons, 1950–1988', *Quarterly Journal of Economics*, **106** (2), 327–68.

World Bank (1997), *World Indicators*, Washington, DC: World Bank.

World Commission on Culture and Development (1995), *Our Creative Diversity*, Paris: UNESCO.

APPENDIX: SOURCES OF DATA AND VARIABLE DEFINITIONS

1. World Bank (1994), *World Data, 1994*.
2. World Bank (1997), *World Indicators, 1997*.

    The above sources were combined as necessary to get the country-wise annual time series data (1960–95) on all national accounts variables involving national price valuations.

    y_{NP-87} – per capita GDP at constant 1987 national prices (in US$).

    $y_{NP-curr}$ – per capita GDP at current national prices (in US$).

3. International Comparisons Project (1995), *Penn World Table*.

    The Penn Table is the source for country-wise annual time series data (1960–92) on all variables involving valuations at international prices including the measure of trade openness.

    y_{IP-85} – per capita GDP at constant 1985 international prices, chain index (in US$).

    $y_{IP-curr}$ – per capita GDP at current international prices (in US$).

015 F13
024 019
847 F4

4. Income distribution, growth and protectionism in Sub-Saharan Africa and the case of Zimbabwe[1]

Jørn Rattsø

1. INTRODUCTION

Most of colonial Africa had strong government regulation of the economy, including foreign trade and capital flows. This is an important background to understand the present debate about liberalization and globalization in Africa. The issue is not to return to the *laissez-faire* policies prevailing before socialist independence movements got rid of colonial rule. The new independent governments of the 1960s inherited a system of controls, and the regulatory apparatus was well designed to promote national planning and public sector dominance towards new goals. The governments chose to use the controls to protect industry and discriminate agriculture. Industrialization was the word of the day. The policy aimed at transferring the agricultural surplus to industrial investment. The attention here is concentrated on this interplay between agriculture and industry, rural and urban. With hindsight we can conclude that the independent governments generally were not successful in arranging the interaction between rural and urban to generate sustainable growth. Productivity in agriculture stagnated and industry never took over as an engine of growth. In this perspective, recent liberalization reforms can be seen as an acknowledgement of this failure and an attempt to find a new growth model. In a political context, the urban and anti-export bias has been understood to be based on a separation between urban and rural constituencies. Bates (1981) argues that governments based their support on urban groups and arranged regulations to keep food prices low, and thereby urban industries profitable. Marketing boards and protectionism have delivered economic conditions for strong government support. On distributional grounds this makes good sense, and the urban constituency must have strengthened over time. But the recent history of policy reforms indicates that when the overall model does not deliver wealth and growth, even policies built on a strong distributional coalition are changed. Distribution and growth in the context of urban and rural are evaluated in this chapter.

The discussion is made in three parts. First, I will address the income distribution aspects of the agriculture-industry divide in the trade policy setting, distinguishing between agriculture/exportables and industry/importables. Distributional consequences of trade policy can be given a fairly simple interpretation in a Ricardo–Viner model. Different stakes in trade liberalization are sorted out, and various arguments related to industry are evaluated. The second part looks at growth interactions between agriculture/exportables and industry/importables. Economic growth is assumed to be determined by productivity growth, and the productivity relationships between the two sectors are important. It is argued that export bias, given the economic structure of the region, can generate an underdevelopment trap. Finally, the mechanisms related to distribution and growth are brought to Zimbabwe to evaluate the experiences of the recent liberalization process.

2. INCOME DISTRIBUTION AND PROTECTIONISM

Trade policy influences sectoral balances and the allocation of production factors and thereby the functional income distribution. The main sectoral balance affected is the relationship between importables and exportables. In large parts of Sub-Saharan Africa, the distinction between importables and exportables is closely linked to the separation between industry and agriculture/raw materials production, and thereby urban and rural. Most industries have been protected, and importables and exportables industrial production often is low-tech. When the economic conditions of importables and exportables production are changed by regulation, labour demand and wages respond. These links are spelled out below. Complex trade regimes are represented by one of their main ingredients, the protection of domestically oriented industries by import regulation, and typically a quota. The anti-export bias of agricultural policy is discussed in the next section.

The framework offered is a compressed Ricardo–Viner model concentrating on the interplay between importables and exportables. It is a simplification of the three-way disaggregation including nontradables, which has been used in many applied analyses since it allows simultaneous discussion of the foreign terms of trade and the real exchange rate. Rodrik (1994) and Rattsø and Taylor (1998) utilize the three-sector framework to understand trade liberalization effects in more general terms. I use the model here to spell out how the income distribution in a stylized Sub-Saharan African context is linked to industry as importable and agriculture as exportable. Rodrik (1998) has produced numerical simulations to quantify distributional implications of trade reform in a related setup.

I assume that the given labour force, L is distributed between the importables sector M and the exportables/agriculture sector X,

$$L_M + L_X = L \qquad (1)$$

Exportables/agriculture is assumed to absorb the labour force not employed in importables/industry. In a dual economy understanding, the wage level W is consequently determined by the constant marginal productivity of labour in exportables/agriculture. I allow for a more general production function for exportables, $X = X(L_X)$, with positive and decreasing marginal productivity of labour, and with land and capital as shadow factors. When the world market price and exchange rate both are set to 1, the wage setting observes the rule:

$$X' = W. \qquad (2)$$

When the capital stock of importables is suppressed, I can apply the production function of importables, $M = M(L_M)$ to get:

$$P_M M' = W. \qquad (3)$$

The relative price of importables is determined by the world market price $P*$ and the tariff equivalent of the quota t, which is a rent, $P_M = P* + t$. Combining (1) – (3), we reach a labour supply curve to importables dependent on the rent:

$$M' \, dt + (P_M M'' + X'') \, dL_M = 0. \qquad (4)$$

The demand for labour in importables must be derived from the market balance, where the quota Q is inserted:

$$P_M M(L_M) + P_M Q = \alpha [P_M M(L_M) + X(L_X) + t \, Q]. \qquad (5)$$

Differentiating the market balance, including an exogenous shift in the quota, we get:

$$-(1-\alpha)(M+Q) \, dt - ((1-\alpha) P_M M' + \alpha X') \, dL_M = (P* + (1-\alpha)) \, dQ. \qquad (6)$$

Solving out from (4) and (6), we can identify the effect of the quota on rents and labour use in importables:

$$dt/dQ = (1/D) (P_M M'' + X'') (P^* + (1 - \alpha)) < 0 \qquad (7)$$

$$dL_M/dQ = - (1/D) (P^* + (1 - \alpha)) M' < 0 \qquad (8)$$

where $D = - (1 - \alpha)(M + Q) (P_M M'' + X'') + M' ((1 - \alpha) P_M M' + \alpha X') > 0$.

Protectionism reducing the quota leads to a higher quota rent and higher employment in importables/industry. The distributional consequences can readily be derived:

$$dL_X/dQ = - dL_M/dQ > 0 \qquad (9)$$

$$dW/dQ = (1/D) (P^* + (1 - \alpha)t) M' X'' < 0. \qquad (10)$$

When profits of the two sectors are defined as π_X and π_M, we find:

$$d\pi_X/dQ = - L_X dW/dQ > 0 \qquad (11)$$

$$d\pi_M /dQ = M \, dt/dQ - L_M \, dW/dQ = \qquad (12)$$

$$(1/D) [P_M M \, M'' + (M - L_M M') X''] (P^* + (1 - \alpha)t) < 0 \text{ when } \varepsilon_M < 1$$

where ε_M is the labour demand elasticity.

The distributional consequences of protectionism are very distinct in this setup. Figure 4.1 describes the structural adjustment in the importables product market and the exportables labour market. Two motivations for the import quota can be explained with the use of the diagram. With world market price P^*, the excess demand for importables contributes to a trade deficit that is undesired or cannot be financed. An import quota also allows the country to move up along the importables supply curve as a way of industrializing. In the diagram, the import quota induces a higher domestic price of importables (tariff equivalent t) and generates higher profits, outlays and quota rents. Sub-Saharan African protectionism in this setup first and for all has been to the benefit of capitalists in domestically oriented industries. Trade liberalization then should work progressively in terms of income distribution.

Elimination of the quota (that is, trade liberalization) implies that farmers/owners in the exportables/agriculture sector are the clear winners

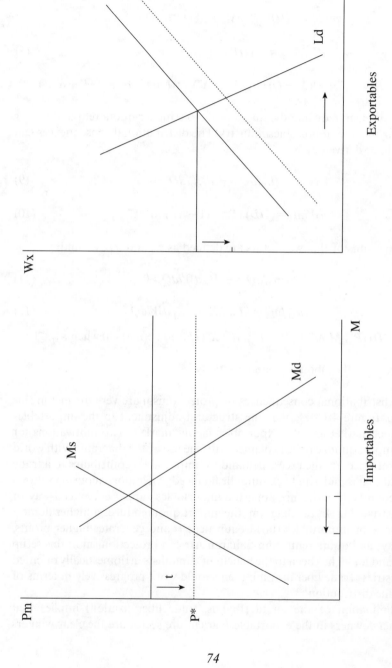

Figure 4.1 Trade policy, importables – exportables interaction

of a reduced wage level when labour is released by deindustrialization. Owners of importables capital are expected to lose together with those enjoying rents from the quota, be it government officials and/or receivers of quota imports. If importables/industrial wage earners are able to take a share of the rents (Rodrik, 1998), their loss will be bigger too. Trade liberalization in this stylized sub-Saharan African structure looks like a clear shift of income from industry to agriculture and from urban to rural areas. Outside the model, if importables contraction is fast and exportables expansion is slow, nontradables and informal production activities may take a loss from the demand side.

While the distributional implications are stark in this simple framework, it is just a starting point for adding more realistic features. The first key issue in any trade liberalization debate is the exportables response. The channels to expansion of exportables may include more than the wage reduction assumed above. Access to importables at lower prices may improve incentives to engage in exportables production – a classic argument about the export stagnation under protectionism. Deregulation of capital flows has the similar effect of raising the attractiveness of foreign exchange earnings. In a world of flexible production conditions, firms that are made unprofitable in the importables sector may shift to exportables production. All of the above factors tend to shift the labour demand curve in exportables outward, thereby contributing to higher wages. A 'successful' liberalization has sufficient exportables response to drive up labour demand and wages.

The second key issue is what happens to industry. The above story is quite pessimistic, except for the possibility of moving old domestically oriented firms into exportables production. With the introduction of increasing returns to scale and imperfect competition, multiple equilibria can occur, and thereby more dramatic shifts. The technical formulation takes advantage of the Dixit–Stiglitz model of product differentiation and monopolistic competition. The industrial sector includes both intermediate inputs and final goods and the differentiated intermediates are produced under increasing returns to scale and serve as input to the final goods production. The production function of the importables final good is extended to include aggregate intermediates I, $M = M(L_M, I)$ where $I = [\Sigma\, z_i^\beta]^{1/\beta}$ (z_i is the volume of intermediate input i, β is related to the elasticity of substitution σ between any two inputs, $\beta = (\sigma - 1)/\sigma$ and $\sigma > 1$). The main trick is this separation between upstream/intermediate goods and downstream/final goods industries, which offers a richer framework by which to understand various trade policies. Both intermediates and final goods are importables, but final goods are typically assumed to be perfectly competitive with constant returns to scale. Lack of space forbids us to expand on the equilibrium of this model version, and I refer to Puga and Venables (1998) for an overview.

Protection of industry in Sub-Saharan Africa has included both inter-mediates and final goods production. In a more standard setting, the protection of intermediates is expected to allow for more domestic intermediates production because of the higher price, but the negative effect for downstream industries may reduce demand for domestic intermediates. Venables (1996) argues that the economy can be stuck in a 'low level equilibrium' of intermediates protection under increasing returns to scale and outlines a most optimistic scenario of trade liberalization. When protection of intermediates is eliminated, the price of intermediates goes down and downstream final output may expand with lower costs. The growth of final goods production attracts entry and competition for upstream firms generating further expansion of downstream industry. The economy can shift to a 'high level equilibrium' with higher output of both intermediates and final goods and even with reduced imports.

In a more realistic Sub-Saharan Africa interpretation, the conclusions may be turned around. The region concentrated on protection against final goods, and import allocations to intermediate and capital goods were given priority. This strategy possibly hoped for a downstream final goods industrial sector large enough to take advantage of scale economies and differentiation of the upstream intermediate industrial production. With hindsight we know that this optimistic scenario of industrialization with protectionism did not work out. But the mechanisms may tell us something about deindustrialization with final goods liberalization. When the domestic price of final goods importables falls with reduced tariffs or tariff equivalents, final goods production falls and brings with it a contraction of domestic intermediates production. The shift may be dramatic when costs of intermediates are driven up by the disadvantage of smaller scales. Given the limited success of the African way of industrializing, however, this should not be taken as a recommendation of continued trade policy the old way.

The third relevant aspect I will throw in is the macroeconomic context. Linking back to Figure 4.1, the liberalization process may influence the demand side of the importables market. The new availability of importables can reduce savings, stimulate demand and increase the trade deficit. Savings can represent postponed consumption under import protection. The model assumption of a common importables good may exaggerate the degree of substitution between domestically and foreign produced importables. Under imperfect substitution, the demand may shift from domestically produced to imported importables. Such a demand shift can strengthen the deindustrialization process and worsen the trade deficit.

3. ANTI-EXPORT BIAS AND GROWTH

The protectionism in Sub-Saharan Africa took many forms, and the most explicit anti-export bias was the discrimination of exportables agriculture. Agriculture was taxed to give room for industrial expansion. When decolonization started, agriculture was the dominant production sector, with a great potential for exports and technological advancement. Possibly, agricultural production growth could have set the stage for industrialization by releasing food and raw materials, generating foreign exchange revenues, and creating a domestic market for manufacturing goods. But the governments chose otherwise. Both ideological orientation for equity and urban pressure led to cheap food policies, implemented with monopoly control of both domestic marketing and international trade in food. Descriptions of agricultural policies such as Krueger et al. (1991) conclude that there has been a 'surprising magnitude of discrimination'. Collier and Gunning (1997) discuss how other policies have contributed to the same, such as allocation of investment, overvaluation of the currencies, and priorities of import rationing.

A case can be made for discrimination of agriculture in favour of industry. This view emphasizes the competition between the two sectors, notably for labour and capital. Agriculture is seen as a low-productivity sector, and resources should not be locked into low returns. Matsuyama (1992) offers a modern restatement of the dual model, assuming full employment and productivity growth only in industry. In his model, higher agricultural productivity reduces the overall growth rate in an open economy. Reducing agricultural productivity is good for economic growth, since labour allocation adjusts to comparative advantage and is released for industry with productivity growth. According to this analysis, sub-Saharan Africa did right by neglecting agriculture. But the model cannot explain why the economies failed to industrialize. This motivates a new look at other interactions between the two sectors.

In our understanding, the analyses emphasizing competition for labour between agriculture and industry are much too optimistic to understand the region. Surplus labour is a more realistic description of the situation; shortage of unskilled labour has not been an important constraint on growth. Under unemployment or surplus labour, choice of policy has more dramatic growth effects than under full employment, and policy effects may be very different.

The discussion below is based on Rattsø and Torvik (1999), where the discrimination of agriculture is analysed in a model of sectoral balances under growth. Let us stick to the exportables/agriculture and importables/industry dichotomy. Importables/industry is assumed to be the potentially leading sector in terms of productivity growth and learning by doing, while agriculture is in a catching up situation with productivity growth proportional to the productivity gap between industrial and agricultural productivity. When the sectoral productivities are A_M and A_E, technically we assume that:

$$\frac{\dot{A}_M}{A_M} = vL_M \tag{13}$$

$$\frac{\dot{A}_E}{A_E} = uH, \tag{14}$$

where the productivity gap $H = A_M/A_E$. In comparable models, Matsuyama (1992) holds agricultural productivity constant, while Sachs and Warner (1995) assume a perfect spillover from industry to the rest of the economy.

The productivity dynamics can be attached to the two-sector model of section 2 given the proper extension of the production functions. When productivity dynamics is added, multiple equilibria and underdevelopment traps can result without increasing returns to scale. I will concentrate here on explaining possible dynamic adjustment mechanisms. Rattsø and Torvik (1999) show the assumptions needed to have the market balances and the static equilibrium only depend on the relative level of productivity between sectors, the productivity gap H. The dynamics will depend on the relationship between the productivity gap and the labour use in importables/industry. When relative productivity H increases, the labour demand in industry is expected to increase, since the wage becomes lower relative to industrial productivity. When the importables/industry production depends on imported intermediates, however, there may be a foreign exchange linkage between the two sectors working in the opposite direction. A shift in relative productivity against exportables/agriculture then can squeeze the importables/industry sector via foreign exchange availability or depreciation and reduce labour use. The dynamics of the model are determined by the strength of these two effects, as seen by the development of the productivity gap over time:

$$\frac{\dot{H}}{H} = \frac{\dot{A}_M}{A_M} - \frac{\dot{A}_E}{A_E} = vL_M - uH. \tag{15}$$

When the productivity gap is constant, productivity growth in the two sectors is the same and determined by the employment in industry (and the parameters v and u). When the productivity gap has a negative feedback on its own growth, the model has a stable steady state with a constant economic growth rate. A story about multiple equilibria and the underdevelopment trap is shown in Figure 4.2. The relationship between H and its own growth rate is drawn as hump-shaped, with the following intuition. When the country is relatively poor, and has a low productivity in industry compared with agriculture (low *H*), improvement in relative industrial productivity stimulates industrial labour use. We are on the upward sloping part of the curve, since higher *H* means higher labour use L_M, which generates more learning and productivity advantage to industry. When the economy grows richer (higher *H*), agriculture is transformed from food orientation to export crops and the foreign exchange linkage between the two sectors (and the agricultural catch-up) ends up dominating. The growth equation starts to fall.

*H** is a stable equilibrium. If $H > H^*$, *H* falls over time as indicated by the arrows until *H* is back at its steady state value. When *H* lies above its stable steady state value, the catch-up potential in agriculture is strong, and productivity in agriculture grows quickly. In addition, and given the dominating foreign exchange linkage, the industrial employment is below its steady state value and the productivity growth in the industrial sector is weak. *H*** is unstable and only a relative productivity of industry above *H*** brings the economy into a growth process with industrialization. If $H < H^{**}$, the productivity gap declines because of low industrial employment and learning. This is the underdevelopment trap. When relative productivity in industry compared with agriculture is low, there is little industrial

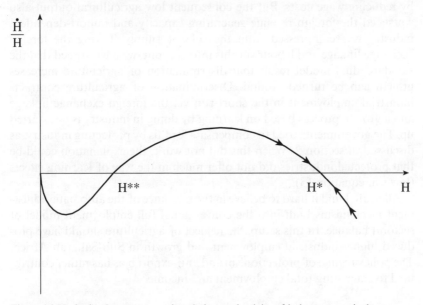

Figure 4.2 Underdevelopment trap, the relative productivity of industry to agriculture

employment and little learning and productivity growth. The economy is stuck in an equilibrium with agriculture as the dominating production sector and limited productivity growth.

The trick here is that agricultural exports can be instrumental to get out of the underdevelopment trap and then serve as an engine of industrial growth. A stimulus to agricultural exports can improve the profitability of intermediate imports to industry and thereby raise industrial employment. Industrial employment means learning by doing and if the relative productivity reaches above the threshold H^{**}, a growth process is started towards the steady state H^* with positive economic growth. The growth mechanism clearly depends on labour surplus, since both agriculture and industry can be stimulated at the same time.

The analysis is related to the literature on the big push, notably the modern restatement by Murphy et al. (1989). In that literature, static increasing returns in industry mean that agricultural demand must be high for industrial productivity to be high. In the present model, agriculture stimulates industrial productivity not primarily through creating demand, but through industrial supply. Alternative adjustment mechanisms with endogenous growth are outlined by Ros (1998).

We have shown that discrimination of agricultural exports can keep the economy in a 'low level equilibrium'. The Sub-Saharan African policy of turning terms of trade against agriculture was meant to stimulate industry by reducing wage costs. But the consequent low agricultural output also worsened the foreign revenue-generating capacity and import-dependent industry was compressed from the side of supply. Taking the foreign exchange linkage and labour surplus into account, we have argued that the standard dual model result that discrimination of agriculture increases growth can be turned around. Discrimination of agriculture contracts industrial employment in the short run via the foreign exchange linkage and a growth process based on learning by doing in industry is not started up. The governments tried to compensate for this by protecting industry, as discussed in section 2. When this did not work, the explanation could be that protected industries did not offer much in the way of learning effects (low v in equation 13).

All in all, I find it hard to believe in the relevance of the automatic adjustment mechanisms built into the conventional full employment model of sectoral balance. In this setup, the neglect of agriculture should have produced higher industrial employment and growth in Sub-Saharan Africa. The policy regime of protectionism and anti-export bias has rather contributed to stagnating total employment and income.

4. THE CASE OF ZIMBABWE

Zimbabwe offers an interesting case study, and I will discuss the relevance of the above mechanisms in this country. Interestingly, industrialization really gained speed with forced import substitution under international sanctions during the Unilateral Declaration of Independence (UDI) period of 1965–80. The new independent government in 1980 took over a semi-industrialized economy. The immediate policies of raising wages and government service spending were quite expansionary, and the government soon became concerned about the foreign exchange implications of their programme. They then resorted to an array of import controls and administered foreign exchange allocation mechanisms inherited from the sanctions-ridden Smith regime. The rationing was enforced by strict import licensing (Green and Kadhani, 1986; Pakkiri and Moyo, 1986; Davies, 1991). The import compression policy was motivated on macroeconomic grounds, but implied an industrial policy with detailed control of capacity utilization and also capacity expansion.

It follows that Zimbabwe in terms of policy regime looked like most of the Sub-Saharan African region in the early 1980s: protectionism, marketing boards, government influence on industry via import allocations and investment allocations. It seems like the industrialization and productivity enhancing effects of protectionism were exhausted already under Smith, and that the long-run disadvantages of an inward looking strategy were experienced under Mugabe. The combined stagnation of agriculture and industry looks like a development trap, and per capita incomes declined.

At first, from about the mid-1980s, the government started to build a number of institutional responses to the foreign exchange constraint. A series of export promoting measures were introduced, designed either to increase the incentive to export or to remove the imported input bottleneck for exporters (Dailami and Walton, 1989; Davies, Sanders and Shaw, 1992; Davies and Rattsø, 1993; Davies, Rattsø and Torvik, 1994). In view of the relative success of this modified regulation strategy in the late 1980s, the abrupt trade liberalization of the 1990s is somewhat puzzling. When the main constraint on the economy in the 1980s, foreign exchange, seemed to be easing, the government embarked upon an orthodox trade liberalization and domestic deregulation package. One way of understanding this in terms of the variables we have played with is that industrial productivity did not take off as long as the industrial sector was protected.

The liberalization programme announced in 1990, called ESAP, presented a broad package of reforms, including all the elements of the standard Washington advice (Government of Zimbabwe, 1991a). A social dimension was added later (Government of Zimbabwe, 1991b). Clearly, a wide range of inter-related political and ideological factors, both domestic and international, contributed to the changed policy perception (Davies and Rattsø, 1996; Shaw and Davies, 1993; Skålnes, 1995). It seems that broad groups (politicians, private industrialists, the international donor community) reached the understanding that the regulation regime was not sustainable on economic grounds.

Preliminary evaluations of the trade liberalization reform point to short-run stabilization and contraction problems (Davies et al., 1998; Rattsø and Torvik, 1998) and question the long-run growth effects (Davies and Rattsø, 1996; ILO, 1993; Ncube et al., 1996; Robinson, 1993). The government admits to some of the new adjustment problems in its most recent long-term programme (Government of Zimbabwe, 1998).

Short-run adjustment problems related to trade liberalization reform are well known and have led to reversals in many countries. They are closely linked to the core rationale of trade liberalization – to improve the efficiency of the economy by having imports substitute domestic import-competing industries and by stimulating exports. The economic mechanisms are easily seen in Figure 4.1, where trade liberalization is associated with this shift of resources from importables to exportables production. If the contraction of importables production is fast as many firms are made unprofitable, and the expansion of exportables is slow and takes time to build up, overall output and employment may go down. When importables production to a large extent consists of industrial output, the contraction of importables implies deindustrialization. The deindustrialization in Zimbabwe may be particularly strong because of the historical background. The international sanctions during the UDI period led to a broad manufacturing base, but also more inward looking industries than in most countries. Bad luck added to the problems, since the trade liberalization coincided with a serious drought (in 1992).

As discussed in section 2, the consequences of eliminating protectionism are harder to sort out when we distinguish between intermediate and final goods importables and between protection against importables and final goods. Liberalization of trade in intermediates, the first stage of the programme in Zimbabwe, is expected to be expansionary for downstream final goods industries. Lack of intermediate imports was seen as the main constraint for further industrialization. But the statistics available and CGE calibration (Davies et al., 1998; Rattsø and Torvik, 1998) do not indicate much output response to the new availability of foreign intermediates. It seems like the industrial sector had adjusted to the import rationing system and was not ready to expand. The second phase of liberalization, eliminating quotas on final goods, clearly pushed many domestic producers out of the market. The liberalization concentrated on abolishing the foreign exchange allocation apparatus, and the tariff structure was left more or less intact. Since final goods imports were kept very low, tariffs and tariff revenues were unimportant. Tariffs had been kept fairly high on intermediate imports, where tariff revenues could be generated. The continuation of this awkward tariff structure contributed to the dismal performance of established industries.

Macroeconomic instability added to the short-run adjustment problems. Macroeconomics is beyond the present essay, and I will only refer to the argument mentioned in section 2. Private savings easily fall when private sectors suddenly have access to foreign goods. The following consumption boom tends to disturb both current account and inflation processes. The inflation shift from below 20 per cent to above 40 per cent in 1992, probably the result of both drought and lower savings, had distributional effects overwhelming the relative price adjustments shown in Figure 4.1.

The long-run effects of the new liberalization regime are still a 'wait and see'. The economics literature on trade policy has primarily appealed to static comparative advantage and efficiency. The export response and the cost efficiency following international competition are two important sources. After the first setback, exports have increased considerably. The new foreign exchange situation, the deregulation of markets and better international transport facilities have given a boost to agricultural exports. Mining exports have increased together with foreign investment. The improved export capacity certainly has reduced the foreign exchange constraint to growth. Industrial exports have been slower to respond and not much evidence is available regarding cost efficiency.

The open question of long-run implications concerns the dynamics and productivity growth. If the economy adjusts to comparative advantage, export specialization in commercial farming and mining will continue. Comparative advantage is hardly related to advanced manufacturing production. If productivity growth is driven by industrial production technology, the new economic structure may be a disadvantage in the long run. It seems to me that Zimbabwe has returned to the basic development issue that this chapter started with – how to industrialize.

5.   CONCLUDING REMARKS

The experiences of Sub-Saharan Africa represent an interesting challenge to understand growth, distribution and reform. In this essay I have tried to throw light on this experience using the urban–rural or industry–agriculture divide in the context of foreign trade.

It is argued that the regulation regimes since independence have made urban/industry protected from world markets, while rural/agriculture has been outward oriented. The recent liberalization process has changed the sectoral balances, and the region is in an interesting transformation to a new balance between exports and imports, agriculture and industry. To analyse this balancing, I have made used of some old wine in new bottles. Dualism, imperfect competition, productivity gaps and underdevelopment traps are old concepts in development economics. They have appeared again under labels such as 'new trade theory' and 'new growth theory'. The 'new' add-on has certainly contributed to clarifications of trade and growth, so there is some new wine involved too. With this little attempt at bringing the concepts in touch with Sub-Saharan African realities, I hope others are motivated to contribute to new old development economics analysis.

NOTE

1. The author is grateful to Rob Davies and Ragnar Torvik for discussions and joint work on Zimbabwe.

REFERENCES

Bates, R. (1981), *Markets and States in Topical Africa*, Berkeley: University of California Press.

Collier, P. and J. Gunning (1997), 'Explaining African economic performance', CSAE, University of Oxford, WPS/97-2-1.

Dailami, M. and M. Walton (1989), 'Private investment, government policy, and foreign capital in Zimbabwe', Working Paper 248, Country Economics Department, The World Bank.

Davies, R. (1991), 'Trade, trade management and development in Zimbabwe', in J. Frimpong-Ansah, S.M. Ravi Kanbur and P. Svedberg (eds), *Trade and Development in Sub-Saharan Africa*, Manchester: Manchester University Press.

Davies, R. and J. Rattsø (1993), 'Zimbabwe', in L. Taylor (ed.), *The Rocky Road to Reform: Adjustment, Income Distribution and Growth in the Developing World*, Cambridge: MIT Press.

Davies, R. and J. Rattsø (1996), 'Growth, distribution and environment: Macroeconomic issues in Zimbabwe', *World Development*, 24 (2), 395–405.

Davies, R., J. Rattsø and R. Torvik (1994), 'The macroeconomics of Zimbabwe in the 1980s: A CGE-model analysis', *Journal of African Economies*, 3 (2), 153–98.

Davies, R., J. Rattsø and R. Torvik (1998), 'Short run consequences of trade liberalization: A CGE model of Zimbabwe', *Journal of Policy Modeling*, 20 (3), 305–33.

Davies, R., D. Sanders and T. Shaw (1992), 'Liberalization for development: Zimbabwe's adjustment without the fund', in G.A. Cornia, R. van der Hoeven and T. Mkandawire (eds), *Africa's Recovery in the 1990s: From Stagnation and Adjustment to Human Development*, Basingstoke: Macmillan, 135–55.

Government of Zimbabwe (1991a), *Zimbabwe: A Framework for Economic Reform 1991–95*, Harare.

Government of Zimbabwe (1991b), *Social Dimensions of Adjustment: A Programme to Mitigate the Social Costs of Adjustment*, Harare.

Government of Zimbabwe (1998), *ZIMPREST: Zimbabwe Programme for Economic and Social Transformation 1996–2000*, Harare.

Green, R. and X. Kadhani (1986), 'Zimbabwe: Transition to economic crises 1981–83: Retrospect and prospect', *World Development*, **14** (8), 1059–83.

International Labour Office (1993), *Structural Change and Adjustment in Zimbabwe*, Occasional Paper 16, Geneva.

Kirkpatrick, C. and C. Weiss (1995), 'Trade policy reforms and performance in Africa in the 1980s', *Journal of Modern African Studies*, **33** (2), 285–98.

Krueger, A., M. Schift and A. Valdes (eds) (1991), *The Political Economy of Agricultural Pricing Policy*, Vol. 3, Africa and the Mediterranean, Baltimore: Johns Hopkins University Press and World Bank.

Matsuyama, K. (1992), 'Agricultural productivity, comparative advantage and economic growth', *Journal of Economic Theory*, **58** (2), 317–34.

Murphy, K., A. Shleifer and R. Vishny (1989), 'Industrialization and the big push', *Journal of Political Economy*, **97** (5), 1003–26.

Ncube, M., P. Collier, J. Gunning and K. Mlambo (1996), 'Trade Liberalization and Regional Integration in Zimbabwe', *mimeo*, AERC and Centre for the Study of African Economies, University of Oxford.

Pakkiri, L. and N.P. Moyo (1986), 'Foreign exchange policies: The case of Zimbabwe', IDRC Workshop on Economic Structure and Macroeconomic Management, Harare.

Puga, D. and A. Venables (1998), 'Trading arrangements and industrial development', *The World Bank Economic Review*, **2** (12), 221–49.

Rattsø, J. and L. Taylor (1998), 'CGE-modelling of trade liberalization in Sub-Saharan Africa: An evaluation', *mimeo*, Norwegian University of Science and Technology and New School of Social Research.

Rattsø, J. and R. Torvik (1998), 'Zimbabwean trade liberalisation: Ex post evaluation', *Cambridge Journal of Economics*, **22** (3), 325–46.

Rattsø, J. and R. Torvik (1999), 'Dynamic interactions between agriculture and industry: Theoretical analysis of the consequences of discriminating agriculture in Africa', *mimeo*, Department of Economics, Norwegian University of Science and Technology.

Robinson, P. (1993), 'Structural adjustment in Zimbabwe: Adjustment and long-term industrial development', Harare: Zimconsult, prepared for ILO.

Rodrik, D. (1994), 'Trade and industrial policy reform in developing countries: A review of recent theory and evidence', in J. Behrman and T.N. Srinivasan (eds), *Handbook of Development Economics Book III*, Amsterdam: North-Holland.

Rodrik, D. (1998), 'Why is trade reform so difficult in Africa?', *Journal of African Economies*, **7**, Supplement 1, 43–69.

Ros, J. (1998), 'Increasing returns, development traps, and economic growth', *mimeo*, Department of Economics, University of Notre Dame.

Sachs, J. and A. Warner (1995), 'Natural resource abundance and economic growth', NBER Working Paper 5398.

Shaw, T. and R. Davies (1993), *The Political Economy of Adjustment in Zimbabwe: Convergence and Reform,* Ottawa: North South Institute.
Skålnes, T. (1995), *The Politics of Economic Reform in Zimbabwe*, London: Macmillan.
Venables, A. (1996), 'Trade policy, cumulative causation, and industrial development', *Journal of Development Economics*, **49**, 179–97.

016 G21 F32
S. 019 G28 623 024

5. The Korean financial crisis of 1997–98 and its implications for the global financial system

Irma Adelman and Song Byung Nak

1. THE CHRONOLOGY OF THE CRISIS

The first overt signs of trouble in Korea became evident in 1996, when the current account deficit widened from 2 per cent of GNP in 1995 to 5 per cent in 1996, the rate of growth of exports slowed down from a phenomenal 31 per cent to a merely very high 15 per cent and that of GNP declined from an exceedingly high 14.6 per cent to a very high 7.1 per cent. At the same time, foreign debt rose from 78 billion dollars (62 per cent of exports) in 1995 to 100 billion dollars (76 per cent of exports) in 1996, most of it[1] short term. The slowdown in export growth was due in part to: a loss of competitiveness arising from the relative appreciation of Korea's currency because of the drastic decline of the yen; a recession in Japan and Europe; and a precipitous drop in the world prices of computer chips, ships, automobiles and garments, which affected over 50 per cent of Korea's total exports.[2] Exporters of these products were therefore losing money on their exports. Together with increases in domestic wages and high domestic interest rates, these losses put a squeeze on corporate profits, which led to a surge in corporate failures. In January of 1997, despite a massive rescue attempt, Hanbo Steel, the fourteenth largest chaebol in terms of assets and seventeenth largest in terms of sales, went into bankruptcy. This was followed by the failure of the Sammi group, another steel producer. Next came two major affiliates of the Jinro group, the nineteenth largest chaebol, that defaulted on their debts in April. They were succeeded by the Dainong retail chain and by the Ssangyong business group, the sixth largest. In July 1997, Kia Motors, the third largest Korean auto maker, went into default. The stock market responded by a precipitous decline; by mid-November, it had dropped 50 per cent from its mid-1997 high. The won went into a free-fall on 19 November, when it tumbled 50 per cent during a two-week span after the daily band for its fluctuation was widened from 8 to 10 per cent and the government announced that it would henceforth refrain from intervening in currency markets; in May of 1998 the won was about 75 per cent below its high in mid-1997. As Korea's financial troubles mounted, the government asked the IMF and other international agencies for standby loans in mid-November; the largest international financial rescue package to date was approved by the IMF board during the first week of December. Nevertheless, Korea's bonds were downgraded by Moody's and Standard and Poor's from A1 status to junk-bond status on 11 December, when the IMF forced disclosure of the true state of Korea's usable external reserves and it became apparent that they were inadequate to cover the debt coming due before the end of the year. The downgrading of Korean bonds made them ineligible for portfolio investment by international banks. The banks not only could not renew maturing loans, but started withdrawing funds from Korea to the tune of a billion a day. The swing in foreign lending in 1997 from plus $100 billion between January and October, to minus $20 billion by the end of the year was catastrophic. With IMF and US help, talks on debt rollover with international commercial banks were started on 29–30 December 1997. On 17 January the US Secretary of the Treasury stated that Korea had stabilized, but the President elect, Kim Dae Jung, warned that with adjustment under IMF conditions 'the worst is yet to come'. On 29 January 1998, agreement between Korea and international commercial lenders was reached on a rollover of $60 billion of its debt, on favourable terms.[3] After a landmark agreement was reached with the union to allow firing of workers as part of IMF adjustment conditions, a general strike called for 11 February was cancelled. In February, one third of Korea's merchant banks were closed, but deposits were guaranteed. Problem loans at banks were 6 per cent of all loans and non-performing loans, on which payments overdue by more than three months were between 15 and 20 per cent. The debt default ratio was 62 per cent in February, as compared with 53 per cent in January and 1.5 per cent in December 1997, with over 10000 firms defaulting on payments since the previous December. Industrial output in February was 1.9 percentage points lower than the previous year; during February, the rate of growth of output was negative. In 1998 the crisis abated and was replaced by a depression. Since 1999 Korea has resumed its high growth trajectory, achieving 10 per cent rates of growth annually in both 1999 and 2000, rebuilding its foreign exchange reserves and repaying its IMF loan. There has also been some restructuring of its financial and corporate sectors.

This chapter is organized as follows. We start by discussing the crisis's origins, the policy measures adopted to handle it, and Korea's future prospects. We end the chapter by discussing the implications of the crisis for development policy options in other countries and for the global financial regime.

The origins of the present Korean financial crisis are complex. Several elements have combined to generate it: vulnerabilities to external shocks, both inherent and strategy-induced; institutional inadequacies, both domestic and global; domestic policy mistakes; and exogenous shocks originating in the external environment. Individually, none of these elements would have sufficed to generate the financial meltdown experienced by Korea between October 1977 and mid-March 1998. In the absence of substantial capital-market liberalization, the policy mistakes and domestic institutional inadequacies in Korea would merely have resulted in a recession, as they did during the previous corporate financial crises of 1972, 1980–81, and 1992. In the absence of exogenous shocks stemming from prolonged recession in Japan and Europe and contagion from financial crises in other East Asian countries, the mistaken real appreciation of the won and the consequent slowdown in exports and economic growth, which made Korea more vulnerable to shocks, would not have taken place. And, if the financial crisis had not been as severe once it got going, Korea would not have had to submit to the overly stringent and partially mistakenly conceived IMF conditionality which, despite being accompanied by the largest financial rescue package in IMF history, did not succeed in stemming the crisis and would slow down Korea's recovery and increase its pain. It took the combination of these factors to produce the magnitude of financial and economic disaster of 1997–98. We now proceed to the analysis of each of the ingredients of the Korean financial crisis, in turn.

2. STRATEGY-INDUCED VULNERABILITIES

First, the development strategy pursued by Korea of export-led growth transformed the economy from one in which exports were of marginal importance into one in which they have become vital. As emphasized by Stiglitz (1998), small open economies are inherently vulnerable to exogenous shocks. While Korea is now the eleventh largest trading economy in the world and the third largest developing country, and thus does not qualify for the label 'small', it is certainly extremely open, with the sum of exports and imports[4] in 1995 being 56 per cent of its gross domestic product. The openness of the economy makes it very sensitive to influences originating in the global economy, such as price shocks (for example, oil) and slowdown in the growth of international trade.

In the crisis of 1997–98, the specific exogenous shocks to Korea were a lengthy recession in Japan and a worldwide decline in demand for computer chips, ships, automobiles and garments. These impacted upon the value of its overall exports, their profitability and their competitiveness, and led to a mild recession during the first two quarters of 1997, from which the economy was starting to recover. Japan's economic slowdown had started in 1990, and had led to a steadily declining exchange rate of the yen relative to the dollar; by mid-1997, the yen had declined to about 45 per cent of its value in 1994. Since Korea's nominal exchange rate was (loosely) pegged to the dollar, Japan's declining real exchange rate meant an automatic currency appreciation of the won. Korea's trade-weighted real exchange rate appreciated by 12 percentage points between 1990 and 1996.[5] This caused a decrease in the rate of growth in the value of Korea's exports and, to the extent that dollar prices were reduced to maintain competitiveness, a reduction in their profitability. But it was the decline in Korea's competitiveness, rather than the reduction in the rate of growth of its exports to Japan, which was the critical element since, in 1995, Korea's exports to Japan were only 13.6 per cent of its total exports while Japan was Korea's nearest competitor for more than 50 per cent of its exports.

After mid-1997, one must add to the exogenous shocks emanating from Japan and the decline in world demand for a large share of Korea's exports contagion from the financial crises in Thailand, Indonesia, Malaysia and Singapore. The contagion took three forms: a decrease in exports to these countries, which, in 1995, had accounted for 7 per cent of Korea's exports; increased competition for its exports due to the precipitous fall in the value of their currencies; and a re-evaluation of Korea's credit-worthiness by international banks. Of these effects, the latter was clearly the most important.

A second source of strategy-induced vulnerability was the major instrument used by Korea's government to promote exports – its management of the allocation of bank credit. This instrument was wielded through government control over subsidized loans, made first by the government-owned banks and then continued through the government's influence over private-bank loans coupled with interest rate ceilings. This instrument was made all the more potent by the relative underdevelopment of Korea's financial system, which made non-bank sources of credit scarce. The stock market and non-financial intermediaries were underdeveloped throughout most of Korea's economic history and curb-market loans, which were freely available, were very expensive.[6] The result was a highly leveraged corporate sector and a banking sector whose financial health was dependent upon that of the corporate sector.

Partly as a consequence of the government's use of interest rate subsidies as a major instrument of development policy, the financial structure of corporations was unsound. More specifically, the debt–equity ratios of the Korean private corporate sector have varied between 3 and 4 throughout its economic history; by contrast, those of the US manufacturing sector have ranged between 0.62 in 1980 to 1.82 in 1990 (as a result of the Reagan–Milken spate of leveraged buyouts), after which they declined to 1.5 in 1992.[7] As a result, the debt–service ratio[8] of the Korean non-financial corporate sector has been enormous: 65 per cent in 1980, 46.4 per cent in 1990, and 53.9 per cent in 1992. Thus rapid growth has been essential to the solvency of the corporate sector, in the equivalent of a corporate Ponzi game. By the same token, the quality of bank assets became highly dependent on the, at times precarious, solvency of the corporate sector.

Furthermore, the fraction of inherently more risky, government mandated, policy loans in the balance sheets of banks was very high. Even though the proportion of new policy loans to new total credit had dropped steadily, from a high of 100 per cent in the 1970s to between 60 and 80 per cent in the 1980s to about 15 per cent in the 1990s, the ratio of policy loans to assets had remained high (30 per cent in 1992). As a result, the inherent solvency of banks was at all times precarious: they had to be bailed out by the Central Bank periodically, and in 1992 net lending from financial institutions to banks amounted to 43 per cent of their total assets. Moreover, since banks were allowed to invest in stocks and real assets on their own account, the values of their portfolios became directly vulnerable to asset price fluctuations as well. Like in Japan, Korea's real estate market went through a price bubble, rising substantially in the 1980s and declining significantly thereafter. In 1992, net real estate purchases by banks were just about as large (89 per cent) as bank net lending and securities constituted 28 per cent of their total assets. And, as indicated in the chronology of the crisis, Korea's stock market plunged from a high value of 1000 for the Korean Dow Jones index in 1991 to 500 in 1995. Not only were banks vulnerable to asset-price bubbles, but they were also exposed to exchange rate risk.[9] Between 1995 and 1997 international claims on Korean banks had risen by 30 per cent, from 77 billion dollars to 103 billion. It is perfectly true that the banks, both local and international, enjoyed implicit government guarantees against the insolvency of Korean banks and could thus take higher risks.[10] Evidently, the vulnerabilities of the Korean economy have been long-standing and could, in and of themselves, suffice to give rise to a vicious economic cycle: an exogenously induced decline in exports, which are vital to the economy, would lead to stress on corporate profits and a decline in the rates of growth of the economy. Deteriorating balance sheets of corporations put the private banking sector's financial viability at risk. The banks respond to these developments by a mix of increased interest rates on loans and curtailment of credit, which, in turn, further deteriorates the balance sheets of the corporate sector, reduces their profits and their ability to service debt, and curtails the growth of their exports and domestic sales. And thus the vicious cycle would continue. In the absence of timely government intervention,[11] a spate of corporate failures, bank failures, and lower rates of economic growth would ensue and lead to a recession ranging in severity from moderate, as in 1972 and 1992, to intense, as in 1981–82, but would not suffice to cause a financial meltdown.

3.   INSTITUTIONAL DEFICIENCIES

3.1   Domestic financial system

The Korean financial crisis was partly the result of serious institutional deficiencies, both domestic and global. The financial system of Korea is at an awkward stage of development: it is in a transitional state between completely nationalized and without a convertible currency, to a fully developed market-based system that enforces prudential regulations and transparent accounting practices in both banks and corporations. In this connection, it is interesting to explore why two East Asian economies, Mainland China and Taiwan, have not had financial crises like Korea's. Mainland China has not started its financial liberalization:[12] its banks are wholly government-owned, by national, regional or local banks; its currency is not convertible; and, only selective foreign investment, under tightly controlled conditions of access and operation, is permitted. While China's competitiveness and exports have been affected by Japan's recession and by the financial crises of other East Asian countries, and while it is estimated that the fraction of non-performing loans held by its state banks is about 20 per cent, the worst that can happen to China is slower overall growth and a currency devaluation. Of course, China is also inherently less vulnerable, being a large country which is relatively closed.

At the other extreme in financial development and liberalization, we have Taiwan. Taiwan has followed a development strategy similar to Korea's, with qualitatively similar vulnerabilities (very open), but its financial system is considerably more advanced. The degree of financial intermediation in Taiwan is twice as high; both bank and non-bank financial institutions are more developed; it has enjoyed double-digit savings rates for considerably longer than Korea, making for financially sounder corporate debt–equity ratios, lower domestic interest rates and higher capitalization rates of banks; it has been running a trade surplus for the last 20 years, as a result of which it has accumulated an extremely large reserve of foreign currency; it has been exporting, rather than importing, capital; and conglomerates play a less significant role in its industrial organization. Also, of course, much of its trade is with the Mainland, which, so far, has been little affected.

It seems that either extreme in financial development is stable to cataclysmic financial crises, while the middle is not.

During the 1960s and 1970s, Korean banks were highly controlled. During the 1960s, the control was exercised by having specialized government-owned banks for special purposes (such as Export–Import, Agricultural Credit Bank and so on) and then, in the 1970s, through direct targeting of loans to specific firms which the government had enjoined to carry out specific activities.[13] The first moves towards financial liberalization in Korea started in 1981–83, when banks were privatized. But, privatization did not carry with it freedom from government controls on lending. While targeted industrial policy effectively ended with the death of President Park in 1980, the government continued to mandate private-bank loans in support of solvency of the corporate sector and its expansion, as well as in support of the government's social goals. Thus, the government encouraged banks to lend for real estate mortgages to would-be home buyers and ordered them not to call loans to corporations in 1992 and again in mid-1997. And it established a main-bank system, borrowed from the Japanese, in which a specific bank is designated by the government to syndicate a loan to a particular corporation for a specific activity. This meant that, although banks were privatized in the early 1980s, policy loans (that is, loans made in support of government policy goals) persisted. The continuation of these loans implied not only that banks wound up with an unsound portfolio of loans, but also that there was little screening of projects and of the credit-worthiness of borrowers and thus that the capacity of banks to engage in financial scrutiny of loan applications was not developed.[14] The problems of unsound banking portfolios was exacerbated by the fact that the banks' balance sheets were not purged of dubious assets when they were privatized. Instead, the newly privatized banks started their economic life with a legacy of questionable loans in their portfolios. However, in return for complying with government directives on lending, banks have had, in effect, virtually unlimited insurance against insolvency, thus encouraging them to make riskier loans[15] and investments. Indeed, banks have consistently borrowed from the Bank of Korea and the government. The institutional structure of the banking system thus promoted the development of unsound balance sheets in banks.

The Korean banking system was privatized and liberalized, but despite controls on lending it has also been inadequately regulated and supervised. Korea's financial system was modelled on Japan's and built around 'relationship banking' rather than, like the Anglo Saxon system, around 'arm's length' relationships. Relationship banking gets around moral hazard issues by forging close communication channels between borrowers and lenders, in which lenders are privy to timely information about business conditions and plans. However, it is also open to manipulation and to persistence of perceptions concerning a company's soundness long after reality has changed.[16] Moreover, in relationship banking the degree of overall transparency, disclosure, and rule-based banking supervision is low. Relationship banking is also not well suited to globalized financial systems, which require generalized, timely and accurate information to function properly.

In addition, starting with the 1980s, Korea had pursued a high real interest rate policy, in order to encourage domestic savings and attract savings away from the curb market. The intent of the policy was to curb inflation[17] while financing high investment rates. But this high interest rate policy encouraged borrowing abroad, especially during the 1990s, when US (and world) interest rates started declining. When restrictions on foreign capital inflows were lifted, Korean banks started borrowing heavily on the foreign market. Between 1990 and 1995, foreign debt shot up by 70 per cent, after declining by 68 per cent between 1985 and 1990, and net foreign liabilities, expressed in won, increased six-fold to 6 billion dollars.[18] Nevertheless, by 1995 foreign debt was only 12 per cent of GNP and 44 per cent of exports. Most of this foreign debt represented borrowing by private banks. Naturally, the foreign borrowing was denominated in dollars, exposing bank borrowing to exchange rate risk. Since Korea was committed to maintaining a stable exchange rate, the short term debt was unhedged. Moreover, about 80 per cent of loans were short-term, making the solvency of banks and, indirectly, chaebols very sensitive to fluctuations in foreign confidence in Korea's economic prospects.

Banking has, on the average, not been a profitable activity in Korea; indeed, the operating surplus of financial institutions has consistently been negative throughout the 1980s and 1990s. Despite earlier moves to free interest rates on deposits and loans, they continued to be set by the Ministry of Finance. Since banks were privatized in the early 1980s, the spread between nominal time-deposit rates and general loan rates has been quite low, averaging about half a percentage point, and that between time-deposit rates and policy loans has been negative, ranging between -9 to -2 percentage points. Thus there was little, if any, cushion for mistakes in lending. When Korean merchant and commercial banks were allowed direct access to foreign lenders, they tried to improve their profitability by increasing the spread between loan rates to corporations and the cost of these loans through their ready access to cheap short-term loans from foreign banks, and by borrowing short and lending long. They also tried to improve their profitability by using some of the funds they borrowed on international capital markets to purchase bonds and derivatives in other developing countries (such as Brazil and Indonesia) that had less privileged access to international financial markets.

Korea's capital market was closed to foreigners throughout most of its development and opened only cautiously and very gradually. Foreign banks were first allowed to have branches in Korea in 1972, but substantial restrictions were placed on their activities. Portfolio investment by foreigners, through special funds which bought Korean securities and whose shares were traded only abroad, was first allowed in 1982, but these funds were limited to owning no more than 10 per cent of paid in capital of large domestic securities companies. The complete prohibition on direct foreign investment in the Korean stock market was lifted only in 1992, but restrictions were placed on these investments. Restrictions on the convertibility of the won on trade-related transactions were revoked only in 1988. In 1985, Korean firms were allowed to raise capital abroad by issuing convertible bonds. In 1990, a managed-float exchange rate system, known as a market-average-exchange-rate system, was adopted. In this system the Ministry of Finance and the Bank of Korea are no longer directly involved in setting exchange rates. But the bands imposed on the daily fluctuations of the won–dollar exchange rate were narrow,[19] and the government continues to exercise indirect influence on the exchange rate through its foreign exchange transactions. Capital account convertibility for capital inflows was started in 1991, but with substantial restrictions. The opening up of Korea's capital market was accelerated after 1994, in preparation for Korea's joining the OECD and under pressure by the United States, when several steps were taken to liberalize the outflow of capital as well. It was envisaged that, by the year 2000, Korea's capital account transactions would be as liberalized as those of OECD countries. This opening up permitted private-sector banks to borrow abroad without significant oversight. Together with the high interest rate policy, it led to a rapid increase in foreign liabilities of banks, from 5.1 per cent of their total liabilities in 1990 to 9 per cent in 1995.

3.2 Global financial system

When Korea's capital markets were opened up, the institutional problems of its financial system were compounded by the institutional deficiencies of the international financial system. As pointed out by Tobin,[20] international markets for foreign exchange are too smooth, permitting the transfer of vast sums to be carried out instantaneously; they are also too large, enabling immense amounts of cash to be brought to bear on any currency at any moment in time; and they also have an inherent tendency to overshoot, generating waves of over-optimistic risk assessments, leading to overlending, followed by over-pessimistic risk assessments, leading not only to the cessation of new loans but also to huge withdrawals of foreign currency.

These enormous swings in capital flows constitute the essence of financial crises.

The sheer size of the foreign exchange market is staggering. During 1993–95, the Bank for International Settlements estimates that foreign exchange transactions averaged 1.3 trillions per day.[21] By 1997, the daily volume of foreign exchange transactions had increased to 2 trillion![22] Moreover, 40 per cent of these transactions are reversed within two days (and 80 per cent within seven days) and are thus clearly speculative in nature. In 1997, the clearly speculative volume of daily foreign exchange transactions was thus 800 billion. No country, however large and however developed its domestic financial institutions, can withstand that kind of onslaught and emerge mostly unharmed. The international financial market is also inherently cyclical in nature. Korea's financial vulnerabilities were longstanding. If anything, they were more serious during the late 1970s and early 1980s than they are now. However, during the 1970s the banking system was nationalized and exchange transactions were tightly controlled. And during the 1980s, when the banking system was privatized, foreign capital movements and portfolio investment by foreigners continued to be either prohibited entirely or severely limited by law.

Despite these vulnerabilities, when Korea increasingly opened up its financial capital markets in the 1990s, it enjoyed an A1 rating from international credit rating agencies, enabling it to build up substantial foreign debt. It continued to enjoy this rating even though it was increasing its foreign indebtedness at too high a rate. Then, about six months after the East Asian financial crisis started in Thailand, Korea's credit rating was downgraded precipitously to junk-bond status, making its debt ineligible for the portfolios of international banks. As a consequence, in late 1997 Korea experienced a huge withdrawal of foreign capital of about one billion per day. It is perfectly true that Korea had some institutional vulnerabilities, was suffering from a mild recession, and made some policy mistakes which made it susceptible to downgrading. But it is equally true that the international financial system is designed like a crowded, high-speed highway system that demands perfect driving at all points of time from all those who participate in it, to avoid the dangers of severe periodic disasters.

The combination of a highly leveraged economy, a low-information, poorly regulated domestic financial system, together with an open capital market operating in a globalized financial system which is excessively liquid, is a disaster waiting to happen. Indeed, the last decade has seen 67 financial crises, one-third of which has occurred in developed countries.

4. POLICY MISTAKES

The Korean government made several policy mistakes during the period leading up to the crisis.

First, the government's exchange rate management may have been faulty. It first continued to peg its exchange rate to the dollar, refusing to devalue in tandem with the devaluation of the yen. As a result, the real trade-weighted exchange rate appreciated between 1994 and 1997. However, the extent of appreciation was relatively small as the trade-weighted real exchange rate in 1997 was only about 12 per cent above that in 1990.[23] The reasons for not devaluing were a mix of economic and political: the economic arguments for a devaluation were not clearcut. On the one hand, Korea had consistently been running a large trade deficit with Japan; the appreciation of the won relative to the yen made imports from Japan cheaper at the same time that it made exports more expensive, raising Korea's real terms of trade and reducing its rate of inflation. Also, the appreciated won made debt servicing cheaper. Moreover, as in the case of Mexico in 1994, a devaluation might have been taken as a sign of weakness and invited the very speculative attack which it was intended to fend off. With an election looming in 1997, a devaluation would reduce Korea's per capita income below the magic figure of $10000, and erode the claims of the ruling party to an impressive economic performance. On the other hand, the result of continuing the dollar-peg during the 1990s was to reduce the competitiveness and rate of growth of exports, increase the trade deficit, and lower the rate of growth of the economy. The rate of growth of exports fell to an average of about 14 per cent annually between 1990 and 1996 as compared with 20 per cent between 1985 and 1990;[24] the trade deficit doubled between 1990 and 1995; the current account deficit quadrupled; and the rate of growth of GNP declined from an average of 10.8 per cent between 1985 and 1990 to an average rate of 7.5 per cent between 1990 and 1995.

Then, once the won started declining at a precipitous rate, foreign investors and lenders and Korean banks and corporations rushed to convert won into dollars to enable them to pay their dollar-denominated obligations and protect the value of their won-denominated assets. This led to a currency attack on the won. At that point, Korea made a futile attempt to defend its overvalued exchange rate, losing about 20 billion dollars in the process. By the end of 1997, Korea's net usable foreign exchange reserves had dwindled to about 12 billion dollars, or about three weeks' worth of imports and only about 60 per cent of the debt falling due by the end of the year. In addition, the devaluation of the won increased the debt burden on Korea's banks and corporations[25] dramatically.

Second, government policy encouraged a very rapid rate of growth of real wages, in excess of the rate of growth of labour productivity. Between 1987, when independent unions were first allowed to organize, and 1994, real wages more than doubled;[26] relative to 1990, the index of real wages in 1994 stood about 11 percentage points above that of labour productivity. Just before the crisis, the *Economist* indicated that the average wage level in Korea was about 30 per cent above that in the UK. Unit labour costs rose more slowly than labour productivity because of the move by firms to respond to high wages by substituting capital for labour, by increasing investment. Again, the motivation was political: to preempt the opposition parties, which represent labour interests, from gaining popular support. It may also be true that President Kim was genuinely populist in his orientation. In response, firms tried to automate very rapidly, an effort to which a large fraction of corporate investment was devoted.

Third, the government adopted a high interest rate, tight money policy, which set domestic real interest rates way above world markets. Prior to the crisis, the nominal interest rate was about 12–13 per cent annually (real interest rate of about 7–8 per cent) compared with a world-market nominal rate of about 6–7 per cent (real rate of 3–4 per cent). This high interest rate policy was continued from the 1980s and intensified both in response to IMF pressures and in order to qualify for membership in the OECD. Since by 1997 the Korean stock market had declined by 50 per cent relative to 1991, in response to the high interest rates and the squeeze on corporate earnings, firms were unable to raise new equity capital on the stock market and had to resort to borrowing. The huge interest rate differential between domestic and foreign loans, in turn, encouraged foreign borrowing, thus deteriorating the soundness of bank balance sheets further and endangering macroeconomic stability. As a result, the ratio of *foreign* to total liabilities doubled between 1990 and 1995.

These policy mistakes were costly. Their consequence was to put a severe squeeze on corporate profits. To put the squeeze on profits in perspective, in 1992[27] the operating surplus net of taxes in manufacturing was only 9.5 per cent of manufacturing GDP. The result of the profit squeeze was to force 8 out of the top 30 chaebols into bankruptcy during the first six months of 1997. In addition, the policy mistakes also increased foreign indebtedness, and placed the solvency of the economy at risk.

But Korea had faced similar profit squeezes and precarious financial positions of corporations and banks before, notably in 1972, 1980–82, and 1991–92. The immediate results had been one-to-two year recessions, but not economic meltdowns of the type Korea is experiencing currently. To tackle the previous crises, several emergency measures had been adopted: there was some institutional restructuring; loans to corporations were rolled over; banks were recapitalized; and then Korea grew its way out of the solvency crises. The major measure in 1972 was a freeze on repayment of unorganized money-market (curb-market) debt; the effect of this freeze was to force private non-bank lenders to provide corporate solvency. Institutional restructuring of the financial system, by privatizing hitherto nationalized banks without absorbing their questionable loans and increasing the role of non-bank financial intermediaries in finance, were the main responses to 1981–83 crisis. The privatization had the effect of infusing new capital into banks, through the purchase of equity by the private sector. In 1991–92, foreign capital inflows were liberalized, banks were asked to roll over corporate debt and their bad debts were absorbed by the government. In all these cases, Korea's fundamental adjustment strategy had consisted of adopting measures to maintain its growth rate: borrowing abroad to cover its current account deficit and increasing its exports to service its foreign debt.[28]

By the same token, while Korea's level of foreign debt was mounting at an unsustainable rate, Korea had experienced much higher levels of foreign debt during its recent history. Between 1980 and 1986, the ratio of its foreign debt to GNP averaged 50 per cent, as compared with only 12 per cent in 1996, and the ratio of its foreign debt to exports averaged 163 per cent, as compared with only 77 per cent in 1996. It is true that, in the 1980s, only about 30 per cent of Korea's debt was less than one year in maturity while 80 per cent of its debt was short term in 1996. It is also true that the foreign debt of the 1980s was sovereign debt, while the foreign debt of the 1990s was largely private debt. But as against that one must put the facts that, during the 1980s, the Latin American debt crisis had enhanced international concerns with lending to developing countries to almost paranoic heights; that, then, the interest rate on loans was variable, renegotiated at six-month intervals; and that world interest rates stood at double-digit levels. Moreover, between 1981 and 1985, Korea's exports were expanding at only 5 per cent a year while increasing at an average rate of 14 per cent annually during 1986–96 and 15 per cent in 1996. Also, even though Korea's foreign debt in the 1990s was not sovereign debt, international banks correctly perceived banking debt in Korea as having an implicit government guarantee.

Nevertheless, international perception of the risk of lending to Korea actually decreased after the first Mexican debt crisis in 1982: during the 1970s, the premium over the London International Borrowing Rate (LIBOR) paid by Korea was 2 percentage points; it fell to 0.25 percentage points in the wake of the 1982 Mexican debt crisis.[29] By contrast, the rating of Korea's bonds by Moody's and by Standard and Poor's dropped abruptly from A1 prior to June of 1997 to junk-bond status in November

1997.[30] The downgrading was in response to Korea's asking the IMF for a standby loan, the stringent conditionality of the proposed IMF loan and the IMF-mandated disclosure of the true state of Korea's net usable foreign reserves. Interestingly enough, between 1990 and late 1997, while Korea's foreign debt was building up at an unsustainable rapid rate, its ranking was A1. Also, during the rapid debt build-up period, Korea's relative Euromoney country risk rating increased from the thirty-second most credit-worthy nation among 180 in March of 1993 to the twenty-second most credit-worthy in March of 1997.[31] So much for the intertemporal rationality of global financial markets!

So what was different during the present financial crisis? The two major differences were contagion from the rest of Asia and a much more open capital market. In 1982, contagion from the Latin American debt crisis had not spread to Korea, since Korea was correctly perceived to have been qualitatively different in its development strategy, more successful, and therefore more credit-worthy. Developed-country banks were then under pressure to lend, since they were receiving a large inflow of petro-dollars on which they were paying high interest rates and the rate of economic growth in the OECD countries had plummeted. But contagion from East Asia did spread to Korea in 1997, because international financial markets perceived it as being quite similar to the other East Asian countries affected by financial crises. Also, the inflow of petro-dollars into US banks had dropped substantially with declining oil prices and the US was growing rapidly, so that it provided a vibrant market for new lending. This meant that, after the 1997–98 crisis started, Korea could not adjust to the decline in its exports and to the decline in its corporate profits by increasing its foreign borrowing to maintain its growth of GNP and exports and bailing out ailing corporations and banks, as it had done successfully in previous crises.

Thus, perhaps the critical, fundamental policy mistake of Korea was the premature liberalization of its capital markets, which enabled private, as distinct from government, borrowing from abroad. The drive toward premature liberalization was the result of President Kim's desire to join the OECD during his term in office, in order to increase his legitimacy and popular support. Joining the OECD requires, as a precondition, free capital markets and macroeconomic stability. In this context, it is indicative that both the last Mexican crisis and the previous Turkish financial crisis occurred only six months after they became members of the OECD.

The pace of liberalization of Korea's capital account, once started, was quite rapid. Constraints on foreign exchange transaction on capital account were weakened substantially in 1993. In 1994, President Kim Young Sam issued a Declaration of Globalization in preparation for joining the OECD, which significantly accelerated the opening up of

Korea's capital markets to foreign security firms and foreign investors. The liberalization of capital markets enabled Korea's private sector to rely unchecked upon foreign borrowing and thereby become excessively sensitive to fluctuations in foreign confidence in the soundness of Korea's economy. When, partly as a result of the financial turmoil in Thailand, Indonesia and Malaysia, international banks got worried about loans to all Asian countries and refused to roll over Korean debt, and when the credit rating of Korea's bonds abruptly plummeted, Korea found itself in serious trouble.

The Korean meltdown need not have taken place if Korea had not opened up its short-term capital market. It is also possible that the crisis could have been avoided if Korea had waited five to seven years before joining the OECD and used the interim period to: 1) strengthen the balance sheets of banks and the corporate sector; 2) grant greater independence to banks in making loans; 3) increase the capacity of banks to evaluate the financial soundness of proposed projects and the solvency of corporations; and 4) raise the transparency of corporate accounting practices. Under both circumstances, the combination of exogenous shocks, vulnerabilities, institutional inadequacies and policy mistakes need only have resulted in a (mild?) recession.[32] After all, there had not been financial meltdowns during previous financial crises and external policy shocks.

Of course, the statement that with a fully mature financial system Korea could have avoided a financial crisis is predicated on the assumption that international capital markets would have recognized that Korea's economy is sounder than, say, Indonesia's and not downgraded its credit rating so precipitously when crises developed in the other East Asian economies. Alas, there is no guarantee that this would have been the case. Financial markets are plagued by various imperfections: moral hazard exacerbated by herd psychology; fallacy of composition; and imperfect information. Thus, despite the fact that quite substantial economic restructuring had taken place before the 1994 Mexican crash, international financial markets did not recognize the difference between the Mexico of 1982 and Mexico twelve years later.[33] Moreover, the last decade has seen serious financial crises in over 20 OECD countries, including the US in the early 1980s, even though their financial systems, by and large, met all of the structural criteria enumerated above.

5. POLICY RESPONSES TO THE CRISIS

The initial responses of the Korean government to the crisis were perverse. Korea was poorly situated to tackle the crisis as it was developing. With an election only a month away, its President, Kim Young Sam, placed the good of the ruling political party ahead of the needs of economic development. Moreover, like the Mexican President in 1994, President Kim Young Sam had surrounded himself with corrupt politicians, who were very influential in formulating and executing economic policy. There was also a split on appropriate economic policy between the Ministry of Finance and the Bank of Korea, which caused costly delays in undertaking corrective steps. Thus, at this critical juncture, leadership commitment to development was lacking and the government's moves to tackle the crisis had low credibility. Indeed, the Korean stock market dropped after each major government response to the crisis was announced.[34]

Prior to the crisis, businessmen had repeatedly asked the President to correct the three policy mistakes described in the previous section. But he turned a deaf ear to their pleas, putting short-term political considerations above the needs of economic development. Not only was leadership commitment to development lacking, but the institutional development of the private banking system, in which banks were only nominally independent of the government, made Korea's financial system vulnerable to corruption. The President's son, who was in charge of economic policy, bartered corporate loans to financially troubled chaebols for substantial bribes, a fact for which he is currently under indictment. Instead of correcting the policy mistakes discussed in the previous section in a timely fashion, the President initially attempted to paper over the evolving corporate crisis.

During 1996, a costly, and ultimately unsuccessful, bailout of Hanbo Steel, the fourteenth largest chaebol, was attempted. Commercial banks were forced by politicians intimately linked to President Kim Young Sam to extend new loans to Hanbo, amounting to 7.2 billion dollars, under threat of firing their presidents; those bank presidents who disobeyed the order to extend loans to Hanbo Steel were put in jail. Thus, corruption played a role in the loans to Hanbo Steel.[35] Hanbo Steel had been started by a low-level retired tax official with no business experience but who maintained close personal relationships with many corrupt politicians who were intimates of the President. Hanbo Steel was seriously mismanaged, had an astronomic debt–equity ratio of 16 and folded in January 1997, despite the rescue attempt. Naturally, the attempted bailout of Hanbo left Korea's merchant banks in a precarious financial position.

During October and November 1997, an unsuccessful effort was mounted to hold the line on the devaluation of the won by selling foreign exchange. It used up 60 per cent of the country's dollar reserves without achieving its objective. The futility of this stabilization effort could easily have been predicted, when one realizes the enormous size of the volume of global foreign exchange transactions. In addition, to maintain its international credit-worthiness, the Bank of Korea shifted large amounts of its reserves to offshore branches of Korean banks to help them repay the short-term debt falling due by the end of the year. The combination of these moves left the Bank of Korea with only 6 billion dollars in usable foreign exchange reserves in early December.

In response to the string of corporate failures during the first two quarters of 1997, in August, after about six weeks of unavailing resistance, banks were ordered by the President to refrain from calling in loans to chaebols. In their search for liquidity, financial institutions had previously increased their attempts to collect on loans to corporations. The mandate to refrain from calling in loans left banks with even more precarious balance sheets. In early December, the government attempted to shore up large conglomerates through a combination of direct budgetary injections of funds and large loans from the Bank of Korea. But these attempts also failed, as the spate of corporate failures continued. A Presidential Commission established in 1998 to examine the soundness of the corporate sector declared 55 corporations insolvent in July 1998. The failed attempt to rescue Hanbo Steel and the failures of the other chaebols have made it clear that Korea's business groups have grown both too big to be allowed to fail and too big to rescue.

Thus, the initial policy responses by Korea's government to the crisis as it developed were both futile and perverse: they increased the vulnerability of Korea's financial system even further without succeeding in solving the corporate crisis. They also ate up Korea's cushion of foreign exchange reserves at a juncture at which the liberalization of financial and foreign exchange markets had made preservation of foreign exchange reserves and financial system soundness critical.

In November 1997, the government announced a fundamental restructuring package to deal with the escalating financial crisis. It entailed: enhancing the financial capacity of the Korean Asset Management Corporation to purchase distressed assets, which would then be purchased by the government within two years; facilitating the restructuring of financial institutions through mergers and injections of new funds by domestic and foreign investment; providing vastly increased deposit insurance by raising the capital of the Deposit Insurance Corporation almost tenfold; liberalizing the capital account further by raising the limits on individual investments by foreigners and guaranteeing corporate bonds with maturities over three years; and strengthening financial disclosure standards and loan classification requirements. But this package was announced less than two weeks before the election, and was not viewed as credible. So, both the stock market and the won continued their declines.

By contrast, the responses of the corporate sector to the crisis have been totally appropriate to the (sorry) conditions in which it found itself. Unable to roll over foreign loans, the banks could not provide new credit to the corporate sector, even for exports, thus giving rise to a general scramble for liquidity. The banks also increased interest rates even more, from a high of 15 per cent to a high of 25 per cent in December 1997. In response, the business groups have all cut investment rates; have reduced management and professional salaries; sold off firms to foreign and, where possible, domestic buyers; reduced their degrees of diversification; and are striving to increase their productivity and competitiveness. So far, the chaebols have more or less held the line on worker layoffs, except by retirement and attrition. The unemployment rate has nevertheless increased, from about 2 per cent in October 1997 to about 6.5 per cent in June 1998,[36] largely as a result of bankruptcies of small- and medium-sized firms. While appropriate, the corporate reactions to the crisis have led to a severe recession. It is estimated that the rate of growth of GNP during the first two quarters of 1998 fell to -1.5 per cent from approximately $+7.1$ per cent in the previous year.

In late November 1997, the government reluctantly approached the IMF for an emergency loan. The policy responses mandated by the IMF, as part of its conditionality, were mixed. The IMF built upon the Korean programme of 19 November 1997, but required an accelerated pace of adjustment and made the conditions of adjustment more stringent. The seven IMF provisions were:

1. To achieve a sounder financial structure the IMF required immediate closure of 14 technically insolvent merchant banks and 2 commercial banks, with full protection of depositors. The closed merchant banks constitute about half the total number of merchant banks. The closed banks were required to submit a restructuring plan to the Ministry of Finance and merchant banks given three months and commercial banks four to implement it; if they do not succeed in implementing the plan, they are to be permanently closed. In December, the government provided 11 trillion won to the two commercial banks to initiate their recapitalization. Other commercial banks were given four months to compensate for impaired assets and security losses.
2. To reduce a future moral hazard problem, by the end of the year 2000 the government was to withdraw its full deposit guarantee and replace it with more limited insurance protection.
3. To improve soundness, bank supervision is to be strengthened by setting up an independent supervisory commission outside the Ministry of Finance; prudential regulation is to be strengthened; and large banks will be required to engage foreign firms to audit their

books. Also, chaebols are to be required to produce consolidated financial statements.[37]

4. To increase competition in the banking system, foreign institutions are to be allowed to participate in friendly mergers with domestic banks and permitted to acquire as much as a 100 per cent stake in merchant banks.

5. Bank governance is to be improved by the government's complete withdrawal from the management and lending decisions of banks; the abolition of policy loans; and corporate bankruptcies are to be allowed to take their course.

6. The IMF availed itself of the opportunity to insist on further opening of Korea's capital markets by raising ceilings on foreign ownership and setting a timetable for eliminating restrictions on direct access to foreign borrowing by corporations. Korea is also required to submit a timetable for complete elimination of trade barriers and trade-related subsidies.

7. In the macroeconomic area, Korea is to raise interest rates; pursue a tight monetary policy; increase its fiscal surplus to 1.5 per cent of GNP through a combination of higher taxes and lower spending; and accumulate foreign exchange reserves.

Though imposing a severe institutional shock upon the economy because of their accelerated time scale, the first five provisions in the IMF agreement are appropriate remedies for lessening chances of a future repetition of the current crisis, even though they did nothing to ameliorate the crisis itself. The sixth and seventh conditions are controversial, however. It is not clear how improving the access of Korean corporations to foreign borrowing (part of the sixth provision) will help avoid a foreign debt crisis in the future. It is also unclear how macroeconomic austerity (the seventh provision) will help the adjustment process. One might legitimately ask the following questions about the fiscal and monetary conditions contained in the seventh provision: How will increasing the credit-crunch in an already credit-starved economy that will be undergoing massive bank closures assist economic recovery? How will imposing higher taxes on a population whose incomes are shrinking ease the pain of restructuring? How will reducing government expenditures, when unemployment is increasing and safety-net provisions must be raised, help ease the human costs of Korea's adjustment? It is not as though Korea had not been pursuing fiscally and monetarily prudent policies. It is also not as though Korea did not attempt to accomplish the combination of macroeconomic stringency and corporate restructuring in 1980–83 and fail. It is also not as though similar medicine, imposed (legitimately) on Latin America during the 1980s, did not lead to what most development economists would call 'a lost development decade' from which most of them have just started to recover after more than ten years of immiseration.

It is also not clear why the macroeconomic austerity provisions were imposed at all. Pre-Keynesian thinking? Reflex? Standard IMF boiler-plate? Or, as Radelet and Sachs (1998) suggest, did the IMF mistakenly view Korea's financial crisis as a macroeconomic crisis, akin to that of Latin America in the 1980s, and recommend its standard macroeconomic fix? If so, the diagnosis of the crisis as due to macroeconomic excesses is incorrect: Korea has had a central government budget surplus between 1993 and 1995, and a very small deficit (0.1 per cent of GDP) in 1996; a small trade deficit (2 per cent of GDP in 1995 and 5 per cent in 1996) and a small capital account surplus (2.5 per cent) over 1990–96. While the money supply was increasing by an average annual rate of 19 per cent, the inflation rate averaged only 5 per cent between 1993–97. Also, the ratio of broad money to GNP was low for an economy at Korea's level of development: it was only 0.46 in Korea as compared with 1.7 in Taiwan and 1.1 in Japan. There was also no indication that there was a build-up of excess capacity. Even though overall capacity in manufacturing increased by 30 per cent between 1990 and 1995, the operating ratio in manufacturing rose by 3.5 per cent over the period.

In addition, there already were some signs of a domestic recession before the IMF intervention: a slowdown in the rate of economic growth in 1996 to about (sic!) 7.1 per cent; a decrease in the rate of growth of exports to (sic!) 15 per cent; a decrease in corporate earnings; a rise in major corporate failures; and an increase in inventories. Under these circumstances, tightening domestic credit further and reducing domestic absorption – the standard macroeconomic crisis conditionality imposed by the IMF – was obviously not an appropriate medicine for Korea's current crisis.[38] The IMF defended raising interest rates further as a measure necessary to attract foreign capital.[39] By May 1998, interest rates in Korea had risen to 30 per cent per year – surely overkill for attracting foreign capital and more than enough to choke off not only investment but also most economic activity, including exports. Indeed, international financial markets were alarmed rather than calmed by the draconian nature of the IMF's conditionality; the drastic downgrading of Korea's credit rating occurred after its first letter of agreement with the IMF was made public.[40]

It is instructive to compare Korea and Japan in this context. Both countries were suffering from recessions, long in Japan, short in Korea. Both countries have inherently unsound banking systems, with a large percentage of non-performing loans (about 20 per cent in Japan and 30 per cent in Korea). Nevertheless, both countries are economic powerhouses with fundamentally sound economies and with very high rates of national savings (35 per cent in both countries). Yet the remedies that the international community initially urged upon the two countries were fundamentally different: Japan was urged to assume the non-performing debts of its banks, create a 'bridge facility' that would continue to extend credit to its corporate sector, and reflate its economy by, in effect, running a large fiscal deficit. By contrast, Korea was initially forced, as a condition of IMF credit, to tighten credit even further, close many of its banks, restructure its corporate sector and sell off corporate assets to foreign firms at what the *Wall Street Journal* described as 'bargain basement prices'. In effect, with similar ailments, the treatment of choice first prescribed by the international community was diametrically opposite in the two countries. While Japan is being urged to shift its aggregate demand schedule outward, Korea was initially being asked to shift it inward. Which remedy is appropriate? In the short run, with a fundamentally sound economy, it would seem that the response urged upon Japan is the correct response for Korea as well. After all, an adjustment strategy similar to that currently urged upon Japan had worked well in Korea during the 1980s. In the intermediate run, both Japan and Korea need to restructure their banking systems substantially so as to make banks subject their loans to more stringent economic scrutiny. They both also need to decrease the debt–equity ratios of their corporate sectors.

After a few months of IMF-imposed austerity, the IMF recognized that it needed to change its macroeconomic prescriptions. It, in effect, acknowledged that Korea had been mis-diagnosed as suffering from over-expansionary policies, mostly because of its continued high rate of economic growth in the past. The 'over-expansionary' diagnosis was applied to Korea despite its very high rate of national savings (35.2 per cent of GNP in 1995); despite the fact that the ratio of its gross domestic investment to GNP was only 0.9 per cent of GNP higher than its rate of national savings in 1995; and despite a very high rate of capacity utilization (103 per cent in 1995 relative to 1990). In late 1998, the IMF retreated from the fiscal and monetary austerity package. It allowed Korea to run a fiscal deficit; permitted the temporary nationalization of illiquid and insolvent private banks so that the treasury could assume responsibility for the banks' non-performing loans and renew the ability of banks to extend credit for exports.

6. THE RECOVERY

Even prior to the monetary and fiscal loosening, by March 1998, less than six months after the crisis broke, Korea had already stepped back from an economic abyss[41] to what was merely a severe recession. Once the loosening occurred, the economy recovered extremely rapidly – within two years.[42] The secret was orthodox Keynesian deficit financing of major dimensions, which pumped new liquidity into the system and enabled firms to renew production and exports, plus resumption of foreign capital inflows. There was also a recovery in global economic growth and an increase in Korean competitiveness, due to lower than pre-crisis exchange rates. By 1999, Korea's GDP was restored to its pre-crisis level and growth increased dramatically, by almost 10 per cent relative to 1998. Some 30000 new small and medium-sized firms were incorporated. Unemployment, though still twice its pre-crisis quantity, was halved and wage rates rose by about 12 per cent. The stock market recovered to its pre-crisis height. Interest rates, which had shot up to twice world-market heights during the crisis, fell to pre-crisis rates, and exchange rates rose from their crisis depths to 80 per cent of their pre-crisis levels. The economy experienced a renewed influx of foreign investment and short-term capital. Korea's international credit rating has been restored. However, the budget deficit shot up, to about 7 per cent of GDP.

But the remarkable recovery remains precarious. Institutional reforms have been limited. The banking system continues to be in receivership. While the government is anxious to re-privatize the banks by selling them to private investors, it has had no takers. Small surprise, given the quality of their assets, and given that foreign banks may now start operating in Korea without burdening themselves with a large portfolio of bad debts. Also, in the past, banking has not been a profitable activity in Korea. The spread between borrowing and lending rates of banks, due to government mandated ceilings on lending rates and floors on deposit rates, was less than 1 per cent, which meant that banks have operated at a loss ever since their privatization in 1980.

Much of the economic recovery has been fuelled by foreign capital inflows. It is estimated that about 40 per cent of Korea's stock-market capitalization is now held by foreign funds and foreign financial institutions. And foreign investment is responsible for a large share of private investment. Since short-term foreign capital is very liquid, quite volatile and subject to herd psychology; this is worrisome.

In addition, the financial soundness of the business sector is still precarious. While the debt–equity ratio of firms has improved, sometimes even dramatically, the improvement is largely cosmetic. The observed halving of the debt–equity ratio, from about 4 to about 2, is not due primarily to debt-reduction; rather, it reflects the rebound of stock-market valuations of the shares of firms. The ratio of retained earnings to operating expenses remains very low, and the cushion offered by internal sources of funds therefore remains very thin. Informed observers of Korean chaebols fear that between one-third and two-thirds of the top 30 may well go into receivership in the near future. If these gloomy forecasts materialize, this may precipitate yet another financial crisis, as foreign mutual funds and hedge funds, frightened by the rash of firm bankruptcies, rush to withdraw their capital from Korea. The withdrawal of funds may be less extensive than in 1997–98, since, with the help of the IMF, foreign loans have been rolled over and their maturity extended. But the effects of withdrawals will permeate the whole economy. Not only will banks and firms be affected but the government will be affected as well since, as part of the roll-over agreement with foreign banks, foreign loans have, in effect, become socialized through government guarantees. The consequences of the depreciation of the won due to the flight of short-term foreign funds from Korea will therefore be spread throughout the economy's institutions.

And despite the dramatic increase in foreign reserves, from about 4 billion dollars by the end of 1997 to over 70 billion dollars by the end of 1999, the government will be in a less favourable position to counteract a new crisis, should it develop, than in 1997–98. In 1997 there was virtually no budget deficit, while by the end of 1999, the government budget deficit had ballooned to 7 per cent of GDP.

7. CONCLUSION

Some neoclassical development economists have attempted to use the Korean financial crisis as an argument against a government-led strategy of economic growth. (Note that they have not pointed to the dangers of openness, which contributed in no small measure to the vulnerability of the economy to external shocks). But it is hard to see how a strategy that, in a mere 30 years, resulted in the growth of the economy from one of the half-dozen poorest in the world to membership in the club of the 20 richest nations, while transforming it from a largely primary economy to an industrial one that competes in international markets with the technologically most advanced nations can be legitimately deemed a failure and used as a cautionary tale.

The Korean 1997–98 crisis cannot be explained by fiscal or monetary excesses. It is not due to a single factor but rather to a confluence in time of a multitude of factors to which both domestic and international circumstances contributed significantly. On the domestic front we have lack of leadership commitment to development, major instances of corruption and policy mistakes, as well as a drifting towards an incorrect mix of government intervention with market forces.[43] During the 1990s, the incorrect mix consisted of: combining government-mandated, corruption-motivated loans to mismanaged business groups, notably Hanbo, with a *laissez-faire* attitude towards the activities of unions which allowed them to push wages above productivity; maintaining a high interest rate regime, with too low a spread between deposit rates and loan rates, while refusing to intervene in the foreign exchange market to prevent overvaluation of the won; an incorrect mix of regulation and liberalization in its financial system, characterized by very little prudential regulation of banks and corporations combined with greater freedom in investing, borrowing and lending; and removing controls on international financial capital markets combined with setting high domestic interest rates, an overvalued exchange rate and maintaining domestic financial repression.

On the foreign front, the most important contributing factors were: the prolonged refusal by Japan to take the necessary measures to reflate its economy; the recession in Europe; the drastic decline in the world price of computer chips, ships and automobiles; the financial crises in other East Asian countries; and the excessively optimistic evaluation of Korea's credit-worthiness between 1990 and 1997 followed by its excessively pessimistic evaluation some time after the start of the crisis in the rest of East Asia.

Thus, mistakes were made by both borrowers (Korea), who were too eager to rely on cheap but volatile foreign short-term loans, and lenders (banks in the rest of the world), who were initially too eager to extend loans to Korea and subsequently too quick to withdraw them. Unfortunately, Korea is paying the major share of the cost for these mistakes while international banks are getting off scot-free. Indeed, international banks have renegotiated their loans to Korean banks at higher interest rates and with the Korean government assuming explicit legal responsibility for the repayment of these loans, thereby reducing the risk of the loans while increasing the risk premium Korea pays for foreign borrowing.

8. IMPLICATIONS FOR OTHER COUNTRIES

An alternative, more fundamental, view of the crisis which we find appealing, which has profound implications for other countries and for the architecture of the global financial system, is that the crisis is the result of a basic incompatibility between an independent fiscal and monetary policy, which Korea tried to pursue, with liberalized, smoothly functioning, unregulated, huge short-term global capital markets. Two of Korea's major policy mistakes were in trying to have an exchange rate policy which was out of alignment with its purchasing power parity and an interest rate which was out of alignment with world interest rates while having largely liberalized its foreign capital inflows and outflows. The Korean crisis demonstrates graphically that this is an economic impossibility.

The crisis indicates how unforgiving short-term global capital markets are to mistakes in economic policy and to institutional inadequacies within countries and how severe the penalties for mistakes are. This is not surprising to specialists in international finance. Keynes (1930), Tobin (1974) and Davidson (1997) have long warned us about the dangerously excessive volatility of world financial markets and urged alternative ways of restructuring them so as to make them more robust. But the Asian economic crisis, which occurred in the best performing economies in the world, brings this forcefully to the fore. Thus, one important lesson from the East Asian crisis is that international capital flows can pose serious threats to national economic stability and that, iconoclastic as it may sound, some mix of regulation, disincentives, or other impediments to short-term capital flows is required.[44]

Global short-term financial markets preclude governments from having independent exchange and interest rate policies. This is something well understood by OECD governments, as the regular, periodic G7 consultations and the drive towards European Monetary Union demonstrate. With respect to interest rates, if, as happened in Korea, the domestic interest rate is set significantly above world market then the result is a rapid and unsustainable build-up of foreign indebtedness; if, as happened in Japan, the domestic interest rate is set substantially below world market the result is an outflow of domestic savings, in the form of portfolio investment in foreign bonds and securities, and of real investment abroad; the consequence is lower domestic economic growth and a heating up of other economies. Globalization of capital markets in a fluctuating exchange rate regime is also incompatible with an independent exchange rate policy, especially one that strives to peg the exchange rate. Attempts to maintain an overvalued currency (as in Korea) require using foreign exchange reserves to sell foreign currency to prevent a devaluation; eventually, the supply of foreign exchange reserves will inevitably be exhausted and the currency will devalue anyhow. Attempts to maintain an undervalued currency (as in Japan) will, in the absence of restrictions on currency outflows, cause an outflow of domestic currency with adverse effects on domestic investment and domestic growth. Thus, financial globalization imposes severe fundamental constraints on the policy levers which governments can exercise in their management of the domestic economy.

So, what are developing-country governments to do in the post-Bretton Woods era? Fundamentally, governments have four types of choices:

1. Governments can relinquish their economic autonomy and renounce
    their responsibilities for macroeconomic management, economic
    development and social policy. This is hardly an appealing, or indeed
    responsible, choice. Developing-country governments that want their
    countries to become developed cannot renounce their policy auton-
    omy. For the economic history of the currently developed follower
    countries during the Industrial Revolution and the post-1950 experi-
    ence of currently developed countries shows clearly that the process of
    successful long-term economic development entails a state-led process
    of systematically changing dynamic interactions between institutional
    change, technological progress, structural change in the economy's
    production profile, and international trade and domestic accumulation
    patterns. The government and its policies must play a key role in this
    process. Long-run success in economic development requires that the
    dynamic restyling of all policies and institutions be mutually consistent
    and that it be embedded in a receptive international and domestic
    setting that is compatible with the shifting major thrust of domestic
    change. To enable governments to play their fundamental developmen-
    tal roles successfully, they must therefore have sufficient economic and
    political autonomy to shift among policy regimes as the requirements
    of economic development, domestic conditions and the international
    environment switch.
2. Developmentally oriented governments can limit themselves to the
    instruments they retain. In particular, having lost control over more
    neutral indirect means of promoting structural change, they can rely
    increasingly on direct, targeted and untargeted, mostly non-market
    mechanisms for achieving economic development. More specifically,
    they can use disguised subsidies[45] to industry, through education,
    infrastructure investment, cheap food and low-wage, anti-union poli-
    cies. They can use targeted subsidies in the form of tax rebates and/or
    monopoly privileges to specific industries, regions and firms. (But here
    they may invite retaliation from OECD countries, under
    GATT/WTO). They can create generalized externalities in the form of
    investment in education, skill-import enticements, state supported
    research, and tax breaks to promote local and foreign direct invest-
    ment. They can build the physical and legal infrastructure for process-
    ing zones and industrial parks. The less developed among the
    developing countries that still retain the capacity to impose infant-
    industry protection under GATT and WTO can use selective tariffs to
    promote climbing the ladder of comparative advantage. Finally, as was
    done in Korea, Meiji Japan and Communist China, they can create
    national commitment to development, through the educational

system, the use of the media and national campaigns to motivate workers, entrepreneurs, bureaucrats and households to exert themselves and save in the interest of the modernization of their countries. Of course, the national commitment route presupposes a culture that is amenable to this and a distribution of assets and access to accumulation opportunities that is relatively egalitarian.

Nevertheless, the pace of modernization developing countries will be able to achieve through the concerted (and coordinated) use of this battery of direct instruments will be much slower than it was during the Bretton Woods era. It will be constrained to a balanced budget, relatively restrictive monetary and fiscal regime. It will likely be costly, as some of the targeted efforts may be economically inappropriate, premature, ill-timed or of the wrong scale. It will also require state institutions for coordination of industrial policies, not unlike the development agencies of the 1960s and 1970s. This statist-capitalism approach will therefore not have much of a chance of success if the domestic political/bureaucratic environment is not capable, honest and committed to modernization. It will also require that the international environment be committed to economic growth, so that world demand for imports from developing countries is expanding.

It is an ironic thought that this 'do what you can' approach, which is the most statist and interventionist, is stimulated by too liberal an international environment imposed on countries and economies that are not ready for endogenous growth and structural change institutionally, socially or politically.

3. Developing countries can work to convince the international community that the current global financial system requires reform. Their efforts along these lines can be augmented by lobbying by developmentally oriented national and international aid establishments of OECD countries. International aid establishments can add their voices to those of developing country advocates of financial reform of global short-term capital markets in the international community. As we have learned from the almost 70 financial crises during the last 15 years or so, and as pointed out by Tobin,[46] international markets for foreign exchange are too smooth, permitting the transfer of vast sums to be carried out instantaneously; they are also much too large,[47] enabling immense amounts of cash to be brought to bear on any currency at any moment in time; and they also have an inherent tendency to overshoot, generating waves of over-optimistic risk assessments, leading to overlending, followed by over-pessimistic risk assessments, leading not only to the cessation of new loans but also to huge withdrawals of foreign currency. They are thus pro-cyclical in nature,

amplifying both domestic and international recessions and prosperity. The enormous swings in capital flows that ensue constitute the essence of financial crises. These crises penalize not only domestic institutional inadequacies and policy mistakes, but also the self-defeating efforts of governments to pursue policies of economic independence during the post-Bretton Woods era. No country, however large and however developed (transparent and accountable) its domestic financial institutions, is immune from currency attacks. Indeed, as pointed out earlier, of the 70 or so financial crises that have occurred lately, fully one-third occurred in developed countries. There is thus common ground for agreement among developed and developing countries that reform of short-term international financial markets to decrease their volatility and restrict the volume of largely speculative short term foreign exchange transactions is desirable. Iconoclastic as it may sound, some mix of regulation, disincentives, or other impediments to short-term capital mobility is required to generate a global environment that is robust and friendly to economic growth and economic development.

Note that the imposition of constraints on short-term capital movements does not require international agreement. It merely requires reducing the inordinate pressures emanating from the US, the IMF and the OECD to liberalize trade in financial services and short-term capital flows. The threat of retaliation against countries imposing barriers to financial liberalization of short-term capital markets must be lifted, and that requires at least tacit international cooperation.

Note also that we do not argue for a completely closed capital market. We do not propose imposing barriers to long-term capital flows in the form of direct investment, which we consider, on the whole, beneficial to domestic development. Nor are we arguing for barriers to repatriation of profits flowing from direct foreign investment. In essence, we are arguing for a return to the Bretton Woods world of constraints on short-term capital flows, including portfolio investment, combined with relatively free international trade.

4. Developing countries could unilaterally delink from international capital markets to preserve their economic independence and stability. They could either, like Malaysia and Russia, eliminate convertibility of their currencies on capital accounts entirely. Alternatively, *à la* India and China, they could delay convertibility of their capital accounts until their economic and financial systems are sufficiently mature. Or, like Chile, they could, unilateraly, themselves introduce differential taxes and higher reserve requirements on short term capital inflows, and foreign deposits and controls on foreign borrowing. These meas-

ures would make it more expensive to engage in short-term foreign borrowing and exchange rate speculation, and thereby provide a greater degree of state independence. But, they may also invite retaliation.

None of these classes of approaches are mutually exclusive. To our mind, the third, financial-system-reform approach, would be the most desirable. But it would also take longest to implement. In the meanwhile, developing countries that want to develop will have to muddle through using a mix of approaches two and four. But, unless they stay within the monetary and fiscal constraints, or unless they adopt both measures of two and four simultaneously, they will continue to suffer from periodic financial crises with devastating real consequences to the economy, to the people and to the State.

We believe that the recent history of financial crises in Asia, Europe and Latin America has clearly demonstrated that unregulated short-term capital markets have a social cost–benefit ratio that vastly exceeds unity. The first part of the cycle, during which the growth prospects of the economy are overestimated by the participants in the international financial markets and foreign capital flows in and growth rises, is more than counteracted by the second, sharply declining, phase which inevitably follows. The first phase generates an increasing current account deficit and currency appreciation and slow-down in exports. When the international community starts worrying about the sustainability of the mounting current-account deficit and the consequent ability of the economy to service its ever-mounting debt, which at some point it inescapably must, a precipitous withdrawal of foreign short-term capital occurs. This generates a prolonged recession that more than undoes the economic gains of the first phase of the cycle. Admittedly, the second phase of the cycle usually leads, under IMF pressure, to some long-run beneficial structural reforms in domestic financial systems and corporate governance. But Korea's earlier history of more gradual reforms demonstrates that, when there is social commitment to development, there are less socially costly ways of achieving these reforms.

Korea's financial crisis also holds another lesson for other developing countries. The contrast between its (and Singapore's) crisis management on the one hand, and Indonesia's and the Philippines' on the other, indicates the importance of social consensus for the relatively painful adjustments which need to be made to cope with the crisis. As pointed out in section 5 of this chapter, Korea spread the costs of the necessary corporate adjustments so that those who could bear the costs of adjustment more easily (the upper middle class and the rich) were hit first. It only reluctantly spread the costs to the rank and file of workers. This ties in well with Rodrik's (1997 and 1998) thesis[48] that in societies in which inequalities are relatively small and in which the institutions which can manage and contain distributional conflicts arising out of globalization are strong, as they are in Confucian societies, the economic shocks arising from globalization can be contained. They can move relatively quickly and with relatively little social friction to the implementation of the necessary corporate restructuring.[49] Conversely, in societies where inequalities are large and institutions for conflict management are weak or absent, the economic and social costs of external shocks will be magnified and perpetuated in time by distributional conflicts.

In the near future, OECD aid establishments can contribute most to the economic development of developing countries not through direct capital transfers and policy advice, but rather by adding their collective voices to developing country pressures for short-term global capital market reform. For in the absence of reform of short-term financial markets, the effects of foreign aid are likely to be more than nullified by a succession of financial crises. And the ability of foreign aid to counteract financial crises once they start is like the effectiveness of applying band-aids to stem haemorrhaging, as the *annual* collective amounts of resources over which aid establishments dispose is only about one-eighth the value of the *daily* short-term, speculative transactions taking place on the world's foreign exchange markets.

NOTES

1. In 1996, the fraction of short-term debt was 54 per cent if short-term debts of foreign banks in Korea and short-term corporate debt are excluded. If these two items are included, the fraction of short-term debt becomes 80 per cent.
2. It is sometimes argued that the oversupply from Korea caused the worldwide decline in the prices of these exports. For computer chips, this argument may be valid; but for the other exports, Korea's share in the global supply was not sufficient to, in and of itself, induce the large price decline.
3. The maturity of its debt was extended to between one and three years, at between 2.25 and 2.75 percentage points above the six-month London Interbank Rate, with 80 per cent of loans between two and three years' maturity, and the banks received government guarantees on $24 billion of the debt. Nevertheless the crisis worsened.
4. In current won. The exports and imports are both derived from customs clearance accounts.
5. Radelet and Sachs, 1998.
6. Curb-market interest rates were about twice as high as bank interest rates for general loans.
7. Computed from the data in the *Statistical Abstract of the United States* by taking the ratio of liabilities to assets minus liabilities; 1992 is the last year for which the data were available.
8. Computed as the ratio of interest payment to total receipts of the non-financial corporate sector in the National Accounts (1994).
9. In 1992, foreign claims and debts on Korean financial institutions were only 1 per cent of their total liabilities.

10. Krugman (1998) attributes the entire crisis to this fact.
11. In previous financial crises the government intervened quickly by forcing lenders on either the curb-market or banks to roll over loans, and recapitalized banks as necessary.
12. Gong Chen, 1998.
13. Cho Soon, 1994.
14. This point is made by Cho Soon, 1994.
15. Krugman (1998) applies this point only to domestic financial institutions, though it is clearly applicable to foreign financial institutions as well, given the practice of making the debtor country repay the full value of its loans from foreign institutions, which thus do not bear any of the risks from their, perhaps over-optimistic, foreign lending.
16. This point was made by Janet Yellen, 1998.
17. Raising domestic interest rates would curb inflation by raising the effective supply of money to the corporate sector even if there is no increase in domestic savings but only a diversion of savings from the curb market to banks. (Econometric studies done at the time indicated that the increase in interest rate actually induced a rise in domestic savings, though it is hard to be sure because the size of the curb market was not known.) The larger supply of finance came about because of the money creation by banks that is absent when savings are not intermediated by the banking system. The increase in funds to the corporate sector enabled firms to operate at higher levels of capacity and carry higher inventories as well as undertake higher levels of investment. This effect was especially strong for medium-sized firms that prior to this change had no access to capital from the banking sector but affected the chaebols, who had no access to working capital from the organized money market, as well. The increase in production that this would cause would, in a Wicksellian–Schumpeterian world, lower domestic inflation. The absence of credit for working capital is also responsible for another feature of Korean enterprise: it explains the tendency of firms to over-invest, since firms could use investment funds to finance working capital while the investment was being planned and carried out, in a corporate shell-game. The high interest rate policy also had a distribu-tional effect among firms of different size, since it lowered the average cost of funds to the small- and medium-sized firms by increasing the overall supply of credit. This effect was large, because when the bank rate on deposits was increased, the curb-market rate fell substantially. But the chaebols did not oppose the high interest rate policy per se; rather, they opposed a tight-credit policy, which, in Korea, manifested itself directly, not only through interest rates. When the Ministry of Finance wanted to tighten credit, before bank privatization it would merely reduce the supply of credit directly and after privatization the Minister of Finance would call up the heads of the private banks and ask them to stop lending.
18. *Economic Statistics Yearbook 1996*. Converted from won to dollars at the 1995 exchange rate.
19. It was widened to 0.8 per cent in 1992.
20. Tobin, 1974.
21. Mahbub Ul Haq, Inge Kaul and Isabelle Grunberg, 1996.
22. George Schultz, William E. Simon and B. Walter, 1998.
23. Radelet and Sachs, 1998.
24. Of course, the entire drop in growth rate of exports cannot be attributed to Korea's loss in competitiveness. Some of it was due to the decline in world demand for computer chips and to the sheer size of Korea's exports.
25. The foreign currency loans to corporations were denominated in dollars even when they were made by local financial institutions.
26. The index of real wages in 1994 stood at 224, taking 1987 as base.
27. This is the last year for which data are available.
28. Richard N. Cooper, 1994.
29. Richard N. Cooper, 1994.
30. Radelet and Sachs, 1998.
31. Quoted from Radelet and Sachs, 1998.
32. The October 1997 *World Economic Outlook* of the IMF predicted a 1998 growth rate of

6 per cent for Korea, a small decline relative to 1997. Quoted from Radelet and Sachs, 1998.
33. Calvo and Mendoza, 1996.
34. On 25 August and on 19 November 1997.
35. In late 1997, the Korean congress and courts investigated the Hanbo corruption case and put several politicians and bank presidents in jail.
36. *Wall Street Journal.*
37. Prior to this reform, firms in the same chaebol would lend to one another. Loans of one firm would appear as assets in the lending firm and as long-term loans to the borrowing firm.
38. This point is also made by Stiglitz (1998) and Radelet and Sachs (1998).
39. Stanley Fisher, 1998.
40. Martin Feldstein, 1998.
41. Interview with Secretary of the Treasury Rubin, on Lehrer Online Newshour (see: http://www.pbs.org/newshour/).
42. The numbers in this paragraph are taken from Fields (1999) and Kakwani (1999).
43. The incorrect mix of state and market is stressed by Larry Westphal, 1998.
44. This is also the conclusion reached by Stiglitz (1998). Calvo and Mendoza (1996) attribute the 1994–95 Mexican financial crisis to the same cause.
45. Open, direct subsidies are illegal under GATT.
46. Tobin, 1974.
47. During 1993–95, the Bank for International Settlements estimates that foreign exchange transactions averaged 1.3 trillions *per day*. By 1997, the daily book of foreign exchange transactions had increased to 2 trillion! Moreover, 40 per cent of these transactions are reversed within 2 days (and 80 per cent within 7 days) and are thus clearly speculative in nature. The clearly speculative book of daily foreign exchange transactions in 1997 was thus 800 billion.
48. I am indebted to Ro Naastepad for calling my attention to the two papers by Rodrik.
49. It is interesting to note in this context that the recent strikes in Korea have been by workers in chaebols protesting against the dismemberment of the chaebols, rather than by unions urging their break-up.

REFERENCES

Calvo, Guillermo A. and Enrique G. Mendoza (1996), 'Mexico's Balance of Payments Crisis: A Chronicle of a Death Foretold', *Journal of International Economics*, **41** (3–4), 236–64.
Cho, Soon (1994), *The Dynamics of Korean Economic Development*, Washington, DC: Institute for International Economics.
Cooper, Richard N. (1994) in Haggard et al. *Macroeconomic Policy Adjustment in Korea 1970–1990*, Cambridge: Harvard University Press.
Davidson, Paul (1997), 'Are Grains of Sand Sufficient when Boulders are often Required to do the Job?', *Economic Journal*, **107** (442), 129–43.
Feldstein, Martin (1998), 'Refocusing the IMF,' *Foreign Affairs*.
Fields, Gary S. (1999), 'The Employment Problem in Korea', *mimeo*, paper presented at an International Conference on *Economic Crisis and Restructuring in Korea*, Korean Development Institute.
Fisher, Stanley (1998), 'The Asian Crisis: A View from the IMF', *mimeo*.
Gong, Chen (1998), 'The Looming Financial Crisis in China', *The China Strategic Review*, 11–19.

Kakwani, Nanak (1999), *'Long Term Trends and Economic Crisis in the Korean Social Sector'*, *mimeo*, paper presented at an International Conference on *Economic Crisis and Restructuring in Korea*, Korean Development Institute.

Keynes, John Maynard (1930), *A Treatise on Money*, London: Macmillan.

Krugman, Paul (1998), 'What Happened to Asia?', *mimeo*. Department of Economics, Massachusetts Institute of Technology, Cambridge, MA.

Radelet, Steven and Jeffrey Sachs (1998), 'The Onset of the East Asian Financial Crisis', Working Paper 6680, National Bureau of Economic Research, Cambridge, MA.

Rodrik, Dani (1997), 'The "Paradoxes" of the Successful State', *European Economic Review*, **41** (3–5), 411–42.

Rodrik, Dani (1998), 'Globalization, Social Conflict and Economic Growth', *The World Economy*, **21** (2), 143–58.

Schultz, George, William E. Simon and B. Walter (1998), 'Who Needs the IMF?', *Wall Street Journal*, 3 Feb.

Stiglitz, Joseph (1998), 'Sound Finance and Sustainable Development in East Asia', *mimeo*, Keynote Address to the Asia Development Forum.

Tobin, James (1974), 'The New Economics One Decade Older', in *The Janeway Lectures on Historical Economics*, Princeton: Princeton University Press.

Ul Haq, Mahbub, Inge Kaul and Isabelle Grunberg (1996), *The Tobin Tax*, New York and Oxford: Oxford University Press.

Westphal, Larry (1998), 'The East Asian Economies: What Happened?', *mimeo*.

Yellen, Janet (1998), 'Lessons from the Asian Crisis', *mimeo*.

E62 E44 (India)
623 016 015 H54

6. The many edges of the fiscal policy sword

C.W.M. Naastepad*

1.   INTRODUCTION

Macro- as well as microeconomic theory have pointed to positive relations between the government budget deficit and inflation, and between the budget deficit and the trade balance. With these positive relations in mind, governments have, under various programmes, committed themselves to reduce their budget deficits in order to keep inflation and trade deficits under control. This has happened most notably in programmes of stabilization and structural adjustment in developing countries.

The experience with programmes of stabilization and structural adjustment in developing countries, however, shows that in many cases these policies have been accompanied by major declines in private investment and growth; nor have they everywhere succeeded in restoring price stability and in reducing current account deficits (Corbo and Fischer, 1995; Rodrik, 1995). This paper suggests that the reason for such failures may have to be sought in the negative impact of deficit reductions on the supply of credit as well as on 'real' supply. Monetized deficit reductions, which typically form the core of an adjustment programme, involve a monetary squeeze which may result in shortages of credit. If credit is used to finance working capital as well as investment, credit shortages may result in a reduced supply of goods and services in the short as well as medium run. In addition, when public investment is complementary to private investment, deficit reductions achieved through a curtailment of public investment restrict the growth of production capacity and hence of supply in the medium run. When supply is reduced more than demand, the adjustment policy may fail in one of its most important objectives, namely to get rid of inflation.

* With thanks to Veena Pailwar and the *Business Standard* for an inspired title (see *Business Standard*, New Delhi, 24 March 1999, page 7).

This chapter presents a real-financial model designed to provide insight into the effectiveness of alternative fiscal policies in restraining inflationary and trade balance pressures while maintaining growth in India. It incorporates a number of crucial structural features of the Indian economy which are reviewed in section 2. Section 3 describes the model in verbal terms. Sections 4 and 5 discuss the results of short- and medium-run fiscal policy experiments with this model. Section 6 concludes.

2. ECONOMIC REFORMS AND THE STRUCTURE OF THE INDIAN ECONOMY

Towards the end of the 1980s, India experienced high and growing inflation and persistent trade deficits. By that time it had become increasingly accepted that both problems were related to the large fiscal deficits run by the government. The government of India reacted to the problems by adopting a programme of stabilization and structural adjustment in 1991. These programmes centre around a correction of the fiscal deficit (Ministry of Finance, 1992; World Bank, 1996; Chopra et al., 1995; Nayyar, 1996).

From Indian data, however, a clear and consistent relation between the fiscal deficit on the one hand and inflation and the trade balance on the other is difficult to discern. On the basis of econometric analysis, Rakshit (1991) finds the relation between the fiscal deficit, inflation and the balance of payments deficit to be insignificant for India, one reason being that fiscal deficits of equal size may reflect widely divergent compositions of public expenditure and patterns of financing. Econometric causality tests have not been able to consistently support a positive causal relation between growth in the money supply (caused, for instance, by monetization of fiscal deficits) and inflation in India (Balakrishnan, 1991). On the other hand, observers of the Indian economy have argued that India's growth is limited by a number of factors on the supply side, most notably the supply of credit, agricultural production capacity and infrastructure. Credit is used to finance ongoing production as well as investment. Disruptions in credit supply may therefore disrupt supply not only in the medium run, but also in the very short run (Committee to Review the Working of the Monetary System, 1985; Rakshit, 1986, 1994). Agricultural output is heavily dependent on investments in irrigation permitting an expansion of gross cropped area and increases in yields (World Bank, 1996; Storm, 1993; Taylor, 1988; Chakravarty, 1987; Raj, 1984; Sen, 1981). Inadequate growth of infrastructural supplies on which all production is dependent has a general depressing effect on output.

The point made in this chapter is that all three supply-side factors are closely related to the budget. Increases in credit supply are associated with the government's mode of financing. Because of the high costs involved in large-scale irrigation infrastructure, investment in irrigation is heavily dependent on the government budget. Similarly, infrastructure (including power, transport and communication) has always been, and until now continues to be, the almost exclusive domain of the government. Despite serious attempts by the government to attract private investment in these areas, the private sector has until now shown little willingness to step in, because of an inability to internalize external effects and a general uncertainty with respect to future returns.

3. THE MODEL

The model is sequentially dynamic. It comprises a real side, describing production, and a financial side, describing the portfolio behaviour of the government, households, banks, non-bank financial institutions and the central bank. The most important question for our purposes is how the two sides interact. Before discussing the real-financial interactions, we will briefly describe the behaviour of the two sides separately.[1]

3.1 The real side

Aggregate production is broken down into three types of production sectors:

1. **Household sectors** (including agriculture and small-scale industry; sectors 1–4 in the model), which operate under competitive conditions; production is supply-determined and markets clear through price adjustments.
2. **Private corporate sectors** (5–7) which operate under oligopolistic conditions; production is demand-determined; prices are formed through a mark-up on variable costs (cf. Chatterji, 1989) and markets clear through quantity adjustments as long as none of the supply-side constraints discussed below becomes binding.
3. **Public sectors** (8–11), where prices are administratively fixed, and output is demand-determined – unless the capacity constraint binds.

Each of these three institutional sectors produces three goods, namely: (a) basic, intermediate and capital goods, (b) consumption goods, and (c) services, each of which are characterized by different input–output relations and demand conditions. The household sector, in addition, incorporates agriculture, which is separated out for reasons of its size and its importance in consumption and intermediate deliveries. The public sector, in addition, incorporates an infrastructural sector, comprising power, communication and transport, which is separated out from the other sectors because of its central importance in overall economic growth.

A distinction is made between three categories of private income, characterized by (empirically observed) different propensities to save and to consume, namely: agricultural income, non-agricultural wage income, and non-agricultural non-wage income. Agricultural income encompasses all income earned in agriculture, including mixed income of the self-employed and labour income. Non-agricultural wage income comprises income from labour earned in all non-agricultural sectors (2–11). Non-agricultural non-wage income includes non-wage income (or the difference between the value of output and the value of inputs including labour) of the non-agricultural household sectors (2–4) and mark-up income generated in the private corporate sectors (5–7). Agricultural income has the lowest propensity to save and non-agricultural non-wage income the highest. Propensities to consume various types of goods differ between agricultural and non-agricultural income.

For each of the 11 production sectors, the model distinguishes sectoral outputs supplied, X_i^{sc}, and the demand for sectoral outputs, X_i. There are three possible supply-side constraints on output:

1. production capacity, as determined by the installed capital stock, $K_{i,t-1}$, times the inverse of the sector's capital–output ratio, $1/\kappa_i$;
2. the availability of working capital credit; and
3. the availability of infrastructural inputs.

There are no supply-side constraints on the public sectors 9–11; it is implicitly assumed that these public sectors always have sufficient access to the required physical and financial inputs.

The maximum output of sector i permitted by the availability of infrastructural inputs is determined by the production capacity of the infrastructural sector and the share of this supplied to sector i. Since infrastructural prices are administratively determined, excess demands for infrastructure are not eliminated through automatic price rises. Instead, a shortfall in intermediate deliveries of the infrastructural good will constrain the supply of sectors using this good as an input. Available infrastructural goods are distributed over sectors 1–7 in proportion to the latters' (planned) intermediate demand for infrastructure.[2]

For each of the production sectors 1–8, the maximum supply-constrained level of output, X_i^{sc}, equals the minimum of the maximum production permitted by productive capacity (X_i^{sk}), available working capital credit (X_i^{sl}) and available infrastructural inputs (X_i^{sz}). When in any of the private production sectors i ($i = 1-7$) supply falls short of demand, prices rise to eliminate excess demand.[3] If demand remains below the level of supply, different sectors exhibit different adjustment mechanisms. In sectors 1–4, prices fall to adjust demand to supply; in sectors 5–11, supply adjusts to demand.

3.2   The financial side

Three institutional sectors are distinguished on the financial side of the model, namely the household sector, the private corporate sector and the government. The household and private corporate sectors borrow to finance their working capital and investment requirements. The demand for working capital loans is determined by (*ex ante*) production plans and the corresponding input needs. The demand for investment loans depends on (*ex ante*) investment plans, which, in the model, depend on past non-wage income.

The household sector as a whole is a net lender, which uses its accumulated wealth to lend to other sectors. The household sector accumulates wealth by adding current-period savings to the sum of its initial (end-of-the-previous-period) financial wealth.[4] The household sector's gross financial wealth, NW_h^f, equals its total (financial plus physical) wealth plus liabilities minus the value of its stock of physical capital at the end of the current period. Households allocate NW_h^f among six financial assets: currency CUR, bank deposits D_h^b, provident fund deposits D^p, deposits with other non-bank financial institutions D^o, claims on the government L_{gh}, and claims on the private corporate sectors L_{ih} ($i = 5-7$). When we subtract from NW_h^f investments in provident funds D^p (which are compulsory) and CUR (which is related to nominal GDP at market prices) we are left with what we may call A_h, that is, the portion of household gross financial wealth available for allocation among the remaining six assets D_h^b, D^o, L_{gh} and L_{ih} ($i = 5-7$). The allocation of A_h among these six assets may be viewed as a constrained optimization problem, to which we apply a CES utility function type of procedure to arrive at the households' portfolio choice. Households maximize utility from total earnings from the six assets, given the per-unit returns on each of them.

The private corporate sectors invest in bank deposits any excess of their funds (net worth plus loans acquired) over financing requirements (equalling the sum of the sector's capital stock, investments, inventory and change in stocks).

Banks accept as their deposits whatever financial savings households and private corporate sectors wish to hold in the form of bank deposits. These deposits are in turn used by banks to engage in new lending to the government and to private producers and investors. Part of the deposits are held by banks as reserves. The reserves which banks are legally required to hold to support their credit creation are called required reserves, R_r, defined as $R_r = crr\,D^b$ where crr is the cash reserve ratio, which is a policy variable. The amount of bank deposits available for lending purposes thus equals $(1-crr)D^b$. To enlarge their credit creation potential, banks can demand additional reserves from the central bank. Such funds, called borrowed reserves, are here denoted by R_{bo}. R_{bo} is a policy variable. The total amount of funds available for lending by banks, L_b^s, equals the sum of $(1-crr)D^b$, borrowed reserves R_{bo}, and the banks' net non-monetary liabilities.

Part of the amount L_b^s is reserved for the government through so-called secondary reserve requirements. This reflects the situation in India (as well as in a number of other developing countries) where banks are obliged to invest a certain percentage – determined by the Statutory Liquidity Ratio, slr_b – of their deposits D_b in government securities and other approved securities. The amount of bank credit available to the private sector (L_b^{s*}) then equals $L_b^s - slr_b D_b$. Banks may also invest in government securities on top of the amount $slr_b D^b$, if this is profitable for them. The returns offered on government securities, however, are generally lower than those obtained in the market. Therefore, if loan demand is sufficiently high, banks will normally not invest in government securities on top of the amount required under the statutory liquidity regulations. In times of slack, however, when banks are left with excess reserves, they do invest in government securities on top of the required amount.

The allocation of L_b^{s*} between the various private sectors is partly a matter of the banks' choice and partly a matter of policy. In India, part of total bank credit is reserved for a number of sectors whose output is essential both as consumer goods as well as inputs into a large part of modern industry, but whose access to bank finance is limited because of the (perceived) high costs of lending to these sectors (resulting from the relatively long geographical and/or cultural distance between potential borrowers and lenders and (a fear of) high loan delinquencies). Sectors identified as priority sectors include agriculture and small-scale industry. Accordingly, in our model, part of total bank credit to the private sector L_b^{s*} is reserved for the priority sectors (all of which are household sectors) through the policy-determined variables π_i^v and π_i^w ($i=1-4$) denoting reservations for investment and working capital credit respectively. The rest, denoted by L_b^{s**} ($L_b^{s**} = [1 - \Sigma_{i=1}^4 \pi_i^w - \Sigma_{i=1}^4 \pi_i^v]L_b^{s*}$) is allocated over the various assets according to their relative profitabilities. The returns on the assets depend on two factors, namely the rate of interest charged and the costs, to the lending institution, associated with loans issued to this particular debtor. These costs include the perceived costs of monitoring loans, default risk, and so on. The shares of the assets in L_o^{s**} are derived from maximization of a CES utility function.

Non-bank financial institutions utilize the deposits mobilized by them, D^n ($D^n = D^p + D^o$), to invest in loans to the government, the private corporate sector and the household sector. As in the case of banks, part of non-bank financial institutions' investments in government debt, $slr_n D^n$, is compulsory. The remainder of non-bank financial institutions' resources, $(1-slr_n)D^n$, is invested in claims on the private and government sectors, depending on their relative profitability (their shares in the non-bank financial institutions' portfolio is again derived from maximization of a CES utility function). Non-bank financial institutions invest in government securities whatever they are obliged to under the statutory liquidity requirements, $slr_n D^n$, plus an amount $\theta_g^n (1 - slr_n)D^n$ determined by the relative profitability of investment in government securities.

In any particular year, the government accepts from banks and non-bank financial institutions the total of their additional investments in government securities. From the household sector, the government accepts whatever households are willing to invest in government debt. When the sum of its current revenues (from taxes and public enterprises), and the flows of loans from banks, ΔL_{gb}, non-bank financial institutions, ΔL_{gn}, households, ΔL_{gh} and the rest of the world, ΔL_{gf}, are insufficient to cover the sum of its consumption and investment expenditures, the government resorts to the central bank for additional loans, ΔL_{gc}.

With the balance sheets of all but one actor in the financial sector (the central bank) being determined, all items in the central bank's balance sheet (the assets L_{gc}, R_{bo} and foreign reserves R_f – which follow from the trade balance – and the liabilities CUR and R_b) are also determined. Let us now study the interactions between decisions made on the real and financial sides.

3.3   Real-financial interactions

Real-financial interactions are illustrated in Figure 6.1. The real and financial sides interact through the channels of savings, and of borrowing and lending. Savings, generated in the real side, are drawn into the financial sector where they end up as additions to the deposits of banks and non-bank financial institutions. The financial institutions use the deposits brought at their disposal (after allowing for primary and secondary reserve requirements) to offer investment and working capital credit loans to private investors and producers. Private demand for credit is determined by

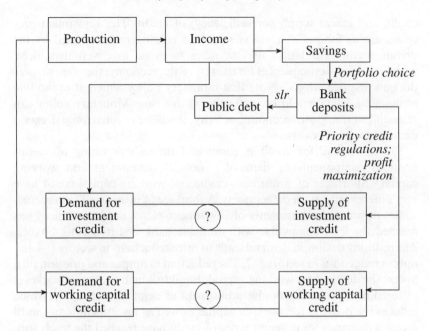

Figure 6.1 Credit creation by banks

private production and investment plans. Macro-balance implies that all credit excess demands be zero or negative; that is, $L_{ib}^{v,d} - L_{ib}^{v,s} \leq 0$ and $L_i^{w,d} - L_i^{w,s} \leq 0$, where L_{ib}^v stands for investment loans from banks, L_i^w stands for working capital loans (always from banks), and the superscripts d and s denote demand and supply respectively. How do credit supply and demand meet?

Note, first of all, that the market for credit in this model clears through quantity adjustments. The interest rate does not play the role of equilibrating supply and demand. This reflects a situation as in India where, until very recently, interest rates were policy-determined. Even after they were (partly) freed, they did not perform this equilibrating role due to oligopolistic conditions in the financial sector. However, interest rates are banished from the model not only as an equilibrating mechanism but also as a factor determining the demand for credit. Keeping the interest rate fixed serves to highlight the credit-rationing mechanisms that are the subject of this chapter.

Macro-adjustment then depends on, firstly, whether or not exogenous shocks (such as policy changes) result in credit shortages, and secondly, on the type of credit that is rationed if credit constraints become binding. Thus, there are two possible (*ex ante*) disequilibria: excess demand for credit; and excess supply (or sufficiency) of credit. The adjustment processes are as follows. An *excess supply* of credit remains unused by the private sector. The banks use the slack to invest in government debt, without further consequences for the rest of the economy: there are no production or price effects.[5] Note that monetary policy aimed at expanding economic activity would be ineffective in this case. Monetary policy can restrain but not 'push' economic activity; it will be effective only if excess demand for credit exists.

Excess demand for credit is eliminated through rationing of credit-financed components of demand – notably, investment and working capital.[6] Shortages of investment credit and working capital credit have very different effects on the economy. A shortage of investment loans necessitates downward adjustments of investment plans, until investment has reached the level compatible with available bank and non-bank finance. The resulting decline in demand leads to price reductions in sectors 1–4 and output reductions in sectors 5–7. The reduction in output and prices in turn lowers the demand for working capital. Equilibrium in the credit market is restored because of this double adjustment of demand and supply, which reduces the demand for working capital as well as investment loans, until sectoral demands for different types of credit have reached the levels supplied by the financial institutions.

Rationing of working capital credit, on the other hand, reduces X^{sl}_i. If the supply of goods and services falls below the level of demand, prices will rise to eliminate the excess demand. The resulting decline in real income and demand affects other sectors' sales and incomes as well. A general fall in demand sets in, until X_i has fallen to the level of X^{sl}_i compatible with available bank finance. Note that, unlike the investment credit constraint, which limits production from the demand side (at least in the short run), the working capital credit constraint affects the economy from the supply side by placing the burden of the adjustment on production plans. Since production is reduced from the supply side, the reduction in output is accompanied by rising rather than falling prices. Similar effects will result from an investment credit constraint in the medium run, when a lower production capacity will put upward pressure on prices.

Let us now see how these real-financial interactions influence the effects of fiscal policy.

4.   SHORT-RUN EFFECTS

By economic logic, balance of payments deficits and high inflation rates are symptoms of an excess of demand relative to output, so the problem is how to restore the balance between aggregate supply and aggregate demand. Behind this problem lies the question regarding the nature of the disturbance producing the imbalance between demand and supply. Stabilization policies are normally based on the idea that persistent and growing fiscal imbalances are the principal cause of macroeconomic and foreign payments imbalances. The remedy to such problems in the short run therefore is sought in immediate reductions in demand, achieved through reductions of the fiscal deficit, and particularly of the monetized deficit which, by reducing liquidity in the system, would restrain private demand as well. In fact, the experiments with the model presented in section 3 throw a different light on this logic, and identify several factors which are of importance in determining the short-run success of deficit reductions.

The experiments are designed as follows. We start from a reference run, representing the fiscal year 1989–90, in which the Indian government was running a relatively large monetised deficit of Rs. crores 14975. This base run is compared with alternative scenarios in which the monetized deficit is reduced by Rs. 10000 crores to Rs. 4975.[7] This is done in four alternative ways, namely by increasing direct tax rates (on agricultural income, wage income and mark-up income respectively), raising indirect tax rates, extending government borrowing from banks, and through government expenditure reduction. In each of the experiments, the policy instrument concerned is adjusted endogenously until the targeted value of the monetised deficit is reached. The values of all other instruments except the one under consideration are kept constant. Each experiment is run under two different export demand regimes: one assuming price-inelastic exports (the price elasticities of export demands, ε_i ($i = 1 - 7$), equal zero) and the other assuming highly price-elastic exports ($\varepsilon_i = -2$). Initial conditions in credit markets are assumed to be tight: no slack exists at the start of the policy change.

The general picture emerging from the experiments is one of output declines (as expected) but the extent to which output falls differs considerably for different modes of deficit reduction. Moreover, the output declines caused by the deficit reduction are not always accompanied by the expected price declines or trade balance improvements. The experiments causing the largest output reductions lead to the smallest price declines. The trade balance worsens when exports are price inelastic. Let us look more closely at the results.

As Table 6.1 shows, the price level declines in all experiments, but these price level declines are 'paid for' by reductions in GDP in all experiments. However, the magnitude of the trade-off between output and prices differs between the experiments. Table 6.2 reports the values for the trade-offs between output and prices in the various experiments. If $\varepsilon_i = 0$, the loss of

GDP for 1 per cent of price decline is largest for a shift from monetization to debt financing. Similarly, among the tax experiments, the experiment causing the largest decline in GDP (at factor cost) leads to the smallest fall in the price level. Also among the direct tax experiments, larger output losses are not always associated with larger price declines. How can the absence of a consistently positive relation between output and prices be explained?

The experiments show that the success of stabilization policy in lowering prices and the trade deficit while maintaining growth depends crucially on how the chosen stabilization policy influences credit supply and the distribution of income. Let us look at these two points in more detail.

4.1 Credit supply

Conventionally, stabilization policies are not believed to cause problems regarding supply in the short run; the only supply-side problems foreseen are those caused by the reductions in overall investment to which these policies may lead, limiting production capacity growth in the medium term. However, an important factor determining supply in the short run is credit to finance working capital. If working capital credit constraints bind, the economy converges at an equilibrium characterized by lower output and higher prices than what would have obtained with the same policy in the absence of credit constraints. In other words, policies leading to working capital credit constraints significantly reduce the deflationary impact of the deficit reduction, despite the additional fall in output which they cause (remember they worsen the trade-off between output and prices). An important factor determining the success of a deficit reduction in reducing pressure on prices therefore is its impact on working capital credit supply.

As the model experiments show, the various modes of reducing the budget deficit differ in their proneness to cause working capital credit shortages. The mechanisms through which credit constraints are brought about also differ between policies. All policies lowering the monetized deficit reduce the availability of credit. This decline in the supply of credit has no further consequences if the demand for credit falls as well – which happens if the policy-induced decline in domestic demand reduces prices and exports are price inelastic. However, if output and prices fall only marginally (for instance because exports show a strong positive reaction to the price decline), credit demand may fall less than credit supply and credit constraints may become binding.

Given tight initial conditions in credit markets, policies particularly prone to result in credit constraints are an indirect tax increase and an increase in debt financing. An increase in debt financing has an immediate

Table 6.1 *Macroeconomic and financial effects of a deficit reduction (in per cent deviation from the base run)*

	GDP m. pr.[a] (1)	GDP f.c.[b] (2)	Price level[c] (3)	Trade deficit (4)	Working capital constraint (5)	Investment credit constraint (6)
Export elasticity = 0						
Increase in tax rate on:						
agricultural income	−6.1	−5.9	−32.5	23.8	—	—
wage income	−6.3	−6.0	−31.9	22.2	—	—
mark-up income	−5.7	−5.5	−29.5	20.7	—	—
commodities	−5.5	−8.6	−28.7	19.9	—	—
Increase in the *slr*	−8.5	−8.2	−2.2	−42.9	1–4, 6, 7	1–6
Expenditure reduction	−6.9	−6.6	−32.3	22.3	—	—
Export elasticity = −2						
Increase in tax rate on:						
agricultural income	−1.8	−1.6	−9.9	−50.4	—	—
wage income	−1.9	−1.8	−9.2	−52.1	—	—
mark-up income	−1.7	−1.6	−8.0	−44.8	—	—
commodities	−4.8	−10.5	−3.7	−37.9	1–4	1–6
Increase in the *slr*	−2.4	−2.2	−7.2	−46.7	1–4, 6, 7	1–6
Expenditure reduction	−2.4	−2.3	−9.0	−56.7	—	—
P.M.: Base run	453986	405827	1	−10346		

Notes:
[a] Real GDP at market prices.
[b] Real GDP at factor cost.
[c] GDP deflator.
Source: Naastepad (1999).

Table 6.2   Macroeconomic trade-offs in deficit reduction

	$\dfrac{\Delta GDPfc}{\Delta p}$	$\dfrac{\Delta GDPfc}{\Delta T}$	$\dfrac{\Delta T}{\Delta p}$
	$(1)^a$	$(2)^b$	$(3)^c$
Export elasticity = 0			
Increase in the rate of tax on:			
agricultural income	0.182	0.248	0.733
wage income	0.189	0.273	0.694
mark-up income	0.185	0.263	0.702
commodities	0.301	0.435	0.692
Increase in the *slr*	3.738	−0.192	−19.485
Expenditure reduction	0.206	0.298	0.689
Export elasticity = −2			
Increase in the rate of tax on:			
agricultural income	0.166	−0.033	−5.094
wage income	0.196	−0.035	−5.660
mark-up income	0.194	−0.035	−5.606
commodities	2.849	−0.278	−10.248
Increase in the *slr*	0.302	−0.047	−6.491
Expenditure reduction	0.252	−0.040	−6.300

Notes:
[a] Calculated as the per cent change in GDP at factor cost (from Table 6.1) divided by the per cent change in the GDP deflator (from Table 6.1).
[b] Calculated as the per cent change in GDP at factor cost (from Table 6.1) divided by the per cent change in the trade balance (that is, the negative of the value for the trade deficit in Table 6.1).
[c] Calculated as the per cent change in the trade balance (the negative of the value for the trade deficit in Table 6.1) divided by the per cent change in the GDP deflator (from Table 6.1).
Source: Naastepad (1999).

adverse effect on credit supply to the private sector. The increase in government borrowing from banks required to compensate for the decline in the monetized deficit is achieved through an increase in the slr_b. The increase in the slr_b reduces the supply of credit by banks to the private sector. Even with unchanged demand for credit, this does not necessarily lead to credit constraints provided there is sufficient slack in the system. However, in the base run of the model banks have only a limited amount of excess reserves at their disposal and therefore, after the increase in the slr_b, they can no longer fully accommodate the private producers' and investors' demand for credit. Working capital constraints become binding in sectors 1–4, 6 and 7, while investment credit constraints bind in sectors 1–6.

The adjustment process that follows depends on the relative strengths of the working capital and investment credit constraints. In case of a shortage for working capital credit, production falls in order to remove the excess demand for working capital credit; a shortage of investment loans forces downward adjustments in investment demand. A decline in investment demand reduces demand with a multiplier. This depresses output and prices. The working capital constraint, however, reduces production from the supply side. If supply falls more than demand, the decline in output will be accompanied by a rise rather than a fall in prices. In the experiment at hand, the overall price level declines, but much less so than if only investment constraints had become binding. Moreover, the decline in the overall price level is the net result of a mix of sectoral price increases and price declines. Prices rise in the consumption goods sectors 3 and 6 as a result of relatively severe working capital shortages relative to the demand for consumer goods. Because of the severe credit shortages, reducing output from the side of supply as well as demand, debt financing leads to a lower level of GDP (at market prices) and a higher price level than in any other experiment. Thus, compared with the tax and expenditure reduction experiments, debt financing is stagflationary.

Debt financing shows much less negative results for output when export elasticities are high than when they are low because when $\varepsilon_i = -2$, debt financing leads to much less severe credit constraints. This is entirely due to the higher level of GDP attained when price elasticities of exports are high. The higher level of GDP results in higher levels of government revenue and this makes it possible to achieve the same reduction in the monetized deficit with relatively small increases in debt financing. Another factor relieving the credit constraints is the lower price level attained in this experiment, which reduces credit needs.

An indirect tax rise causes excess credit demands by raising mark-up prices. The indirect tax rate itself is one of the costs on the basis of which the mark-up price is calculated. Consequently, an increase in the indirect tax rate directly raises mark-up prices. This reduces the demand for mark-up priced goods. With flexible output in mark-up priced sectors, the decline in demand leads to a fall in the output of these sectors. In the flex-price sectors, the indirect tax increase cannot be shifted forward to consumers and therefore it reduces income in these sectors. The resulting decline in consumption demand lowers prices in the flex-price sectors and output in the fixed-price sectors. The decline in flex prices further reduces income in the flex-price sectors, contributing to the decline in demand. The major difference with the adjustment process following, for instance, a direct tax increase is that mark-up prices rise and, output of mark-up priced sectors being flexible, this causes a relatively large decline in the output of mark-up priced goods. Thus, the price level declines less and production falls more. This relatively high level of domestic prices leads to relatively high costs of inputs and investment goods, which keeps the demand for both working capital credit and investment credit up.

This relatively high price level does not lead to binding credit constraints when exports are fixed but it does when price elasticities of exports are high. This is because the increase in foreign demand in response to the (small) domestic price decline raises output, which adds to the economy's working capital needs *ex ante*. The pressure in the credit market is the result of changes in credit supply as well as in credit demand. On the supply side, the decline in bank deposits (and hence in credit supply) is large relative to the other tax experiments. This can be explained in part by a relatively large decline in private savings (private savings decrease by 41 per cent in this experiment as compared with 27 per cent in the agricultural and wage tax experiments and 47 per cent in the mark-up tax experiment) and in part by household portfolio reshufflings in response to price rises (the higher price level caused by the indirect tax increase leads to a higher need for currency, leaving a smaller share of household financial wealth to be invested in bank and non-bank deposits). The tight credit market situation leads to an excess demand for working capital credit in sectors 1–4 (the price-clearing sectors) and to investment credit constraints in sectors 1–6. The result is that the price level declines less while output falls more than in any other experiment in this set ($\varepsilon_i = -2$).

Why do working capital constraints bind in some sectors and not in others? The reason lies in the demand side of the credit market, since the distribution of available credit supply over the different sectors does not change initially. Sectors 1–4 are more liable to working capital constraints because their demand for working capital is tied to their fixed production plans, while sectors 5–7 adjust their production plans to changes in the demand for their output. In general, differences in excess working capital credit demands between sectors are caused by differences in the structure of each sector's vector of inputs in combination with the relative price changes brought about by the change in policy, together determining credit needs. Similarly, differences in investment credit needs depend on the structure of a sector's capital stock in combination with the vector of prices of capital goods.

Note that the above results depend critically on the assumption of tight conditions in credit markets at the start of the policy change. With sufficient slack in the financial system, a shift from monetization to debt financing or from monetization to indirect taxation would not lead to credit constraints.

For completeness: what happens in the direct tax and expenditure reduction experiments? The trade-off between output and prices is lower in the case of direct taxation than in the case of indirect taxation. This can be explained as follows. A direct tax increase lowers after-tax income. This reduces consumption demand. The decline in demand leads to lower prices in the flex-price sectors 1–4 and to lower output in the fixed-price sectors 5–11. The lower prices of goods 1–4 lead to lower mark-up prices to the extent that these flex-price goods are used as inputs into the production of mark-up priced goods. The deflation to some extent restores demand in real terms. What we see is a combination of price and demand declines, with the decline in prices partly offsetting the decline in real demand. Since the decline in demand to a large extent affects the fixed-production sectors (because these produce a large share of total consumer goods, and it is consumption demand which falls), the adjustment falls predominantly on prices while real output remains relatively high. Credit constraints do not become binding. The lower after-tax income does reduce savings and hence bank deposits and credit supply, but the demand for credit falls even faster because of the price decline. This process of adjustment is similar for the three direct tax policies. Although the output and price results differ – because the different direct tax rate policies have different implications for the structure of demand and hence for the vector of prices and sectoral output levels – they are much closer to each other than to the results generated by the indirect tax experiment.

Expenditure reduction leads to a larger decline in output and larger output/price trade-offs than direct taxation. This is so irrespective of the trade regime in operation. The reason is that expenditure reductions fall flatly on demand while direct tax reductions are paid partly by reducing savings and only partly by reducing demand.

4.2 Distribution of income

Distributional effects of fiscal policy influence its macroeconomic impact because of the following two empirically observed facts. Firstly, economies often are a mix of price-clearing and quantity-clearing production sectors. Trade-offs between output and prices will be larger when quantity-clearing sectors dominate the adjustment process. Secondly, economies consist of a mix of income groups which differ in their propensities to save, as well as in their marginal propensities to consume various goods. This second point is related to the first, since different income groups differ in their propensities to consume quantity-clearing versus price-clearing goods. The output and price effects of fiscal retrenchment will depend on which categories of income bear the burden of the adjustment.

How distributional issues affect the macroeconomic impact of a deficit reduction is illustrated by the direct tax experiments. Among the direct taxes, taxation of mark-up income is less detrimental to output than taxation of wage income because of the relatively high propensity to save from mark-up income. Given the model's consumption function, taxes are paid partly by reducing savings and partly by reducing consumption. This means that taxing a higher-saving category of income leads to a higher share of the tax increase being paid by reducing savings. What this does to output and prices depends on what drives the economy (or, the model's closure). In a demand-driven system, savings are a leakage and a decline in savings will not affect output. Since none of the direct tax experiments lead to binding credit constraints, the system remains demand-driven. Hence, taxation of a high-saving category of income is less detrimental to output than taxation of a lower-saving category of income.[8] The mark-up tax policy also leads to a smaller output/price trade-off than all other experiments except the agricultural income tax policy.

The policies achieving the smallest output/price trade-offs are those that lead to the largest reduction in demand for price-clearing sectors. The smallest trade-off between output and prices is achieved by the agricultural tax experiment. The reason lies in the high propensity to consume agricultural goods out of agricultural income. Because of this, a decline in after-tax agricultural income falls relatively hard on agricultural goods. Since the supply of agricultural goods is fixed in the short run (being determined by production capacity) while their prices are flexible, the decline in demand in this experiment is to a large extent absorbed by prices while real output remains relatively intact.

Of course, there may be serious drawbacks to achieving low output/price trade-offs by taxing agricultural income. Firstly, a drop in the share of agricultural income in total income, which is what the agricultural tax increase leads to, is likely to have repercussions for agricultural investment and production capacity and hence for agricultural prices in the medium run. Given agriculture's importance as a supplier of essential consumption goods as well as of inputs into agro-industries, this is likely to have serious macroeconomic repercussions. Secondly, in India agriculture employs roughly 65 per cent of the labour force. A reduction in agriculture's income share is therefore likely to have a significant effect on the country's rate of un(der)employment.

So far for the relation between the deficit, output and prices. The trade balance effects of the various policies are related to their output and price effects and are fairly straightforward. Improvements in the trade balance are associated with declines in output (which reduce imports) as well as prices (which raise external competitiveness) if $\varepsilon_i = -2$ and with declines in output and higher prices (raising the nominal value of exports) if $\varepsilon_i = 0$. When the price elasticity of exports is high, policies leading to the largest price declines (that is, the direct tax experiments) are associated with the smallest output/net export trade-offs. By contrast, when export elasticities are zero, the smallest output losses are associated with policies leading to the smallest price declines. Thus, with low export elasticities, deflating the economy does not help to remove trade imbalances because the price declines lower the value of exports which may lead to trade balance deteriorations despite falling output levels. On the other hand, if exports are highly price elastic, policies successful in generating export booms *ex ante* may run into supply-side (production and/or working capital credit) constraints because of the relatively high (*ex ante*) levels of prices and output to which they lead.

This leads to two conclusions. Firstly, trade-offs between macroeconomic can be mitigated by choosing among alternative modes of reducing the budget deficit. Secondly, since supply and demand conditions in financial as well as real markets may differ for different economies or for the same economy at different points in time, it would be misleading to put forward a single policy as the best policy for achieving a deficit reduction. The general policy lesson emerging from the experiments is that a policy striving to reduce prices and the trade deficit by reducing the monetized deficit is incomplete if it ignores the changes in financial flows associated with the policy change. The matrix of public and private resource requirements will be different for different modes of deficit reduction. To ensure that real and financial policies are mutually consistent, a resource flow policy should be an integral part of the design of any fiscal policy.

The most important limitation of the experiments discussed in this chapter is that they do not take into account the medium-term effects of the policies under study, which operate mainly via investment. The most important threat in the medium run is that, following the decline in (after-tax) incomes, investment falls and production capacity is reduced. This has consequences for future sectoral production capacities and hence the structure of excess demands and prices. Such effects are taken into account in section 5.

5.   STABILITY AND GROWTH IN THE MEDIUM RUN

The medium-run experiments are compared with a base run which follows as closely as possible the actual course taken by the Indian economy under the stabilization and structural adjustment policies pursued in the period 1989–90 to 1992–93. The experiments seek to improve upon this scenario, and ask: could an alternative fiscal policy be designed which leads to higher growth, lower inflation and a lower trade deficit? The experiments are designed as follows.

We compare equal increases in public investment, financed in four alternative ways: direct taxation, indirect taxation, bank debt and monetization. Public investment in infrastructure and agriculture (in real terms) is raised by 10 per cent above the base-run levels in the first two years of the experiment. The expenditure expansion takes place only in the first two years in order to be able to assess the impact of policy changes also after discontinuation of the policy. In the last two years, public investment falls back to the base-run level. To ensure comparability, the monetized deficit is kept constant in all experiments in all years except, of course, in the monetization scenario. To permit the real expansion fuelled by the public sector expansion in the first two years to take place, some minimum degree of accommodation by the central bank is required. In all experiments, borrowed reserves are raised by 20 per cent in the first two years of the simulation period, and brought back to base-run levels thereafter. All experiments are conducted under optimistic expectations regarding exports: the price elasticity of foreign demand for India's exports (of goods 1–7 in the model) is assumed to equal −2. Finally, all experiments are carried out under the assumption that, at the start of the policy change, very little slack exists in the financial institutions.

As can be seen from Table 6.3, none of the four experiments shows very smooth results over time. There are breaks in the time path, particularly in the second year of the experiment – when private investment starts responding to the increase in income generated by the expansion in the previous year – and in the third year of the experiment, when the policy is discontinued. In the first year, the increased public investment has only demand effects: production and income of the capital goods sectors rise and this has multiplier effects on output and incomes in the other sectors. The increase in demand leads to higher production in sectors where underutilization of capacity prevails and to higher prices in sectors where production is supply-constrained. The overall price level rises in all experiments.

In the second year of the experiment, the second year's public investment expansion again raises output with a multiplier. Moreover, the increase in income caused by the increase in public investment in the first year has positive effects on private investment plans in the second year. Both effects raise (*ex ante*) investment expenditure and overall demand. On the other hand, the increase in public investment of the previous year leads to an expansion of production capacities of the infrastructural and agricultural sectors and, as a consequence, an increase in their (potential) supply relative to demand,

Table 6.3   Impact on growth, inflation and trade of an expansion of public investment for alternative modes of financing[a]

	1989–90 (1)	1990–91 (2)	1991–92 (3)	1992–93 (4)	Average[b] (5)
Financing requirements (increase with respect to base run)					
Direct tax	22.6	36.4	−5.2	−12.4	
Indirect tax	6.5	8.6	−1.9	−3.2	
Debt to banks	8.1	14.4	15.9	14.7	
Monetization	3.4	7.8	8.3	5.1	
Price level (per cent deviation from base run)					
Direct tax	0.40	−0.07	−0.59	−0.23	−0.06
Indirect tax	0.57	0.17	−0.51	−0.27	−0.07
Debt to banks	2.06	1.27	−0.12	2.17	0.74
Monetization	2.73	4.59	2.67	−0.53	−0.15
GDP at 1989–90 market prices (per cent deviation from base run)					
Direct tax	0.18	0.08	−0.13	0.05	0.01
Indirect tax	0.18	0.08	−0.10	0.07	0.02
Debt to banks	−0.56	−0.09	−1.12	−0.36	−0.09
Monetization	0.62	1.03	0.86	0.74	0.19
Trade balance (per cent deviation from base run)					
Direct tax	4.32	2.13	−89.44	−9.14	−2.00
Indirect tax	5.62	3.31	−88.46	−10.11	−2.22
Debt to banks	7.29	4.01	−37.58	22.13	4.33
Monetization	16.46	19.99	50.99	−37.40	−9.33

Notes:
[a] Results are given in per cent deviation from the base run. To make sure: $T = 100 * (E − B)/B$ where T is the value given in the table; E is the value of the corresponding variable in the experiment concerned; and B is the value of the variable in the base run.
[b] Difference between the average annual growth rate attained in the simulation and the base-run average annual growth rate. (Since 1989–90 is the first year of the policy change, the average annual growth rates are calculated with base year 1988–89.)
Source: Naastepad (1999).

dampening the upward pressure on prices resulting from the demand expansion. In the third and fourth years of the experiment, public investment falls back to its base-run level, while private investment remains influenced by previous-year income changes.

The expansionary and inflationary consequences of the policy change are clearly influenced by the manner in which the increase in public investment is financed. This is because the various modes of financing have very different demand and supply effects. Increases in output are largest in the case of monetization and smaller in the case of a tax-financed expansion. In the third and fourth years of the experiment, when public investment falls back to its base-run level, the increase in output (with respect to the base run) drops to close to zero in the tax experiments while remaining relatively high in the monetization experiment (0.86 and 0.74 per cent over its base-run level). Price increases are also larger with monetization in the first three years, but not in the fourth year. The difference between the tax and monetization experiments lies in the operation of credit constraints. Let us look at what happens to credit demand and supply.

In year 1, the increase in production caused by the public sector expansion raises the demand for working capital while the increase in prices (pushing up the costs of production and of capital goods) raises the demand for both types of credit. The supply of credit rises as well, on two accounts: the income growth generates additional savings and hence bank deposits (expanding the banks' lending capacity), while borrowed reserves rise exogenously. This increase in credit supply is sufficient to meet the increase in the demand for credit. In year 2, the increase in the demand for investment credit is larger than in the first year because of the response of private investment to the previous-year income growth. Excess demands for investment credit arise (see Table 6.4). Note that the tight credit situation does not necessarily apply equally to all sectors, because sectoral demands for credit do not rise proportionally. This is due to differences in the vector of capital goods used by each sector, and to the disproportionate developments in sectoral prices. The investment credit constraints remain relatively mild however, particularly in the case of monetization. Even the tax-financed experiments achieve slightly higher than base-run levels of real GDP, because the investment credit constraints do not bind sufficiently to suppress total (public plus private) investment below its base-run level.

In year 3, both types of credit demand are above base-run levels owing to the higher planned private investment (in response to the income growth in the previous year) and the associated multiplier effects on production. The supply of credit, however, is not higher than in the base run because the expansionary monetary policy (which accompanied the fiscal expansion in the first two years) is discontinued. As a result, working capital and investment credit constraints become binding (see Table 6.4). (Again, credit shortages do not arise in all sectors because of differences in the vectors of inputs and of capital goods used by each sector.) There are two opposing effects on the price level. The working capital credit constraints in the two price-clearing household sectors (2–3) place upward pressure on prices by reducing output from the supply side. On the other hand, as a result of the policy-induced capital stock expansions of the first two years, the increase

Table 6.4   Infrastructure and credit constraints resulting from public sector expansions[a]

	1989–90	1990–91	1991–92	1992–93
Expansion of public investment				
Direct taxation				
Infrastructure constraint	–	–	–	–
Working capital constraint	–	–	2–3	–
Investment credit constraint	–	2, 4–7	4–7	–
Indirect taxation				
Infrastructure constraint	–	–	–	–
Working capital constraint	–	–	2–3	–
Investment credit constraint	–	2, 4–7	4–7	–
Monetization				
Infrastructure constraint	–	–	–	–
Working capital constraint	–	–	2–3	–
Investment credit constraint	–	2, 4–7	4–7	–
Bank debt				
Infrastructure constraint	–	–	–	–
Working capital constraint	1–7	–	2–3	–
Investment credit constraint	1–6	2, 4–7	4–7	–

Note:
[a] Note that this table reports only on the presence of constraints, not on their severity. The severity of credit constraints differs significantly between the experiments.
Source: Naastepad (1999).

in agricultural and infrastructural supplies, and the moderating effect of this on prices, is largest in year 3. The investment credit constraints contribute to the dampening effect on prices. The net result in the tax experiments is a price decline, which reduces the nominal value of savings and hence of bank deposits. Bank deposits decline below their base-run level. The resulting relatively severe credit constraints cause output to fall below base-run levels. In the monetization experiment, the credit constraints are much less severe, allowing output (as well as prices) to remain above base-run levels.

Why are the credit constraints less severe in the case of monetization? This is explained by differences between the modes of financing in their impact on credit supply. A monetized expansion represents an 'injection' of expenditures equal to the expansion of the deficit. As this amount is spent, income is generated. Part of this income is again spent, and part of it is saved. Part of the savings ends up as deposits in banks, where it can be used to lend to the government and private agents in response to these agents' financing needs. Precisely how much deposit money is created depends on the size of the public expenditure expansion; on how much of the resulting increase in income generated by the increase in government spending is placed in banks; to which production sectors the banks choose (or are obliged) to lend; and on whether demand for such additional loans exists. Thus, the relation between the monetized deficit and money depends on private production and investment plans and portfolio decisions. But the amount of deposit money created (and hence the expansion of the banks' lending capacity) will be larger in the case of monetization than in the case of taxation, because taxation takes away part of the additional income created by the public expenditure 'injection'.

In the fourth year, none of the credit constraints bind, but private investment drops below base-run levels in the tax experiments because of the growth decline of the previous year. Prices decline as well (with respect to their base-run levels). As a result, real GDP falls back to its base-run level. In the monetization experiment, by contrast, real GDP remains well above its base-run level because overall demand stays high. At the same time, the overall price level drops below its base-run level, and below the level attained in the other experiments. The reason for the deflation lies in the larger capital stocks of agriculture and infrastructure, which remain higher than in the base run owing to the relatively large capital stock additions of the first two years. The deflation can be expected to last for a number of years after the fourth year, until the capital stock expansions made possible (directly and indirectly) by the public investment expansion have worn out. Because the price decline is larger than in any other experiment, the monetization experiment also leads to a larger trade balance improvement than the other experiments.

Although tax financing gives very similar macroeconomic results for direct and indirect taxation (see Table 6.3) there is, however, one important difference. The indirect tax itself is one of the costs on the basis of which mark-up prices are calculated. Consequently, an increase in the indirect tax rate directly raises mark-up prices. This reduces the demand for mark-up priced goods and – the output of mark-up priced sectors being flexible – their output. Thus, the increase in the price level caused by the indirect tax itself leads to fewer goods being traded at higher prices. This is the major difference with the adjustment process following a direct tax increase. The result is that real GDP at factor cost (that is, the sum of factor incomes – not reported in the tables) remains lower with indirect than with direct taxation.

A public investment expansion financed through bank debt gives a dismal performance. The increase in the *slr* substantially reduces the availability of credit to the private sector. This in itself does not necessarily lead to credit constraints provided there is sufficient slack in the system. However, in the model's base run the banks have only a limited amount of excess reserves at their disposal and therefore, after the increase in the slr_b, they can no longer fully accommodate the private demand for credit. This leads to relatively severe credit constraints. If credit were used to finance only investment, the result would have been a fall in output coupled with deflation. Working capital constraints, however, reduce output from the supply side, causing sectoral excess demands and upward pressure on prices. In the experiment, the result of the operation of both types of constraints together is a decline in output coupled with inflation, and a trade balance deterioration.[9]

Thus, we can conclude that (1) higher growth rates and reduced inflation can be achieved through selective increases in public investment directed at relaxing supply-side constraints on growth, but (2) the success of such a policy depends crucially on the mode of financing the increase in public investment. As could be expected, the gains in terms of real GDP growth are highest when the additional investment expenditure is financed through monetization. Remarkably, however, ultimately monetization also leads to the lowest inflation and the largest trade balance improvement. The reason lies in the favourable impact of this policy on credit supply. What is required for an expansionary policy is an increase in the supply of goods and services in line with the increase in the demand for them. Only the monetized expansion provides the required additional resources. This wider availability of financial resources dampens inflation, for two reasons. Firstly, the higher availability of working capital credit allows production to attain a higher level than in the other experiments; this dampens inflation in the short run. Secondly, the higher availability of investment loans permits an expansion of production capacity, which reduces pressure on prices in the medium run.

6. CONCLUSIONS

Fiscal correction aimed at a sustained reduction in the (monetized) budget deficit constitutes the core of the structural adjustment programmes adopted by India and many developing countries in response to macroeconomic imbalances. The underlying argument is that a (monetized) budget deficit reduction will lead to price and balance of payments stability by removing excess demand in the short run and by promoting efficiency in the medium to long run. This argument, however, implicitly assumes that deficit reductions do not have negative supply-side effects. This chapter, by contrast, has argued that the reduction of the (monetized) budget deficit has potentially large and negative supply-side effects. In the short run, variations in fiscal policy have a significant impact on working capital credit supply, and hence on goods supply and inflation. In the medium run, fiscal policy affects the growth of sectoral production capacities, directly via the financing of public investment in key sectors such as agriculture and infrastructure, and indirectly via its impact on investment credit supply, which in turn is a crucial determinant of private investment growth.

To highlight the supply-side effects of the public budget, I have presented above a multi-period real-financial CGE model (for India), which focuses on credit rather than money and explicitly analyses the relation between the budget and the credit creation process. The model goes beyond earlier modelling approaches by: incorporating credit rationing; recognizing the dual role of credit for working capital and investment; and allowing for endogenous switches between credit-constrained, capacity-constrained and demand-constrained regimes. The simulation experiments with this model show that the government budget has potentially strong real effects via its influence over the supply of credit. This effect runs via credit rationing. However, as the experiments show, a simple relation between the budget deficit and credit supply does not exist. This is explained by the great variety in modes of financing and in the composition of public expenditures underlying otherwise equal budget deficits.

Conclusions from experiments with this model are:

1. By influencing credit supply, budgetary policy may lead to credit rationing. The occurrence and severity of the credit constraints are heavily influenced by the mode of financing underlying the budget, and by initial conditions in financial markets.
2. The macroeconomic effects of credit shortages depend on the type of credit that is in short supply:
   • when investment credit is rationed, a new equilibrium is reached through declines in output as well as prices; and
   • when working capital credit is rationed, the economy adjusts through declines in output and price *in*creases.
3. When credit is rationed, fiscal policy is not effective: the real output effects of increases in public expenditure are very small, mainly because public expenditure crowds out private expenditure. Monetary policy is effective. Monetization of fiscal expansion crowds in private expenditure through two channels:
   • a general expansion of demand and profits; and
   • an expansion of credit supply.

4. When credit is not rationed, fiscal policy is effective, because public expenditure crowds in private expenditure through a general expansion of demand and profits.

More specifically, two important macroeconomic policy lessons can be learnt. First, the simulation experiments show that the impact of the debt financing of public expenditure depends on conditions in financial markets. If there is sufficient slack in financial markets, debt-financed government expenditure will not crowd out private expenditure and may even promote growth, contrary to conventional wisdom. However, if there is no slack, as in our experiments, debt-financed public expenditure will crowd out private expenditure. Second, the simulation outcomes demonstrate that the growth and inflationary effects of a monetized deficit depend critically on what the deficit finances – both directly (government expenditure) and indirectly (through its impact on credit supply). If the monetary expansion following a rise in the monetized deficit is targeted to reducing supply-side constraint in agriculture and/or infrastructure, it may contribute to growth without raising prices.

NOTES

1. For a full description of the model's equations and an elaborate explanation of how the model developed in this paper differs from existing real-financial CGE models, see Naastepad (1999).
2. To avoid further modelling complications, it is assumed that all categories of final demand for the infrastructural good as well as intermediate demand by sector 8 for its own good, as also the intermediate demand of public sectors 9–11, get priority.
3. In sectors 5–7 prices rise through upward adjustments in the mark-up rate.
4. Apart from the savings of production sectors 1–4, household sector savings include savings from all wages (earned in all sectors).
5. It is assumed that the government uses the extra credit to reduce its foreign debt.
6. The rationing rule applied in the experiments described in this chapter is that available credit is distributed over the various private parties in proportion to their excess demands for credit.
7. To get an idea of the size of the adjustment: Rs. crores 10000 of monetary financing supports almost one-tenth of total public current plus investment expenditure or about one-quarter of the public saving–investment gap.
8. Note that, if credit constraints had become binding, the system would have become savings-driven and the ranking of the results in terms of effects on output and prices would have been different.
9. The third year, when the discontinuation of the public expansion leads to a slight decline in the price level and a corresponding (relatively small) improvement in the trade balance, is an exception.

REFERENCES

Balakrishnan, P. (1991), *Pricing and Inflation in India*, Delhi: Oxford University Press.

Behrman, J. and T. Srinivasan (eds) (1995), *Handbook of Development Economics, Volume III*, Amsterdam: North-Holland.

Chakravarty, S. (1987), *Development Planning, The Indian Experience*, Oxford: Clarendon Press.

Chatterji, R. (1989), *The Behaviour of Industrial Prices in India*, Delhi: Oxford University Press.

Chopra, A., C. Collyns, R. Hemming and K. Parker (1995), 'India: Economic reform and growth', *IMF Occasional Paper 134*, Washington DC: International Monetary Fund. With W. Chu and O. Fratzscher.

Committee to Review the Working of the Monetary System (1985), *Report of the Committee to Review the Working of the Monetary System*, Mumbai: Reserve Bank of India. Chaired by S. Chakravarty.

Corbo, V. and S. Fischer (1995), *Structural adjustment, stabilization and policy reform: Domestic and international finance*, in Behrman and Srinivasan (1995), Chapter 44, pp. 2845–924.

Ministry of Finance (1992), *Economic Survey 1991–92*, Delhi: Government of India.

Naastepad, C.W.M. (1999), *The Budget Deficit and Macroeconomic Performance – A Real-Financial Computable General Equilibrium Model for India*, Delhi: Oxford University Press.

Nayyar, D. (1996), *Economic Liberalization in India: Analytics, Experience and Lessons*, Hyderabad: Orient Longman.

Raj, K. (1984), 'Some observations on economic growth in India over the period 1952–53 to 1982–83', *Economic and Political Weekly*, **19** (41), 1801–4.

Rakshit, M.K. (1986), 'Monetary policy in a developing economy', *mimeo*, Helsinki: WIDER.

Rakshit, M.K. (1991), 'The macroeconomic adjustment programme: A critique', *Economic and Political Weekly*, **26** (34), 1977–88.

Rakshit, M.K. (1994), 'Money and public finance under structural adjustment: The Indian experience', *Economic and Political Weekly*, **29** (16/17), 923–37.

Rodrik, D. (1995), *Trade and industrial policy reform*, in Behrman and Srinivasan (1995), Chapter 45, pp. 2925–82.

Sen, A. (1981), 'The agrarian constraint to economic development: The case of India', *PhD thesis*, Cambridge: University of Cambridge.

Storm, S. (1993), *Macroeconomic Considerations in the Choice of an Agricultural Policy – A Study into Sectoral Interdependence with Reference to India*, Aldershot: Avebury.

Taylor, L. (1988), 'Macro constraints on India's economic growth', *Indian Economic Review*, **23** (2), 144–65.

World Bank (1996), *India – Five Years of Stabilization and Reform and the Challenges Ahead*, Washington DC: IBRD.

PART II

International capital flows

F32
ō 19 ōlₗ

7. An analysis of the impact of short-term capital flows on income in developing economies

Amit Bhaduri

Keynes' as well as Kalecki's analysis of the problem of income determination through aggregate demand was set, almost self-consciously, in the context of a closed economy. The generalization of this analysis to an economy open to foreign trade through various ramifications of the 'foreign trade multiplier' has one common thread running through it. Imports, like savings, are assumed to be induced by income. Thus, with both savings and imports as increasing functions of income, the effect of the foreign trade multiplier on aggregate demand is derived in terms of the saving and import propensities as the two sources of leakage from demand.

With capital inflow in the liberalized regime of trade and finance in a developing country, the problem needs to be viewed somewhat differently. Capital inflow is an autonomous variable decided by private traders in the international foreign exchange market. In many situations relevant to developing countries, we may plausibly postulate that higher imports, and therefore a higher trade deficit, are not only sustained but driven by the volume of autonomous capital inflows into a country. Thus, in contrast to the more traditional Keynesian model, imports may be assumed to be induced not by income but by capital inflow. Its consequence is evident. A higher capital inflow in a liberalized trade regime permits sustaining a higher trade deficit, which in turn has a contractionary impact on income through the standard multiplier mechanism (Bhaduri and Skarstein, 1996). More formally, in familiar notations of national income accounting, Gross Domestic Product (GDP) is defined as:

$$X = GDP = C + I + E - M$$

where C = consumption, I = investment, E = exports and M = imports. Deducting consumption expenditure (C) from both sides, we obtain saving (S):

$$S = X - C = I + E - M. \tag{1}$$

Moreover, for simplicity, we assume the average and marginal saving propensity to be a fixed proportion of *GDP (X)*, that is:

$$S = sX, \quad 1 > s > 0. \tag{2}$$

The solution of demand-determined *GDP* is given from (1) and (2) as:

$$X = (1/s) [I - (M - E)]. \tag{3}$$

If a higher level of capital inflow (F) simply sustains a higher trade deficit, but does not affect either investment (I) or the exchange rate, it is evident from (3) that such capital inflow will be contractionary through the multiplier mechanism in its impact on demand-determined output. This is shown explicitly by rewriting (3) as:

$$X = (1/s)[I - F], \tag{4}$$

where $F = (M - E)$, that is, the level of trade sustained by the capital inflow F.

Despite the elementary nature of the above algebraic calculation, it has an important economic message which deserves emphasis, especially because it goes against the conventional wisdom about trade liberalization sustained through capital inflow. As equation (4) shows, a higher inflow of foreign finance F, could reduce income through the multiplier mechanism for a given level of investment. However, the multiplier mechanism driving the contraction of aggregate demand and income in equation (4) does not depend merely on the substitution of less competitive, 'inferior' domestically produced goods by 'superior' imported goods to enhance consumers' welfare, as conventional theory would often have us believe. This is because the substitution of domestic by imported goods provides only the initial impulse to the Kahn–Keynes multiplier process. However, as the output of domestic goods decreases through substitution, so do profits, wages and employment in these domestic industries. This sets in motion a further decline in demand and output of domestic industries in a chain reaction captured by the usual convergent geometric series of the multiplier process, as implied by (4). Note that these successive rounds of contraction in demand and output need not involve any further substitution of domestic by foreign goods. Therefore, they also do not imply that the decline in domestic output in these successive rounds is due to its lack of international competitiveness, because they could be driven entirely by the contraction in domestic demand (Bhaduri, 1998).

The unambiguously contractionary impact of a foreign capital inflow on the level of domestic aggregate demand and output represented by equation (4) is clearly an extreme case. Yet it may not be altogether irrelevant in some situations. Tanzania, for example, was advised by the International Monetary Fund, in the 1980s, to liberalize its imports by bringing most imported items under the 'Open General Licence' (OGL) scheme, while major aid donors agreed to sustain the higher trade deficit of the liberalized trade regime through augmented capital inflows, mostly in the form of official development assistance (ODA). The higher ODA, supporting a larger trade deficit through current account liberalization under the OGL scheme without much variation in the exchange rate as assumed in the analysis above, resulted in a strong contractionary impact on domestic demand and output. In an altogether different context, it is arguable that the massive transfer of income from the west to the east of united Germany, right after the political as well as exchange rate reunification, had a similar effect. A large part of the transferred income, as well as accumulated private saving in the eastern region, were spent on imports from West German industries at the unified exchange rate to set in motion a similar contractionary process of demand for goods produced by the eastern region of Germany.

Equation (4) is, however, misleadingly simple for an open economy. It assumes that the entire capital inflow of the developing country is available for sustaining only its trade deficit. Some recent calculations on the other hand suggest that, on average, debt servicing and other factor payments account for some 30 per cent and the change in reserve for another 20 per cent of capital inflows to developing countries. The remaining 50 per cent is available for covering trade deficits $(M-E)$ of developing countries as a whole (UNCTAD, 1999). Thus,

$$F = Z + \Delta R + (M - E), \tag{5}$$

where F = gross capital inflow, ΔR = change in foreign exchange reserve, and Z = net factor payment for simplicity. Since, by definition, $GNP(Y)$ is $GDP(X)$ minus net factor payment (Z), that is:

$$Y = X - Z \tag{6}$$

we may substitute this in (1) and use (5) to obtain:

$$Y - C = S = I + \Delta R - F. \tag{7}$$

Therefore, if saving is assumed to be a fraction(s) of GNP (rather than GDP), we obtain in place of (4):

$$Y=(1/s)\,[I-(F-\Delta R)]. \tag{8}$$

In other words, the contractionary effect of a foreign capital inflow at a given level of investment discussed earlier in equation (4) remains qualitatively similar to that in equation (8). The support such inflow provides to the trade deficit, net of the change in reserve (ΔR), operates through the multiplier leading to demand contraction. And the two formulas (4) and (8) coincide so long as there is no change in reserve.

Although our theoretical analysis so far suggests that a capital inflow net of reserve change covering the trade deficit has a contractionary effect on the level of economic activity, this contradicts the recent experiences of many developing countries which have enjoyed rapid expansion in the levels of output and economic activity as well as subsequent financial crisis in regimes of significant capital flows. To incorporate formally into the analysis these possibilities, we need to recognize that real investment might be stimulated or depressed through a complex set of financial influences exerted by capital flows.

The stimulating effects of capital inflows on investment through the 'monetarist' channel of the interest rate reduction can be seen most clearly through a modified IS/LM analysis. Suppose, for simplicity, that all capital inflows are in the form of reserves held by the financial system of the country, so that no output contraction operates through the channel of the trade deficit identified earlier. Since, by standard accounting, the liabilities of the financial system to the public correspond to some definition of the supply of 'money' (M^s), this must be matched by its corresponding asset position which is domestic credit advanced (A) plus foreign reserve (R), that is:

$$M^s = A + R, \tag{9}$$

implying that an increase in reserves through unspent capital inflow would be associated with an increase in money supply in a 'non-sterilized' regime.

As in standard IS/LM analysis, the increased money supply lowers the interest rate (i) to stimulate investment and depress savings. In consequence, income expands as a result of the capital inflow in a non-sterilized, cheap money regime. Formally, this is easily checked from the equation:

$$I(i, Y) = S(i, Y), \tag{10}$$

implying that:

$$di = [(S_Y - I_Y)/(I_i - S_i)]\,dY = -k\,dY, k > 0, \tag{11}$$

where k is the magnitude of slope of the IS curve, which is negative under the usual assumptions.

The money market equilibrium, the LM side, is given from (9) as:

$$M^d = L(i, Y) = A + R = M^s$$

$$\text{or, } L_i d_i + L_Y . dY = dR = F. \tag{12}$$

From (11) and (12), it follows:

$$dY = F/(L_Y - k L_i). \tag{13}$$

Since under the usual assumptions of the transaction demand for money, $L_Y > 0$, and the speculative demand for money $L_i < 0$, it follows that the denominator on the right hand side of (13) is unambiguously positive, implying that income expands, that is, $dY > 0$ due to a capital inflow $F > 0$ in a non-sterilized monetary regime.

It should be noted in the above chain of reasoning that, in so far as a large foreign capital inflow has this tendency to depress the domestic interest rate through a larger money supply, it stimulates not only investment, but also private consumption by lowering saving through greater hire-purchase, housing loans and so on. These effects encapsuled in $S_i > 0$ are likely to be felt more strongly in industrially advanced countries with wider networks of financial intermediation and consumers' credit than in most developing countries. More importantly, a lower interest rate by raising the prices of bonds might also create a positive 'wealth effect' for private bond holders. In so far as the commercial banks are major holders of government bonds to meet their 'statutory liquidity ratio' in many developing countries (for example, in India until the liberalization of the early 1990s; see World Bank, 1995 for an overview), the increased bond price expands their base for lending. On the whole, the aggregate demand effect is likely to be expansionary, because private bond holders, experiencing a positive wealth effect, spend more, while commercial banks also follow an easier credit policy due to their expanded liquidity base.

This institutional elaboration of the IS/LM-type analysis of the impact of a capital inflow on aggregate demand and output is, however, not very plausible in a globalized setting for short-term capital mobility. The main reason is that the lower interest rate is also likely to induce capital outflow by creating a differential between the domestic and the international interest rate, unless the *expected* appreciation of the domestic exchange rate resulting in expected capital gains nullifies this effect of the gap in interest rates.

Perhaps a more plausible channel to consider is the influence of foreign capital inflow on domestic equity prices rather than bank-financed debt. Capital inflow might involve that foreign institutional (for example, hedge funds) and other investors borrow from domestic banks against foreign currency to purchase financial assets denominated in domestic currency. It would almost certainly have the effect of stimulating domestic investment and demand-determined output, if such purchases are absorbed mostly by the issue of new equities in the *primary* market. Nevertheless, this is far less likely than such purchases being directed towards the *secondary* equity market for the acquision of existing ownership rights. To the extent it increases the financial value of the firm (as seen by the stock market) in relation to the replacement value of its physical capital – Tobin's *q* ratio (Tobin, 1969) – it might have a stimulating effect on real investment, although the empirical evidence in its favour is not very strong even in advanced capitalist countries (for example, Ndikumana, 1999; Semmler and Franke, 1996). In most developing countries, the quantitative importance of the equity market in comparison to the market for government securities and bank credit is considerably less. The investment-stimulating effect of a short-term capital inflow through the stock market (for example, Tobin's *q* ratio) is therefore unlikely to be large. At the same time, the rising price of equities in a bullish stock market due to capital inflow may divert investment more towards speculative acquisition of stocks in the secondary market. This could create a financial bubble, rather than providing support to long-term real investment. The important point to note is that the same story-line, with only slight modification, can be repeated for investment being diverted into land and real estates. Prime land and real estates, being in more or less fixed supply at least in the short run, tend to resemble fairly closely in this respect the secondary market for reputed financial assets. Acquisition of existing ownership rights becomes the name of the game in both cases. To summarize the impact of capital inflow on aggregate demand and income through the channel of the equity market, we reconsider the equality between investment and saving in an open economy. From (5) and (7), we write:

$$S\,(Y,\,F)=I\,(Y,\,F)+B(Y,\,F) \qquad (14)$$

where $B=E-(M+Z)$ that is, the surplus on current account.

On total differentiation and rearrangement of terms in (14),

$$\frac{dY}{dF}=\frac{I_F-S_F-B_F}{S_Y-I_Y-B_Y}. \qquad (15)$$

Note that the current account surplus is usually expected to diminish with income expansion, yielding $B_Y<0$, which sufficiently guarantees that the denominator of (15) is positive under the Keynesian income adjustment stability condition $S_Y > I_Y$, normally assumed to ensure the negative slope of the IS curve.

To the extent that the capital inflow results in exchange rate appreciation to make imports cheaper and exports more expensive, the current account surplus will diminish with larger capital inflow, provided the so-called Marshall–Lerner condition on trade elasticities is satisfied. This yields $B_F < 0$. Similarly, by raising stock prices a higher capital inflow would create a 'wealth effect' and raise consumption to depress saving, yielding $S_F < 0$. Thus, unless I_F is sufficiently large in magnitude and negative, the numerator of (15) will be positive. This means that the effect of capital inflow on income would be positive, unless it depresses real investment strongly. Note that, by chain rule, we may rewrite:

$$I_F \equiv \partial I / \partial F = (\partial I / \partial p)(\partial p / \partial F) \tag{16}$$

where p = price of equity. In line with our preceding discussion, the equity price in the secondary market would tend to go up, financed by capital inflow, that is $(\partial p / \partial F) > 0$. However, whether the higher equity price stimulates investment through a higher Tobin's q ratio-like effect or it depresses real investment by generating a financial or real estate bubble remains an open question. Thus, the sign of $(\partial I / \partial p)$ in (16) is indeterminate. When the 'bubble effect' is strong, this sign may become negative and sufficiently large in magnitude to turn the numerator of (15) negative. A financial or real estate bubble created by capital inflow will then have a contractionary effect on the level of income. It is indeed a frequently observed pattern that a stock market and real estate boom go hand in hand with income expansion in the initial phase (because $\partial I / \partial p$ remains small in magnitude), but they fail to move in unison and begin to move in opposite directions (as $\partial I / \partial p$ becomes negative and large in magnitude). This is often the prelude to an economic crisis for a developing country that had been enjoying inflows of short-term international capital.

REFERENCES

Bhaduri, A. (1998), 'Implications of globalization for macroeconomic theory and policy in developing countries', in D. Baker, G. Epstein and R. Pollin (eds), *Globalization and Progressive Economic Policy*, Cambridge: Cambridge University Press.

Bhaduri, A. and R. Skarstein (1996), 'Short period macroeconomic aspects of foreign aid', *Cambridge Journal of Economics*, **20** (2), 195–206.

Ndikumana, L. (1999), 'Debt service, financing constraints and fixed investment: Evidence from panel data', *Journal of Post Keynesian Economics*, **21** (3), 455–78.

Semmler, W. and W. Franke (1996), 'The financial-real interaction and investment in business cycle', in G. Deleplace and E.J. Nell (eds), *Money in Motion: The Post Keynesian and Circulation Approaches*, London: Macmillan.

Tobin, J. (1969), 'A general equilibrium approach to monetary theory', *Journal of Money, Credit and Banking*, **1** (1), 15–29.

UNCTAD (1999), *Trade and Development Report*, New York: United Nations.

World Bank (1995), *The Emerging Asian Bond Market*, Washington, D.C.: The International Bank for Reconstruction and Development.

F32

F21   616
E22   519

8.   Globalization of capital markets: Some analytical and policy issues[1]
Mihir K. Rakshit

1.   INTRODUCTION

The 1970s marked a watershed in the development of global financial markets in more ways than one. First, the Bretton Woods system came to an end with the floating of the yen and major European currencies against the dollar in March 1973, and the gradual switchover by more and more countries to flexible exchange rate regimes. Second, with the move towards capital account convertibility by most industrialized nations and the accumulation of huge external assets by oil producing countries, there was a sharp rise in the quantum of international capital movements. Third, and the most important for our purpose, there occurred a quantitative and also a qualitative change in the flow of foreign capital to (non-oil producing) developing countries. Capital inflows in these countries registered a quantum jump during the period 1972–83 and again from the late 1980s.[2] What is no less significant, while the earlier capital flows to developing countries consisted almost entirely of official and government guaranteed loans, since 1973 private capital flows have assumed increasing importance and there has been a sharp decline in loans from official sources.[3]

These developments in international financial markets, together with the trend towards lowering of barriers to trade in goods and services, were widely expected to promote efficient allocation of world resources and add significantly to the economic prosperity of *all* countries, both developed and developing. Emerging market economies in general were expected to reap substantial benefits in as much as it was in these countries that net investment of foreign capital went up by leaps and bounds, and these investments were driven almost exclusively by market forces.[4] However, the relaxation of controls on capital movements and the surge in private foreign investment in developing countries have also been associated with frequent financial upheavals in these economies. Following large-scale capital inflows through multinational banks, there was a series of banking and currency crises in Brazil, Mexico and other Latin American countries in the early 1980s. Similar has been the experience of Venezuela (1993–95), Mexico (1994–95), Hungary (1995), the Asian 5[5] (1997–99), Czech Republic (1997), Brazil (1998–99) and Russia (1998–2000) during the closing decade of the millennium. In the light of these events, especially after the outbreak of the Asian currency crisis, there has been a sea change in the climate of opinion among economists[6] regarding the role and desirability of unhindered capital movements across national boundaries. Such movements are in fact increasingly being viewed as a major source of financial instability and currency crisis in emerging market economies, if not in industrialized countries.[7] What is more, increasing integration of the global financial market seems also to have magnified the contagion effect, with the crisis in one country spreading to not only other regional economies, but also to countries located in other parts of the world. Important recent instances of currency crisis in an economy producing significant contagion effects are the Mexican crisis (December 1994), the fall of the Thai baht (July 1997) and the Russian debt default[8] (August 1998).

The purpose of the present paper is to put the current debate on the role of international capital mobility in a proper perspective. Section 2 provides an overview of the basic economic rationale and the mutually beneficial effects of trans-border capital flows. Section 3 examines the interaction, under alternative economic regimes, of real and financial sectors in governing transfer of resources from one country to another. In terms of the economic mechanism discussed in section 3, we try to identify in the next section the major problems associated with unhindered capital movements and suggest measures for containing their deleterious impact without any significant loss of benefits countries can derive from foreign capital or investment abroad. The final section summarizes the main results.

2. GAINS FROM INTERNATIONAL CAPITAL MOBILITY

The benefits of unrestricted mobility of capital across national boundaries are not very difficult to appreciate in terms of elementary economic principles. The most important of these benefits consists of efficient allocation of global resources by way of transfer of capital from the less to the more productive parts of the world. What is no less significant, as in the case of trade in goods and services, *all* countries, irrespective of whether they borrow or lend, stand to gain from the resulting reallocation of the world's capital stock (see Box 8.1).

That aggregate world output goes up through capital mobility is not

Box 8.1   Production and distribution with and without capital mobility

Consider a two-country world where country A and country B own *OE* and *O'E* amounts of capital respectively (see figure below). MP_a denotes the marginal productivity of capital in A and MP_b that in B. In the absence of any international capital mobility, net national (and domestic) product equals *OCDE* in A and *O'FRE* in B, and there is a gap in marginal returns on capital in the two countries[67], r_{oa} and r_{ob}. When capital is free to move across national frontiers, search for higher returns will induce flow of capital from B to A until the returns in the two countries are equalized at *r**. Under the new equilibrium (at *G*), *EI* amount of foreign capital is invested in A, and its net *domestic* product goes up to *OCGI*. However, since out of the rental income totalling *Or*GI*, *EIGH* goes to B's capitalists investing in A, the increase in A's net *national* product amounts to *DGH*, rather than *DGIE*. It may similarly be shown that though capital outflow reduces B's net *domestic* product by *EIGR*, receipt of rental income amounting to *EIGH* raises B's *national* product by *RGH*. Thus unhindered mobility of capital raises world income by *DGR*, of which *DGH* accrues to A and *RHG* to B.

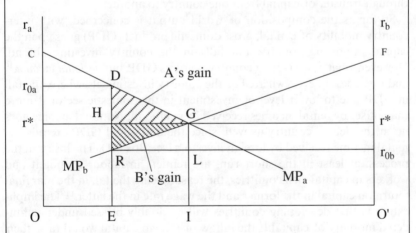

The similarity between international trade and inter-country movement of capital extends also to their impact on income distribution. While every country gains from trade, all income earners do not:[68] workers lose and capitalists gain in the country importing relatively labour-intensive goods in exchange for capital-intensive ones, but the effect is the opposite when

imports are more capital intensive. In order to appreciate the income distributional impact of capital mobility, assume that there are only two
factors of production, capital and labour. Without any foreign capital inflow,
workers in A receive Cdr_{oa} out of $CDEO$ amount of income, and the rest
goes to capitalists. Under unrestricted capital mobility, workers gain to the
tune of $r_{oa}DGr^*$, while capitalists' income falls by $r_{oa}DHr^*$. It may similarly
be shown that the impact on the two groups of income earners is in the
opposite direction in B. The economic reason behind this asymmetric
effect is fairly simple: with no change in the employment of labour in the
two countries, capital inflow reduces the marginal productivity of capital
but raises that of labour, while capital outflow has the opposite effect on
the marginal productivity of the two factors.

difficult to appreciate. Thus if, in the absence of capital movements, marginal productivity of capital is 100 units in the capital abundant, but 150 units
in the capital scarce country, transfer of one unit of capital from the former
to the latter will raise world production by 50 units.[9] Search for higher
profits ensures that, with free mobility, marginal returns on capital across
countries are equalized, leaving no further scope for raising world output
through transfer of capital from one country to another.

So far as the composition of world output is concerned, with inter-
country mobility of capital, gross domestic product (GDP) goes up in the
capital importing country, but falls in the country investing abroad.
However, what matters for a country is not its GDP, but *national income*,[10]
and this goes up everywhere. For the country investing elsewhere, the fall
in GDP due to lower level of investment in the domestic sector is more
than offset by rental incomes received from abroad. National income goes
up in the debtor country as well, since the additional GDP exceeds the
rental income received by foreign investors (see Box 8.1). The losers in the
process, at least in the short run, are rentiers in labour-abundant and
workers in capital-rich countries, the reason being the fall in the marginal
return on capital in the former and the wage rate in the latter.[11] The implication is that developing countries will be doubly blessed under unhindered mobility of capital:[12] the inflow of foreign capital would raise their
national income and produce a salubrious impact on income distribution
as well.

From a long-run developmental perspective economists put much more
emphasis on the role of foreign capital in transferring technical, managerial or organizational know-how from advanced to backward economies.
In such cases gains from capital mobility are recognized to be much larger,

and these gains accrue to the economy in a variety of ways. First, for a *given amount of investment* by foreign firms with superior technology, and so on, the increase in both net domestic product and national income of the country will be larger than what would be obtained without any productivity differential between foreign and domestic firms.[13] Second, the productivity differential enlarges the scope of capital movement from developed to developing countries, and enhances thereby the extent of benefit accruing to both groups of nations. Third, diffusion of technical and organizational know-how from foreign to domestic firms raises over time productivity of all factors in the domestic economy irrespective of their place of employment.[14]

The implication is that not only does the economy gain in terms of enhanced national dividend, but *both* workers and capitalists may enjoy higher levels of income. Last and the most important, the inter-country capital movement, by acting as a vehicle for the transfer of knowledge from advanced to backward parts of the world, can trigger off a cumulative process of experimentation, learning and innovation in developing countries as well, and constitute a most effective means of their economic transformation. The main point to note in this connection is that while the benefits of inter-country capital flows highlighted in the earlier analysis (and Box 8.1) are due solely to allocative efficiency and are mostly of a once-and-for-all nature, the effects operating through the transfer of knowledge generally cause cumulative shifts in the production function itself and can help to set a backward economy on course to self-sustained growth.

2.1 Two-way capital movement

Our analysis seems to suggest that, with no impediments to cross-border investment:

- capital will flow from advanced to less developed economies; and
- for any country there will not be any significant difference between the *gross* and *net* outflow or inflow of capital.[15]

Investors everywhere seek to invest in the most profitable place of business so that not only should foreign capital tend to flow to the country with relatively higher prospective return on investment, but the country's domestic investors also would have little incentive to acquire assets abroad. For similar reasons a country investing elsewhere would not be a good destination of foreign capital. The two presumptions relating to the nature of inter-country capital movement are not, however, supported by the behaviour of the global capital market over the last three to four decades. The

overwhelming part of international capital flows has been from one industrialized economy to another, rather than from developed to developing
countries. It is also interesting to note that the balance of payments of most
countries were characterized by substantial inflows as well as outflows of
capital, that is, the countries were both borrowers and lenders in the international capital market.[16]

That the international capital flows could be from underdeveloped to
advanced economies, rather than the other way round, is not as intriguing
as may appear at first sight, once we step out of the simple framework of
the two-factor production function. The return on capital, it is important
to recognize, depends significantly on availability of skilled labour, infrastructural facilities, a country's law and order situation, the nature of
government control over economic activities, and the efficacy of fiscal and
monetary policy in attaining macroeconomic stability. Even when developing countries are possessed of a vast army of unskilled labour (or natural
resources) and multinational firms can set up productive units embodying
superior technology, the net return on foreign capital may be quite low in
these countries if the supply of workers with the requisite skills[17] is scarce;
there are serious bottlenecks in transport, telecommunications, ports,
financial services or power supply; mafia raj or corruption is rampant;[18]
government controls or taxes tend to produce large distortions; the legal
process of enforcing, or contracts settling, disputes is painfully slow; and
the economy is prone to wide cyclical swings.[19]

Perhaps the most remarkable feature of the international capital market
over the last three decades has been the two-way movement of capital
between developed economies. Such movements may be traced to two sets
of factors. First, the relative superiority of a country in respect of technical know-how or organizational structure tends to vary widely across
different sectors: while Japanese firms may be much more efficient than
their US counterparts in producing automobiles, the situation seems to be
the opposite in respect of banking and insurance. Given such differences,
Japanese investment in the US automobile industry and setting up of US
financial firms in Japan can generate considerable economic gains for both
nations. Note also that, even in the same industry, firms of different countries differentiate their products or cater to different segments of the
market. Such differentiation, driving the growth of intra-industry trade
among countries, also promotes two-way capital flows in the same industry, especially when proximity to buyers enables firms to respond quickly to
changing demand conditions or exploring/creating niche markets for their
products.[20]

Even in the absence of any significant benefit in terms of production,
two-way capital flows secure considerable welfare gains for all nations by

reducing the degree of risk to which investors would otherwise be exposed, and by enabling countries to attain a more even distribution of their consumption over time. Consider first the simple case of consumption smoothing[21] with no use of foreign capital for purposes of production. Without any facility for borrowing from or lending to the rest of the world, a country's consumption will be constrained by its income and hence can display wide inter-temporal variations when production is prone to large shocks, international prices of exportables or importables show sharp fluctuations and costs of carrying inventories are extremely high. However, since the shocks causing fluctuations in income tend to vary across different countries, a fall in income in some parts of the world will tend to be balanced by a rise in income elsewhere. In other words, the inter-temporal fluctuations in world consumption are significantly less than that experienced by individual countries. Under these conditions international borrowing and lending permit all countries to attain a more even time profile of their consumption and hence generate welfare gains even though there may be little change in production in different parts of the world.[22]

More generally, a country can reduce the risk of fluctuations in income and consumption by diversifying its assets or not putting all its eggs in the same basket. One way of attaining this is to invest in a wide range of industries that are subject to dissimilar random shocks. However, such an option is generally inefficient[23] in view of the operation of scale economies and the principle of comparative advantage. Nor does the option insulate the country from trade cycles or region-specific shocks (for example, political upheavals or natural calamities) that affect all industries in an economy. A more efficient solution to the problem lies in owning income earning assets across a number of countries.

To appreciate the economic rationale of the simultaneous inflow and outflow of capital characterizing the balance of payments of practically all economies, consider (once again) a two-country world, both countries owning equal amounts of capital and having the same expected return and risk[24] on investment, when there is no capital mobility. If investors in the two countries can partially swap their assets,[25] the average return on the new portfolio of investors remains unaffected, but there will be a reduction in risk, when the two economies are subject to dissimilar shocks, in respect of their nature or timing. Indeed, the larger the number of countries in which investors can acquire assets and the smaller is the correlation between returns on investment in different economies, the larger will be the volume of *gross* capital flows across countries and the greater the reduction in risk enjoyed by asset holders through diversification.

However, such diversification does not reduce the risk and uncertainty to which the most vulnerable section of society is exposed, namely the labourers. Consumption smoothing would still require that the government or insurance companies in a country borrow or lend in the international capital market so that they could provide larger social security benefits and ensure inter-temporal consumption smoothing.

Were the benefits of simultaneous purchase and sale of assets in global capital markets due to consumption smoothing alone, the extent of welfare gains would have perhaps been fairly moderate. The most important impact of cross-holding of assets is said to operate through an enhancement in average growth rates that all countries in the world can enjoy.[26] To see why, let us go back to the world consisting of two countries A and B, each having only two domestic investment projects: I_s (safe investment) and I_r (risky investment). Assume that the return on I_s is 10 per cent, while that on I_r is 20 per cent. If the variance of the returns on I_r is high enough in relation to that on I_s, and nationals of the two countries are forced to hold only domestic assets, both countries opt for I_s, yielding an average return of 10 per cent. When investors are permitted to hold assets in both countries, distribution of funds between the two risky investments reduces the variance to which the individual asset holder is exposed and may well tilt the balance in favour of risky assets in A and B.[27] This will promote economic growth through two routes. First, the doubling of the return on capital raises the average growth rate in the two countries, for *given levels of investment* and population growth. Second, the higher returns induce larger savings and permit a higher rate of capital accumulation. Combination of the two factors has the potential of causing a sea change in the development process of any economy, emerging or emerged.[28]

2.2   Capital mobility as a policy disciplining device

While examining the impact of cross-border capital flows, we implicitly assumed the fiscal and other policies of the concerned governments as given. As we shall note at a later stage of our analysis, the effects of capital mobility depend crucially upon the type of policies pursued by the authorities. Experience of a wide array of economies, especially the developing ones, suggests that when the domestic sector is insulated from forces operating in the international capital market, the government tends to run large budget deficits, borrowing from the public or relying on seignorage.[29] Not only do such increases in the government's claim on resources of the economy crowd out private investment, but for many a government there does not appear to exist sufficient incentive to curb wasteful and unproductive expenditure for extending patronage or securing short-term political gains. Such policies, to be sure, put a stumbling block to the long-term development of the economy, but can nevertheless be sustained for a considerable period of time. However, when capital account convertibility is in force, public profligacy and distortionary policies are followed by a currency crisis fairly soon and thus make the government highly unpopular. International capital movement may thus act as a disciplining device by forcing the government to adopt policies that would make the domestic economy investor friendly and prevent capital flight. The implication of this line of reasoning is that the salubrious effects of international capital mobility, considered in the earlier subsections, are magnified through a change in the domestic policy regime in the right direction.

3.   THE ECONOMIC MECHANISM UNDER CAPITAL ACCOUNT CONVERTIBILITY

The mutually beneficial effects of international capital mobility enumerated above seem to make the case for capital account convertibility quite open and shut. How can we then account for the extreme reluctance of countries, until recently, to permit free flow of funds across their borders?[30] Empirical evidence also casts serious doubts on the gains countries (are supposed to) secure through unhindered inflow and outflow of capital. Using a sample of 100 developed and developing countries for the period 1975–89, Rodrik (1998) found little evidence of any significant impact of capital account convertibility on the growth rate of a country. Similar results were obtained by Alesina, Grilli and Milesi-Ferretti (1994), Razin and Yuen (1994), and Carrasquilla (1998) from their studies of the OECD and developing countries. Nor is there much empirical support for the hypothesis concerning the growth promoting impact of international risk sharing through globalization of financial markets.[31]

What is more disquieting, the adoption of capital account convertibility has very often led to two types of problems for developing countries. First, contrary to the canonical conclusion concerning consumption smoothing, international capital mobility appears to have added to the volatility of consumption in emerging market economies (Rodrik, 1997). Second, opening the floodgates of cross-border flow of funds has also been associated in many cases with financial turmoil and currency crisis. From a sample of 27 capital inflow surges between 1976 and 1996 in 21 emerging market economies, the World Bank (1999) found that in 'about two-thirds of the cases, there was a banking crisis, currency crisis or twin crisis in the wake of the surge'.

It is this link between capital movements and financial upheavals that has turned the tide of the mainstream view on going in for full capital account convertibility by countries in general, and the emerging market economies in particular. However, empirical evidence alone is not enough in drawing policy conclusions; we need also to keep in view the economic mechanism through which capital account convertibility affects the macroeconomic outcome under alternative scenarios.

3.1   Two faces of cross-border investment: financial and real

In the previous section (and Box 8.1) we have indicated how inter-country movement of capital leads to efficient allocation of global capital stock and contributes to an increase in income in both capital importing and capital exporting nations. However, when an economic agent in (say) country A invests in country B, there is at this stage no transfer of *physical* capital from A to B; all that has happened is that the agent has acquired a bank deposit, shares, bonds or other income earning assets.[32] Hence it is necessary to appreciate how, to what extent or whether, capital account convertibility shifts (physical) capital from less to more productive parts of the world.

Even when A's acquisition of financial assets in B does (eventually) result in inter-country movement of physical resources, the mechanism of transfer and the adjustment process play an important role in governing the macroeconomic outcome. It is also important to recognize in this connection that a transfer of most pre-existing capital stocks from one country to another is too costly or uneconomical, if not impossible. We need not have bothered about the inter-country movement of capital if it could only be in the form of uprooting of railway lines or dismantling existing factories and plants and shifting them to some other part of the world. The mechanism of transfer of real resources from A to B essentially involves an increase in (real) investment in B at the expense of that in A.

The above considerations suggest why the magnitude and behaviour of current account balance, indicating the net outflow of real resources from a country to the rest of the world, figure so prominently in most discussions on capital account convertibility. In order to appreciate the economic significance of the current account balance and possible routes through which international capital mobility may affect the net flow of resources in to or out of a country, it is useful to consider some elementary relations where all variables are expressed in real terms.

Remembering that gross national product (GNP):

$$= \text{Private consumption } (C) + \text{public consumption } (G)$$
$$+ \text{gross investment } (I) + \text{exports of goods and services}^{33} (X)$$
$$- \text{imports of goods and services } (M), \tag{1}$$

$$\text{saving } (S) = GNP - (C + G), \tag{2}$$

and the current account balance (CAB):

$$= \text{current receipts from the rest of the world } (X)$$
$$- \text{current payments to the rest of the world } (M), \tag{3}$$

it is useful to express CAB in alternative forms:

$$\text{CAB} = \text{increase in the country's } net \text{ asset in the rest of the world} \tag{4a}$$
$$= X - M \tag{4b}$$
$$= GNP - (C + G + I) \tag{4c}$$
$$= S - I. \tag{4d}$$

Relation (4c) implies that the current account balance reflects the excess of goods and services at the disposal of a country[34] over and above what it has used up for its own consumption or capital accumulation. This excess thus represents the net transfer of (real) consumable or investible resources from the country to the rest of the world, and the proximate source of the transfer is (a) the goods and services exported by the country less its imports (4b), or (b) the excess of the country's saving over domestic capital accumulation (4d). It is also clear that when a country acquires *net* financial claims on others, by way of additional holding of foreign bonds or other financial assets, there is a corresponding *net outflow* of goods and services to the rest of the world.[35]

The relations set forth, it is important to recognize, are accounting identities and do not indicate any causal connection between the variables. However, they do suggest that in order to appreciate the way capital account convertibility can cause net inflow or outflow of capital, it is necessary to examine the economic mechanism linking trade, investment and saving on the one hand and operation of domestic and international financial markets on the other. Indeed, not only the degree of capital account convertibility, but also fiscal and monetary policies, the exchange rate system and the trade regime in force play an important part in governing the cross-border transfer of real resources.

Note first that a net transfer of real resources can take place only if the concerned governments permit some capital movements across their national boundaries: with no capital account convertibility whatsoever, export proceeds from the rest of the world will necessarily have to equal payments on account of imports.[36] However, capital account convertibility, though necessary, is not sufficient for a reallocation of the world's investible resources on the basis of their (risk-adjusted) relative returns in different countries. Thus if convertibility on current account is strictly limited, permitting domestic investors to invest abroad and foreigners to acquire assets in the domestic sector will not be of much help in promoting the net inflow or outflow of capital. To see why, take the case of a country where initially capital account transactions are strictly forbidden and trade restrictions equate exports and imports at some exchange rate. If the country now introduces full convertibility on capital account, adopts a fully flexible exchange rate system, but the maximum permissible quantities of exports and imports are kept at the old level, there will be neither any inflow or outflow of capital after the markets adjust to the new regime. In this instance capital account convertibility has failed to effect any *net* transfer of resources across the national frontier.[37] For reaping the full benefits of liberalization on capital account, it may thus be argued, there should be full convertibility of the currency on both capital and current accounts.

3.2 Economic mechanism under unrestricted trade and capital movements

As suggested in relation (4), the transfer of resources from one country to another will be governed by decisions of economic agents relating to investment, saving, exports and imports. Apart from income levels, the most important factors affecting these decisions are exchange rates, prices of goods and services in different countries and returns on domestic and foreign financial assets. While the outcome of capital account convertibility may thus be seen to depend on interaction among several markets, the proximate impact of such convertibility is felt in markets for foreign exchange and financial assets.

In the absence of capital account convertibility the exchange rate is governed by exports, reflecting the supply side of foreign currency market, and by imports, constituting the mirror image of the demand side. Under unrestricted capital movement, however, it is the decision of domestic and foreign investors regarding holding of financial assets of different countries that plays the dominant role in currency markets and establishes a close link between exchange rates and returns on financial assets in different parts of the world. When all financial instruments (say bonds) are perfect substitutes,[38] their returns should be the same everywhere. The relation between the exchange rate and interest rates, in the absence of any premium for risk relating to the future exchange rate, is then given by:[39]

$$r = \frac{E^d}{E}(1 + r^*) - 1$$

$$\cong r^* + \frac{E^d - E}{E} \tag{5}$$

where r = domestic interest rate; r^* = foreign interest rate; E = current exchange rate (domestic currency per unit of foreign currency); and E^d = expected exchange rate after one period. When financial assets of different countries are not perfect substitutes and asset holders are not risk neutral, relation (5) needs to be modified; but given the nature of the financial instruments, investors' attitudes to risk and so on, a higher domestic interest rate will still be associated with a higher foreign interest rate, a lower E, or a higher expected exchange rate.

The relation between exchange rates and interest rates across countries lies at the heart of the mechanism through which capital mobility gives rise to a transfer of investible resources from one part of the world to another. The outcome also depends significantly on: (a) whether the economic system is Keynesian or neo-classical; and (b) whether the central bank of a country opts for a fixed or flexible exchange rate regime.

3.3   The neo-classical mechanism

The simplest to consider is the case of a small open economy where the exchange rate is fixed, price–wage flexibility generates full employment, and domestic financial assets (say bonds) are perfect substitutes of their foreign counterparts. In such an economy the net capital inflow (or outflow) equals the investment–saving gap at the interest rate prevailing in the international financial market,[40] and is brought about through adjustments in domestic prices and hence in real exchange rates and the country's trade balance. In the economy we have been considering that monetary policy is inoperative (the supply of money being demand determined), but fiscal measures will produce an immediate impact on the country's current account balance. Thus an expansionary budget raises the country's investment–saving gap, and the resulting addition to net capital inflow is induced through an increase in trade deficit due to higher prices and the consequent appreciation of the *real* exchange rate.[41]

Under a fully flexible exchange rate regime, not only investment and saving propensities but also factors directly operating in the domestic money market and in the sphere of international trade affect the book of capital inflow and outflow. The reason is that the flexibility of the exchange rate, as is evident from relation (5), permits divergence between domestic and foreign rates of interest and makes the economic system truly interdependent, even while price–wage flexibility ensures full employment everywhere. An expansionary fiscal policy still raises the country's current account deficit through an appreciation of the *real* exchange rate, but this effect is moderated somewhat by the rise in domestic interest rates.[42] Exchange rate flexibility also restores the central bank's role in influencing the course of domestic economic events. Thus enlargement of the money supply through (say) open market purchase of securities now tends to reduce the domestic interest rate, enlarge the investment–saving gap and raise the trade deficit through an appreciation of the (nominal as also the real) exchange rate. Indeed, since substitutability among financial assets of different countries is far from perfect, there can be considerable differences in interest rates across countries even when a fixed exchange rate system is in force. In this case, as may be easily verified, the mechanism of international capital movement will be similar to the one just considered.

3.4 Capital mobility in a Keynesian world

When production is demand constrained, changes in income, apart from those in interest rates or exchange rates, act as an important factor behind transfer of resources from one country to another. It is not very difficult to see that in this case also under a fixed exchange rate regime an expansionary fiscal policy[43] induces a rise in capital inflow, as the trade balance falls along with an increase in income. However, since there is no change in either the nominal or real exchange rate,[44] the entire adjustment in the country's current account balance takes place through the rise in income and the consequent increase in trade deficit.

When the exchange rate is flexible, currency appreciation or depreciation also plays a major role in affecting the direction and scale of cross-border resource transfer. Indeed, given an initial shortfall of the actual from the full employment output, a fiscal stimulus aimed at closing the gap will generate a larger current account deficit (than under the fixed exchange regime) in view of the currency appreciation associated with enlargement of income.[45] In this case there is no change in either the nominal or the real exchange rate,[46] and the entire impact on the current account balance operates through the increase in income and the consequent widening of the import–export (and investment–saving[47]) gap in the economy. However, the impact of an expansionary monetary policy on the net inflow of foreign capital is uncertain. Such a policy raises GDP, reduces domestic interest rates and effects a depreciation of the country's currency. Thus while expansion of income tends to enlarge the trade deficit, the impact of the exchange rate depreciation is in the opposite direction. The trade balance may thus move either way.[48]

4. ON THE NEED FOR CONTROLLING CAPITAL FLOWS

The foregoing analysis of inter-country transfer of resources abstracts from a number of real world factors; but the framework linking the financial and real sectors enables us to appreciate how the actual outcome under capital mobility may differ significantly from the mainstream conclusions discussed in section 2. It is important to identify the major sources of this departure, both for putting the current debate on capital account convertibility in its proper perspective and to draw policy conclusions in the context of the structural features and economic conditions of the countries concerned.

The traditional results relating to the mutually beneficial effects of international capital movements subsume that:

- resources are fully employed everywhere;
- capital flows themselves do not stand in the way of attaining full employment or macroeconomic stability; and
- the transfer of capital from one country to another is governed by long-term returns on investment in different countries.

Returns on assets as well as their riskiness, as perceived by both domestic and international investors, vary significantly with the degree of capacity utilization of a country. Under conditions of demand deficiency, expected profitability of investment tends to be low and financial instruments issued by domestic producers attract high risk premia.[49] The result is generally a capital outflow to the rest of the world, something which may not be warranted by the country's technical know-how and resource endowment. Similarly, capital inflows induced by an unsustainable boom produce gross distortions in the allocation of the world's investible resources. Maintenance of full employment and macroeconomic stability thus constitutes an important prerequisite for reaping the benefits of a globalized capital market.

4.1 Macrostabilization with capital account convertibility

The problem, however, is that international capital movements make macrostabilization difficult by: (a) making the domestic economy vulnerable to external shocks; and (b) robbing the fiscal or monetary authorities of much of their policy autonomy. Even without any capital account convertibility, impulses occurring in the rest of the world are transmitted to a country through changes in its demand for exports or supply of imports. Under a globalized capital market external turmoil buffets an economy through not only trading but financial links as well, as domestic and foreign investors try to shift their funds into or out of the country. In other words, in the absence of capital movements external factors can influence a country's interest rates, share prices or the exchange rate only through markets for exportables and importables. But when financial assets can be easily transferred from one part of the world to another, any development, actual or expected, that affects money and capital markets elsewhere will have an immediate impact on domestic financial markets also. Remembering that these markets are much more volatile than commodity and labour markets, it is not very difficult to appreciate why the frequency and magnitude of external shocks tend to increase manifold when a country removes all restrictions on capital movements.[50]

Globalization of financial markets also makes attainment of macroeconomic balance much more difficult for individual nations. The first source of difficulty lies in informational problems and increased uncertainty. The policy makers now have to gather a much wider range of data and keep track of the evolving scenario in both the domestic and international economy. Even when the requisite machinery for collection and processing of all relevant information has been put in place, it is by no means simple to assess the emerging trend of crucial variables because: (a) so many factors, including future policies of other countries, affect the outcome; and (b) financial markets are driven by investors' expectations and these are characterized more often than not by herd behaviour and egregious exuberance or under pessimism.[51]

The second and no less serious difficulty arises from the fact that under unrestricted flow of funds across countries, the traditional instruments for countering anti-cyclical tendencies in the system lose much of their cutting edge. Since the contributions of Mundell (1963) and Fleming (1962) economists have been aware of how full capital account convertibility in a fixed exchange rate regime robs the central bank of its policy autonomy.[52] The burden of maintaining full employment is thus to be borne primarily by fiscal authorities. Budgetary policies are, however, difficult to change and put into operation quickly, in response to new developments in domestic and international spheres. Again, the impact of such policies, even when properly implemented, may not be very significant because of factors similar to those giving rise to the Ricardian equivalence.[53] The problem becomes particularly serious in an open economy when the source of macroeconomic instability originates on the trading front. To see why, consider the case where the demand for the country's exports suffers a setback, setting a negative foreign trade multiplier in motion. With no change in the fiscal stance, the budget as well as the current account deficit will go up along with the fall in GDP and employment.[54] An increase in government expenditure or reduction in tax rates, if successful in restoring full employment, would make these two deficits larger. However, against this increased liability of the government and the country, no additional income earning assets have been created in order to service the larger debt in the future. Rational households and firms may thus harbour serious doubts regarding the sustainability of such deficits, reduce their current consumption and investment demand, and neutralize, partially or wholly, the expansionary impact of fiscal instruments.

The solution to the policy problem does not lie in the adoption of a flexible exchange rate system either. Under such a system the central bank can, to be sure, affect the domestic interest rate through changes in money supply. The effects of monetary policies on output and employment, it may also be noted, are transmitted through both interest rates and the exchange rate, and the two effects operate in the same direction.[55] However, fiscal policies now lose much of their potency as an anti-cyclical device.[56] There are also serious limits to the central bank's power to maintain macroeconomic balance in a rapidly changing international environment.

The first problem is Keynesian and arises from the low interest-elasticity of aggregate demand and the difficulty of effecting significant changes in interest rates.[57] Nor is the impact of monetary policy through the exchange rate quite unambiguous or likely to be significant. Thus when currency depreciation constitutes the main source of the expansionary impact of a cheap money policy, the country is in effect exporting unemployment to its trading partners and may invite their retaliatory action. Again, when banks and firms have borrowed in the international market, a sharp fall in the exchange rate puts them in serious financial troubles and negates thereby the effect operating through the trade balance. Finally, under a globalized capital market there is an inherent tendency for market forces to generate large fluctuations in exchange rates and to heighten the uncertainty faced by traders as also by producers and firms having significant external exposure in their balance sheets. Hence all central banks, even when they have not opted for a pegged exchange rate system, find it necessary to keep day-to-day exchange rate variations within a narrow band and permit only gradual upward or downward adjustment of the rate over time. The central bank, constrained by such exchange rate objectives,[58] may not thus on its own be able to moderate cyclical tendencies in the real sector.

4.2 Capital mobility under full employment: some disquieting characteristics

Even with full employment of resources everywhere, integration of global capital markets may not be welfare improving. For one thing, unhindered capital movements tend to promote inequality in both the intra- and inter-country distribution of income. Since the mobility of labour is highly restricted, but funds can easily flow across national frontiers, not only is it extremely difficult to tax capital, but also very often governments compete with each other to provide tax concessions and various forms of direct and indirect subsidies in order to retain or attract capital, domestic or foreign.

Apart from the fact that this is nothing but a zero-sum game and grossly distorts the allocation of world's investible funds among nations, for discharging their basic responsibilities the governments are also forced to rely on heavier taxes on labourers. Hence the tendency for the post-tax distribution of income to move against workers in all countries.

Again, contrary to the orthodox conclusion, capital mobility very often favours developed countries at the expense of the poorer nations. The first source of this bias arises from the substantial foreign exchange reserves central banks need to maintain for smoothing out large fluctuations in exchange rates, induced under full capital account convertibility. Forex reserves, let us remember, are a form of loan to other nations. Since these reserves are held in the form of 'vehicle' currency,[59] financial assets, supplied by countries like the US and Germany, the accumulation of foreign exchange reserves by central banks has resulted in a significant resource transfer to these countries from the rest of the world. Indeed, the relatively high liquidity enjoyed by the US financial assets has also tilted private capital flows heavily in favour of these assets. No wonder then that the richest nation of the world is also the most heavily indebted one, and in spite of zero or negative saving, the US has been able to sustain a fairly decent rate of capital accumulation.

There are other and more crucial respects in which the neo-classical perception relating to the effect of capital movement appears to be flawed. We have indicated how financial globalization may cause an outflow of investible resources from poorer parts of the world.

It may perhaps be argued that, given the existing differences in inter-country resource endowments, including those in physical, financial and administrative infrastructure, transfer of capital from the poorer to the richer nations is in perfect accord with the principles of allocative efficiency and enlarges the national income of both sets of countries. However, such a view ignores some crucial elements of the problem, apart from the adverse impact on workers in less developed countries. The most important of these elements are scale economies, learning by doing and cumulative process of growth or decay of nations. In the context of the operation of such factors it is not very difficult to appreciate why globalization of capital markets can trigger off a decline of backward economies, as the (relative) fall in their GDP makes them still less attractive to international investors, and removal of infrastructural and related constraints becomes increasingly difficult. Before loosening capital controls, the poorer countries thus need to put their own house in order and develop facilities in the absence of which incentives to invest will remain abysmally low.

The allocative inefficiency of cross-border capital movements considered above is due primarily to historical legacies standing in the way of optimal deployment of global resources from a longer-term perspective. Experience of the world economy over the last two decades has brought to light other serious limitations of market-driven capital flows, especially to emerging economies which have broken through the vicious circle of underdevelopment and started enjoying sustained growth. The huge inflow of foreign funds these countries attracted gave rise to the 'moral hazard' problem[60] and made the countries highly vulnerable to shocks, both domestic and external.

The bias in favour of high risk ventures, reflecting the moral hazard problem, becomes large when firms rely primarily on loans for financing their investment. The problem arises even for domestic debts, but becomes qualitatively different and much more serious when firms and banks borrow from the rest of the world. Note first that the lenders' costs on account of gathering the relevant information and monitoring the operation of foreign firms are much larger than in the case of domestic firms. Second, when banks or financial intermediaries like mutual funds or pension funds distribute their portfolio among a large number of firms in several countries, there is little incentive for fund managers to assess the credit worthiness of individual borrowers. Hence the close connection between the integration of global financial markets and the aggravation of the moral hazard problem.

Moral hazard associated with capital inflows can cost an economy dear, both directly and indirectly. The direct cost arises from distortions in choice of investments, as firms go in for high risk projects even if their expected yields are relatively low. Considerably more important is the indirect cost due to increased susceptibility of the country to banking and currency turmoil. Distortions in the pattern of investment under moral hazard, let us note, raise the probability of default or bankruptcy and hence of a financial crisis through a 'run' on banks. In the absence of capital account convertibility such crises may be resolved fairly quickly through central bank intervention. However, when the country is burdened with substantial external liabilities and no capital controls are in place, default on foreign debts, even though partial, may seriously undermine the confidence of international investors and push the country into a currency crisis. It is for this reason that everybody recognizes the need for strengthening the financial system in general and overcoming moral hazard in particular, before a country liberalizes the capital account of its balance of payments.

4.3 Capital flows and currency crisis: some general observations

Resolution of the moral hazard problem is necessary, but not sufficient for preventing currency crisis. Failure of some business ventures or of banks is a normal economic phenomenon even in the absence of moral hazard. When capital movements are highly restricted and the country does not have any significant external liability, such failures or defaults do not end up in a currency crisis. Again the central bank, acting as the lender of last resort and ensuring the supply of adequate liquidity in the system, can contain the deleterious impact of bankruptcies of some producers or bankers on the rest of the economy. However, such damage control exercise becomes largely ineffective when capital can move freely across the national frontiers and the country is already burdened with substantial liabilities to the rest of the world.

Note first that even when the country does not have any significant foreign liability, flight of domestic capital due to banking troubles or corporate default can trigger off a currency crisis. Indebtedness to the rest of the world magnifies the problem since: (a) currency depreciation produces a negative impact on the balance sheets of domestic entities having external debts; (b) foreign investors are much less informed and hence tend to over-react to adverse developments; and (c) it is the foreign, and not so much the domestic investors, who have to be extremely wary of exchange rate movements.[61] Hence the higher probability of currency crisis with larger capital inflows, other things remaining the same.

An immediate policy implication of the above is the need for controlling capital inflows, taking account of their benefits and costs. It is important to distinguish between two categories of capital controls, the first amounting to monopolistic exploitations, the second purported to undo the negative externality characterizing the market-driven outcome in the system.

When a country is relatively 'large', the marginal cost of borrowing from the international market is higher to the country than to its individual borrowers. The cost–benefit calculus then suggests that the government should restrict the scale of capital inflow in order to maximize net gains to the country.[62] In this case it is important to recognize that not only is the gain to the country at the expense of foreign lenders, but such restrictions reduce *aggregate* benefits and hence are distortionary from the global viewpoint (Box 8.2).

The economic rationale of the second type of control lies in the fact that individual borrowers do not take into account the greater risk of currency crisis associated with larger external indebtedness. The implication is that there is a divergence between the social and private cost of borrowing from abroad. In this case a tax on capital inflow for eliminating the gap is optimal for the country as well as for the world as a whole (Box 8.2).

Box 8.2   The case for capital controls: A pedagogic exposition

Consider the case where a country is 'large' in the international capital market, but its individual borrowers are not. In the figure below, *MR* denotes the marginal returns on domestic investment financed through borrowing from abroad,[69] and hence represents the country's demand for foreign loans at different rates of interest. The 'large' country assumption implies that the supply of foreign loans, *CB*, is upward rising. With no capital control whatsoever, the country borrows I_0 from external sources at r_0 rate of interest. Note however that at I_0 amount of capital inflow, the marginal cost of borrowing to the country as a whole is c_0, but that to an individual borrower only r_0, remembering that *CB* is the country's average cost curve of borrowing, while the marginal cost curve is given by *MCB*. The *net* gain to the country from foreign capital inflow is maximized when the country borrows *I** rather than I_0. Hence the case for limiting the scale of foreign borrowing below what would obtain under free market equilibrium.

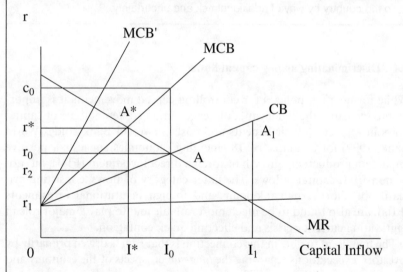

Note, however, that in this case the gains from capital controls are secured through the country's monopsony power and hence such controls are distortionary from the global viewpoint. The reason lies in the fact that *CB* represents the marginal returns on investment elsewhere. Hence at *A**, the marginal return on investment in the rest of the world is r_2, but that on domestic investment *r**. Thus global production is less at *A** than at A, implying that in this instance capital controls violate the Pareto optimality conditions.

Consider now the second case where the country is small and its investors can borrow from the international capital market at r_1 rate of interest. However, larger external borrowing requires the central bank to hold larger foreign exchange reserves, and raises the probability of financial turmoil and adds to disruption in the real sector. The implication is that the *marginal* cost of foreign borrowing is not downward sloping, but upward rising (say *CB*). Note that since individual borrowers can borrow at r_1, absence of any control will push foreign borrowing to I_1, where the marginal cost of such borrowing (at I_1A_1) exceeds r_1. Optimality then requires OI_0 amount of capital inflow.

The important point to note in the second case is that, here the reduction in capital control is optimal from both the national and global viewpoint. The reason is that *CB* is the marginal cost of capital inflow to the country and is upward rising due to: (a) the loss (here fixed at r_1) of withdrawal of investment from the rest of the world; and (b) the marginal cost to the country by way of additional risk and uncertainty.

4.4 Discriminating among capital flows

While formulating policies for controlling capital movements it is important to recognize the significant differences among different types of capital flows in respect of their benefits and costs. A World Bank study (World Bank, 1999) for a sample of 18 emerging economies suggests a positive impact on productivity growth of foreign direct investment (FDI), but not of non-FDI, capital inflows. The latter category of flows, consisting primarily of short-term bank loans and foreign institutional investments (FIIs), are also found to be much more volatile and to play a major role in aggravating currency crisis and effecting quick contagion.

The first point to note in this connection is that FDI is driven primarily by investors' expectations regarding the *long-run* prospects of the economy and its various sectors. It is also difficult for such investors to exit from an enterprise in which they have acquired controlling interest. Finally, FDI, and not FII or bank loans, constitutes the principal means of transfer of knowledge – relating to technology, management and so on – from one country to another. No wonder then that FDI tends to crowd in further investment, contributes to productivity growth and remains relatively unaffected amidst financial turmoil or cyclical fluctuations.

Non-FDI capital flows, let us recall, are supposed to confer substantial benefit through consumption smoothing, reduction of risk and enhanced average yield on investment. On all these counts the effects have, however, actually been the reverse: capital inflows into developing countries have been pro-cyclical;[63] have been associated with heightened financial turbulence;[64] and have had little, if not negative, impact on output growth. The reason for such perverse effects may be traced primarily to wild swings in short-term expectations, herd behaviour of investors and negligible costs of transferring funds from one country to another. Given the fixed and not-too-insignificant cost of gathering information regarding economic fundamentals of a country or viability of a firm and the lengthy menu of assets available to choose from with integration of world financial markets, it is economical for an individual investor to widely diversify his portfolio without any serious scrutiny of the economy- and enterprise-specific factors affecting the riskiness and expected returns of different options. High liquidity of financial assets and low cost of switching among them also imply that flow of funds from one country to another will be driven primarily by expectations relating to *short-term* movements[65] in exchange rates, interest rates and share prices. The problem, however, is that since investors are generally ill-informed, they tend to be swayed by ephemeral developments, financial markets display herd behaviour and expectations become self-fulfilling. It is thus not very difficult to see why non-FDI capital flows are predominantly pro-cyclical or why extensive liberalization of capital account transactions throughout the world has been associated with increasing incidence of currency crisis and quick contagion, even though economic fundamentals of some afflicted economies were quite strong.

Finally, we need to examine whether central bank intervention can moderate the deleterious impact of non-FDI flows and enable countries to enjoy the benefits of capital mobility. For this purpose the central bank has to stabilize the foreign currency market, but keep the exchange rate close to its long-term equilibrium trajectory. However, globalization of financial markets severely limits the central bank's ability to prevent large deviations of the actual from the equilibrium exchange rate, or to ward off speculative attacks against currencies.

Given the flimsy basis of short-term expectations and the predominance of herd behaviour, undue panic or exuberance is quite normal in currency markets. It is not too difficult for a central bank to take care of surges of capital inflow: it can prevent a sharp appreciation of the exchange rate by buying the foreign against domestic currency, and neutralizing the associated expansionary impact on money supply through open market sale of securities. However, in case of a capital flight, foreign exchange reserves of the central bank may be quite inadequate to keep the exchange rate stable and avert a currency turmoil.

The implication is that, in order to avoid a currency crisis incorporating non-FDI capital flows, a central bank has to keep 'adequate' foreign exchange reserves. When short-term flows dominate international capital movements, the reserves need to be correspondingly large. Since a major part of non-FDI inflows has thus to be kept in the form of liquid foreign assets, the net contribution of such inflows to the country's national income or economic welfare generally turns out to be negative, especially when it is recognized that large reserves are no guarantee against currency crises and that central bank measures to avert a crisis, even when successful, involve heavy cost to the economy in terms of lost employment and output. The behaviour of world currency markets in recent years has suggested how even the Bank of Japan and other central banks with substantial foreign exchange reserves have failed to prevent large swings in their exchange rates and preserve macroeconomic stability. One reason for this failure lies in the enormous amount of foreign exchange transactions in relation to foreign exchange reserves an individual country can manage to hold. The disproportionality between the two magnitudes is indicated by the fact that the daily volume of foreign-currency trading was over $2 trillion at the beginning of the new millennium, but the *combined* forex reserves of rich countries amounted to only $1.6 trillion. Under such a scenario piling up foreign exchange reserves, especially by emerging economies, adds to their cost, but little improvement in their ability to ward off speculative attacks against currencies. The case for controlling non-FDI capital flows thus appears quite open and shut, though there can be serious differences of opinion regarding the degree of control and the type of measures required in this context.

5. SUMMARY AND CONCLUSIONS

1. The last quarter of the twentieth century was characterized by a rapid integration of the world's financial markets, as first the developed and then the developing countries increasingly liberalized transactions on the capital account of their balance of payments. However, surges of international capital flows during this period were also associated with a substantial increase in the incidence of banking and currency crises, especially in emerging market economies. In the context of the Asian crisis in particular economists have been wondering whether the costs of financial globalization outweigh its benefits, and have been searching for optimum control on capital movements.

2. Mainstream economics suggests different routes through which unrestricted flow of funds across the world becomes mutually beneficial for

both capital exporting and capital importing countries. Apart from the gains due to optimal allocation of the world's investible resources, countries can derive substantial benefits by way of inter-temporal consumption smoothing; reduction of risk through cross-holding of assets; and hence flow of funds to investment packages having higher expected returns along with lower risk.[66] Perhaps the most important benefit arises through diffusion of knowledge and technology and the resulting cumulative advancement of all economies, both emerging and emerged.

3.   Financial globalization implies that the flow of funds from one country to another is driven by current and expected share prices, interest rates and exchange rates. The result is a close connection among prices in financial markets in different parts of the world.

4.   An important fall-out of such close connection among financial markets is the serious difficulty national governments face in maintaining full employment or effecting macro-stabilization. The reason lies in: (a) the frequent and large shocks to which countries become subject; and (b) relative ineffectiveness of fiscal and monetary policies in attaining the desired objectives. Exchange rate fluctuations and pronounced pro-cyclicity of capital inflows, especially in developing countries, suggest that globalization of financial markets hinders rather than helps inter-temporal consumption smoothing.

5.   Even when countries manage to maintain full employment, capital mobility tends to: (a) promote inequality in both intra- and inter-country distribution of income; (b) cause serious moral hazard problems by way of diverting investment to ventures with high risk but low expected rate of return; and (c) emit wrong signals to economic agents regarding the long-term factors operating in the system.

6.   Perhaps the most important cost of capital mobility arises from currency crisis to which countries become prone. Indeed, given the extraordinarily large volume of global foreign exchange transactions and the self-fulfilling nature of expectations relating to currency and share prices, there is no adequate defence against speculative attack against a country's currency. However, the volatility of the currency market is due not to capital flows on account of FDI, but to inter-bank loans and FIIs. Hence arises the need to exercise control over the latter category of capital movements in order to remove the most important source of distortion under a globalized financial system.

NOTES

1. Research support for the work reported in this chapter was provided by ICRA.
2. Between 1973 and 1982, the aggregate external debt of non-oil producing developing countries went up by more than 450 per cent, from $130 billion to $600 billion. Again, while the annual average net capital flows to developing countries (excluding changes in reserves) was a little less than $50 billion during 1984–98, the average nearly trebled to $146 billion over 1990–96, with the flows reaching their peak at $194 billion in 1996 before subsiding, in the wake of the Asian crisis, to $129 billion in 1997 and $105 billion in 1998. See IMF (1983, 1998).
3. The marginalization of such loans in recent times is indicated by the fact that in 1996 out of a total net capital inflow of $194 billion in developing countries, official sources accounted for only $2.6 billion (IMF, 1998a).
4. The general perception was that not only had official aid and loans to LDCs been given in many cases on non-economic grounds, but bureaucratic corruption and inefficiency also led quite often to substantial seepage from, or wasteful use of, these funds.
5. Consisting of Thailand, Malaysia, Indonesia, the Philippines and Korea.
6. See, for example, Jagadish Bhagwati (1998) and Joseph Stiglitz (1998).
7. In the early 1990s developed countries like Britain, Norway, Sweden and Finland also suffered from financial turmoil.
8. See Rakshit (1997) for an analysis of the contagion effects of the Thai crisis. Rakshit (1999) indicates how the Russian financial troubles impacted on the Brazilian economy and ultimately forced the Central Bank of Brazil (in mid January 1999) to let the real float against dollar and other currencies.
9. Since production goes down by 100 units in the former, but rises by 150 units in the latter.
10. Which is nothing but GDP less net factor income from abroad. Thus if a country's GDP is 100, but interest or profit on foreign capital amounts to 20 units, the country's national income will be 80 units. For a capital exporting country the national income would be its GDP *plus* income from investments abroad.
11. Export of capital leads to a lower capital–labour ratio and hence raises the marginal productivity of capital, but reduces that of labour. The results on wages and rentals are the opposite in the capital importing country.
12. Even in capital exporting countries everybody *could* gain through a system of taxes-cum-transfers.
13. In the absence of such a differential, gains from capital mobility are due entirely to the initial inter-country difference in marginal productivity of capital. Note that, in Box 8.1, with capital inflow from B to A, marginal productivity of capital declines along MP_a, signifying that foreign investment does not cause any improvement in factor productivity in the domestic sector.
14. Alternatively, if domestic firms fail to catch up with their foreign counterparts, competition will ensure that domestically owned capital is employed in foreign-owned (or managed) firms. Note also that the direction of capital movement depends not so much on the initial difference between the actual returns on capital in the two countries, but on the gap in their *potential* returns. Thus the actual return on capital in LDCs may be lower than that in developed countries; however, if the potential return on foreign investment backed by superior technology is higher in LDCs, they will enjoy capital inflow.
15. Gross outflow of capital refers to a country's investment (or acquisition of assets) abroad, while net outflow is nothing but gross outflow less the amount foreigners invest in the domestic economy. Operation of factors considered in the previous subsection would make a country either a lender (or investor) or a borrower in the international capital market, but not both.
16. In 1996, foreigners invested a whopping $547.6 billion in the US, but the US investment abroad was not insignificant either, and amounted to $352.4 billion (IMF, 1997, p. 5).
17. For adoption of superior technology.
18. So that the major part of the surplus is siphoned off by gangsters or bureaucrats or pol-

iticians. What is no less important, the aggregate surplus itself is reduced through distortions in the functioning of firms. It is interesting to note that when there are a number of illegal claimants on a firm's surplus or the clout of the dominant claimants is expected to be short-lived, profitability of investment can become negative, with extortions killing off the goose that lays the golden egg.

19. While lack of effective demand reduces the average return on capital over its life time, pronounced cyclicity makes the return highly variable and acts as a disincentive to invest.

20. It may also be noted that superiority of a country's producers in a particular industry is generally overall and does not extend to *all* operations, technical or managerial, in running the enterprise. Hence when foreign and domestic firms operate side by side in the same line of business, they may learn from each other and enjoy rapid advancement in their productivity.

21. For a rigorous analysis see Obstfeld and Rogoff (1996).

22. Welfare gains from international consumption loans follow from the law of diminishing marginal utility. The law implies that a consumer enjoys larger utilities from a given aggregate level of consumption if it is more evenly distributed over time. Without any time preference, the maximum utility is attained when consumption is the same in all periods. If the consumer prefers current to future consumption, the inter-temporal distribution of consumption is optimal when the marginal utility from future consumption, discounted by the subjective rate of time preference, equals the marginal utility from current consumption. Under a perfectly functioning loan market the inter-temporal distribution of goods consumed will be such that the subjective rate of time preference of all consumers equals the (common) rate of interest and there is no further scope of mutually beneficial borrowing and lending. The logic applies to international consumption loans as well.

23. Especially for small economies.

24. As given by (say) the variance of the returns. The greater is the dispersion of probable returns around their mean or average value, the larger will be the value of the variance and the investment considered more risky.

25. Through purchase and sales in the international capital market.

26. The enormous significance of even marginal changes in growth rates may be appreciated from the following example. Between 1870 and 1990 a real per capita GDP growth of 1.75 per cent per annum raised the US per capita income by a factor of 8.1. Were the annual growth rate less by 1 percentage point, the per capita GDP in 1990 would have been only 2.5 times the value in 1870 and only 30 per cent of the actual value in 1990 (Barro and Sala-i-Martin, 1995).

27. The result is easily generalized. Given the investment options and probability distribution of their returns, an optimum distribution of funds among various options enables an asset holder to attain some highest possible expected return corresponding to a given variance of yields on the aggregate funds. The relationship between the highest possible expected returns corresponding to different degrees of risk (as denoted by the variance) is a rising one: higher expected returns can be obtained only by holding more risky assets at the expense of less risky ones. Enlargement of investment options shifts this relationship, raising the maximum attainable return at each degree of risk. Thus given the degree of risk aversion on the part of asset holders, there will be a shift towards investments with higher expected returns, as possibilities of wider diversification of funds reduce the risk on a portfolio with high-yield investments.

28. Recall the enormous power of compounding over long periods, as illustrated in note 26.

29. Government expenditure financed through printing notes or an increase in reserve money.

30. Between the onset of the First World War (1914) and the early 1970s, movement of capital between nations, especially on private account, remained severely limited. It is also worth noting that the Bretton Woods agreement set current, but not capital, account convertibility as the goal for trading nations in the post Second World War era.

31. While Obstfeld (1995) estimates the potential gain through this route to be significant, the conclusion is not supported by empirical estimates of Tesar (1995), and Levine and Zervos (1998).

32. Even when the agent purchases a house or a factory, the acquisition does not *by itself* involve transfer of physical resources from A to B.

33. Includes factor incomes from abroad.

34. That is, the amount the country can consume or invest *without borrowing* from, or raising its liability to, the rest of the world.

35. This correspondence does not, however, hold at the level of an individual economic agent or between any two countries: it is possible for (say) Singapore to use its net export earnings from the EU to invest in the US bond market.

36. Strictly speaking, absence of net transfer also implies no official aid as also no change in net foreign exchange reserves of the central bank.

37. Even though the net transfer is zero, there could be considerable amounts of cross-holding of assets among domestic and foreign economic agents under the new regime.

38. This also implies that riskiness is also the same for all bonds.

39. Note that the l.h.s. equals return on holding domestic bond and the r.h.s. the yield on one unit of domestic currency invested abroad for one period (and repatriated thereafter). In the second step on r.h.s. we have ignored $r^* \left[\dfrac{E^d - E}{E} \right]$ in view of its quantitative insignificance.

40. And the full employment income of the economy. Note that under the fixed exchange rate system $r = r^*$ (in relation (5)), and this, together with the full employment income, gives the investment–saving gap.

41. This is the major reason why the IMF insists on a cutback on fiscal deficit when countries seek its financial support in order to tide over their balance of payments difficulties.

42. Which reduces the investment–saving gap obtaining under the new equilibrium configuration.

43. Or enlargement of the investment–saving gap due to operation of some autonomous factors.

44. Remembering that commodity prices are sticky in a Keynesian set-up.

45. Note that given the domestic money supply, a higher income tends to raise domestic interest rates, causes an inflow of foreign funds, and results in an appreciation of the country's currency until equation (5) is restored.

46. Remembering that under a Keynesian set-up, prices do not change significantly in response to variations in GDP.

47. Note that an expansionary fiscal policy, at the initial income and interest rates, raises the investment–saving gap. The increase in income and interest rates under the new equilibrium reduces the gap, but cannot eliminate it altogether.

48. Note, however, that when monetary rather than fiscal expansion is used to effect *a given increase in the GDP level*, the extent of capital inflow will be less. The reason is that, interest rates (instead of going up, as happens under fiscal expansion) tend to go down so that there is a larger depreciation of domestic currency, *à la* equation (5).

49. In terms of equation (5), the implication of higher risk premium is that with given E, E^d and r^*, the domestic interest rate needs to be higher in order to induce investors to hold the country's financial assets.

50. We have already noted how rapid development of global financial markets since the mid 1970s have been associated with rising incidence of banking and currency turmoil.

51. We shall take up the problem later in our discussion of the link between capital mobility and currency crisis.

52. Recall from equation (5) that in such a regime there is no scope for a policy-engineered change in r when the size of the domestic financial market is small and bonds of different countries are perfect substitutes. When the two conditions are not satisfied, r can differ from r^*, but monetary instruments still remain attenuated.

53. The theorem states that when private economic agents expect the government to vary its tax collections over time in order to satisfy the inter-temporal budget constraint, tax financed and loan financed government expenditure will be equivalent in their impact on current (aggregate) demand for goods and services.

54. The fall in income reduces imports and moderates thereby the rise in trade or current

account deficit; but the adjustment in income cannot reverse the *direction* of change in the initial deficit.

55. Thus the expansionary impact of an increase in money supply will be due to a simultaneous fall in interest rates and the exchange rate.

56. Thus a budgetary expansion, through an increase in domestic interest rates, attracts foreign funds and induces an appreciation of the country's currency. The result is a worsening of the trade balance and a downward thrust on output and employment. In the Mundell–Fleming framework, the trade-balance effect will completely neutralize the expansionary impact of budgetary policies.

57. Even when the economy is not caught in the liquidity trap.

58. We shall presently discuss how international capital flows make attainment of these objectives extremely difficult.

59. That is, currencies in terms of which external accounts are settled and transactions take place. By far the overwhelming part of forex reserves are held in terms of dollars, though some European countries found it useful to hold marks (before the introduction of the Euro).

60. See Stiglitz and Weiss (1981) and Rakshit (1998). The basic factors giving rise to moral hazard are: (a) lenders' lack of adequate information regarding prospects of proposed ventures; and (b) higher expected yield from riskier investment on *equity capital* than that on total funds employed. The reason lies in the fact that if the (high risk) project fails, stock holders share the loss with the lenders; but in case the project succeeds, not only will the operating surplus be very large, but the entire amount less the prestipulated interest will accrue to the owners. The implication is that the larger the debt–equity ratio of a firm, the greater will be its incentive to undertake riskier ventures.

61. Remembering that what matters for investors is the real rate of return and this equals the nominal rate of return in terms of their *national currency* less the rate of inflation prevailing in their own country.

62. This is similar to the 'optimum tariff' argument relating to external trade.

63. So that the gap between the boom-time and bust-time consumption was widened rather than narrowed.

64. A World Bank (1999) study, based on the experience of a large number of emerging economies in general and that of Argentina, Mexico and Hungary in particular, notes: 'FDI is far less volatile and less subject to reversals. It even continues to increase in downturns. Non-FDI private-to-private flows, in contrast, are much more volatile. Portfolio equity most closely resembles FDI, but is more volatile. Debt portfolio investment (including private-to-public) is volatile and intensifies the severity of financial crises. Non-FDI and debt portfolio flows increase in the years just before a crisis, then reverse sharply after the crisis occurs. These features magnify boom–bust cycles and, hence, the severity of financial crises in small, financially open developing countries.'

65. Even investors aware of long-term fundamentals find it worth their while to 'outguess the market' in respect of short-term price movements (Keynes, 1936).

66. Compared with the packages chosen in the absence of capital account convertibility.

67. While drawing MP_a and MP_b we have assumed that international trade is perfectly free. Were all assumptions of the text-book model of trade satisfied, there would have been no differences in the return on capital in the two countries, and international capital movements would have lost their main *raison d'être*: mobility of goods would have acted as a perfect substitute for mobility of factors. However, transport costs, inter-country difference in technical know-how or acute dissimilarities in resource endowments generally stand in the way of factor price equalization across countries. Hence arises the need for factor mobility in order to attain allocative efficiency at the global level.

68. Though in any country gains outweigh the losses in the aggregate. The implication is that gainers can overcompensate the losers or everybody in the economy could be made better off with an appropriate tax-cum-transfer system (provided the system is costless).

69. In other words, MR denotes the (gross) marginal return on foreign borrowing, given the level of domestic investment financed from internal sources.

REFERENCES

Alesina, A., V. Grilli and G.M. Milesi-Ferretti (1994), 'The Political Economy of Capital Controls', in L. Leidermand and A. Rozin (eds), *Capital Mobility: Impact on Consumption and Growth*, New York: Cambridge University Press.

Barro, R.J. and X. Sala-i-Martin (1995), *Economic Growth*, New York: McGraw-Hill.

Bhagwati, J. (1998), 'The Capital Myth: The Difference between Trade in Widgets and Dollars', *Foreign Affairs*, May/June.

Carrasquilla, A. (1998), 'On Regulating Capital Account Transactions', *mimeo*, Inter-American Development Bank.

Fleming, J.M. (1962), 'Domestic Financial Policies under Fixed and under Flexible Exchange Rates', *IMF Staff Papers*, March.

International Monetary Fund (1983), *World Economic Outlook*, Washington, DC, October.

International Monetary Fund (1997), *International Capital Movements: Developments, Prospects and Key Policy Issues*, November.

International Monetary Fund (1998), *International Capital Markets: Developments, Prospects and Key Policy Issues*, September.

Keynes, J.M. (1936), *The General Theory of Employment, Interest and Money*, London: Macmillan.

Levine, R. and S. Zervos (1998), 'Stock Market, Banks and Economic Growth', *American Economic Review*, **88** (3), June.

Mundell, R.A. (1963), 'Capital Mobility and Stabilization Policy under Fixed and Flexible Exchange Rates', *Canadian Journal of Economics and Political Science*, November.

Obstfeld, M. (1995), 'Risk-Taking, Global Diversification and Growth', *American Economic Review*, **84** (5), 1310–29.

Obstfeld, M. and K. Rogoff (1996), *Foundations of International Macroeconomics*, Cambridge, Massachusetts: MIT Press.

Rakshit, M. (1997), 'Crisis, Contagion and Crash: Asian Currency Turmoil', *Money and Finance*, No. 4, December.

Rakshit, M. (1998), 'Financial Fragility: Sources and Remedies, Part I', *Money and Finance*, No. 7, October–December.

Rakshit, M. (1999), 'Currency Crisis in Brazil', *Money and Finance*, No. 10, July–September.

Razin, A. and C. Yuen (1994), 'Convergence in Growth Rates: A Quantitative Assessment of the Role of Capital Mobility and International Taxation', in L. Luiduman and A. Razin (eds), *Capital Mobility: The Impact on Consumption, Investment and Growth*, New York: Cambridge University Press.

Rodrik, D. (1997), *Has Globalization Gone Too Far?*, Washington, DC: Institute for International Economics.

Rodrik, D. (1998), 'Who Needs Capital-Account Convertibility?', *Princeton Essays in International Finance*, Princeton University: Department of Economics, International Finance Section.

Stiglitz, J.E. (1998), 'The East Asian Crisis and Its Implications for India', Commemorative Lecture, New Delhi.

Stiglitz, J.E. and A. Weiss (1981), 'Credit Rationing in Markets with Imperfect Information', *American Economic Review*, **71** (3), 393–410.

Tesar, L.L. (1995), 'Evaluating the Gains from International Risksharing', *Carnegie–Rochester Conference Series on Public Policy*, Amsterdam: North-Holland.
World Bank (1999), *Global Economic Prospects and the Developing Countries*, Washington, DC.

9. Aid in the twenty-first century: Reconciling the real and the desirable

Frances Stewart

1. INTRODUCTION

Significant levels of aid from rich to poor countries – that is, the transfer of resources by gift or at highly subsidized interest rates – will, I believe, come to be viewed as peculiar to the second half of the twentieth century. This is because aid had historic functions in this period, with the end of colonialism, the acquisition of political independence among Third World countries, and the Cold War. This was a transitional period in which fundamental choices were being made about the nature of economic development, and whether *laisser-faire* capitalism, Keynesian/welfare state capitalism or centrally planned socialism would dominate. Aid was a major instrument influencing choices among these alternatives. At the end of the twentieth century these choices appear to have been largely made in favour of *laisser-faire* capitalism (with elements of Keynesian or welfare state interventions in some places), and thus from the perspective of donors aid is much less useful.

Aid is also motivated by altruism, it is claimed. Both empirical investigation and casual observation would suggest that altruism has been a stronger motive among small aid donors (for example, the Scandinavians), and for some types of aid (non-governmental organizations (NGOs), humanitarian aid), than for official development aid from large donors (see for example, Maizels and Nissanke, 1984). The role of altruism as a significant source of human motivation in general is being downplayed in the late twentieth century as the role of the market and financial incentives expands. Moreover, downward pressures on government expenditure (in donor and recipient countries) also imply a lesser potential for official–official transfers. Thus the altruistic motive is also diminishing in force.

Hence one would expect a much smaller role for aid in the twenty-first century: on the one hand, the self-serving objectives have been largely realized; on the other hand, altruism is likely to deliver even less than it did previously. This does not mean *no* aid transfers. There will continue to be some of both kinds – to exert foreign and economic policy pressure, secure markets and so on, and to fulfil some genuine altruistic concerns. But it is not helpful for potential recipients to continue to focus on the hope of increasing old style aid (for example, on the 0.7 per cent target) at the expense of a realistic appraisal of what sort of aid is likely, and what is the best way of using it.

This chapter is intended to do two things: first to examine the diminishing role of aid and consider new functions from a realistic perspective; and second, to explore what type of aid (and North–South relationship more generally) is desirable for the twenty-first century from a development perspective. The next section expands on the suggestion just made about the diminishing functionality of aid, briefly reviewing actual trends and concluding with a discussion of how one would expect the role of aid to evolve, given these considerations. Section 3 considers the past record of aid from the perspective of development. Section 4 explores what might be a desirable approach to aid and North–South relations more generally in the twenty-first century, from a development perspective. Section 5 comes to some conclusions about possibilities of reconciling the real and the desirable.

2. THE CHANGING ROLE OF AID

2.1 The diminishing functionality of aid

For donors, aid serves a number of self-interested objectives, including *political* (as an instrument of foreign policy) and *economic* (an instrument of trade and investment policy). Bilateral aid tends to be directed at immediate gains for the particular country's interests; multilateral aid provides general leverage over recipient countries' trade, investment and technology policies in ways that serve the interests of the donors as a group. The transfer of resources at less than market costs is the price donors pay for these returns.

The combination of the end of colonialism and the Cold War provided a powerful motive for aid. Since countries had acquired political independence they could no longer be controlled directly; moreover, the existence of the apparently successful Soviet Bloc provided an alternative economic and political model. Hence, for both East and West, there was a struggle for hearts, minds and markets among the newly independent countries. Aid was a major instrument in this contest, as shown by the disproportionate amounts of aid received by 'frontline' states (for example, South Korea, Turkey, Pakistan, Cuba, North and South Vietnam). Military and economic aid was highly correlated. More immediately economic gains were assured by tied aid, 'trade and aid' provisions, the use of donor-country technical consultant companies which usually recommended donor-country machinery for aid projects and so on. This is not to say that none of the aid was motivated altruistically; all aid was presented with an altruistic veneer, and some was genuinely motivated in this way. Moreover, it was felt, rightly, that successful development would be the most effective way of defeating the alternative socialist model, so much aid was intended to achieve both objectives – to support the Western model and to bring about development.

The collapse of the Soviet model meant not only that there were fewer foreign-policy/military-security reasons to support aid, but also that the socialist model no longer presented a real alternative. But the interventionist Keynesian type model still persisted – indeed, it was the dominant model among developing countries in the Western camp. The restrictions governments of developing countries imposed, associated with the Keynesian model, reduced profitable opportunities and worsened terms of trade for the industrialized countries. Thus in the 1970s import restrictions were prevalent, as were limitations on Foreign Direct Investment (FDI), while many parts of the productive sector were dominated by parastatals diminishing the role of multinational companies. Moreover, corporate taxation was significant in many countries, and a failure to observe strict intellectual property 'rights' reduced profit-making opportunities for Western companies. Hence in the 1980s multilateral aid (supported by bilaterals) was used systematically to eliminate these restrictions under the policy conditionality of the International Monetary Fund (IMF) and World Bank which was applied country by country. The Uruguay round, the World Trade Organization and planned new international rules on intellectual property and multinational investment (for example, through the Multinational Agreement on Investment) are carrying this programme forward for the world as a whole, but aid has played a much lesser role in these negotiations (which may be indicative of future mechanisms for achieving policy change).

There is no question but that these pressures from the donor community were hugely successful in shifting countries away from the Keynesian model, with a diminished economic role for the government, in moves which have been described as 'liberalization' (for example, privatization, import liberalization, abolition of constraints on FDI, capital market liberalization). The liberal agenda is not yet complete (as indicated by the IMF's intention to take on capital market liberalization; and the moves to privatize the previously central government functions, such as health and education provision, prisons, pensions and so on), but the end appears to be in sight. Moreover, the changes have achieved their own momentum, so aid is no longer so essential to leverage the changes. Thus, once heavy dependence on private capital has occurred, countries are constrained from reversing liberalization, and persuaded to undertake more, for fear of losing the confidence of international markets. The changes have brought about a new political economy so that weakened governments not only *cannot* but also *do not want* to challenge powerful companies, and come to favour further liberalization under pressure from emerging domestic private interests. This, of course, is a crude generalization covering many countries and many changes: undoubtedly some governments retain some autonomy and persist with aspects of the Keynesian model (for example, Costa Rica), but virtually all countries in the world are marching to the same tune, albeit at different paces.

Hence in so far as the main purposes of aid were: (a) to help fight the Cold War; and (b) to shift the economic model from Keynesianism to *laisser-faire*, they have largely been achieved and one would therefore expect aid to diminish. And this, as is well known, is what has happened. In aggregate aid fell from 0.34 per cent of Gross National Product (GNP) of donor aid countries (DAC) in 1984–85 to 0.27 per cent in 1995. This conceals divergent trends among donors. Much the biggest drop was from the US, where aid fell from 0.24 per cent of GNP to just 0.10 per cent. Most other countries dropped by much less (see Table 9.1) while in a few countries aid rose as a percentage of GNP (for example, Denmark, Switzerland, Portugal). The differences broadly support the views advanced above since the US, as the leader of the Western countries and strongest adherent of the *laisser-faire* model, would be expected to be most affected by the changes discussed here. In principle, altruistically motivated aid might be expected to hold up best, although, as argued in the introduction, altruism seems to be being diminished as a significant motive for behaviour in the current *zeitgeist*; moreover, those countries that have focused more on altruistic type aid have been disappointed in its effects, especially in its failure to promote independent self-sustained development and to reach the poorest and are therefore reviewing their efforts (for example, Sweden). The data indicate that 'altruistic' donors have also reduced their aid efforts.

2.2   Probable aid trends in the new international political economy

There remain important functions for aid in the new international political economy, although these are rather different from those that obtained in the last half century. These include:

Table 9.1   Net aid flows as percentage of GNP

Normal donors	1984–85	1995
Australia	0.47	0.36
Austria	0.33	0.33
Belgium	0.56	0.38
France	0.62	0.55
Germany	0.46	0.31
Ireland	0.23	0.29
Italy	0.27	0.15
Japan	0.31	0.28
New Zealand	0.25	0.23
Portugal	0.05	0.27
Spain	0.09	0.24
Switzerland	0.30	0.34
UK	0.33	0.28
US	0.24	0.10
Unweighted average	0.32	0.29
More altruistic donors		
Canada	0.50	0.38
Denmark	0.83	0.96
Finland	0.38	0.32
Netherlands	0.97	0.81
Norway	1.02	0.87
Sweden	0.83	0.77
Unweighted average	0.76	0.69
Aggregate average (weighted)	0.34	0.27

Source: Development Assistance Committee Report, 1996 (Paris, OECD).

- New functions for aid related to new foreign policy and security considerations. The new international economic order (or lack of it), unlike the old one, does not contain a single cause or enemy bloc, but rather a multiplicity of objectives and focal points. For each objective and focal point aid may be an important instrument, used as an incentive and a facilitator. For example, aid may assist policy objectives in the Middle East (towards the Israel/Arab conflict, or between Arab states). Aid may be used during conflicts (to support one or the other side), after conflicts to reinforce peace, and perhaps to prevent conflict. The objectives and focal points of developed countries, or blocs of countries, differ. France, for example, has particular objectives in Africa which are likely to sustain its aid there. The UK tends to have residual post-colonial focal points. Russia and Japan have particular interests in neighbouring countries, as well as those that provide key resources, and so on. The planned expansion of NATO will almost certainly involve military aid, and possibly economic aid as well. Hence some aid is likely to continue to be needed for foreign policy reasons, but its precise location is likely to be fluid, changing with changes in perceived interests.

- Aid as a mechanism for achieving some generally desired 'public' goals. These goals include preventing proliferation of dangerous weapons (nuclear, chemical, biological), securing environmental objectives (restrictions on CO_2 omissions, for example, or preservation of tropical forests). Aid may be useful as a means of persuasion.
- Aid for policy conditionality to complete the liberalization agenda, avoid back-slipping, and perhaps for the achievement of new goals, including those noted in the point above.
- Aid to facilitate the activities of the private sector (especially the foreign private sector) – for example, co-financing for infrastructure, technical assistance to improve regulatory functions.
- Aid to help prevent mass migration – for Europe this involves aid to Northern Africa and parts of Eastern Europe; for the US, aid to Latin American countries.
- Aid to support development within regional blocs and thus to cement the blocs as a whole, to prevent large imbalances that may lead to bloc break-up or mass movement of workers within the bloc, and generally to contribute to the prosperity of the bloc. This type of aid, which is not necessarily North–South in nature, may be quantitatively the most important – for example, transfers within the European Community greatly exceed North–South aid from Europe to developing countries.
- Aid to prevent collapse of one part of the system, with dangers of infecting the rest (as in East and South East Asia, or Mexico or Russia). Such aid is likely to be temporary and on 'hard terms'.
- If a new alternative to Western capitalism threatens on any significant scale – for example, from religious fundamentalism or from a powerful eastern bloc led by China – development aid might get a new momentum in order to challenge this, like the previous contest with communism. But this seems unlikely in the next ten years or so.

This is a long list, and doubtless it misses out some functions for aid in the New Order. However, none of the functions individually (nor taken together) is likely to lead to very high levels of aid, especially given the antipathy to public expenditure of the majority of people in most developed countries. A decline of aid to between 0.1 per cent and 0.25 per cent of Gross Domestic Product for these self-interested concerns would seem likely, excluding transfers within blocs like the EU. To this, one should add: (i) as much or more for the countries that have strong altruistic motives, but since these are among the smallest countries the addition to the total will not be great; and (ii) new aid donors from the newly developed. Countries such as China, South Korea when recovered, Taiwan and Chile will themselves be motivated to undertake aid for the same set of reasons as existing aid donors (that is, those listed above). For some functions, the list of donors might even extend to quite poor countries with strong intra-regional objectives (for example, Museveni's Uganda, among the poorest countries in the world, might provide resources to Southern Sudan or the Congo for foreign policy reasons).

2.3 Implications for aid distribution

Setting aside altruistic aid, one can draw some implications for aid distribution from this analysis of functions:

1. Aid that is rational from a foreign policy perspective need bear no relation to that which might seem desirable from a redistributive and poverty-reducing one. Indeed the opposite is probable as very poor countries are rarely politically significant enough to feature in foreign policy objectives.
2. Similarly, aid that is rationally distributed from the point of view of achieving public environmental goals (forestation, CO_2) will only coincidentally be the same as a poverty-reducing aid distribution.
3. Aid that is rationally distributed from the perspective of facilitating private capital, via policy conditionality or infrastructure, for example, is liable to be distributed to *poorer countries*, as the richer countries can afford their own infrastructure and are less likely to be bought on the policy-reform issue. But it is unlikely to go to the *poorest people* within the countries, nor to the *poorest countries*, as governments are not in a position to offer strong policy reform. That is to say, this type of aid may go to China, India and South Africa, but is less likely to go to Afghanistan, Nepal and Burkina Faso.
4. Aid to prevent financial collapse is unlikely to be focused on especially poor countries or people within them.

5. Some of the motives listed above do justify development aid – for example, the motive of preventing mass migration and of challenging new fundamentalisms. But the migration threat does not emanate from the poorest countries or the poorest people. The challenge from fundamentalism might well be centred on the poorest countries and people, but as noted earlier this is not yet a serious motive for aid.

The conclusion seems to be that for the most part the new motives for aid (which, of course, are not new at all but have been in operation side by side with the old motives for some time) are not likely to lead to a developmentally promising distribution of aid. From this perspective the situation is worse than that in the old era, because the Cold War battlelines were worldwide, encompassing very poor countries. (But the other side of the coin was that some of them suffered acutely by having the Cold War fought physically on their territory.) For the new era, it seems that anti-poverty aid will have to come mainly from the altruistically motivated portion of aid.

2.4   Characteristics of altruistic aid

Actually, of course, motives for aid are mixed so there isn't one type of aid which is altruistic as against all the other types. But the altruistic motive pushes aid in different directions from the rest. The purest form of altruistic aid is that given by the public in developed countries to NGOs for distribution in developing countries. This only accounts for a fraction of total (and even of NGO-administered) aid. In addition, there is that part of official aid that has largely altruistic motives. Altruistic aid goes to:

1. The poorest countries.
2. Poor people in lower-middle-income countries.
3. Emergency humanitarian aid in response to natural and man-made disasters.

In principle, all three categories of aid can be expected to be poverty reducing. Over the past 15 years, an increasing portion of aid has been directed towards emergency aid. Assuming this continues, total flows of aid for poverty reduction in normal circumstances (1. and 2.) are likely to form a reduced portion of a reduced total, that is, to diminish quite sharply compared with the past.

2.5   Summary of likely developments in aid levels and distribution in the first half of the twenty-first century

The conclusions from the discussion above are that in the twenty-first century, aid is likely to diminish as a proportion of donor-country GDP, but not to disappear. The proportion of aid going to poor countries or poor people is likely to lessen, while within the diminished total, emergency aid is likely to absorb an increasing amount. This is my conclusion about the probable reality. The next section will consider what would be desirable, in a reasonably realistic context, and therefore what policies might best be pursued.

3.   AID AND DEVELOPMENT: THE RECORD

Before spending too much time bemoaning the trends just outlined, it is helpful briefly to survey what the 'golden' era of aid achieved. The political achievements can be argued to have been substantial in contributing to a victory in sustaining countries in the Western camp during the Cold War, and in effecting the widespread shift in economic model away from socialism and Keynesian models towards a more *laisser-faire* capitalist model, as noted above. But my perspective here is a Human Development one, and for this economic growth and private and social poverty reduction are the key elements. Any survey of aid in these dimensions has to come to the conclusion that *not very much* was achieved from the perspective of economic development and poverty reduction.

3.1   Aid and growth

'The main empirical result . . . is a negative one, namely that there appears to be no statistically significant correlation in *any* post-war period, either positive or negative, between flows of development aid and the growth rate of GNP in developing countries when other causal influences on growth are taken into account' (Mosley, 1987, p. 139). 'Inter-country statistical analyses do not show anything conclusive – positive or negative – about the impact of aid on growth' (Cassen et al., 1994, p. 29). '. . . studies have found no evidence that more aid leads to higher growth' (Burnside and Dollar, 1997, p. 5). These statements echo many other studies. However, Burnside and Dollar find positive returns to aid flows when they are accompanied by 'sound' policies (that is, open trade regimes, fiscal responsibility and avoidance of high inflation).

3.2 Aid and poverty

The record of aid as a mechanism for reducing poverty is weak. It is generally accepted that official flows are unlikely to reach the poorest of the poor, who are not linked into the channels through which aid flows. But the record in terms of the moderately poor is not good either. Aid tends to go to modern sector projects which rarely reach the poor; or to be given as a lump sum conditional flow where policy requirements are often poverty-creating.[1] '. . . evidence was accumulating that more aid on any scale – while it helped to temporarily alleviate the plight of victims of crisis – was not likely to engender significant and sustainable advantages for the neediest in the developing world' (Browne, 1997, p. 14). Aid which finances social sector investments may help reduce social poverty, but only where: (a) it does not displace government investment in these sectors; and (b) the recurrent costs are sustainable. Tanzania provides an instructive example of massive expansion of priority social services generating a sharp drop in social poverty, which proved temporary as poor macroeconomic performance and a massive build-up of debt undermined the government's ability to sustain the services, and there was a consequent reversal with a rise in social poverty. In any case, the proportion of aid going to social priorities is quite low according to the United Nations Development Programme, ranging between 2.0 per cent (Germany and Australia) and 20 per cent (Norway) among bilateral donors, with an average of just 6.5 per cent among 15 DAC donors in 1988–89 (UNDP, 1992, p. 43).

Aid can make a contribution to poverty reduction in a context where there are strong government (or NGO) policies supporting the poverty reduction objective (as, for example, in Costa Rica in the mid-1980s, Botswana during the droughts of the early 1980s, or for support of the Grameen Bank in Bangladesh). But thrown into a situation where poverty reduction is not a priority, it fails to make a significant impact.

3.3 Humanitarian aid

Again the record has varied widely, but is often not impressive. At its worst, it has been too little, too late, and deliberately mishandled by the protagonists so that it permits starvation of the enemy, fuels the conflict and prolongs suffering (as in the Sudan, see Keen, 1994; de Waal, 1997). Where the government aims to distribute food to as many people as possible (as in Mozambique in the 1980s), or aid goes via effective NGOs (which appears to be the case in Afghanistan), it can prevent massive starvation, but even then it may lead to sharply rising disease (as people move to camps – see de Waal), indirectly finance the war (through the foreign exchange generated) and undermine local food production. At the same time, emergency aid is accompanied, and in terms of humanitarian effects, offset by military aid. For example, according to Pentagon data, Liberia, Somalia, Sudan and Zaire, all countries undergoing civil war, owe the US $430 million for arms sales loans.[2]

Thus the past record of aid is not such that, taken as a whole, its reduced role need be much regretted, even though particular countries (for example, South Korea in the 1950s) got a boost from a large inflow of aid, and particular projects have successfully reached the poor and enabled them to generate self-sustaining incomes.

Moreover, the aid relationship is not a healthy one: it is an unequal relationship, encouraging dependency, with an implicit assumption that the rich are superior and have the right to patronize the poor, while a focus on aid diverts attention away from other aspects of the North–South relationship which are of greater importance. These include debt, terms of trade, intellectual property rights, migration, private capital flows and so on.

4.   DESIRABLE DIRECTIONS FOR NORTH–SOUTH RELATIONS

The decline in aid represents an opportunity for rethinking its role and North–South relations more generally. In my view (along with many others) a change in philosophy is needed from the language of gifts to that of rights. As the internationally agreed conventions on Human Rights agree, people throughout the world have certain rights because they are human. These rights have been defined as negative rights (political freedoms) and as positive rights (rights to food, water, education, health services and more generally 'development'). Of course, international agreement to certain rights doesn't mean anything unless the rights can be enforced – which they cannot be, at present. Nonetheless they represent a starting point for focusing desirable directions of change.

In principle, who should be liable to meet the rights if they were enforceable? Possibilities range from the family, the local community, local or provincial governments, the central government, the regional association of countries where there is one, or finally the international community. A reasonable approach would be to suggest that the rights should be met at the lowest level possible, given resource constraints. Where there are resource constraints at the lowest level (the family, that is, where the household is below the poverty line), then support is needed from outside. This support might consist of provision of services, transfer of money or food, creation of employment opportunities, or improved terms of trade for existing employment. Ensuring that the conditions are met for rights to be realized needs to be done on a cooperative basis by all the other levels of authority, that is, by cooperation within the country between the local community and the government; and outside the country between the government (and also local NGOs) and the international community (foreign NGOs, bilateral or multilateral donors). In this ideal world, the role of the international community is to assist the government in realizing individual positive rights, where there is a national resource deficiency, and in realizing the collective right to development.

Aid is not necessarily the best way to provide such assistance: the total international relationship needs to be considered, including trade (access and terms of trade), private capital flows and the debt situation. If rights can be realized via private capital flows and trade, then this is normally preferable to aid, since it is more sustainable. In such conditions aid's role may be to support trade and capital flows, not to substitute for them, and to provide a safety net when there are adverse fluctuations.

Only where rights cannot be realized through trade and private capital, nor through domestic resources, does aid need to play a major role. Given the tremendous expansion of trade and private capital flows in recent years, aid is likely to be the main source of support only in a minority of countries – the least developed countries and countries in or having recently suffered major conflict.

The most difficult situation arises where national resources are sufficient to meet a people's rights, but the government and market operate in such a way to oppose this. It might be argued that in such countries aid has a special role. But experience suggests that it is almost impossible to realize rights in a comprehensive way when the combined efforts of government and market are working in the opposite direction. NGOs may achieve some 'mopping up', but reforms, political and economic, are what is really needed. In that context, aid could be used as a lever, conditional on the necessary reforms. But it may well not work.

This approach to aid is not totally inconsistent with the predicted trends in aid discussed above. These trends, for example, are consistent with heavier reliance on private capital flows and trade and with the use of aid to facilitate and top up these flows. They are also consistent with the distribution of altruistic aid on the basis of Human Rights principles. However, the foreign policy motivated aid may only coincidentally be consistent with the requirements of a Human Rights approach, although it may sometimes be possible to use foreign policy motivated aid in a way that supports the Human Rights agenda – for example, if providing support for the Palestinians for foreign policy reasons, using the aid to support the fulfilment of rights. Often, however, the foreign policy agenda may prevent this.

Table 9.2   Matrix of aid requirements

Human Rights deficit due to:	Source of foreign finance	
	Foreign exchange earnings/private capital flows adequate	Foreign exchange earnings/private capital flows inadequate
Country poverty	I	III
Distribution of income (private or social)	II	IV

What the proposed approach requires is to put all types of aid described above into a Human Rights framework, and rationalize it in this framework, country by country. In practical terms, the implications are as follows:

1. For each country, a Human Rights set of accounts needs to be established and deficits identified, differentiating between those cases where deficits arise from country-wide poverty, and the major need is to promote development, from those where the main problem is poor private income distribution leading to private income poverty (PIP) or failure of government to provide adequate services leading to social income poverty (SIP).
2. Similarly, resource flow accounts should be developed, indicating actual (and potential) non-aid sources of foreign finance, including foreign exchange earnings, remittances, private capital flows and (negatively) debt service obligations.

A matrix of aid needs can then be established, as shown in Table 9.2.

Countries with a deficit on Human Rights will fall into one of the four quadrants shown in Table 9.2. Failure of Human Rights has been treated as single phenomenon. A further subdivision is needed according to whether it is PIP or SIP which forms the major deficiency, or both – that is, subdivide each quadrant into Ip, Is, Ips; and similarly IIp, IIs, IIps and so on (where p indicates mainly PIP, s, mainly SIP and ps both). One should also note that private flows may be more or less adequate (that is, able to supply most of the needs, or only a small proportion) rather than being totally adequate or inadequate.

3. For every country, aid should be regarded as a second-best and temporary option; it is greatly preferable to enhance foreign exchange earnings (through better terms of trade, supporting production of

exportables and policies to encourage switching) since such an option is more likely to be sustainable, to be associated with generation of employment opportunities, and to avoid aid dependency and policy conditionality. Long-term private capital flows also have some advantages compared with aid – in terms of sustainability, technology transfer and managerial support. However, much more caution is needed with respect to short-term private capital.

4. Appropriate aid policies then differ according to which quadrant a country falls into, and which category within it; for example:

Quadrant I: this is an unusual case, since private flows are normally low for low-income countries, so for practical purposes this quadrant may be filled by very few cases. But there are some low-income countries, for example China and India, which have good access to private flows and growth of foreign exchange earnings. There is a case for providing only limited aid in these cases, given the constraints on total aid levels. If the problem is Ip, then access to markets and support for income earning opportunities are most needed. If Is, then the aid may be directed towards provision of social goods, or, better, supporting government in revenue raising and redirection of government expenditure towards these goods. These are cases where International Safety Nets may be needed to deal with fluctuations in private foreign capital.

Quadrant II: these are cases where substantial flows of aid are not justified. All efforts need to be addressed towards persuading the governments to redirect resources.

Quadrant III: this category is the most aid-needy, being poor and having inadequate private flows. But while there is a strong short-term case for aid, the aim should be to establish self-sufficiency by providing the sort of resources which will promote foreign exchange resources and encourage private flows.

Quadrant IV: these are middle-income countries, which, potentially, should be able to attract sufficient private foreign resources and/or earn them via exports. Hence these are prime targets for policy reform of two types: (a) to bring about a situation in which private flows/earnings will be sufficient; and (b) to secure redistribution of income internally.

5. Accepting the approach represented by Table 9.2 implies a thorough review of aid distribution, with a concentration on Quadrant III countries, the elimination of most aid from Quadrants II and IV, and a substantial reduction of flows to Quadrant I countries. Moreover, from the perspective of achieving the fulfilment of Human Rights even aid to Quadrant III countries will often not be justified, as it will only be justified from this perspective if it seems probable that the aid will assist development and appropriate distribution – this may often not be the

case. That is, altruistically motivated aid flows of any magnitude are justified only where it seems reasonable to expect a 'partnership' to promote Human Rights.[3] This apparently ruthless redirection of aid would not be as ruthless in practice as in theory because of continued 'functional' aid to many countries which would not qualify on Human Rights and capital inadequacy grounds.

6. Potentially, following this approach would release large amounts of aid within the current total flows. In 1994–95, 30.5 per cent of allocable aid went to least developed countries (broadly Quadrant III countries), and another 17 per cent to low-income countries (Quadrant I). Over half the allocated aid total went to other countries (Quadrants II and IV). Unallocated flows accounted for an additional fifth of the allocated flows. From a geographic perspective, we get a similar picture: 29 per cent of DAC aid went to Sub-Saharan Africa (mainly Quadrant III), 12 per cent to South and Central Asia and 26 per cent to other Asian and Oceania countries, of which about half was probably for Quadrant I (that is, 19 per cent), making approximately 52 per cent of present flows going to Quadrants II and IV.

7. An additional constraint on 'useful' pro-Human Rights aid follows from avoiding governments for which pro-Human Rights partnerships are unlikely, further limiting the countries to which this type of aid should go. Realistically, this might reduce the number of countries in the 'good government, Quadrant II' category to perhaps half. We are then left with a situation in which about one-quarter of current aid goes to the target countries (that is, good government, Quadrant II). Redirection of one-third of the remaining aid would double aid to these countries.

8. Conditionality and partnership: pressure for pro-Human Rights conditionality would appear to be needed for countries in each quadrant. But there are severe problems about making this operational. First, in general such conditionality is not likely to be effective where governments are generally elitist (that is, especially countries in Quadrants II and IV where distribution of income is poor and where, potentially, change in policies has most to offer). Moreover, with the proposed changes in aid distribution, most of the countries in Quadrants I, II, and IV would be excluded as aid recipients, thus eliminating possibilities of using aid as a policy conditionality tool. Aid will be focused on countries where appropriate Human Rights distribution of resources is probable – that is, the Partnership countries. Knowledge that aid is concentrated on Partnership countries may, however, lead to policy change so that additional countries would then qualify for aid. But apart from this incentive, policy change towards Human Rights would

rest on international monitoring and advocacy – not a very effective approach, but probably as effective as any other.

8. NGOs: NGOs are better at reaching the poorest than official aid. Moreover, they can also support local popular organizations which may alter the local political economy towards Human Rights. Hence NGOs may have an especially important contribution to make in countries where the source of the problem is maldistribution of private and social income (the Quadrant II and IV countries).

9. Humanitarian aid: despite its frequent misuse, this type of aid remains necessary, but with greatly improved mechanisms to improve timing and distribution. Of greater long-term importance is to redirect development efforts in conflict-prone countries to help avoid emergency by promoting inclusive forms of political, economic and social development.[4]

4.1 Realism versus desirability

The big issue is whether the directions for aid considered desirable – as discussed above – are consistent with the distribution likely to emerge from the changed motivation for aid discussed in section 2. Obviously not entirely: as noted above, the functional approach to aid will probably largely bypass the poorest countries, apart from those suffering humanitarian disasters, although there are a few cases where poor countries represent threats or opportunities for rich countries, economically or politically. But we can only expect a relatively low level of aid for low-income countries arising from the functional motives. The needs of the countries in the non-priority quadrants, however, can be expected to be largely met out of functional aid so that altruistic aid can concentrate entirely on the countries in Quadrant III. The problem is that much of altruistically motivated aid is probably *already* largely concentrated on these countries; assuming such aid includes all aid from Scandinavian countries, Canada and The Netherlands (the altruistic donors) plus 10 per cent of the aid of every other donor, the total comes to around 25 per cent of net flows – roughly the same proportion as the estimated share of total aid to good government/Quadrant III countries (taking the estimates of around 30 per cent for Quadrant III in 7. in the previous section and deducting 5 per cent for non-Partnership countries).

Hence given a trend decline in total aid flows, a rise in the proportion of altruistic aid will be needed to meet the Human Rights agenda. Such a rise does seem possible, especially among progressive political regimes. Therefore the development lobby (including the North–South Roundtable) should focus on the, perhaps, realistic objective of securing such a redirection rather than on trying to promote the unrealizable 0.7 per cent target.

5. CONCLUSIONS

In brief, this paper has argued that:

1. Aid in the twenty-first century is likely to fall, but will not be eliminated as it serves several useful economic and foreign policy functions.
2. This is not a tragedy since the record of aid over the past 40 years has not been good, especially in reaching the poor.
3. Aid should be put in a Human Rights framework.
4. It should be redirected towards countries which are prevented from realizing Human Rights by their poverty and which lack access to sufficient foreign exchange earnings/private capital to do so. Within this group only countries whose governments seriously aim to pursue these objectives should be supported.
5. Aid should aim to work itself out of a job by promoting foreign exchange earnings and long-term private capital.
6. There is a need for national and international safety nets. These need not be aid-financed, although aid may play a role. But the most important requirement is that mechanisms are in place, internationally and nationally.
7. The role of development agencies in the twenty-first century should: shift away from a prime focus on aid giving towards monitoring Human Rights and sources of finance; identify the policy reforms needed; and review international trade, finance, investment and technology policies with the aim of seeing that they are in the interests of developing countries.

NOTES

1. See Cornia, Jolly and Stewart (1997) and Stewart (1995).
2. Information taken from Browne (1997, fn. 28).
3. This is the policy and terminology contained in the British Department for International Development's White Paper (DFID, 1997).
4. Some of the ways of doing so are outlined in Stewart (1998).

REFERENCES

Browne, S. (1997), 'The rise and fall of development aid', *Working Papers 143*, Helsinki: WIDER.
Burnside, C. and D. Dollar (1997), 'Aid spurs growth – in a sound policy environment', *Finance and Development*, **34** (4), 4–7.

Cassen, R. and Associates (1994), *Does Aid Work?*, Oxford: Clarendon Press.

Cornia, G.A., R. Jolly and F. Stewart (1987), *Adjustment with a Human Face*, Oxford: OUP.

de Waal, A. (1997), *Famine Crimes: Politics and the Disaster Relief Industry in Africa*, Oxford: James Currey.

Department for International Development (1997), *White Paper on Aid*, London: Government Printing Office.

Keen, D. (1994), *The Benefits of Famine: A Political Economy of Famine and Relief in Southwestern Sudan, 1983–1989*, Princeton: Princeton University Press.

Maizels, A. and M. Nissanke (1984), 'Motivations for aid to developing countries', *World Development*, **12** (9), 879–900.

Mosley, P. (1987), *Overseas Aid: Its Defence and Reform*, London: Wheatsheaf.

OECD (1996), *Development Cooperation: 1996 Report*, Paris: OECD.

Stewart, F. (1995), *Adjustment and Poverty: Options and Choices*, London: Routledge.

Stewart, F. (1998), 'The root causes of conflict: Some conclusions', paper prepared for WIDER project on 'The Political Economy of Humanitarian Emergencies', Helsinki: WIDER.

UNDP (1992), *Human Development Report*, New York: OUP.

10. Globalization and FDI in Asian developing countries

John H. Dunning

1. INTRODUCTION

This chapter seeks to do three main things. First, it examines the extent to which Asian developing countries have participated in the trend towards a globalizing world economy over the past two decades or so. Second, it looks more specifically at the ways in which one of the main engines of globalization, namely inbound investment by foreign institutions and individuals in Asia and outbound investment by Asian multinational enterprises (MNEs), and individuals have contributed towards a deepening economic interdependence between Asian countries and the rest of the world. Third, it presents some recently published data on trends of European foreign direct investment (FDI) in Asian developing countries, and of how some 310 leading MNEs and international experts view future corporate investment priorities up to the year 2001.

Where possible, we shall adopt a three-fold classification of Asian developing countries, which corresponds to that used by the United Nations Development Programme (UNDP),[1] namely high human development, medium human development and low human development countries (see Appendix 2). The Human Development Index, compiled by the UNDP, while incorporating gross domestic product (GDP) per capita, also embraces variables such as developing countries, but also embraces other variables, such as life expectancy and adult literacy. A list of the Asian countries assigned to each group is set out in Appendix 1. We are aware that there are other criteria for classifying Asian developing countries, apart from their stage of human development. For example, in some situations, size is a critical variable; and, where appropriate, we shall distinguish between small and medium to large Asian countries. The contents of this chapter will be mainly descriptive, and no formal econometric analysis of the data will be undertaken. However, we will attempt to relate our statistical findings to the main body of extant theory and also offer some additional hypotheses of our own.

2. GLOBALIZATION AND DEVELOPING COUNTRIES

Our interpretation of the term globalization, and of how it differs from internationalization, is contained in a quotation by Anthony McGrew in a jointly edited book *Globalization and the Nation State* which was first published in 1992 (McGrew and Lewis, 1992).

> Globalization refers to the multiplicity of linkages and interconnections between the states and societies which make up the present world system. It describes the process by which events, decisions, and activities in one part of the world come to have significant consequences for individuals and communities in quite distant parts of the globe. Globalization has two distinct phenomena: scope (or stretching) and intensity (or deepening). On the one hand, it defines a set of processes which embrace most of the globe or which operate worldwide: the concept therefore has a spatial connotation. On the other hand, it also implies an intensification on the levels of interaction, interconnectedness or *interdependence* between the states and societies which constitute the world community. Accordingly, alongside the stretching goes a deepening of global processes. (p. 23)

In short, then, globalization is leading to the structural transformation of firms and nations, and is creating new relationships and new dependencies. Sometimes the transformation takes place at a regional level: much of the integrated production networks of MNEs is so focused. Sometimes it occurs at a global level. For example, the contemporary global financial system is one in which national markets throughout the world, though physically separate, operate as if they are in the same place (Stopford and Strange, 1991). One scholar has put it even more dramatically by averring that global financial integration is 'the end of geography'.[2] The main causes of globalization are well known. I shall focus on just two. The first is the pressure on firms – by consumers and competitors alike – to continually introduce new products and upgrade the quality and/or reduce the price of existing goods and services. At the same time, the escalating costs of research and development, coupled with ever-shortening product life cycles, are compelling firms both to curtail the scope of their value added activities and to search for wider markets. Moreover, in order to effectively and speedily exploit their core competencies, firms are finding they need to combine these with the core competencies of other firms and those of governments. Hence the emergence of strategic alliances and networks which, together with FDI, are the main instruments fashioning deep economic interdependence.

The second cause of globalization – which in many ways is better described as a removal of an obstacle – is the renaissance of market-supporting policies pursued by national governments and the growth of market-led regional integration. In the last 5 years alone, more than 30 countries have abandoned central planning as the main mode of allocating scarce resources; while, as we shall see later, over 80 have liberalized their inward FDI policies. The privatization of state-owned enterprises, the liberalization and deregulation of markets – especially for services – and the removal of a bevy of structural distortions, have all worked to stimulate cross-border corporate integration, both within MNEs and between independent firms, or groups of firms.

In this chapter I will consider just nine indices of globalization, and Table 10.1 sets out how these vary between the three groups of Asian developing economies, other developing countries, developed countries and all countries. These indices are:

1. Trade as a percentage of GDP in 1996.
2. Changes in (1), 1980–96.
3. Share of world exports of 'growth' products, 1995.
4. Changes in (3), 1980–95.
5. Inward plus outward direct investment stock as a percentage of GDP, 1996.
6. Changes in (3), 1980–96.
7. Inward plus outward foreign portfolio investment as a percentage of GDP, 1996.
8. Changes in mergers and acquisitions (M&A), 1990–96.
9. Use of international communications media, 1994.

The findings of Table 10.1 are self-evident. Briefly highlighted they are:

- Asian economies are more globalized than other developing economies, and enjoy a larger share of the exports of 'fast growth' products to the OECD. As might be expected, smaller Asian countries tend to be more globalized than their larger counterparts.
- The propensity of Asian economies to be more deeply integrated into a global economy tends to increase as economic development proceeds. As other research (Dunning, 1981, 1986 and Dunning and Narula, 1996) has shown, there is a GNP per capital threshold before a country is able to attract substantial amounts of inward direct investment and another threshold before it engages in outward direct investment. These thresholds are also seen to vary with the size, industrial structure and general economic environment of the developing countries, but, as identified in Table 10.1, only Group 1, Asian and a handful of Latin American, countries are experiencing 'balanced' globalization – by which we mean they are: (a) sharing in export

Table 10.1   Indices of globalization of Asian economies, 1980–96

	Trade				Foreign investment				International communications	
	% of GDP 1996	Change % 1980–96	% of growth trade^a	Change % of growth trade	FDI as % of GDP 1996	Change % 1990–96	FPI as % of GDP 1996	Change M&As 1990–96	Int. Tel.^b calls 1994	Internet^c users 1994
1. Asian developing economies	72.1	489.1	384.6	134.8	26.7	1196.9	19.5	491.7	32.9	16.6
a. Group 1	114.5	580.3	596.4	47.3	31.5	1246.3	26.5	302.9	97.2	49.6
b. Group 2	45.2	419.5	381.4	293.1	25.9	2123.3	10.7	317.9	1.2	0.2
c. Group 3	20.3	190.9	176.0	64.1	3.1	721.4	2.8	7005.5	0.4	0.0
2. Latin American economies	24.8	106.9	122.1	72.6	18.8	586.8	34.1	164.2	NA	NA
3. African economies	134.1	29.53	–47.7	NA	44.9	443.9	NA	996.1	NA	NA
a. Sub-Sahara	NA	NA	–29.3	NA	29.4	112.1	NA	200094.1	1.4	NA
b. Other	NA	NA	4.6	NA	12.1	300.5	NA	896.1	NA	NA
4. All developing economies	62.1	178.4	92.8	NA	20.5	853.8	25.6	358.8	2.5	1.5
5. All industrial economies	25.4	165.9	186.8	NA	17.7	462.2	46.5	40.4	35.1	232.2
6. All economies	36.8	170.0	157.8	NA	21.4	515.3	50.6	71.7	9.4	60.9
7. Smaller Asian economies[1]	174.1	581.4	585.5	34.3	58.8	1321.2	58.8	170.6	81.8	32.0
8. Larger Asian economies[2]	43.2	532.4	411.4	165.3	15.2	8815.6	3.1	930.2	1.6	2.2

Notes:
NA = Not available.
1. Defined as countries with a population of 20 million or less in 1996.
2. Defined as countries with a population of over 20 million in 1996.
a. For 1995 data.
b. Minutes per person, 1994.
c. Per 100000 people, 1994.
Source: *World Investment Report* (1998a), *World Economic Forum* (1995), *The World Competitiveness Report* (1998), *UNDP Human Development Report* (1997), *The IMF Balance of Payments Statistics* (1985, 1998).

growth of dynamic products: (b) engaging in outward as well as inward and outward FDI and M&A activity; and (c) making good use of international communications facilities.

• Almost certainly part of the more outward-looking stance of Asian (and other developing) countries reflects a trend towards regionalization rather than globalization. Thus, for example, it is estimated (UNCTAD, 1997) that 75 per cent of all inward direct investment in Asian developing countries between 1990 and 1995 originated from elsewhere in Asia, while about the same proportion of the manufacturing exports from these same countries in 1995 went to other Asian countries. On the other hand, it is clear that Asian developing countries are gaining an increasing share of world *outward* FDI – or at least they were up to 1996[3] – as their own firms take a more global perspective on the sourcing of products such as footwear, clothing, consumer electronics, semi-conductors, toys, computer software and some kinds of technology; and as they seek to make inroads into European and US markets.

• There is some suggestion that an increasing proportion of cross-border strategic alliances is now involving Asian firms. According to a survey of Booz, Allen and Hamilton (1997), the average value of a cross-border strategic alliance concluded by Japanese and other Asian firms was four times greater than that of US firms in the mid-1990s; while approaching two-thirds of developing Asia is viewed by the leading Western MNEs as offering the best prospects for new forms of cross-border collaboration, for acquiring complementary technological and other skills, and for exploiting new markets.

What are the main explanations for the facts just described? We might highlight just three of these. The first is the increased liberalization of markets in Asian developing countries, and a more positive attitude to the inbound investment, and a growing belief that, to be competitive in international markets, the leading Asian firms need to engage in outward direct investment. Almost certainly, one important contributor to the current economic crises in the Far East is the imprudent haste at which both firms and governments of Asian developing countries have tried to 'catch up' with their Western counterparts.

The second factor is the growing competition among firms – and particularly MNEs from industrialized countries – both to protect existing and to exploit new markets, and to be more cost effective in their global sourcing and production strategies. This has fostered a new international division of labour; and, because of their favourable real costs, and investment incentives offered by their governments relative to those of their competitors, Asian developing countries have gained the lion's share of new FDI and inward strategic alliance over the last decade.[4]

The third factor is the forceful, yet market-friendly, development strategies pursued by governments of Asian developing countries, which in the main have been consistent with the tenets of globalization (and increasingly so over the last decade). However, again, through zealous and incautious expansionist macroeconomic policies, and the fostering of easy credit by the financial sector, Asian governments may well have contributed towards the economic downturn and growing indebtedness of their economies.

3. FOREIGN INVESTMENT AND THE DEEPENING INTERDEPENDENCE OF THE ASIAN ECONOMIES

One of the key attributes of a deepening economic dependence, or interdependence, of a country with the rest of the world is the extent to which that country is invested in by foreign institutions and individuals, and/or the extent to which its own institutions and individuals invest in other countries. In this section we shall primarily concentrate on FDI as a globalizing vehicle. However, in so far as the growth of inbound foreign portfolio investment (FPI) mirrors the strength and vitality of the local capital market, and the confidence with which foreign institutions view the local economy, while outbound FPI normally reflects the availability of locally generated savings, and the perceived opportunities for investing in foreign countries, we shall briefly consider this variable as well.

Table 10.2 sets out some details of the significance of inbound and outbound foreign investment to the three groups of Asian economies, and the 'balance' between the two over the last two decades. In particular it examines:

1. The proportion of inward and outward FDI stock of the GDP,[5] 1980 and 1996.
2. The balance between inward and outward FDI stock, 1980 and 1996.
3. The growth of inward and outward FPI flows between 1983–89 and 1990–96.
4. The value of shares quoted on the domestic stock market as a proportion of GDP, 1980–82 and 1994–96.

What do these data show? We would highlight four main points:

- As a proportion of their GDP, the combined inward and outward and direct stock of Asian developing countries rose from 4.4 per cent in 1980 to 20.5 per cent in 1996. The corresponding increases for South,

Table 10.2 Foreign investment and Asian economies, 1980–96

| | FDI as % of GDP | | | | Inward/ outward FDI balance (ratio) | | Growth of FPI (%) | | Market capital as a % of GDP | |
| | Inward | | Outward | | | | Outward | Inward | | |
	1980	1996	1980	1996	1980	1996	1990/96	1990/96	1980/82	1994/96
1. Asian developing economies	7.8	14.6	4.4	6.0	15.9	2.13	598.47	2307.9	20.2	53.5
a. Group 1	14.9	22.9	12.5	20.5	2.5	0.88	686.47	2430.8	54.2	114.2
b. Group 2	7.9	22.2	0.5	1.0	27.8	11.75	783.93	3021.5	0.8	27.9
c. Group 3	0.7	8.4	0.1	0.1	17.6	19.36	NA	1471.3	5.6	26.5
2. Latin American economies	6.4	17.4	0.4	1.5	16.2	11.73	−86.02	190.6	4.3	25.8
3. African economies	3.2	16.6	0.1	4.1	21.7	4.01	−295.08	−1232.6	NA	148.0
a. Sub-Sahara	3.1	22.0	0.1	4.5	30.2	1.46	NA	NA	NA	NA
b. Other	3.3	11.2	0.2	3.6	15.2	13.04	NA	NA	NA	NA
4. All developing economies	4.3	15.6	0.5	4.9	8.6	3.18	84.31	413.8	2.7	39.9
5. All industrial economies	4.8	7.6	6.5	10.1	0.7	0.75	227.34	235.3	33.5	64.9
6. All economies	4.6	10.6	4.9	10.6	0.9	0.98	217.02	236.4	24.9	70.6
7. Smaller Asian economies	15.0	31.8	8.3	31.8	2.7	0.62	686.35	2654.8	119.0	178.3
8. Larger Asian economies	2.4	7.5	0.1	7.5	38.5	5.98	160.58	595.1	3.1	25.3

Note: NA = Not available
Source: As per Table 10.1 and Emerging Stock Markets Factbook (1998, 1990).

East and South East Asian developing countries were 5.1 per cent and 23.9 per cent. These rates of increase are about the same as those for countries in South America (6.8 per cent and 21.9 per cent) and North Africa (3.5 per cent and 12.8 per cent) but not (and rather surprisingly as it is usually perceived to be marginalized in the globalization process) for Sub-Saharan Africa (4.1 per cent and 23.0 per cent) (UNCTAD, 1998a).

* The most pronounced trends towards globalization have occurred in China (classified as a Group 2 country) and Group 1 Asian developing countries. Most noticeably the significance of inbound FDI has increased the most in China and some Group 3 countries, for example Vietnam, Nepal and Myanmar. At the same time, Hong Kong, taiwan and Korea have each moved along their investment development paths to become important outward investors. It is also noteworthy that an increasing proportion of Asia outward direct investment, particularly by Group 1 countries, has been directed to advanced industrial countries outside Asia (Dunning et al., 1997); and, in part at least, has been geared to gaining access to new resources and markets rather than to exploiting a particular competitive advantage of the investing firms.

* While, until the mid-1980s, most of new FDI in and by Asian developing countries took the form of greenfield investment, in the last decade the share in global M&As accounted for by these countries has risen sharply. In 1990, for example, the total value of these M&As involving South, East and South East Asian firms as buyers or sellers was 4.9 per cent; by 1997 this figure had risen to 9.0 per cent (UNCTAD, 1998a). However, in both years, two-thirds of the Asian firms' sales and more than four-fifths of the purchasing Asian firms were from China and Group 1 countries.

* Since the early 1980s there has been a huge increase in inbound portfolio investment into Asian developing countries – particularly in bonds and notes. In 1985 such countries accounted for 2.4 per cent of global inbound FPI; by 1996 this proportion had risen to 4.2 per cent. Corresponding figures for outbound FPI from Asian developing countries were 0.7 per cent and 3.1 per cent. In 1990 FPI into Asia was still only 2.5 per cent of FDI. By 1994–95 this proportion had risen to 50.1 per cent. Partly the increase, which again was strongly concentrated in China and Group 1 countries, reflects the development of the capital markets in these countries. The last column of Table 10.2 shows that the market value of Asian domestic capital markets was 53.5 per cent of their GDPs in 1996, compared with 39.9 per cent for all developing countries.

What are the explanations for these facts? In terms of the Ownership Locational Internationalization (OLI) paradigm of international production (Dunning, 1993, 1995), the marked increase in inbound FDI reflects the rising locational advantages of Asian compared with other developing countries; and/or a greater propensity of FDIs to internalize the markets for their competitive (that is, ownership specific) advantages. The opening up of several markets into which FDI had been previously restricted (for example, in Korea) and the gradual upgrading of indigenous, but location-bound, created assets (especially skilled labour, the institutional framework and technological infrastructure) needed by foreign firms to exploit their own particular core competencies, explain much of the growth of inward FDI. At the same time, Asian firms have come to evolve their own unique competitive advantages, which together with rising domestic wage rates and encouragement both from the indigenous banking system and their home governments, explain the upsurge in outbound investment over the last decade or so. Of course, the opening up of The People's Republic of China to inbound FDI was the greatest single stimulus to that country's entry into the global market economy. In 1997, China accounted for 41.1 per cent of the inbound FDI stake into South, East and South East Asian developing economies. Hong Kong was responsible for nearly one-half of such investment, and Singapore and Taiwan another third between them. However, it is estimated that more than two-thirds of that investment went to Mainland China – that is, was symptomatic of a trend towards regionalization rather than globalization.

Whether one prefers Ozawa's stages of economic development (Ozawa, 1992, 1996) or our own 'investment development path', explanation of the dynamics of FDI in and out of developing countries, the deepening of the structural integration between Asian economies and the rest of the world, and the continual upgrading of indigenous resources facilitated by both inward and outward FDI, have exhibited an entirely predictable pattern over the last two decades. Moreover, in explaining why Asian developing countries – be they in Groups 1, 2 or 3 – have generally recorded higher levels of FDI than those of other developing countries, particularly in the last decade, one finds the more export- and market-oriented friendly approach of Asian governments, a more entrepreneurial culture and the Confucian ethic of the Asian people, and a greater quality control and a consensus approach to decision taking by Asian firms, have all helped these economies to embrace the challenges and opportunities of the global economy more easily than their counterparts in Africa and Latin America.

While recent economic events are most certainly slowing down the pace of globalization in East Asian countries,[6] the demands on Asian firms to become even more competitive in their home and foreign markets are likely to become even more pressing. And though outbound FDI is likely to be curtailed until the early 2000s, and some expansion plans shelved,[7] it is also likely that the depreciating currency of several Asian countries (notably Malaysia, Hong Kong, Korea and Indonesia) will lead to more inbound FDI – particularly from Europe and the US – including some acquisitions of, or alliances with, Asian firms now facing financial difficulties. In the longer run, however, we anticipate a renewed upgrading in the resources and capabilities of the Asian 'tigers', particularly in sectors which, if they are to be internationally competitive, their firms also need to be part of a global network of valued added activities.[8]

4. EUROPEAN FDI IN DEVELOPING ASIAN ECONOMIES

With these thoughts in mind let me now turn to consider recent, and likely future, trends of European FDI in Asia. In doing so I shall rely very heavily on a European Commission/UNCTAD report, *Investing in Asia's Dynamism: European Union Direct Investment in Asia*, published in 1996; an Invest in France Mission/DATAR/Arthur Anderson study on *International Investment: Towards the Year 2001*; and a study by the European Round Table of Industrialists on *Investment in the Developing World*, also published in 1997.

Table 10.3 sets out some data on FDI by EU countries in selected Asian countries between 1980 and 1993, and compares it with that of other Triad investors. This reveals that, over this period, the EU's stock of all FDI in the named Asian countries fell from 16.4 per cent to 12.9 per cent, but that this mainly reflected a rise in non-Triad (mostly intra-Asian) FDI in the region. In the case of the Group 1 countries and most Group 2 countries about which data are available, the increase in the European stake more or less kept pace with that of the US and Japanese stake. However, in China, European – and to a lesser extent US – MNEs have lagged well behind their Asian counterparts; and this pulled down the share of all EU FDI in Asia quite considerably.

When one looks at individual Asian countries, one sees the share of European FDI (relative to that of US and Japanese FDI) – being the highest in Singapore and Malaysia – the UK and/or other European investors have long had cultural, ethnic political or economic links. By contrast, in the Philippines and Thailand, the US has a larger than average stake, while the Japanese presence is seen to be most marked in Indonesia and Korea, and that of Mainland China is concentrated in Hong Kong and Taiwan. Again this picture is largely consistent with traditional FDI theory.

Table 10.3   FDI by the Triad in developing Asia (millions of dollars and percentage)

| | Stocks | | | | | | Flows | | | |
| | 1980 | | 1985 | | 1993 | | 1985–87 | | 1990–93 | |
	Value	Share of total FDI	Value	Share of total FDI	Value	Share of total FDI	Value	Share of total FDI	Value	Share of total FDI
Hong Kong										
European Union	NA	NA	182	12.4	647	12.3	33	17.2	17	12.5
Japan	NA	NA	308	21.0	1788	34.1	84	44.2	67	49.5
United States	NA	NA	788	53.7	1474	28.1	80	42.2	15	10.7
Triad total	NA	NA	1278	87.2	3910	74.6	197	103.6	99	72.8
All countries	NA	NA	1466	100.0	5244	100.0	190	100.0	135	100.0
Korea, Republic of										
European Union	123	6.6	241	6.6	2220	19.8	31	7.4	360	34.8
Japan	1026	55.0	1002	52.3	4466	39.8	224	53.6	226	21.8
United States	491	26.3	1073	29.5	3259	29.1	120	28.7	333	32.2
Triad total	1640	87.9	3216	88.5	9945	88.7	375	89.6	919	88.8
All countries	1866	100.0	3634	100.0	11209	100.0	419	100.0	1034	100.0
Singapore										
European Union	1342	39.6	2040	30.4	5271	26.9	147	16.5	342	16.3
Japan	567	16.7	1600	23.9	6167	31.5	355	39.8	489	23.3
United States	1001	29.6	2440	36.4	6851	35.0	268	30.0	572	27.3
Triad total	2910	85.9	6081	90.7	18289	93.4	771	86.2	1404	66.9
All countries	3387	100.0	6708	100.0	19581	100.0	894	100.0	2098	100.0

Malaysia

European Union	1720	26.6	2264	26.6	5842	17.1	84	10.3	837	15.2
Japan	1135	17.6	1602	18.8	7435	21.8	284	34.7	1142	20.7
United States	413	6.4	604	7.1	3586	10.5	65	7.9	709	12.9
Triad total	3268	50.6	4470	52.5	16864	49.5	144	17.6	2688	48.8
All countries	6462	100.0	8510	100.0	34091	100.0	818	100.0	5508	100.0

Group 1 countries total

European Union	3185	27.2	4727	23.3	13980	19.9	295	12.7	1556	17.7
Japan	2728	23.3	4512	22.2	19856	28.3	947	40.8	1924	21.9
United States	1905	16.3	4905	24.1	15170	21.6	533	23.0	1629	18.6
Triad total	7818	66.7	15045	74.0	49008	69.9	1487	64.1	5110	58.2
All countries	11715	100.0	20318	100.0	70125	100.0	2321	100.0	8775	100.0

Indonesia

European Union	851	8.3	2672	17.4	9967	14.7	269	25.7	1205	13.4
Japan	3462	33.7	5009	32.6	13937	20.6	329	31.4	1379	15.3
United States	437	4.3	974	6.3	3701	5.5	123	11.7	450	5.0
Triad total	4750	46.2	8655	56.4	27605	40.8	721	68.8	3034	33.7
All countries	10274	100.0	15353	100.0	67625	100.0	1047	100.0	8999	100.0

Philippines

European Union	114	9.3	349	13.5	748	17.1	15	12.3	71	21.7
Japan	206	16.8	362	14.0	890	20.3	12	9.5	111	33.7
United States	669	54.6	1461	56.6	1937	44.1	79	65.2	55	16.7
Triad total	988	80.7	2172	84.2	3576	81.5	105	87.1	237	72.1
All countries	1225	100.0	2580	100.0	4389	100.0	121	100.0	329	100.0

Table 10.3 (cont.)

| | Stocks | | | | | | Flows | | | |
| | 1980 | | 1985 | | 1993 | | 1985–87 | | 1990–93 | |
	Value	Share of total FDI	Value	Share of total FDI	Value	Share of total FDI	Value	Share of total FDI	Value	Share of total FDI
Thailand										
European Union	156	15.9	350	15.8	1484	10.7	24	9.2	210	10.3
Japan	285	29.0	622	28.0	4.579	32.9	100	38.5	602	29.4
United States	322	32.8	721	32.5	2412	17.3	69	26.7	311	15.2
Triad total	762	77.7	1693	76.2	8476	60.9	193	74.4	1122	54.8
All countries	981	100.0	2221	100.0	13918	100.0	259	100.0	2050	100.0
China										
European Union	300	13.6	584	8.3	2018	3.5	113	5.5	300	2.6
Japan	128	5.8	502	7.2	4288	7.5	245	12	782	6.7
United States	372	16.9	1106	15.8	4680	8.2	312	15.2	830	7.1
Triad total	800	36.3	2192	31.2	10986	19.2	670	32.7	1911	16.4
All countries	2202	100.0	7015	100.0	57172	100.0	2048	100.0	11631	100.0
Group 2 countries total										
European Union	1421	9.7	3955	14.6	14217	9.9	421	12.1	3501	10.5
Japan	4081	27.8	6495	23.9	23.694	16.6	686	19.7	5316	15.9
United States	1800	12.3	4262	15.7	12730	8.9	583	16.8	3686	11.0
Triad total	7300	49.7	14712	54.1	50643	35.4	1689	48.6	12502	37.3
All countries	14682	100.0	27169	100.0	143104	100.0	3475	100.0	33473	100.0

218

Notes:

NA = Not available.

[a] Manufacturing only.

[b] Data for 1985 stock are 1984.

[c] Basaef on approvals.

[d] Data for 1980 and 1985 stocks are 1981 and 1985, respectively.

[e] Stocks are gross fixed assets of foreign companies for stock and flows are changes in gross fixed assets.

[f] Data for 1985 stock are 1986 and data for 1985–87 flows are 1986–88.

[g] Includes another East Asian economy.

[h] Data for 1985–87 flows are only 1987 flows.

[i] Data for 1985 stock are 1967.

[j] Singapore is included in (newly industrializing economies (NIEs). Bronei Darussalam and Vietnam are excluded.

[k] Data for 1980 and 1985 stocks are 1984 and 1987.

Source: UNCTAD, Division on Transnational Corporations and Investment, FDI database.

What, however, is perhaps a little surprising is the increase in the share of the EU since the 1980s in countries with strong US or Japanese connections, for example the Philippines and Korea, and a decrease in their relative participation in countries in which they have strong historical ties, namely Singapore and Malaysia. It would seem then that there has been some convergence in the geographical origin of Triad FDI in the Asian countries over the last decade, and that is paralleling the trend in other parts of the world, for example the US and Europe.

Part of the explanation for these changing shares of EU FDI is that, while the pre-1980s patterns of FDI strongly reflected the competitive advantages, psychic ties and natural resource needs of the investing countries, in more recent years most FDI has been in sectors in which competitive advantages tend to be more *firm* than *country* specific, and in which large MNEs from each of the Triad countries are well represented. The auto, chemical, electronics, clothing and footwear, and telecommunications industries are cases in point. It is our belief that both the geographical origin and the industrial structures of inbound investment – particularly in Group 1 Asian developing countries – will continue to converge,[9] and reflect as much the degree of multinationality or strategies of the investing firms as their countries of origin.

Other data on the sales of foreign affiliates in Asia and exports to Asia from the three Triad countries or regions suggest that, in the mid-1990s, EU firms exported slightly more to Asia than their Asian subsidiaries produced and sold. This was in contrast to the rest of the world, where the main modality of servicing foreign customers was through FDI rather than exports. In the case of US and Japanese firms, too, the relative significance of deep integration was higher in other regions than developing Asia.

Economists usually distinguish between different kinds of trade and FDI according to their *natural resource* and/or *created asset* intensity.[10] Table 10.4 shows quite clearly the growing importance of capital and technology-intensive trade and investment, relative to more traditional natural resource and labour-seeking FDI. It also shows that relative to their share of all manufacturing FDI, that of EU MNEs in technology/capital-intensive FDI has increased the most, and that their 'revealed' comparative advantage[11] in both these kinds of FDI is higher than that for the US and Japanese.

Turning now to recent surveys of European business and their attitudes towards investing in Asia, we would make two points.

- The regulatory environment in most Asian countries – and particularly in smaller Group 1 countries – is perceived to compare reason-

Table 10.4   Shares of developing Asia in world manufacturing FDI stock and manufactured exports of the EU, Japan and the US by industry groups, 1985 and 1993 (percentage)

Item	European Union		United States		Japan	
	1985	1993	1985	1993	1985	1993
Outward FDI						
Resource intensive[a,b]	4.9	1.9	1.8	5.2	28.9	29.1
Labour intensive[c]	1.6	2.1	1.8	4.1	50.4	34.8
Technology/capital intensive[d]	3.4	4.7	5.1	9.8	25.3	27.3
All manufacturing	3.4	3.7	3.7	7.5	30.8	29.1
Exports						
Resource intensive[a,b]	2.0	3.8	12.5	15.0	45.5	65.1
Labour intensive[c]	4.2	5.8	13.9	13.2	30.9	44.6
Capital/technology intensive[d]	5.8	7.4	13.7	20.1	22.0	33.5
All manufactured exports	4.1	6.2	13.4	18.0	26.1	37.4

Notes:
[a] Food, beverages and tobacco, paper and wood products, coal and petroleum products, rubber products, non-metallic mineral products and metals. Coverage of industries varies, to some extent, for the different categories in FDI and exports.
[b] Data are for 1994.
[c] Textiles and 'other manufacturing'.
[d] Chemicals, mechanical equipment, electrical and electronic equipment, motor vehicles and other transport equipment.
Source: UNCTAD, Division on Transnational Corporations and Investment, FDI database; and UNCTAD trade statistics database.

ably favourably with that in other developing countries, particularly in respect of alliance formation and investment protection. Of the 10 countries identified in Table 10.5, Korea was ranked the least liberal in its attitudes towards FDI. In another survey conducted by the European Round Table of Industrialists (1997)[12] (which embraced a rather different sample of developing countries) most of the Asian developing countries were classified as being 'quite open' in 1996 and/or were opening up to FDI at above-average speed.

• Of the transaction cost-related barriers to FDI in Asia, set out in Table 10.6, those related to bureaucracy, corruption and lobbying were the ones most frequently mentioned by an opinion survey of some 300 businessmen conducted by the World Economic Forum

Table 10.5 Survey results on the FDI regime in Asian developing countries[a]

Economy	Local K market * (A)	Acquisition of control (B)	Equal treatment * (C)	Employment of foreigners (D)	Strategic alliances (E)	Cross-border ventures * (F)	Investment protection (G)	Image of country * (H)	Overall assessment (I)
Group 1									
Singapore	3.8	8.2	7.6	7.6	8.4	9.0	7.3	9.0	7.6
Hong Kong	9.2	9.3	6.6	7.0	8.5	8.5	5.1	8.6	7.8
Republic of Korea	7.8	4.8	5.3	4.4	5.3	5.3	5.9	5.8	5.6
Malaysia	6.1	4.9	5.0	5.5	7.4	7.8	7.2	8.4	6.5
Thailand	7.0	5.2	7.0	5.9	7.8	7.7	6.4	7.4	6.8
Taiwan	5.8	N/A	7.6	N/A	N/A	6.7	N/A	6.8	6.7
Group 2									
Philippines	7.5	6.0	7.2	6.9	7.5	7.4	6.7	6.4	6.9
Indonesia	6.2	6.2	5.8	6.2	7.5	6.6	6.5	6.2	6.4
China	5.7	6.5	5.4	6.2	5.2	5.9	7.8	7.9	6.3
Group 3									
India	6.3	6.6	5.3	6.5	6.6	4.3	5.7	4.1	5.7
Other developing Asia	8.4	6.2	7.5	5.8	6.8	7.9	6.5	3.9	6.6
Average, 11 Asian economies	7.0	6.2	6.3	6.0	7.0	6.8	6.4	6.6	6.5

Developed countries[b]	8.1	8.1	6.7	6.9	7.3	8.3	6.1	6.4	7.2
Countries and countries in transition[c]	7.2	7.7	5.9	7.3	5.7	7.3	5.6	5.2	6.5

Notes:
N/A = Not available.
* Indicates 1997 data.
[a] Survey results are scaled from 0 (least favourable to FDI) to 10 (most favourable to FDI) in terms of the items (A)–(G).
(A) Access to local capital is restricted for foreign companies (0)/is not restricted (10).
(B) Foreign investors may not acquire (0)/are free (10) to acquire control in a domestic company.
(C) Foreigners are not treated (0)/are treated (10) equally to citizens in all respects.
(D) Immigration laws prevent (0)/do not prevent (10) your company from employing foreign skills.
(E) Strategic alliances are not common (0)/are common (10) between domestic and foreign firms.
(F) Cross-border ventures cannot be negotiated with foreign partners without government-imposed restraint (0)/can be negotiated freely (10).
(G) Investment protection schemes are not (0)/are (10) available for most foreign partner countries.
(H) Image of your country abroad (0) hinders the development of business/(10) supports the development of business.
(I) Average assessment according to criteria (A)–(F).
[b] Average for Australia, Canada, France, Germany, Italy, Switzerland, United Kingdom and the United States.
[c] Average for Argentina, Brazil, Chile, Colombia, Czech Republic, Hungary, Mexico, Poland, Russia and Venezuela.
Source: World Economic Forum (1995, 1997).

Table 10.6   Transaction cost-related barriers to FDI in Asian developing countries[a]

Economy	Cultural barriers * (A)	Country image * (B)	State control (C)	Transpa-rency * (D)	Bureau-cracy * (E)	Corrup-tion * (F)	Lobbying (G)	Distri-bution system * (H)	Tele-commu-nications (I)	Techno-logical infrastruc. (J)	Labour Regulation * (K)	Overall assess-ment (L)
Group 1												
Singapore	8.5	9.0	7.1	7.4	7.6	9.4	7.8	9.2	9.3	8.6	3.2	7.9
Hong Kong	8.5	8.6	9.0	6.4	7.0	6.9	6.5	8.2	9.3	6.3	8.2	7.7
Rep. of Korea	4.9	5.8	4.6	3.1	2.5	4.6	5.3	3.5	7.4	5.5	8.0	4.8
Thailand	6.6	7.4	5.1	2.9	4.1	2.6	3.7	5.5	4.9	4.3	6.9	4.9
Malaysia	6.7	8.4	5.7	6.1	5.5	4.8	4.9	7.3	7.2	5.3	7.9	5.8
Taiwan	8.5	6.7	NA	4.6	4.0	4.4	NA	6.2	NA	NA	4.9	NA
Group 2												
Indonesia	7.3	6.2	4.4	4.2	3.6	2.3	3.6	4.5	5.9	4.0	5.8	4.6
Philippines	8.8	6.4	4.7	4.8	2.8	2.0	3.6	3.9	3.7	3.1	5.6	4.1
China	6.7	7.8	4.1	5.8	1.8	2.5	4.5	3.7	5.3	2.7	5.0	4.2
Group 3												
India	7.4	4.1	4.0	2.7	2.7	1.9	3.9	3.3	4.0	3.8	2.8	4.1
Other Asia	8.0	3.9	5.9	2.6	3.0	2.4	4.1	5.8	6.3	6.3	7.2	5.6
Average, 11 Asian economies	7.6	5.7	4.6	4.0	2.8	2.2	3.9	4.2	5.0	4.0	5.9	4.5
Developed countries[b]	7.3	6.7	6.1	5.0	3.9	7.0	4.5	7.4	7.8	6.5	4.9	6.3
Developing countries and countries in transition[c]	8.0	5.2	5.1	3.5	2.5	2.7	4.2	4.8	4.9	3.5	4.8	4.6

Notes:

NA = Not available.

[a] Survey results are scaled from 0 (least favourable to FDI) to 10 (most favourable to FDI) in terms of the items (A)–(L).

* Indicates 1997 data.

(A) National culture is closed (0)/open (10) towards foreign cultures.

(B) Image of your country abroad is distorted (0)/reflects reality accurately (10).

(C) State control of enterprises distorts (0)/does not distort (10) fair competition in your country.

(D) The government does not often communicate its intentions successfully (0)/is transparent towards citizens (10).

(E) Bureaucracy hinders (0)/does not hinder (10) business development.

(F) Improper practices (such as bribing or corruption) prevail (0)/do not prevail (10) in the public sphere.

(G) Lobbying by special interest groups distorts (0)/does not distort (10) government decision making.

(H) Distribution systems are generally inefficient (0)/efficient (10).

(I) Telecommunications infrastructure does not meet (0)/meets business requirements very well (10).

(J) Technological infrastructure is developed slower (0)/faster (10) than in your competitor countries.

(K) Labour regulations are (0) too restrictive/(10) are flexible enough.

(L) Average assessment according to criteria (A)–(K).

[b] Average for Australia, Canada, France, Germany, Italy, Switzerland, United Kingdom and the United States.

[c] Average for Argentina, Brazil, Chile, Colombia, Czech Republic, Egypt, Hungary, Mexico, Peru, Poland, Russia and Venezuela.

Source: *World Economic Forum* (1995, 1997).

(1995, 1997). These were again most marked in Group 2 Asian countries and in India. Including developed countries in our analysis, it is clear that, as countries move along their investment development paths (Dunning and Narula, 1996), the transaction cost-related barriers to inbound FDI fall. Table 10.6 also shows that relative to other developing countries, Asian countries do well on all counts identified except with respect to the quality of their local capital markets. In particular, they were perceived to have particularly good telecommunications and technological infrastructures; and their governments were thought to be more transparent at successfully communicating their intentions.

A final table, Table 10.7, drawn from the Invest in France Mission/DATAR/ Arthur Anderson report (1997), compares the perceptions of some 310 MNE executives and international experts about past and future FDI intentions. The replies are categorized both by the home region of the investing companies and by the region of investment. The table shows that, over the past five years, and among developing regions, Asian countries have been ranked the highest by all groups of foreign investors. Even more impressive, it is anticipated that over the next five years developing Asia will have a higher priority for new FDI than either Western Europe or North America.[13] As might be expected, Asian and Japanese MNEs grade the developing Asian region higher than do their US or Western European counterparts; however, it is the Western-based firms which are most upgrading their investment expectations in Asia.

The data set out in Tables 10.4 to 10.7 suggest that historically speaking, and with a few major exceptions, Western European MNEs have generally underestimated the growth potential of the dynamic Asian economies. Partly this is most certainly due to the greater 'psychic' distance between Europe and many Asian countries than as between Japan and the US and these countries; and the fact that, in engaging in low-cost production outside their home countries, European MNEs have preferred to use neighbouring regions (for example, Southern Europe and North Africa) rather than more distant locations. Partly too, European MNEs are (or believe they are) at a competitive disadvantage in supplying goods to Asian markets *vis-à-vis* their Japanese or Asian counterparts. More recently, the 'benign' neglect[14] of Asia by European MNEs has been exacerbated by the further liberalization of trade and FDI in the EU and by the partial renaissance of the market economy in Central and Eastern Europe.

While the increased attention now being given by European MNEs to Asia suggests some reprioritization of their geographical preferences – as witnessed, for example, by a sharp increase in approved new projects by

Table 10.7 *Investment priorities by region: Past, present and future (Opinion of 310 MNEs and international experts)*

	Home country		Western Europe (1)		North America (1)		Japan (1)		Developing Asia (1)		Latin America		Africa		Central-Eastern Europe	
	Past	Future	Past	Future	Past	Future	Past	Future	Past	Future	Past	Future	Past	Future	Past	Future
By home region																
North America	7.6	6.8	5.8	5.6	4.4	4.4	2.5	2.8	4.1	6.7	3.5	4.5	0.6	0.9	1.9	3.4
Asian NIEs	5.7	5.3	2.9	3.7	3.8	4.4	2.2	1.7	7.0	7.5	1.7	2.1	0.6	0.8	1.6	2.1
Japan	7.7	7.4	4.4	4.7	5.9	5.7	0.0	0.0	6.7	7.6	1.8	3.1	0.7	1.0	1.7	2.9
Western Europe	6.9	6.0	5.6	5.5	3.7	4.0	1.4	1.7	4.0	5.5	2.5	3.7	1.0	1.1	3.2	4.4
By size of revenue																
>10 billion $	6.9	6.2	5.6	5.3	4.2	4.3	2.2	2.6	5.3	7.1	3.3	4.5	1.2	1.3	3.3	4.5
1 to 10 billion $	6.7	5.9	5.7	5.4	4.4	4.5	2.0	2.1	4.4	6.2	2.6	3.8	0.9	1.0	2.7	3.8
<1 billion $	7.1	6.3	4.6	5.0	3.5	4.0	1.0	1.5	4.5	5.8	2.0	2.7	0.5	0.8	1.6	2.7
NA	7.7	6.7	4.6	4.7	4.2	4.5	1.6	2.1	4.7	6.3	2.6	3.7	0.7	0.9	2.7	4.0
By industry																
Manufacturing	7.0	6.2	5.3	5.2	4.6	4.7	2.0	2.4	4.9	6.5	2.5	3.6	0.7	0.8	2.5	3.7
Services	7.1	6.2	5.0	5.2	3.0	3.5	1.1	1.5	4.2	5.7	2.4	3.5	0.9	1.1	2.5	3.7
By type of respondent																
Companies	6.7	6.0	5.4	5.2	4.2	4.3	1.8	2.2	4.8	6.3	2.7	3.9	0.9	1.1	2.7	3.9
Expert	7.6	6.6	4.6	5.0	3.9	4.3	1.3	1.7	4.5	6.3	2.4	3.2	0.6	0.8	2.2	3.3
Total	7.0	6.2	5.2	5.1	4.1	4.3	1.7	2.0	4.7	6.3	2.6	3.7	0.8	1.0	2.5	3.7

Note: (1) Excluding home country. Past = last five years. Future = next five years (1996–2001). Scale from 0 to 10.0. 0 = no priority. 10 = maximum priority. Average of answers.
Sources: Invest in France Mission/DATAR/Arthur Anderson (1997).

European investors in India, and an increasing number of bilateral and tax treaties concluded between EU member states and Asean countries in the first half of the 1990s[15] – it is too early to judge whether, over the next decade or so, they can make substantial inroads to markets already largely secured by Asian and US MNEs. Perhaps the best opportunities lie in the penetration of the giant Chinese and Indian markets and of the newly emerging economies of the Indian sub-continent (including Myamar).[16] For historical and cultural reasons, India, perhaps, offers the greatest opportunities; although relative to other Western investors, the European presence in Malaysia and Indonesia has always been quite strong. Clearly, too, more needs to be done in creating additional new and closer Asia/European trade, technology and FDI networks; particularly in the light of closer trans-Pacific links likely to follow as APEC gets up steam. It is here, in particular, that the European Commission and the European Investment Bank can provide useful institutional support and financial help, particularly to small firms as they seek both to evaluate and exploit opportunities for FDI, and for alliance formation between European and Asian firms.

5. CONCLUSIONS

This chapter has demonstrated that over the last decade many Asian developing countries have been at the forefront of the globalization process, and that the more advanced of these are becoming important outward investors, not only elsewhere in Asia but in industrialized Western nations. It has further shown that inbound FDI is playing an increasingly important role in helping Asian developing economies to upgrade their economic structures in tune with the demands of the international market place, and to help them gain access to foreign resources and markets (UNCTAD, 1997). In this connection the recent export performance of US manufacturing subsidiaries in Asia is most impressive.[17] The emergence and growth of domestic capital markets has also facilitated the inflow of FPI,[18] which has further stimulated both investment and exports by indigenous firms.

A final section of the chapter showed that, except in Asian countries which have close historical and cultural ties, European FDI in developing Asian countries has lagged behind that of other countries. This is partly because European investors have given Asia a lower investment priority than other regions, and partly because other Asian and US MNEs had already gained an export foothold in these markets. On the other hand, in the last five years there has been a slight shift in the geography of new European FDI (notably from the UK) towards developing Asia; and according to the European industrialists' survey, this shift is likely to accelerate over the next five years.

Finally, while the events of the last two years will undoubtedly slow down the globalization process of the Asian economies – and particularly the outbound FDI by their MNEs – we do not anticipate that this will lead to a major shift in the economic philosophy or outward-looking stance of these countries. We would agree with *The Economist* (1998) that the remedy for the current bout of Asian 'economic flu' lies in more prudent monetary and debt policies, a further liberalization of domestic financial systems, stricter bank regulation and supervision, exchange rate flexibility and a restructuring of some of the larger Asian (for example, the Korean) chaebols. In turn, these reforms coupled with a continuation of market facilitating macro-organizational strategies should lead to leaner, fitter and more stable Asian economies and even more competitive Asian MNEs. It is this, as much as any short-term repercussions of the crisis which the Western industrialized nations should be most concerned about. And one way they may be able to capitalize on the current weakness of Asian currencies is for their own corporations to gain a further foothold (via FDI and alliance formation) in what, after all, remains and is likely to remain one of the most dynamic growth regions in the world.

NOTES

1. United Nations Development Programme.
2. O'Brien (1992), quoted in Kobrin (1993).
3. For example, South and South East Asian countries accounted for 14.2 per cent of global outward direct investment in 1996, compared with 8.7 per cent in 1992. This share, however, dropped back to 11.8 per cent in 1997.
4. See especially the Appendices in UNCTAD (1997).
5. This measure is preferred to that of FDI flows to gross domestic capital formation partly because FDI flows sometimes include reinvested projects and sometimes they do not; and partly because FDI flows are essentially a financial measure whereas capital formation is a real expenditure measure.
6. Both indirectly and as a result of the rippling effects these events have on the rest of the world. For example, in December 1997, the IMF revised downwards its projections for world economic growth (GDP) by a one percentage point in 1997 and 0.8 percentage point in 1998, with particular sharp reductions for the Asian economies of 3.8 per cent for Korea, 5.4 per cent for Indonesia and Malaysia and 7.0 per cent for Thailand (IMF Survey, 1998). In 1997, the outward direct investment flow from Korea was $4287 million, compared with $4670 million in 1996. The corresponding figures for Malaysia and Thailand were $3100 million and $3700 million and $500 million and $931 million respectively (UNCTAD, 1998a). See also Appendix 1, Table 10A1.3 to this chapter.
7. For example, in 1998 a number of Korean MNEs including Hyundai and Samsung Electronics announced they were postponing or shelving expansion plans for their UK subsidiaries.

8. At the same time it is possible that the ownership and/or control structure of Asian globalization might change, and that Western firms may play a more important role than they have done up to now.
9. At least at a two or even three digit SIC level. However, within these industries, the principle of comparative advantage still holds good and different countries tend to specialize in the production of different kinds of products.
10. The former is sometimes referred to as Heckscher–Ohlin (H–O) trade, and the latter as Schumpeterian (S) trade.
11. Obtained by dividing the share of a particular type of FDI or exports by the share of all FDI and exports.
12. The European Industrialists survey excluded Singapore and Hong Kong from the Asian developing countries, but included Bangladesh, Vietnam, Pakistan and Sri Lanka.
13. This survey was undertaken between June and October 1996. A later survey published in 1998 confirms the high rating given to both China and the Asia/Pacific region, right up to the year 2002. See Invest in France Mission/Arthur Anderson (1998).
14. An expression coined by the European Commission, see UNCTAD (1997), p. 59.
15. According to the European Commission/UNCTAD, 1996 (pp. 64–5) survey, by November 1994, 109 such tax treaties and 103 investment treaties had been concluded.
16. Where in December 1996, EU countries accounted for 40 per cent of the (approved) FDI stocks (Mason, 1997).
17. In 1993, for example, US manufacturing subsidiaries in Asian developing countries exported 69.9 per cent of their sales. The corresponding proportion for Latin-American subsidiaries was 41 per cent, for African subsidiaries 50.4 per cent and for subsidiaries in all countries 51.1 per cent (US Department of Commerce, 1995).
18. Between 1983–89 and 1990–95 the annual average flows of inward portfolio investment to Asian countries increased nearly eight times (from $1840m to $14512m). However, due primarily to substantial privatization schemes in Brazil, Mexico and Argentina, and in Central Europe, the inflow of portfolio capital to other developing countries over the same period of time was 28 fold (from $8719m to $20048M).

REFERENCES

Booz, Allen and Hamilton (1997), *Cross Border Alliances in the Age of Collaboration*, Los Angeles: Booz, Allen and Hamilton.

Cuyvers, L., P. de Lombaerde and D. van Den Bulcke (1997), 'European Round Table of Industrialists (ERT)', *Investment in the Developing World*, Brussels: ERT.

Dunning, J.H. (1981), 'Explaining the international development path of countries: towards a dynamic or developmental approach', *Weltwirtschaftliches Archiv*, **119**, 30–64.

Dunning, J.H. (1986), 'The investment development cycle revisited', *Weltwirtschaftliches Archiv*, **122**, 667–77.

Dunning, J.H. (1993), *Multinational Enterprises and the Global Economy*, Wokingham, England and Reading, Mass.: Addison Wesley.

Dunning, J.H. (1995), 'Reappraising the eclectic paradigm in an age of alliance capitalism', *Journal of International Business Studies*, **XXVI** (3), 461–91.

Dunning, J.H. and Narula, R. (1996), *Foreign Direct Investment and Governments*, London and New York: Routledge.

Dunning, J.H., R. Narula and R. van Hoesel (1996), *Explaining the New Wave of Outward FDI from Developing Countries*, occasional paper 2/96–013, Maastricht: MERIT.

Economist, The (1998), 'Keeping the hot money out', *The Economist*, 24 Jan 1998, 85–6.

European Commission/UNCTAD (1996), *Investing in Asia's Dynamism*, Brussels: Office for Official Publications of the European Communities.

European Round Table of Industrialists (1997), *Investment in the Developing World*, Brussels: European Round Table of Industrialists.

IMF (1998), 'Interim assessment revises global growth projections downwards', *IMF Survey*, **27** (1), 12 Jan., 1–4.

IMF (various), *Balance of Payments Statistics Yearbook Summary Tables*, Washington, DC: IMF.

International Finance Corporation (1990), *Emerging Stock Markets Factbook*, Washington, DC.

International Finance Corporation (1998), *Emerging Stock Markets Factbook*, Washington, DC.

Invest in France Mission/DATAR/Arthur Anderson (1997), *International Investment: Towards the Year 2001*, New York: UN.

Invest in France Mission/DATAR/Arthur Anderson (1998), *International Investment: Towards the Year 2002*, New York: UN.

Kobrin, S.J. (1993), *Beyond Geography: Inter-Firm Networks and the Structural Integration of the Global Economy*, Philadelphia: William H. Wurston Center for International Management Studies, The Wharton School, Working Paper 93–10.

Mason, M. (1997), *Foreign Direct Investment in Burma/Myanmar: Trends, Determinants and Prospects*, mimeo. New Haven: Yale University.

McGrew, A.G. and P.G. Lewis (1992), *Global Politics: Globalization and the Nation State*, Cambridge: The Polity Press.

O'Brien, R. (1992), *Global Financial Integration: The End of Geography*, London: Pinter Publishers.

Ozawa, T. (1992), 'Foreign direct investment and economic development', *Transnational Corporations*, **1** (1), 27–54.

Ozawa, T. (1996), 'Japan: The macro-IDP, meso IDPs and the technology development path', in J.H. Dunning and R. Narula (eds), *Foreign Direct Investment and Governments*, London and New York: Routledge.

Stopford, J. and S. Strange (1991), *Rival States, Rival Firms: Competition for World Market Shares*, Cambridge: Cambridge University Press.

UNCTAD (1997), *World Investment Report: Transnational Corporations, Market Structure and Competition Policy*, New York and Geneva: UN.

UNCTAD (1998a), *World Investment Report 1998: Trends and Determinants*, New York and Geneva: UN.

UNDP (1997), *Human Development Report 1997*, Oxford: OUP.

US Department of Commerce (1995), *US Direct Investments Abroad: Provisional Results, 1993*, Washington, DC: US Department of Commerce.

World Economic Forum (1995), *World Competitiveness Report 1995*, Geneva: IMD and World Economic Forum.

World Economic Forum (1997), *World Competitiveness Yearbook*, Lausanne and Geneva: IMD and World Economic Forum.

World Economic Forum (1998), *World Competitiveness Report*, Oxford: Oxford University Press.

APPENDIX 1

Table 10A1.1   FDI inflows by selected regions, 1990–97 (billions of dollars)

	1990	1991	1992	1993	1994	1995	1996	1997 (p)	Growth (%)	
									1990–94	1994–97
Africa	2.3	2.8	3.2	3.7	5.3	4.8	4.6	4.4	130.4	17.0
Central and Eastern Europe	1.2	2.5	4.4	6.3	5.9	14.3	12.4	14.4	391.7	144.1
Latin America and the Caribbean	9.3	15.3	16.2	18.2	29.6	31.1	41.8	53.0	218.3	79.0
South, East and South East Asia	20.1	21.2	27.7	47.6	56.4	66.1	83.1	86.2	180.6	52.8

Note: p = provisional.
Source: Geneva: FDI/TNC database.

Table 10A1.2   FDI inflows, by host region and economy, 1986–97

South, East and South East Asia	1986–91 Annual Ave.	1992	1993	1994	1995	1996	1997
High human development							
Singapore	3592	2204	4686	5480	6912	9440	10000
Malaysia	1605	5183	5006	4342	4132	5300	3754
Hong Kong	1711	2051	1667	2000	2100	2500	2600
Thailand	1325	2114	1730	1322	2003	2426	3600
Korea, Republic of	863	727	588	809	1776	2308	2341
Taiwan	1034	879	917	1375	1559	1402	2248
Brunei Darussalam	–	4	14	6	7	9	5
Total	10130	13162	14608	15334	18489	23385	24548

Medium human development

China	3105	11156	27515	33787	35849	42300	45300
Indonesia	1777	1777	2004	2109	4348	7960	5350
Vietnam	68	385	523	742	2000	2156	1200
Philippines	501	228	1238	1591	1478	1408	1253
Sri Lanka	41	123	195	166	63	170	140
Maldives	5	7	7	6	5	7	10
Total	5497	13676	31482	38401	43743	54001	53253

Low human development

India	177	233	574	1314	1929	2587	3264
Pakistan	188	335	347	419	639	690	800
Cambodia	–	33	54	69	151	350	200
Myanmar	68	171	149	91	115	100	80
Bangladesh	6	4	14	11	2	9	145
Nepal	2	1	4	6	5	5	20
Mongolia	–	2	8	7	10	5	7
Korea, Democratic People's Rep.	95	42	6	7	3	4	2
Total	536	777	1142	1910	2841	3741	4518

Source: UNCTAD, *World Investment Report* (1998a).

233

Table 10A1.3   FDI outflows, by host region and economy, 1986–97

South, East and South East Asia	1986–91 Annual Ave.	1992	1993	1994	1995	1996	1997
High human development							
Hong Kong	2373	8254	17713	21437	25000	26356	26000
Singapore	658	1317	2021	3104	3906	5900	5900
Korea, Republic of	923	1208	1361	2524	3529	4670	4287
Taiwan	3191	1869	2451	2460	2678	3843	5222
Malaysia	311	514	1325	1817	2575	3700	3100
Thailand	92	147	233	493	886	931	500
Brunei Darussalam	–	–	–	–	–	–	–
Total	7548	13309	25104	31835	38574	45400	45009
Medium human development							
China	745	4000	4400	2000	2000	2114	2500
Indonesia	7	52	356	609	603	512	2400
Philippines	–1	5	374	302	399	136	136
Sri Lanka	2	2	7	8	7	8	8
Vietnam	–	–	–	–	–	–	–
Maldives	–	–	–	–	–	–	–
Total	753	4059	5137	2919	3009	2770	5044

Low human development							
India	3	24	41	83	117	239	100
Pakistan	12	−12	−2	1	6	3	3
Cambodia	–	–	–	–	–	–	–
Myanmar	–	–	–	–	–	–	–
Bangladesh	–	–	–	–	–	–	–
Nepal	–	–	–	–	–	–	–
Mongolia	–	–	–	–	–	–	–
Korea, Democratic People's Rep.	–	–	–	–	–	–	–
Total	15	12	39	84	123	242	103

Source: UNCTAD, *World Investment Report* (1998a).

Table 10A2.1   Countries associated with high, medium and low human development categories

High human development
  Hong Kong
  Singapore
  Korea, Republic of
  Brunei Darussalam
  Thailand
  Malaysia
  Taiwan
Medium human development
  Sri Lanka
  Philippines
  Indonesia
  China
  Vietnam
Low human development
  Myanmar
  India
  Pakistan
  Cambodia
  Nepal
  Bangladesh

Source: UNDP (1997).

11. Firm-level determinants of outward FDI from the Korean and Taiwanese electronics industry: An econometric analysis

Roger van Hoesel

1. INTRODUCTION

For a long time the promotion of manufactured exports has been regarded as the most important source of economic growth of South Korea and Taiwan. At present, however, their cross-border business activities are no longer confined to exports. Since the end of the 1970s, Korean and Taiwanese companies have also started to invest abroad. Although this relatively new phenomenon has already been analysed to some extent at the more aggregate level (compare van Hoesel, 1996; Lee, 1994), much less is known about the firm-level determinants of outward investment. The primary goal of this chapter is therefore to investigate which firm-level factors determine whether a Korean or Taiwanese firm would rather invest abroad than export. But, as Chen (1992) noted, most of the indicators that are commonly tested in studies on the firm-level determinants of outward investment are typically ascribed to Multinational Enterprises (MNEs) from Early Industrialized Economies (EIEs). It therefore follows that a second question (almost automatically) has to be raised, namely whether the determinants that are derived from conventional MNE theory also apply in the case of MNEs from Late Industrialized Economies (LIEs). In other words, are the characteristics of Korean and Taiwanese MNEs similar to those of MNEs from EIEs?[1]

The numerous empirical studies carried out to test firm-level determinants of outward investment are in most cases based on samples of American, European or, especially in more recent years, Japanese companies.[2] In view of the fact that most Foreign Direct Investment (FDI) from Korea and Taiwan is still very recent, it is not surprising that the evidence from these LIEs is scarce. An early attempt to test variables that were expected to determine FDI by Korean manufacturing companies was made by Jeon (1992). This investigation concerned companies that had invested abroad before 1990, which restricted the sample to the (very) early outward investors. In addition, the equations estimated were certainly not limited to firm-level variables. 'National' variables (such as the growth of the Korean economy and geographic proximity) as well as typical industry character- istics (for example, market concentration) were also included.[3] No distinc- tion was made according to different sectors, ignoring industry differences with regard to the tendency to invest abroad (see for instance Dunning, 1993).[4]

Chen (1992) tested a number of possible determinants of outward FDI of manufacturing companies in Taiwan, on the basis of a survey that was held at the beginning of 1988, about investment intentions of individual compa- nies. Unfortunately, the value of the dependent variable (0 or 1) was based on *intentions* rather than the actual decision to invest abroad or export. Since in 1988 investments from Taiwan were still very limited, it was not possible to use realized FDI data. In addition, no distinction was made between investments that took place in industrialized and developing economies. Since the motivations to invest in either category of countries can be very different, it is likely that – at least partly – the characteristics of the compa- nies investing in one of the categories will also differ. Moreover, although the author admitted that important industrial differences may exist with regard to the propensity to invest abroad, firms from all manufacturing subsectors were lumped together in one single sample.[5] In a more recent study, Chen, now with Ku and Liu (1995), obviated important objections to Chen's 1992 paper by making the distinction between FDI in industrialized and develop- ing economies. Also, *intentional* investment projects were replaced by actual (albeit approved) investments. Although a dummy was included to take into account differences among industries, it did not work out very well. The industry dummy was only inserted to distinguish between industries that were the most active foreign investors. The results underlined the dominant effect of industrial origin on the propensity to invest abroad and suggest that a sample across industries is highly inappropriate.

The above remarks clearly call for a test that uses firm-level data within a specific industry. For these reasons our analysis is confined to electronics firms in South Korea and Taiwan which in both economies are among the most important sources of outward investment. The remainder of this chapter is set up as follows. In section 2, the model used for the economet- ric estimates and the data collection is elucidated. In section 3, hypotheses are formulated and variables defined. In section 4, the results are discussed and finally in section 5 conclusions will be drawn.

2. THE MODEL AND DATA COLLECTION

We assume that in principle, each firm is a potential outward investor. In practice, however, not all electronics companies will have invested overseas. Hence, for a relatively large number of observations the dependent variable has a value of zero. The dependent variable, outward direct investment (ODI_i), can have no negative values, but is either zero (case I) or positive (case II). The econometric equation should 'explain' not only whether case I occurs or not, but also if case II occurs what the size of ODI_i is. For this purpose, Tobit models were developed that are specifically equipped to deal with dependent variables that are partly discrete and partly continuous.[6] The Tobit model looks as follows:

$$X_i\beta + u_i > 0 \Rightarrow ODI_i = X_i\beta + u_i$$

$$X_i\beta + u_i \leq 0 \Rightarrow ODI_i = 0.$$

ODI_i expresses both the investment or non-investment status of the i_{th} company and the extent of foreign involvement (measured by the size of FDI by individual companies). X_i represents a vector of explanatory variables. In the Tobit model, the βs are estimated through a maximum likelihood procedure.[7] To suppress the scale of variation, all independent variables (with the exception of the dummy variables) are expressed in natural logarithms ('linear-log' or 'semi-log').[8]

Another assumption made is that the explanatory variables discussed in section 3 are not relevant in every case. Since we assume that the motivations to invest in industrialized economies may to some extent differ from those applicable to investments in developing economies, it can be argued that part of the explanatory variables relevant in explaining FDI are different. Therefore three separate equations for both economies are estimated:

1. Firm-level determinants of FDI in all economies.
2. Firm-level determinants of FDI in industrialized economies.
3. Firm-level determinants of FDI in developing economies.

The data needed for this analysis were gathered from various sources (see references). Because certain data were not available from published sources, it was necessary to involve the cooperation of the local authorities. The variables used for the Korean sample refer to their values in 1993. The information for most explanatory variables (namely firm size, technological capabilities, commercial capabilities, human capital, productivity, labour intensity and foreign ownership) was extracted from *Maekyung:*

Annual Corporation Reports (Mae-il, 1994). Data on antidumping measures against electronics companies were derived from *Import Restrictions against Korean Products by Major Industrialized Countries* (Korean Foreign Trade Association, 1994). Export figures were taken from the *Annual Directory of Electronic and Electrical Manufacturers in Korea* (Electronics Industry Association of Korea, 1994). Information on Korean conglomerates came from the *Business Korea Yearbook 1994–95*. Unpublished data on individual investment projects (namely size and destination of investments) were provided by the Bank of Korea. In principle only those companies for which information could be gathered for all variables were included in the sample, yielding a total of 141 observations.[9] A major exception concerns technological capabilities, for which information unfortunately was only available for a very limited number of companies.

Starting-point for the Taiwanese sample was the electronics companies (defined as 'electronics and electrical' (CCIS 22) and 'computers and peripherals' (CCIS 25)) belonging to the top 1,000 manufacturing companies as published in *The Largest Corporations in the Republic of China 1992* (China Credit Information Services, 1992) (which records 1991 data). From this list, companies with total sales exceeding NT\$400 million in 1991 were selected. In total, this resulted in a sample of 173 companies in CCIS 22 and 75 companies belonging to CCIS 25. The company information listed in this data source (namely firm size, labour intensity and foreign ownership) was complemented by variables (namely technological capabilities, human capabilities, export orientation and productivity) included in (or calculated from) the 1991 census data (*Industrial and Commercial Census; Taiwan-Fukien Area, the Republic of China*).[10] Since the most recent census data referred to 1991 data, information on the other explanatory variables was also collected for that year. Because the companies listed in the census are anonymous, the values of the variables had to be matched with those published in *The Largest Corporations*. Eventually, 64.5 per cent of the 248 companies (n = 160) were identified, forming the total sample for the estimates. Moreover, information on the membership of the Brand International Promotion Association (Bipa) was provided by the association itself. Unpublished data on individual investment projects were provided by the Investment Commission of the Ministry of Economic Affairs. The most serious limitation of the sample is that no data on investment projects in Mainland China are available. Given the political sensitivity of these investments, the Investment Commission does not provide information on these projects. Even if these data were available, however, they would reflect a serious bias since a great majority of the projects are small scale and likely to be unregistered.

3. HYPOTHESES AND VARIABLES

In this section, hypotheses are formulated about the relationships between firm characteristics (namely explanatory variables) and outward investment. The proxy variables used to measure these characteristics are also defined. As noted above, outward investment refers to the likelihood that a company actually invests abroad and – if investment has already taken place – the consequent size of outward investment. For matters of convenience, reference will mostly be made to 'FDI' or 'outward direct investment'. If a particular hypothesis is only assumed to be relevant in case of investments in either industrialized or developing economies, this will be mentioned explicitly.

3.1 Firm size

There are many reasons why the size of a firm is generally regarded as an important determinant of outward investment.[11] Horst (1972b), for instance, refers to the fixed costs incurred in investing in foreign production for which the larger firms often can get financing more easily than smaller firms. Moreover, a certain minimum size ('critical mass') of tangible and intangible assets is needed to invest abroad (see for instance Jeon, 1992). In addition, due to their sheer size, larger firms reach the limits of domestic markets and involvement in overseas markets more rapidly than smaller firms (UNCTC, 1992). Moreover, large firms are often associated with concentrated (or even oligopolistic) market structures which imply certain ownership advantages that encourage FDI (see for instance UNCTC, 1992). *It is therefore argued that a positive relationship exists between the size of a firm and outward investment.* Firm size will be measured by total sales of companies (*SIZE*).

3.2 Intangible assets

According to mainstream MNE theory, the possession of intangible assets is an essential prerequisite for FDI (Caves, 1971a; Helpman, 1984; Dunning, 1993). In order to undertake FDI, a firm must possess intangible assets that can be transferred internationally at low opportunity costs for use within the firm (Pugel et al., 1996). In this study, we distinguish between technological capabilities, marketing strengths and the quality of human capital.

Technological capabilities
Some form of technological superiority is mostly seen as indispensable to compete successfully in foreign markets (Caves, 1971b and 1993; UNCTC,

1992; Dunning, 1993). It usually is assumed that this superiority is based on R&D efforts. Investment projects in advanced economies especially are market-seeking and therefore have to be competitive in the host country. *Therefore the hypothesis will be tested that technological capabilities are positively correlated with overseas investment in industrialized economies.* Technological capabilities (*RDINT*) are proxied by the ratio of R&D expenditures and total sales. For 69.4 per cent of the firms in the Taiwanese sample, data on *RDINT* were available. Two equations are therefore estimated: one for the total sample excluding *RDINT* and one for the sample for those companies for which data on *RDINT* are available. In the Korean sample, unfortunately only for 23.9 per cent of the firms could data on *RDINT* be collected. Since the degrees of freedom would be too few, an estimation of the full equation was not attempted. Instead, a simple Pearson's correlation coefficient was calculated to get an impression of the relationship between *RDINT* and outward direct investment.

Marketing strengths
According to Kumar (1994), the goodwill associated with a firm's brand names or trade marks in the form of consumer loyalty is considered to be one of the most important intangible assets possessed by EIE MNEs. Other researchers (for example, Caves, 1971b; UNCTC, 1992) have also argued that skills in marketing and product differentiation can develop into key ownership advantages that may lead to overseas production. A firm's ability to differentiate products is supposed to be more easily transferable than the introduction of a new technology. Close coordination with, for instance, R&D functions is not as much needed in the case of product differentiation. On the contrary, Lall (1980) argued that a successful marketing policy requires to be carried out in proximity of the end markets. If such expertise is to be exploited effectively, this – *inter alia* – implies feedback to the production units, for instance with regard to the recommended product adaptations or developments which again may require implementation by local production facilities. Since most goods produced in developing economies are not marketed in the host country but are sold elsewhere, marketing capabilities are assumed to be especially relevant in the case of FDI in industrialized economies. *It will therefore be tested whether a positive relationship exists between a company's marketing capabilities and its foreign involvement through FDI in industrialized economies.* In the case of Korea, the ratio of (direct and indirect) selling expenditures and total sales is used as a proxy for marketing capabilities (*MARKINTI*). Unfortunately, such data are not available for Taiwanese firms. Consequently, the membership of Bipa was used as a proxy. Bipa in Taiwan acts as a platform for indigenous companies that intend to build up or improve international brand

awareness for their products. A dummy variable (*MARKINT2*) will take a value of 1 if a company is a member of Bipa, while zero will be used in other cases.

Human capital
Next to the (more specific) technological and commercial determinants of FDI, a more general, complementary, indicator for the possession of intangible assets is tested that reflects the quality of human capital. It has been argued by Lall (1980), UNCTC (1992) and Chen et al. (1995), that many firms develop important advantages in a form that is not specifically related to its technological or commercial capabilities. Such skills can not, by definition, be transferred outside of a company but can contribute to successful operations overseas. In addition, the (complicated) coordination of cross-border production operations requires a high quality of the firm's human capital – both in industrialized and developing economies. Caves (1971b) refers in this respect to 'entrepreneurial resources' as a determinant of outward investment. According to Caves, MNEs expand abroad in order to give full employment to coordinating activities of their fixed stock of entrepreneurial talent. *It is hypothesized that the general quality of human capital embodied in a firm is positively related to the amount of FDI.* Following Lall's approach (1980), average annual earnings per employee are used as a proxy variable to measure the general quality of human capital (*HUMCAP*) for both Korean and Taiwanese firms.

3.3 Productivity

Historically, the strength of (leading) firms in such LIEs as Korea and Taiwan is typically based on their shopfloor operations (compare Hikino and Amsden, 1994). The question then arises whether manufacturing capabilities are a relevant determinant in explaining outward investment from Korea and Taiwan. We therefore included labour productivity in the analysis. It is difficult, however, to determine a priori the sign of this relationship. On the one hand, one might argue that high productivity levels make overseas production redundant, since such companies are less sensitive to rising industrial wage levels (Jeon, 1992). On the other hand, high productivity might be perceived as a source of ownership advantage typically needed to overcome the disadvantages related to being alien in a foreign market *vis-à-vis* indigenous firms. In any case, it will be *hypothesized that a relationship exists between (labour) productivity and outward investment.* For Taiwan, labour productivity (*LABINT2*) was proxied by using the total value of production per person employed. As this information was not available in the case of Korea – following Pilat

(1993) – value added per employee was used to measure labour productivity (*LABPROD1*).

3.4 Export orientation

A common assumption in the literature on firm-level determinants of outward investment is that firms which for a substantial part depend on sales outside the home economy will – at some stage, and if other characteristics are present – move production to important target countries (Agarwal, 1980). This is often referred to as the 'export-market defence motive'[12] (Chen, 1992; Chen et al., 1995). With regard to investments in developing economies, it can be added that companies selling in the international market face continuous price pressure from (global) competitors. In case of strong domestic factor price increases (for example, wage level) it may be decided to shift production to other countries with more favourable factor prices (namely wages). *It is therefore put forward that the export orientation is positively related to FDI.* Export orientation (*EXP*) is measured by the export value divided by total sales.

3.5 Labour intensity

Similarly, it is argued that the effect of wage increases (and consequently the need to shift production abroad) is more negative for labour-intensive companies than for those firms for which labour costs account for only a modest part of their total production costs. This is likely to be especially relevant to economies such as Korea and Taiwan, that traditionally possessed a comparative advantage in labour-intensive industries but in recent years have experienced extremely fast wage rises in the industrial sector. To make use of low wage levels abroad, companies are assumed to invest in developing economies. Following Chen (1992) and Jeon (1992), *we therefore expect that FDI in developing economies is positively related to the labour intensity of individual firms.* Labour intensity (*LABINT*) is proxied by the ratio of the number of employees to the value of fixed assets.

3.6 Foreign ownership

Chen et al. (1995) drew attention to the relationship between the origin of the equity ownership and the decision to invest abroad. Referring to the so-called 'corporate decision' approach to FDI (Aharoni, 1966), it is argued that competitive pressure and opportunities to make profits are not sufficient conditions to engage in FDI. Other aspects, such as the objectives of individual managers, their limited decision-making horizons and the existence of information costs, may still prevent companies from investing overseas. Accordingly, foreign managers of MNE subsidiaries in Taiwan show limited initiative to invest abroad. In more general terms, it has to be admitted that investment decisions by most MNEs are still taken and implemented at the level of corporate headquarters in the home economy rather than at the subsidiary level in a host country.[13] The hypothesis therefore reads that the likelihood to invest abroad is related to the nationality of the ownership. In other words: *firms that are to a large extent owned by foreign companies are less likely to invest abroad.* To capture the influence of foreign ownership on outward investment, a dummy variable (*FOR*) is included that equals 1 in the case that foreign ownership of a firm in the sample exceeds 50 per cent and 0 otherwise.

3.7 Protectionism

Horst (1972b) has argued that exporters often establish production facilities behind a country's high tariff rather than to continue to serve markets through exports. In other, more recent, studies it is also argued that import barriers tend to increase FDI as local production is used as a means of supplying those markets (see for instance Pugel et al., 1996; UNCTC, 1992). Belderbos (1994) showed that the surge in Japanese FDI in the electronics industry in North America and Europe in the second half of the 1980s was for a substantial part a response to export barriers for Japanese products, especially because of antidumping measures. Dumping occurs when a good is sold abroad for a lower price than the seller charges for the same good in his home market (Hindley, 1988). GATT (WTO) authorized the imposition of antidumping duties on dumped exports.[14] To avoid paying antidumping levies, the Japanese companies set up production activities in North America and the EU.[15] The exports of Korean electronics companies are also known to have been frequently hit by antidumping duties in industrialized economies (Bark, 1993). Since there are no a priori reasons to assume that Korean electronics companies respond differently to such measures, it is *expected that protectionist (namely antidumping) measures against individual (Korean) companies are positively related to the decision to invest in industrialized economies.* Since no such measures have been observed against Taiwanese firms operating in the electronics industry, this hypothesis will only be tested for Korean firms. To measure this effect, a dummy variable (*DUMP*) is included with a value of 1 in the case that a company has been hit by antidumping measures and 0 otherwise.

3.8 Company structure

A frequently hypothesized determinant of FDI is the possibility to raise capital at preferential rates (Dunning, 1993). As is generally known, the Korean economy is strongly dominated by conglomerates ('chaebols'). Although the chaebol, as opposed to Japanese conglomerates (especially the so-called horizontal 'keiretsu'; see Belderbos, 1994), until very recently did not include financial/banking activities, it is known that members of the chaebol typically have had favourable access to additional capital. For a long time, preferred access to (often relatively cheap) credits provided by Korea's government-controlled banks was an important source for the chaebol (Il Sakong, 1993). An additional, financial advantage for chaebol *vis-à-vis* non-chaebol companies concerns the intragroup financial resources available through cross-lending and cross-guaranteeing of loans and the cross-holding of equity of member firms (Kang, 1996). Another, non-financial, advantage of belonging to a chaebol is that most of them also possess trading companies. These trading companies often act as overseas advance guards that not only sell the chaebol's products overseas, but also collect important information about overseas markets. *It is therefore argued that a positive relationship exists between being a member of a chaebol and outward investment.* Since such conglomerates are not present in the Taiwanese electronics industry, this hypothesis is only tested for the Korean sample. If a sample firm is a member of one of the conglomerates (*CONG*), the dummy variable will take the value 1 and 0 otherwise.

To sum up, the following equations are estimated in this chapter:

1. *All countries* The equation for investments in all countries (namely industrialized as well as developing economies) will be estimated to investigate the common significance of part of the aforementioned determinants of FDI. For Korea, the size of the company (*SIZE*), human capital (*HUMCAP*), export orientation (*EXP*), foreign ownership (*FOR*), labour productivity (*LABPROD1*) and company structure (*CONG*) are assumed to be significant, both in industrialized and in developing economies. In the case of Taiwan, the significance of company size (*SIZE*), human capital (*HUMCAP*), export orientation (*EXP*), foreign ownership (*FOR*) and labour productivity (*LABPROD2*) will be tested. In other words:

$$ODI_{KORi} = F(SIZE, HUMCAP, EXP, FOR, LABPROD1, CONG);$$
$$\text{and } ODI_{TWNi} = F(SIZE, HUMCAP, EXP, FOR, LABPROD2).$$

2. *Industrialized countries* With regard to FDI in industrialized economies, we hypothesize that for Korea, as well as the variables listed under (1), marketing capabilities (*MARKINT1*) and protectionist measures (*DUMP*) have to be included in the equation. In the case of Taiwan, marketing capabilities (*MARKTINT2*) and technological capabilities (*RDINT*) are added. As a result, the equations look as follows:

$$ODI_{KORi} = F(SIZE, HUMCAP, EXP, FOR, LABPROD1, CONG,$$
$$MARKINT1, DUMP); \text{ and } ODI_{TWNi} = F(SIZE, HUMCAP, EXP,$$
$$FOR, LABPROD2, MARKINT2, RDINT).$$

3. *Developing countries* Regarding FDI in developing nations, it is hypothesized that for both economies, as well as the explanatory variables included in equation (1), labour intensity (*LABINT*) is a significant determinant. As a result, the equations to be estimated look as follows:

$$ODI_{KORi} = F(SIZE, HUMCAP, EXP, FOR, LABPROD1, CONG,$$
$$LABINT); \text{ and } ODI_{TWNi} = F(SIZE, HUMCAP, EXP, FOR,$$
$$LABPROD2, LABINT).$$

In Table 11.1, the independent variables included in the respective models and the expected signs of the relationships are listed.

Compared with the earlier empirical studies on Korean and Taiwanese FDI, and as discussed in the previous section, the present study shows a number of important improvements. As a matter of fact, by including only companies operating in the electronics industry, it is possible to control for the dominance of industry characteristics over firm determinants. Moreover, by including investment projects that were approved as late as 1993, the investigation is not limited to pioneering firms which may show deviant patterns from 'average' investing firms. In addition, as will be discussed in the next section, new hypotheses are tested. Contrary to the previous studies on Taiwanese investments, the use of a Tobit model also takes into account investment size.

4. EMPIRICAL RESULTS

This section presents the estimation results for the Korean (4.1) and Taiwanese (4.2) samples (see Appendix 1 for the definition of variables).

Table 11.1   Independent variables and expected signs

	(1) All economies		(2) Industrialized economies		(3) Developing economies	
	Korea	Taiwan	Korea	Taiwan	Korea	Taiwan
SIZE	+	+	+	+	+	+
RDINT[a]	ni	Ni	ni	+	ni	ni
MARKINT1	ni	Ni	+	ni	ni	ni
MARKINT2	ni	Ni	ni	+	ni	ni
HUMCAP	+	+	+	+	+	+
LABPROD1	+/−	Ni	+/−	ni	+/−	ni
LABPROD2	ni	+/−	ni	+/−	ni	+/−
EXP	+	+	+	+	+	+
LABINT	ni	Ni	ni	ni	+	+
FOR	−	−	−	−	−	−
DUMP	ni	Ni	+	ni	ni	ni
CONG	+	Ni	+	ni	+	ni

Notes:
ni = not included.
[a] For Korea, Pearson's correlation coefficient between *RDINT* and *ODI* for a limited
number of observations will be calculated.

4.1 Korea

In Appendix 2, the correlation matrix shows that no high degree of correlation can be found between the explanatory variables. The results of the empirical analysis are reported in Table 11.2.

4.1.1 All countries
First, the variables were tested which were assumed to be important in explaining all investment projects, irrespective of their destination. Table 11.2 shows that, with the exception of the membership of a conglomerate (*CONG*), all explanatory variables have the expected sign. The size of the firm (*SIZE*) turns out to be a highly significant determinant in explaining the likelihood of and subsequent extension of overseas investment projects. Moreover, the hypothesis that the overall quality of the human capital embodied in a firm (*HUMCAP*) influences FDI in a positive manner is also supported – albeit at the 10 per cent level. In addition, a heavy reliance on markets outside the home country (measured by the export orientation of firms (*EXP*)) turns out to be positively related to outward investment. Likewise, the suggested negative effect of foreign ownership of companies

Table 11.2 Results: Tobit estimates Korea

Explanatory variables[a]	(1) All economies	(2) Industrialized economies	(3) Developing countries
SIZE[b]	27.981***	23.851***	9.438***
	(6.914)	(4.918)	(5.55)
MARKINT1	ni	−1631.37	ni
		(−0.527)	
HUMCAP	11.804*	18.234**	1.520
	(1.476)	(1.845)	(0.4233)
LABPROD1	−24.525**	−23.823*	−15.106***
	(−2.275)	(−1.898)	(−2.653)
EXP	17.710***	19.383***	6.023***
	(3.289)	(2.850)	(2.636)
LABINT	ni	ni	−6.708**
			(−1.672)
FOR	−35.082**	−25.349*	−18.281**
	(−2.188)	(−1.409)	(−2.182)
DUMP	ni	26.435**	ni
		(1.919)	
CONG	−14.015	−18.567*	−6.626
	(−1.080)	(−1.304)	(−1.165)
Observations	141	135	141
Pos. observ.	37.6%	23.7%	29.8%
L.L.[c]	−658.277	−402.547	−495.459
Goodness-of-fit[d]	$\chi^2(6) = 100.99$***	$\chi^2(7) = 88.232$***	$\chi^2(8) = 82.178$***

Notes:
[a] The explanatory variables in the table correspond to the log-linear specification of the model.
    * significant at 10% level.
  ** significant at 5% level.
*** significant at 1% level.
[b] Figures in brackets are asymptotic t-values. A one-tailed test is used in all except in the case of the coefficient for which no a priori prediction could be offered (namely labour productivity).
[c] L.L. refers to log likelihood of the estimated model.
[d] $\chi^2(n)$ indicates the likelihood ratio statistic on the null hypothesis that the coefficients of all explanatory variables except the constant term are zero, where n reflects the degrees of freedom (compare Greene, 1993).
Source: Van Hoesel (1999).

(*FOR*) on overseas activities through FDI is confirmed here. Interestingly, the estimates indicate that indeed a significant relationship exists between the manufacturing capabilities of firms (*LABPROD1*) and outward investment. That the sign of the relationship is negative renders support to the proposition that a high level of productivity encourages a company to keep production activities in Korea and serve overseas markets through exports instead of FDI. No statistical evidence is found for the hypothesis that membership of a conglomerate positively influences FDI. The estimate not only has a low asymptotic t-value, but also a negative sign. A possible explanation for this poor result is that for the existing sample, the assumed (financial and non-financial) advantages of conglomerates in reality is only confined to those chaebols for which electronics is a core activity.[16] Since for these other conglomerates sales in the electronics sector are often primarily limited to the home market, overseas investment – as far as operations in electronics are concerned – is not a real alternative for them.

4.1.2 Industrialized countries

Subsequently, the variables which determine FDI in industrialized economies were tested. Again, most variables (with the exception of *CONG* and *MARKINT1*) showed the expected sign. As in the case of the first equation, *SIZE*, *HUMCAP*, *LABPROD1* and *EXP* turned out to be significant. Whereas in the case of *HUMCAP* the statistical significance here is stronger than in the previous analysis (at the 5 per cent instead of 10 per cent level), the opposite holds for *LABPROD1* (at the 10 per cent instead of 1 per cent level). The statistical relationship between foreign ownership and outward FDI is significant at the 10 per cent level. Conforming to the expectations, the results show that protectionist measures (namely antidumping cases; *DUMP*) taken by authorities in industrialized economies against Korean electronics products have indeed encouraged the companies involved to invest in these countries. As far as the importance of marketing capabilities (*MARKINT1*) is concerned, the results do not support the hypothesis of a positive relationship with FDI as the sign is negative. This outcome suggests that in the case of Korean electronics companies, marketing capabilities as such are no ownership advantage that – *inter alia* – explains outward investment.[17] The negative (instead of the expected positive) relationship between being a member of a conglomerate and FDI is found to be statistically significant at the 10 per cent level.

It has already been noted that, due to the limited number of observations, technological capabilities (*RDINT*) could not be included in the equation estimate. The Pearson's correlation coefficient between *RDINT* and outward FDI in industrialized economies amounted to -0.154. Although one has to be very cautious in drawing inferences, this result suggests that the empirical support for the hypothesized positive relationship between technological capabilities and FDI in these countries is not strong.

4.1.3 Developing countries

As far as the determinants of FDI in developing economies are concerned, the estimates reveal that in all but two cases (*CONG* and *LABINT*) the variables show the expected signs. As in the foregoing estimates, *SIZE*, *LABPROD1* and *EXP* register statistically significant relationships. Moreover, with regard to FDI in developing economies the results confirm the expected negative impact of foreign ownership of firms in the electronics industry on outward investment from Korea. As opposed to FDI in industrialized economies, the general quality of human capital for investments in developing economies – though of the expected sign – is much less important, as is shown by a t-value substantially below the critical value. Surprisingly, labour intensity (*LABINT*) influences – at the 5 per cent level – FDI in a *negative* (instead of the expected positive) manner. In other words, the results suggest that especially the more labour extensive (namely capital intensive) firms shift production to developing economies. This outcome suggests that the assumed 'macro' relationship between labour intensity and FDI does not hold at the firm level for the sample. Moreover, this result suggests that the more advanced (namely labour extensive) companies shift parts of their production activities to economies with relatively low industrial wage levels. A possible explanation for this is that FDI by these companies is not so much a result of the high wage levels in Korea (in their case, labour is a relatively small portion of total production costs), but rather should be seen as part of their strategies to pursue an international division of labour. Given the large distinction in Korea's industrial structure between the more sophisticated (namely labour extensive) companies and the relatively unadvanced (namely labour extensive) small- and medium-sized firms, it would be no surprise if especially the former category of companies are able to pursue such a strategy.

4.2 Taiwan

Appendices 3 and 4 show the correlation matrices for the explanatory variables for Taiwan. In Appendix 3, the pair-wise correlation coefficients are depicted for all firms in the sample excluding the variable *RDINT*. In Appendix 4, the coefficients are listed for the explanatory variables of companies for which also values for *RDINT* are available. In some cases, relatively high values of pair-wise correlation coefficients are shown which (in combination with high standard deviations) suggest the presence of multicollinearity – a feature often observed in this kind of cross-section analysis (Pugel et al., 1996). In Table 11.3, the results of the equation estimates are presented.

4.2.1 All countries

In column 1 of Table 11.3, the results are shown of the equation estimate including all the variables that are assumed to influence Taiwan's FDI, both in industrialized and in developing economies. All variables have the expected signs. The size of companies (*SIZE*) turns out to be a highly significant factor in determining whether a firm invests abroad or not and, if so, the magnitude of that investment. The hypothesis that the export orientation (*EXP*) of firms is positively linked to its outward investment behaviour is also supported. The same holds for the nationality of ownership (*FOR*) of the companies in the sample: foreign ownership strongly influences the likelihood of investing abroad in a negative way. Although labour productivity (*LABPROD2*), as in the Korean sample, shows a negative relationship with FDI, the asymptotic t-value is much too low to suggest statistical significance. The same holds for the overall quality of human capital (*HUMCAP*).[18]

Since, as we noted before, the information on *RDINT* is only available for a portion of the sample, two equations are estimated regarding FDI in industrialized economies: one using the whole sample excluding *RDINT* as an explanatory variable (2a) and a second one on the basis of the partial sample including *RDINT* in the equation (2b).

4.2.2 Industrialized countries (excluding *RDINT*)

Again, all explanatory variables showed the expected sign for the hypothesized relationships with FDI. Also in the case of FDI in industrialized economies the assumed positive impact of *SIZE* on FDI is confirmed. The same holds for *EXP* and *FOR*, which show a positive and negative statistically significant relationship with FDI. To explain FDI in advanced economies, a proxy capturing the marketing capabilities (*MARKINT2*) of firms was also included. Although the dummy variable used (namely membership of Bipa) merely indicates the *willingness* to invest in commercial capabilities rather than the actual expenditures made, the results in the table suggest that those companies that are serious about increasing their commercial capabilities are also more eager to invest abroad. Although *HUMCAP* is again of the expected sign, the assumed relationship statistically is not significant. Also *LABPROD2* has the same sign as in the Korean case but again shows a low t-statistic.

Table 11.3 Results: Tobit estimates Taiwan

Explanatory variables:	(1) All economies	(2a) Industrialized economies (excluding *RDINT*)	(2b) Industrialized economies (including *RDINT*)	(3) Developing economies
SIZE	7.933*** (5.890)	4.9441*** (4.254)	6.189*** (4.479)	6.505*** (4.660)
MARKINT2	ni	7.972*** (3.211)	7.215*** (2.603)	ni
HUMCAP	4.975 (1.060)	2.809 (0.718)	−0.146 (−0.033)	4.791 (0.889)
LABPROD2	−1.342 (−0.601)	−2.362 (−1.207)	−2.549 (−1.035)	3.359 (1.273)
EXP	3.338** (2.089)	3.312** (1.959)	3.581** (1.810)	0.890 (0.654)
LABINT	ni	ni	ni	2.973 (1.213)
FOR	−23.824*** (−4.753)	−15.293*** (−3.804)	−14.667*** (−3.461)	−18.556*** (−3.241)
RDINT	ni	ni	1.823*/** (1.620)	ni
Observations	160	160	111	160
Pos. observations	33.1%	28.8%	30.6%	16.3%
L.L.	−596.449	−510.876	−373.694	−294.673
Goodness-of-fit	$\chi^2(6)=71.836$***	$\chi^2(6)=68.19$***	$\chi^2(7)=58.16$***	$\chi^2(6)=48.158$***

Notes: See Table 11.2.

4.2.3 Industrialized countries (including *RDINT*)

For the smaller sample including only those firms with observations regarding technological capabilities, the results are for most explanatory variables similar to those in the previous equation. Also for this sample, *SIZE*, *MARKINT2* and *EXP* are statistically significant variables in explaining outward investment by Taiwanese companies in the electronics industry. In addition, the hypothesis that the technological capabilities of individual firms (proxied by R&D intensity, *RDINT*) influence FDI in a positive manner is confirmed at the 10 per cent level (and almost at the 5 per cent level). The statistical significance of *HUMCAP* in this estimate has become minimal, though still of the expected sign.[19] As in the previous equations for Taiwan, the coefficient estimated for *LABPROD2* shows a negative sign but has a statistically insignificant asymptotic t-value.

4.2.4 Developing countries

Finally, equation 3 was estimated to test the hypotheses related to investments in developing economies. As in the foregoing cases, all variables have the a priori expected signs. For our sample, *SIZE* is also a very significant variable in explaining FDI in this category of countries. Moreover, the results confirm the assumed negative relationship between *FOR* and outward investment. Although there seems to be some evidence for the hypothesis that a positive relationship exists between the labour intensity of individual Taiwanese electronics companies and the likelihood to invest in developing countries (to make use of prevailing lower wages), the statistical support is insufficient. Also in the case of FDI in developing countries, *HUMCAP* shows low statistical significance. Furthermore, the estimated coefficient of *EXP*, though of the correct sign, has a low asymptotic t-value. Contrary to the Korean sample and previous estimates for Taiwan, the estimate for *LABPROD2* here has a positive sign (though a low asymptotic t-value), suggesting that the higher its productivity, the more likely a company will invest in developing countries. Given the relatively high pairwise coefficient for *LABPROD2* and *LABINT* and *LABPROD2* and *HUMCAP*, as well as relatively high standard errors for these variables, the latter outcome could be caused by some degree of multicollinearity.[20] Multicollinearity is known to be a typical sample problem (Stewart, 1991). As noted earlier, some bias in the sample indeed may be expected since small investment projects are often not registered and FDI in the People's Republic of China is also not included. Given the fact that multicollinearity probably exists, it is dangerous to delete these variables on the basis of these estimates.

5. SUMMARY AND CONCLUSIONS

In this chapter, the importance of firm-level characteristics in explaining outward FDI from Korea and Taiwan in the electronics industry was investigated. In Tables 11.4 and 11.5 the results of the present study are summarized and compared with those of previous studies discussed in section 1.[21] What inferences can be drawn from this exercise?

Table 11.4   Summary of results on Korean FDI

	Present study			Jeon (1992)	
	All	DCs	LDCs	DCs	LDCs
Size	+	+	+	+	ni
Marketing capability	ni	I	ni	I	ni
Human capital	+	+	I	ni	ni
Productivity	−	−	−	ni	ni
Export orientation	+	+	+	ni	ni
Labour intensity	ni	ni	−	ni	+
Foreign ownership	−	−	−	ni	ni
Protectionism	ni	+	ni	+	ni
Company structure	I	−	I	ni	ni

Notes:
ni = not included; I = insignificant.

Table 11.5   Summary of results on Taiwanese FDI

	Chen (1992)	Chen et al. (1995)			Present study		
	All	All	DCs	LCDs	All	DCs	LDCs
Size	+	+	+	+	+	+	+ +
Technological capabilities	ni	I	+	I	ni	ni	+ ni
Marketing capabilities	ni	ni	ni	ni	ni	+	+ ni
Human capital	ni	I	+	I	I	I	I I
Productivity	ni	ni	ni	ni	I	I	I I
Export orientation	+	+	I	+	+	+	+ I
Labour intensity	I	I	I	I	ni	ni	ni I
Foreign ownership	ni	−	−	−	−	−	− −

Notes:
ni = not included; I = insignificant.

In the case of Korea, the size of companies in all cases turned out to be a significant explanatory variable.[22] The same holds for their reliance on foreign markets (that is, export orientation). The hypothesis that foreign ownership is negatively related to FDI was also confirmed in the present study. Moreover, although the quality of human capital also registered as important for 'all economies', its significance especially held for FDI in advanced economies. The investigation further revealed that protectionist measures against Korean products make a difference in the decision to invest abroad or export. Being hit by antidumping measures taken by industrialized economies turned out to encourage Korean companies to invest there. Although Jeon (1992) looked at non-tariff barriers, his study found a similar impact of protectionist measures. Also interesting is the negative significant relationship found in the present study between labour productivity and FDI.

Not all hypotheses were confirmed in the present investigation, however. Marketing capabilities of individual firms turned out to have no influence on the decision to invest overseas. This outcome suggests that marketing has played (until recently) a minor role for Korean electronics companies. This impression is confirmed by Jeon (1992). Moreover, no evidence was found that belonging to one of the conglomerates made a (positive) difference in investing abroad or not. Surprising (and contradictory to Jeon's study) was the negative relationship found between labour intensity and FDI in developing countries.

Also in the Taiwanese electronics industry, the size of companies turned out to be a significant determinant for investments abroad – a result that was also found in the previous studies by Chen (1992) and Chen et al. (1995). The same held for the hypothesized negative relationship between foreign ownership of companies and outward investment. This outcome parallels the findings by Chen et al. (1995). In addition, again conforming to the study by Chen et al. (1995), it was found that technological capabilities positively influence FDI in industrialized economies. The assumed importance of sales outside Taiwan was confirmed when all investments were taken into account, but after having separated FDI in developed and developing countries, statistical significance only could be determined in the former case.[23] The present investigation further showed that – as opposed to the Korean firms – for Taiwanese electronics companies, the likelihood to invest in developed countries (and the subsequent magnitude of those investments) is also positively influenced by the marketing capabilities of individual firms.

Although Chen et al. (1995) found a statistically significant positive relationship between human capital and FDI in developed countries, this result could not be confirmed – probably due to multicollinearity. Moreover, no evidence was found for the hypothesized influence of productivity on the likelihood to invest abroad. In addition, the impact of labour intensity on FDI in LDCs could not be proven convincingly.

Although the Tobit analysis described in this paper is a powerful research instrument, it also has its limitations. The (cross-section) analysis, for instance, was based on characteristics observed at one point in time. This implies that rapid changes in the values of explanatory values (and also their influence on FDI) are not taken into account. Since the industrial transformation of both Korea and Taiwan takes place at a very rapid pace, a deeper insight into the dynamic aspects of the internationalization of the companies involved is still needed. Moreover, the investigation for a major part was based on hypotheses derived from 'conventional' insights. The results show that at least part of these 'conventional' firm characteristics leading to outward FDI are also relevant in the case of Korean and Taiwanese electronics firms. In addition, however, it was shown that in the case of Korean firms more idiosyncratic features, such as labour productivity (underlining the typical strength in manufacturing) and protectionist measures, influence FDI behaviour.

NOTES

1. Although the firm-level determinants of FDI do not necessarily coincide with their ownership specific advantages, according to Lall (1986, p. 30) this kind of analysis does shed some light on the nature of the 'perceived competitive advantage' of these firms in their overseas operations.
2. For an extensive summary of the principal empirical evidence regarding determinants of FDI, see UNCTC (1992).
3. As early as in 1980, Lall emphasized the distinction between industrial and firm characteristics that influence (outward) FDI behaviour.
4. The dummy included in the Less Developed Country (LDC) sample was not meant to distinguish between FDI prone and non-FDI prone industries but rather to test the importance of the 'invest-to-safeguard-raw-materials' motive for certain industries.
5. The only distinction made in this respect was a dummy included to measure the importance of dependence on raw materials.
6. Initially, the use of logit or probit models was also considered (in which case the dependent variable takes a value of 0 or 1) to estimate the equations. In that case, 1 represents an investment in a production location abroad, whereas 0 indicates that no investment has taken place. Although in principle the data allow for a distinction between investments by manufacturing companies in overseas production units from investments in sales subsidiaries, in practice there were strong indications that the distinction did not always match reality. Companies that had received approval to set up production sites abroad sometimes only operated a sales subsidiary and vice versa.
7. For an extensive discussion on the properties of Tobit models, we refer to Maddala (1983) and Greene (1993).
8. Linear formulations were also tried out; they yielded similar but less significant results, however.
9. Because for six companies no information was available on marketing capabilities, the

equation estimating FDI in industrialized economies (for which marketing capabilities were assumed to be a determinant) was based on 135 observations.

10. The census data tapes were made available at Chung-Hua Institution for Economic Research where the author carried out part of the research.

11. Some authors argue that 'size' itself can be perceived as a composite variable for other variables affecting propensity to invest abroad. It is nonetheless argued here that size *per se* is a determining factor.

12. In anticipation of the criticism that many surveys have failed to distinguish between motives for and determinants of FDI (Dunning, 1993, p. 139), we emphasize that export orientation is a determinant of FDI, whereas defending the (former) export market is the motive to invest.

13. The most notable exception concerns outward FDI from Hong Kong. Taiwanese companies are not allowed to invest directly in the People's Republic of China (PRC), and therefore set up shell companies in the city state from where investments in the PRC are made.

14. The maximum amount of such a duty is the 'margin of dumping' – that is, the difference between the price at which the good is sold on the home market of the exporter and the price of the good when exported.

15. In some cases, the threat of import barriers at the beginning of an antidumping investigation was sufficient to start production in the countries that were considering taking measures.

16. In 1991, Daewoo, Lucky-Goldstar, Hyundai, Samsung and Sunkyoung indicated that electronics was a key business sector. Including a different dummy with a value of 1 for electronics companies belonging to a chaebol (and 0 otherwise), however, still renders a 'mixed' variable since this would also include the (substantial number of) electronics firms that are part of a chaebol but mainly focus on domestic markets and therefore are not potential outward investors.

17. It should not be forgotten that the data on which the estimation is based refer to the situation in 1993. There are indications that (at least some of the leading) firms in Korea in recent years have increased their marketing budgets in a substantial way, however.

18. The relative high pair-wise correlation between *HUMCAP* and *LABPROD2* and standard errors (of which the latter are not present here) probably can be attributed to the presence of multicollinearity. Since deleting *LABPROD2* (which showed the highest standard deviation) leaves the significance of other variables intact and slightly lowers the t-value of *HUMCAP*, we suspect that only the statistical significance of *LABPROD2* is negatively influenced.

19. A high standard deviation and substantial pair-wise correlation coefficients with *LABPROD2* and *FOR* suggest that this may be attributed to multicollinearity. Deleting *LABPROD2* from the equation leaves the other estimates and levels of significance intact, which underlines their robustness. The result for *HUMCAP* remains very low, however. Since *FOR* is an important significant explanatory variable that cannot be deleted, the equation is kept intact.

20. To counter the correlation among the variables, separate equations were estimated in which each time one 'suspect' variable was eliminated. This did not improve the results significantly, however.

21. The (mainly non-firm-level) determinants that were included in previous studies, but were not tested in the present investigation, are not listed in the table. Since especially Jeon (1992) included a relatively large number of non-firm-level explanatory variables in his model, the possibilities to compare the results of both studies are rather limited.

22. Jeon (1992), who tested the importance of company size only for FDI in industrialized economies, found a similar result.

23. In the study by Chen et al. (1995), the relationship between export orientation and FDI was significant in LDCs but insignificant in DCs.

REFERENCES

Agarwal, J.P. (1980), 'Determinants of Foreign Direct Investment: A Survey', *Weltwirtschaftliches Archiv*, **116** (4), 739–73.

Aharoni, Y. (1966), *The Foreign Investment Decision Process*, Boston: Harvard Graduate School of Business Administration.

Bark, T. (1993), 'The Korean Consumer Electronics Industry: Reaction to Antidumping Actions', in J.M. Finger (ed.), *Antidumping: How it Works and Who Gets Hurt*, Ann Arbor: The University of Michigan Press, pp. 121–35.

Belderbos, R. (1994), *Strategic Trade Policy and Multinational Enterprises; Essays on Trade and Investment by Japanese Electronics Firms*, Amsterdam: Thesis Publishers.

Business Korea Co. (1994), *Business Korea Yearbook 1994/1995*, Seoul.

Caves, R.E. (1971a), 'International Corporations: The Industrial Economics of Foreign Investment', *Economica*, **38** (149), 1–27.

Caves, R.E. (1971b), 'Causes of Direct Investment: Foreign Firms' Shares in Canadian and United Kingdom Manufacturing Industries', *The Review of Economics and Statistics*, **56** (3), 279–93.

Caves, R.E. (1993), 'Japanese Investment in the United States: Lessons for the Economic Analysis of Foreign Investment', *The World Economy*, **16** (3), 279–300.

Chen, T.-J. (1992), 'Determinants of Taiwan's Direct Foreign Investment; the Case of a Newly Industrializing Country', *Journal of Development Economics*, **39**, 397–407.

Chen, T.-J., Y.-H. Ku and M.-C. Liu (1995), 'Direct Foreign Investment in High-Wage and Low-Wage Countries: The Case of Taiwan', in E.K.Y. Chen and P. Drysdale (eds), *Corporate Links and Foreign Direct Investment in Asia and the Pacific*, Pymble: Harper Educational.

China Credit Information Services (1992), *The Largest Corporations in the Republic of China 1992*, Taipei.

China Credit Information Services (various years), *The Largest Corporations in Taiwan*, Taipei.

Dunning, J.H. (1993), *Multinational Enterprises and the Global Economy*, Wokingham: Addison-Wesley.

Electronics Industry Association of Korea (1994), *Annual Directory of Electronic and Electrical Manufacturers in Korea*, Seoul.

Greene, W.H. (1993), *Econometric Analysis*, 2nd ed., New York: Macmillan.

Helpman, E. (1984), 'A Simple Theory of International Trade with Multinational Corporations', *Journal of Political Economy*, **92** (4), 451–71.

Hikiono, T. and A.H. Amsden (1994), 'Staying Behind, Stumbling Back, Sneaking Up, Soaring Ahead', in W.J. Baumol, R.R. Nelson and E.N. Wolff (eds), *Convergence of Productivity: Cross-national Studies and Historical Evidence*, Oxford: Oxford University Press, 285–315.

Hindley, B. (1988), 'Dumping and the Far East Trade of the European Community', *The World Economy*, **11** (4), 445–64.

Hoesel, R. van (1996), 'Taiwan: Foreign Direct Investment and the Transformation of the Economy', in J.H. Dunning and R. Narula (eds), *Foreign Direct Investment and Governments: Catalysts for Economic Restructuring*, London: Routledge.

Hoesel, R. van (1999), *New Multinational Enterprises from Korea and Taiwan: Beyond Export-led Growth*, London: Routledge.

Horst, Th. (1972b), 'The Industrial Composition of US Exports and Subsidiary Sales to the Canadian Market', *American Economic Review*, **62** (1) (March), 37–45.

Il, Sakong (1993), *Korea in the World Economy*, Washington: Institute for International Economics.

Jeon, Y.-D. (1992), 'The Determinants of Korean Foreign Direct Investment in Manufacturing Industries', *Weltwirtschaftliches Archiv*, **128** (2), 527–41.

Kang, M.H. (1996), 'The Korean Business Conglomerate: Chaebol Then and Now', Berkeley: Institute of East-Asian Studies – Korea Research Monograph.

Korean Foreign Trade Association (1994), *Import Restrictions against Korean Products by Major Industrialized Countries* (in Korean), Seoul.

Kumar, N. (1994), *Multinational Enterprises and Industrial Organization; the Case of India*, New Delhi: Sage Publications.

Lall, R.B. (1986), *Multinationals from the Third World; Indian Firms Investing Abroad*, New Delhi: Oxford University Press.

Lall, S. (1980), 'Monopolistic Advantages and Foreign Involvement by US Manufacturing Industry', *Oxford Economic Papers*, **32** (1), 102–22.

Lee, K. (1994), 'Structural Adjustment and Outward Direct Foreign Investment in Korea', *Seoul Journal of Economics*, **7** (2), 179–211.

Maddala, G.S. (1983), *Limited-Dependent and Qualitative Variables in Econometrics*, Cambridge: Cambridge University Press.

Mae-il Kyung Jae Shin Moon Sa (1994), *Maekyung: Annual Corporation Reports* (in Korean), Seoul.

Pilat, D. (1993), *The Economics of Catch Up: The Experience of Japan and Korea*, Groningen: Groningen Growth and Development Centre Monograph Series, No. 2.

Pugel, Th.A., E.S. Kragas and Y. Kimura (1996), 'Further Evidence on Japanese Direct Investment in US Manufacturing', *The Review of Economics and Statistics*, **LXXVIII** (2), 208–13.

Stewart, J. (1991), *Econometrics*, New York: Philip Allan.

UNCTC (1992), *The Determinants of Foreign Direct Investment; A Survey of the Evidence*, New York: UN.

APPENDIX 1

Table 11A1.1   Variable definitions

Symbol	Variable definition
SIZE	Total sales
MARKINT1	Direct and indirect selling expenditures/total sales
MARKINT2	Dummy: 1 if Bipa member; 0 otherwise
HUMCAP	Average annual earnings/number of employees
LABPROD1	Value added/employee
LABPROD2	Total output/employee
EXP	Exports/total sales
LABINT	Number of employees/gross assets
FOR	Dummy: 1 if foreign ownership > 50 per cent; 0 otherwise
DUMP	Dummy: 1 if hit by antidumping measure; 0 otherwise
CONG	Dummy: 1 if member top 20 conglomerate; 0 otherwise
RDINT	R&D expenditures/total sales

Source: Van Hoesel (1999).

APPENDIX 2

Table 11A2.1   *Correlation coefficients for independent variables – Korea*

	SIZE	HUMCAP	EXP	FOR	MARKINT1	LABINT	LABPROD1	DUMP	CONG
SIZE	1.00000								
HUMCAP	-0.033854	1.00000							
EXP	0.048549	-0.25046	1.00000						
FOR	-0.063294	0.27050	-0.022705	1.00000					
MARKINT1	0.15076	0.23711	-0.20721	-0.0061818	1.00000				
LABINT	-0.13723	-0.26124	0.053743	0.15368	-0.10898	1.00000			
LABPROD1	0.17521	0.21618	0.0026177	0.084045	-0.067844	-0.33689	1.00000		
DUMP	0.46091	-0.092475	-0.0034102	-0.11437	0.15544	-0.13981	0.17173	1.00000	
CONG	0.41247	-0.029256	-0.021159	-0.052838	0.20782	-0.13749	0.25525	0.36802	1.00000

APPENDIX 3

Table 11A3.1 *Correlation coefficients for independent variables – Taiwan I*

	SIZE	LABPROD2	RDINT	MARKINT2	FOR	LABINT	HUMCAP	EXP
SIZE	1.00000							
LABPROD2	0.13700	1.00000						
RDINT	0.0093572	0.11444	1.00000					
MARKINT2	0.092076	0.085903	0.26196	1.00000				
FOR	0.16637	−0.00085388	−0.15891	−0.20221	1.00000			
LABINT	−0.15216	−0.44903	−0.34250	−0.13599	0.36267	1.00000		
HUMCAP	0.20867	0.50160	0.42501	0.082011	0.050746	−0.51225	1.00000	
EXP	−0.0049505	0.093585	−0.25848	0.041529	0.14387	0.29832	−0.37428	1.00000

Source: Van Hoesel (1999).

APPENDIX 4

Table 11A4.1 Correlation coefficients for independent variables – Taiwan II

	SIZE	LABPROD2	MARKINT2	FOR	LABINT	HUMCAP	EXP
SIZE	1.00000						
LABPROD2	0.076930	1.00000					
MARKINT2	0.14414	0.057380	1.00000				
FOR	0.089928	−0.029995	−0.19809	1.00000			
LABINT	−0.14594	−0.44131	−0.13972	0.38261	1.00000		
HUMCAP	0.22919	0.46198	0.099628	0.031938	−0.49883	1.00000	
EXP	−0.059102	0.054732	−0.045409	0.13604	0.33355	−0.38623	1.00000

Source: Van Hoesel (1999).

PART III

Equity, employment and environment

12.   Liberalization and economic performance in developing and transition countries

Lance Taylor

1.   INTRODUCTION

As seen from the year 2000, economic policy in developing and post-socialist economies during the preceding 10–15 years had one dominating theme. Packages aimed at liberalizing the balance of payments, on both current and capital accounts, showed up throughout Latin America, Eastern Europe, Asia, and even in parts of Africa. Along with large but volatile foreign capital movements (often but not always in connection with privatization of state enterprises), this wave of external deregulation was the central feature of 'globalization' for the non-industrialized world.

In two recent research projects, the implications of external liberalization have been investigated through the use of quantified narrative histories for a number of countries, based on methodologies to decompose and analyse changes over time in effective demand, productivity growth, employment and the sectoral/functional income distribution. The studies were done by nationals of the countries concerned – all highly respected internationally and at home. They appear in collections edited by Ganuza, Taylor and Vos (2000) and Taylor (2000).[1] The former concentrates on countries in Latin America and the Caribbean, while the latter includes papers on Argentina, Colombia, Cuba, India, South Korea (hereafter simply 'Korea'), Mexico, Russia, Turkey and Zimbabwe. The results are sobering. At their infrequent best, liberalization packages have generated modest improvements in economic growth and distributional equity; at their worst they have been associated with sharp deteriorations in economic performance (despite higher capital inflows). The obvious implication is that the liberalization strategy needs to be seriously rethought. A good place to start is with current views about its likely effects.

2. VIEWS ABOUT LIBERALIZATION

Liberalization arrived abruptly. Stabilization and structural adjustment efforts through the mid-1980s had concentrated on fiscal and monetary restraint and realignment of exchange rates. Then in the late 1980s and early 1990s came drastic reductions in trade restrictions and domestic and external financial liberalization, almost simultaneously in most countries. Complementary policies included deregulation of domestic financial markets, tax systems and labour markets.

All these changes are very recent. It will take time before their full effects on growth, employment, income distribution and poverty can be fully assessed. But external liberalization marks such a dramatic switch in development policy away from traditional regimes of widespread state controls and import-substituting industrialization that one would expect large consequences.

The old policy model had been criticized for failing to promote efficient and competitive industrial production, for creating insufficient employment, and for failing to reduce income inequality. Its rapid abolition raises a new set of fundamental questions. Will the liberalization of trade and capital flows help countries meet social goals such as reductions in inequality and poverty, better provision of health and education, and social security? Will a world system in which national economies are highly integrated in commodity and capital markets (in terms of both increased transactions flows and tendencies toward price equalization) attain these goals of its own accord? Can social policies be deployed to ease the task?

The main official justification for the reforms was stated in terms of the visible increases in economic efficiency and output growth that they were supposed to bring. Governments and international institutions promoting them were less explicit about their distributional consequences. The predominant view is that liberalization is likely to lead to better economic performance, at least in the medium to long run. Even if there are adverse transitional impacts, they can be cushioned by social policies, and in any case after some time they will be outweighed by more rapid income growth. This conclusion is fundamentally based on supply-side arguments. The purpose of trade reform is to switch production from non-tradable goods and inefficient import-substitutes towards exportable goods in which poor countries should have comparative advantage. Presumed full employment of all resources (labour included) enables such a switch to be made painlessly. Opening the capital account is supposed to bring financial inflows that will stimulate investment and productivity growth. In a typical mainstream syllogism, Londoño and Székely (1998) postulate that equity is positively related to growth and investment. These in turn are asserted to be positively related to structural reforms, so the conclusion is that liberalization supports low-income groups.

A second position is more radical in that its proponents such as Sen (1999) argue that social policies *should* be deployed to help the poorest, on the implicit assumption that the forces determining the income distribution, the extent of poverty and social relationships are largely independent of liberalization, globalization and market processes more generally.

Finally, others argue that while there may be supply-side benefits from trade and capital market reforms, one should not overlook aggregate demand, its potentially unfavourable interactions with distribution, and the impact of capital inflows on relative prices. The old import-substitution model relied on expansion of internal markets with rising real wages as part of the strategy. Under the new regime controlling wage costs has come to centre stage. So long as there is enough productivity growth and no substantial displacement of workers, wage restraint need not be a problem because output expansion could create space for real income growth. But if wage levels are seriously reduced and/or workers with high consumption propensities lose their jobs, contraction of domestic demand could cut labour income in sectors that produce for the local market. Income inequality could rise if displaced unskilled workers end up in informal service sector activities for which there is a declining demand.

Rising capital inflows following liberalization tend to lead to real exchange rate appreciation, offsetting liberalization's incentives for traded goods production and forcing greater reductions in real wage costs. Appreciation in turn may be linked to high real interest rates, which add to production costs and penalize capital formation. Higher rates may also draw in more external capital, setting off a high interest rate/strong exchange rate spiral. Via the banking system, capital inflows feed into international reserves and domestic credit expansion. On the positive side, more credit may stimulate aggregate spending through increased domestic investment. However, credit expansion can also trigger a consumption boom (with purchases heavily weighted toward imports) or a speculative asset price bubble (typically in equity and/or real estate). The demand expansion may prove to be short-lived if the consequent widening of the external balance is unsustainable, or if capital flees the economy when the bubble begins to deflate. Lack of prudential financial regulation makes the latter outcome all the more likely.

The thrust of these observations is that the effects of balance of payments liberalization on growth, employment and income distribution emerge from a complex set of forces involving both the supply and the demand sides of the economy. Income redistribution and major shifts in relative prices are endogenous to the process. Nor is social policy a panacea for rising inequality and distributional tensions. Only a few countries such as Korea in 1998–99 and Chile and Colombia through much of the 1990s took advantage of strong fiscal positions to introduce large-scale programmes to offset some of liberalization's adverse distributional effects. Elsewhere they were simply allowed to cascade through the system. The bottom line is that there can be no facile conclusions about liberalization, nor about how its consequences can be contained. To date, social costs in many countries have outweighed the benefits, and this situation may persist for an extended period of time.

3.   THE APPROACH OF THE COUNTRY PAPERS

The authors of the country studies in the two projects largely adhere to the third, 'structuralist' world view. Structuralism is not accepted in all circles. But the strength of the papers is that their shared methodological stance eases the task of cross-country comparisons and points to coherent policy conclusions. Their analyses in depth are able to support generalizations about likely outcomes of the globalization/liberalization policy mix in diverse national circumstances. How did the authors separate effects of specific policy changes from other factors, such as external shocks and other policy initiatives? They addressed this standard problem in economic analysis with a mixture of the following approaches:

- Well-informed country 'narratives' discussing policy changes and observed outcomes in a 'before and after' approach. The country stories started with a basic set of questions and hypotheses and a simple analytical framework suggesting possible channels of causation as outlined below. Authors sub-divided their period of analysis into 'episodes' with relatively homogeneous policy packages and economic circumstances. They could then trace the effects of liberalization from one episode through another.
- Still within the realm of 'before and after', the decomposition analyses of aggregate demand, the factoral income distribution, employment and productivity growth mentioned above were applied wherever data availability made them possible. They give essential comparative information on changes in output, employment and inequality that actually took place.
- Counterfactual policy simulations ('with and without') were incorporated in some case studies, based on country-specific models.

Table 12.1 A classificatory scheme of the growth and distibutional effects of globalization

Effect on growth	Distributional impacts		
	Favourable	Neutral	Unfavourable
Positive	Chile (post-1990)	Peru Uruguay	Argentina (until 1997–98) Chile (until 1990) Dominican Republic El Salvador Mexico (post-1995)
Neutral	Costa Rica	Brazil Cuba Turkey	India Korea Mexico (until 1995)
Negative		Colombia	Argentina (post-1997–98) Jamaica Paraguay Russia Zimbabwe

4. INITIAL SUMMARY OF RESULTS

An immediate conclusion is that the effects of globalization and liberalization have not been uniformly favourable. In a classification that is overly simplistic but still suggestive, changes in growth rates and the primary income distribution for the countries included in the studies are summarized in Table 12.1.

The general impression given by Table 12.1 is a tilt toward the southeast – slower growth and deterioration in the primary income distribution. Just two countries had a clear distributional improvement, and only Chile after 1990 managed to combine high growth with decreasing inequality (in contrast to increasing inequality over the preceding liberal 15 years). Stable or more rapid growth on a sustained basis was observed in a few small, open economies that benefited from capital inflows and a somewhat illiberal policy orientation discussed below. Two-thirds of the countries had rising inequality, and the five toward the extreme southeast to a greater or lesser extent were 'disasters'.

5.   A MODEL OF LIBERALIZATION

Along with the aggregate outcomes just summarized, liberalization had strong differential effects on prices and quantities in different sectors. For many but not all countries, an appropriate disaggregation of the non-financial, price/quantity side of the economy focuses on traded and non-traded goods. The key relative price is the real exchange rate or ratio of traded to non-traded goods price indexes. In more populous, less intrinsically open economies one also has to consider other price ratios such as the agricultural terms of trade (India, Turkey) or the relative price of energy products (Russia). In Sub-Saharan African countries such as Zimbabwe, as well as in primary product exporters in Latin America and the Caribbean, the terms of trade between an urban-industrial and rural-agricultural sector come to the fore. In all cases, a mixture of price and quantity adjustments to liberalization is evident. Since it is broadly applicable, the traded/non-traded separation is explored in the discussion to follow. Direct effects of removing barriers to trade and capital movements show up first in the traded (or tradable) goods sector, but spillovers in both directions with non-traded goods have been immediate and substantial. Amadeo and Pero (2000) and Ros (1999) point out the major connections in similar fashions.

The framework is a 'fix-price–flex-price' model à la Hicks (1965) and many others. Traded goods are assumed to be produced under imperfect competition. The simplest model involves a discriminating monopolist manufacturing goods that can both be exported and sold at home, as in Ocampo and Taylor (1998). Households at home buy both domestically made and imported consumer goods. Prior to liberalization, firms have established mark-up rates over variable costs in both their markets – the levels will depend on the relevant elasticities. Variable cost is determined by the market prices and productivity levels of unskilled labour and intermediate imports; skilled labour and physical capital are fixed factors in the short run. The traded goods price level P_t follows from the domestic mark-up over variable cost.

With stable mark-up rates, traded goods comprise a Hicksian 'fix-price' sector, with a level of output x_t determined by effective demand. The level of production of non-traded goods is also determined by demand, but the sector may well have decreasing returns to unskilled labour in the short run. Higher production x_n is made possible by greater unskilled employment (or labour demand) L_n^d. However, cost-minimizing producers will hire extra workers only at a lower real product wage w/P_n, where w is the unskilled nominal wage (fixed in the short run but subject to adjustment over time as discussed below) and P_n is the price of non-traded goods. In other words, a higher price–wage ratio P_n/w is associated with greater non-traded goods production and employment, and (if there are decreasing returns) reduced labour productivity. If P_n/w is free to vary, then non-traded goods aggregate into a 'flex-price' sector. With stable mark-up rates in the traded goods sector, the intersectoral price ratio P_t/P_n will fall as P_n/w rises, that is, a rising price of non-traded goods is associated with real appreciation as measured by the ratio of traded to non-traded goods price indexes (a commonly used proxy is the ratio of wholesale to retail price levels).

In a number of countries, an important component of the non-traded sector comprises the finance, insurance and real estate (or FIRE) sub-sectors. As argued below, both the national interest rate i and the level of financial activity have tended to increase with liberalization – higher values of i and P_n/w go hand in hand, with distributional consequences to be discussed below.

Figure 12.1 gives a graphical presentation of the model.[2] The key quadrant lies in the extreme northeast. It shows how prices and output in the two sectors are determined. Along the schedule for 'non-traded goods equilibrium', a higher traded goods output level X_t is assumed to generate additional demand for non-traded goods. As it is met by an increase in supply, the non-traded price–wage ratio P_n/w will rise. In the market for traded goods, depending on income effects a higher level of P_n/w can be associated with either higher or lower demand. The 'traded goods equilibrium' schedule illustrates the former case – demand for x_t is stimulated by an increase in P_n/w. As drawn in Figure 12.1, the short-run macro equilibrium defined by the intersection of the two curves is stable.

This equilibrium helps determine the status of several markets in the economy. For example, unskilled labour demand in the non-traded sector (L_n^d) is determined in the northwest quadrant. Employment in the traded goods sector is shown in the second quadrant from the top on the right. A lower employment level in traded goods liberates labour that can be used in the other sector, as shown in the second quadrant from the top on the left. As the figure is drawn, labour supply L_n^s exceeds demand L_n^d in the non-traded sector, that is, there is open or disguised unemployment as measured by the difference $(L_n^s - L_n^d)$. Finally, in the extreme southeast quadrant, bigger trade deficits are associated with higher levels of X_t and P_n/w.

6.   EFFECTS OF LIBERALIZATION

As indicated above, in many developing economies both current and capital accounts of the balance of payments were liberalized nearly simultaneously in the late 1980s or early 1990s. Given this history, one has to consider the two policy shifts together. However, for analytical clarity it is

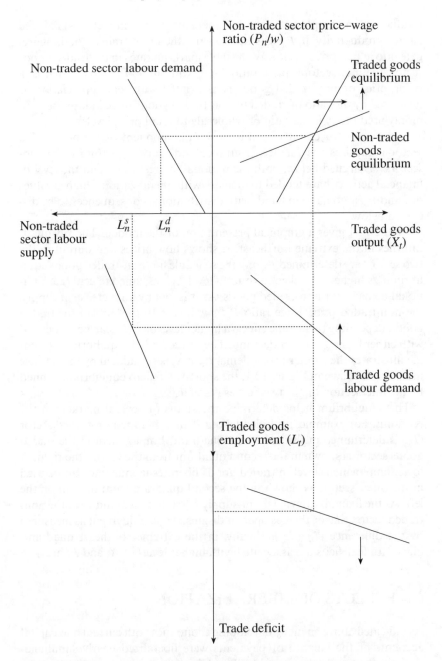

Figure 12.1 Initial equilibrium positions in traded and non-traded goods markets and probable shifts after current and capital account liberalization

useful to dissect them one at a time. In addition, effects of other reforms have to be considered as well, in particular domestic financial, tax and labour market deregulation. We begin with the capital account, followed by the current account, to end with some comments regarding the other sets of reforms.

6.1   Capital account liberalization

Countries liberalized their capital accounts for several apparent reasons – to accommodate external political pressures (Korea and many others), to find sources of finance for growing fiscal deficits (Turkey, Russia), or to bring in foreign exchange to finance the imports needed to hold down prices of traded goods in exchange rate-based inflation stabilization programmes (Argentina, Brazil, Mexico). Whatever the rationale, when they removed restrictions on capital movements, most countries received a surge of inflows from abroad. They came in subject to the accounting restriction that an economy's *net* foreign asset position (total holdings of external assets minus total external liabilities) can only change gradually over time through a deficit or surplus on the current account. Hence, when external liabilities increased as foreigners acquired securities issued by national governments or firms, external assets had to jump up as well. The new assets typically showed up on the balance sheets of financial institutions, including larger international reserves of the central bank. Unless the bank made a concerted effort to 'sterilize' the inflows (selling government bonds from its portfolio to 'mop up liquidity', for example), they set off a domestic credit boom. In poorly regulated financial systems, there was a high risk of a classic mania–panic–crash sequence along Kindleberger (1996) lines – the famous crises in Latin America's Southern Cone around 1980 were only the first of many such disasters.

When the credit expansion was allowed to work itself through, interest rates could be low. However, other factors entered to push both levels of and the spread between borrowing and lending rates upward. One source of widening spreads is related to asset price booms in housing and stock markets, which forced rates to rise on interest-bearing securities such as government debt. Another source playing a role at times originated from central banks trying to sterilize capital inflows, and so pushing up rates as well. Finally, in non-competitive financial markets, local institutions often found it easy to raise spreads. High local returns pulled more capital inflows, worsening the overall disequilibrium.

Unsurprisingly, exchange rate movements complicated the story. In many countries, the exchange rate was used as a 'nominal anchor' in anti-inflation programmes. Its nominal level was devalued at a rate less than the rate of inflation, leading to real appreciation. In several cases, the effect was rapid, with traded goods variable costs in dollar terms jumping upward immediately after the rate was frozen.

The same outcome also showed up via another channel. As countries removed capital controls and adopted 'floating' rates, they lost a degree of freedom in policy formulation. From standard macroeconomic theory we know that in a closed economy the market for bonds will be in equilibrium if the money market clears as well. When proper accounting restrictions (including a fixed level of net foreign assets in the short run) are imposed on portfolio choice in an open economy, this theorem continues to apply (Taylor, 1999). That is, an open economy has just one independent 'asset market' relationship, say an excess supply function for bonds of the form:

$$B - B^d[i, i^*, (\epsilon/e)] = 0.$$

In this equation, B and B^d are bond supply and demand respectively. The latter depends positively on the domestic interest rate i, and negatively on the foreign rate i^* and on expected depreciation ϵ as normalized by the current spot rate e.[3] Total bond supply B will change slowly over time as new paper is issued to cover corporate and (especially) fiscal deficits.

For given expectations, the formula suggests that the interest rate and spot exchange rate will be related inversely. If, for the reasons mentioned above, the domestic rate i tended to rise, then the exchange rate would appreciate or fall. Or, the other way round; if the exchange rate strengthened over time, then interest rates would be pushed upward. This tendency would be amplified if real appreciation stimulated aggregate demand in the short run – the other side of the coin of the well-known possibility that devaluation can be contractionary in developing economies (Krugman and Taylor, 1978). Abandoning capital controls made the exchange rate/interest rate trade-off far more difficult to manage. Some countries did succeed in keeping their exchange rates relatively weak, but they were in a minority. Summarizing, capital account liberalization combined with a boom in external inflows could easily provoke 'excessive' credit expansion. Paradoxically, the credit boom could be associated with relatively high interest rates and a strong local currency. These were not the most secure foundations for liberalization of the current account, the topic we take up next.

6.2 Current account liberalization

Current account deregulation basically took the form of transformation of import quota restrictions (where they were important) to tariffs, and then consolidation of tariff rates into a fairly narrow band, for example between 0 and 20 per cent. With a few exceptions, export subsidies were also removed. There were visible effects on the level and composition of effective demand, and on patterns of employment and labour productivity.

Demand composition typically shifted in the direction of imports, especially when there was real exchange appreciation. In many cases, national savings rates also declined. This shift can partly be attributed to an increased supply of imports at low prices (increasing household spending, aided by credit expansion following financial liberalization), and partly to a profit squeeze (falling retained earnings) in industries producing traded goods. The fall in private savings sometimes was partially offset by rising government savings where fiscal policy became more restrictive. Many countries showed 'stop–go' cycles in government tax and spending behaviour.

Especially when it went together with real appreciation, current account liberalization pushed traded goods producers toward workplace reorganization (including greater reliance on foreign outsourcing) and downsizing. If, as assumed above, unskilled labour is an important component of variable cost, then such workers would bear the brunt of such adjustments via job losses. In other words, traded goods enterprises that stayed in operation had to cut costs by generating labour productivity growth. Depending on demand conditions, their total employment levels could easily fall.

The upshot of these effects often took the form of increased inequality between groups of workers, in particular between the skilled and unskilled. This outcome is at odds with widely discussed predictions of the Stolper–Samuelson (1941) theorem, according to which trade liberalization should lead to an increase in the remuneration of the relatively abundant production factor in low- and middle-income countries (unskilled labour) with respect to the scarce factor (capital or skilled labour). Of course, besides considering exchange rate and capital flow effects on remunerations, the model just presented departs from the standard Heckscher–Ohlin trade theory framework underlying Stolper–Samuelson by working with more than two production factors and allowing for open unemployment, factor immobility and product market imperfections. These considerations along with changes in the sectoral composition of output, as emphasized in Figure 12.1, are important factors in determining the distributive effects of trade liberalization (Wood, 1997). With liberalization stimulating productivity increases leading to a reduction of labour demand from modern, traded-goods production, primary income differentials widened between workers in such sectors and those employed in non-traded, informal activities (for example, informal services) and the unemployed.

7. GRAPHICAL ILLUSTRATION OF THE EFFECTS OF LIBERALIZATION

It is easy to trace through the implications of these changes in Figure 12.1, beginning with the traded goods equilibrium schedule in the northeast quadrant. The sector was subject to several conflicting forces:

- By switching demand toward imports, current account liberalization tended to reduce output X_t. This demand loss was strengthened by real appreciation and weakened or even reversed by devaluation. Removal of export subsidies hurt manufacturing and raw materials sectors in some cases.
- Domestic credit expansion and a falling saving rate stimulated demand for both sectors, although high interest rates may have held back spending on luxury manufactured items such as consumer durables and cars (in countries where they were produced). Income generation via FIRE activity helped stimulate the non-traded sector.

The outcome is that the shift in the traded goods equilibrium schedule was ambiguous, as shown by the double-headed arrow in Figure 12.1. The contractionary forces just mentioned did not impinge directly on non-traded goods; as shown, the corresponding market equilibrium schedule shifted upward. The likely results after both schedules adjusted were a higher non-traded price–wage ratio P_n/w, a fall in the intersectoral terms-of-trade P_t/P_n and an ambiguous change in X_t. In some cases (notably Cuba, Russia and Zimbabwe), the increase in the 'flex-price' P_n was associated with an inflationary process shifting the income distribution away from wages and toward public revenues or profits. The outcome was a reduction in effective demand through 'forced saving' by wage-earners with high propensities to consume, as analysed by Keynes and contemporaries in the 1920s and Kaldor after World War II.

Turning to employment and productivity changes, new jobs were typically created in the non-traded sector, that is, L_n^d went up along the demand schedule in the northwest quadrant. With overall decreasing returns in the sector, its real wage w/P_n and labour productivity level X_n/L_n^d could be expected to fall.

In the traded goods sector, higher labour productivity meant that the labour demand schedule in the middle quadrant on the right moved toward the origin. Regardless of what happened to their overall level of activity, traded goods producers generated fewer jobs per unit of output. Reading through the lower quadrant on the left, L_n^s or unskilled labour supply in non-traded goods tended to rise. The effect on overall unemployment

$(L_n^s - L_n^d)$ was unclear. Wage dynamics appeared to be driven by institutional circumstances in partly segmented labour markets, with details differing country by country. In many cases, stable or rising unemployment and unresponsive wages caused the overall income distribution to become more concentrated. The differential between skilled and unskilled wage rates tended to rise.

The final curve that shifted was the one setting the trade deficit in the extreme southeast quadrant. Higher import demand and (typically) lagging exports meant that it moved away from the origin – for a given output level, the deficit went up. The corresponding increase in 'required' capital inflows fed into the shifts in the capital account discussed above.

7.1   Other reforms

When assessing the effects hypothesized above in real-country contexts, one has to take account of other measures that were implemented simultaneously in many places and which compounded the effects discussed above. We briefly mention three other major areas of liberalization.

1. *Domestic financial sector deregulation*   The effects of capital account liberalization have to be understood in conjunction with the domestic financial sector reforms that also took place in many countries before or around 1990. The lifting of interest-rate ceilings, lowering of reserve requirements, and easing of entry for new banks and other financial institutions were conducive to private credit expansion fuelled by foreign capital inflows. With inadequate bank regulation and supervision in most countries, these changes in regulatory policy exacerbated the risk of banking crises along the lines described above (Vos, 1995).

2. *Labour market liberalization*   Typically, only small changes have occurred in this area. However, distributional outcomes can be strongly influenced by the degree of wage rigidity and labour market segmentation. In most cases institutional wage setting in modern sector firms continues to prevail (as assumed above), as well as regulations stipulating high severance payments in case of dismissal of employees. Strongly segmented labour markets are still a main characteristic in many countries. The bargaining power of organized labour may well have declined, reducing the political space for real wage adjustments.

3. *Tax reforms*   Broadly speaking, countries moved toward taxation of consumption through valued added taxes and away from direct taxation, roughly a shift away from taxing the wealthy and toward lower- and middle-income groups. Substantial lowering of marginal rates on income and corporate taxes has been common.

8.   ECONOMIC PERFORMANCE OVER TIME

The country papers deployed several decomposition techniques to trace economic changes over time.[4] One showed how effective demand was influenced by mutually offsetting pressures among national investment and saving, exports and imports, and government spending and taxes. Another followed sectoral employment growth in terms of growth rates of demand and productivity, a third was an analysis of interactions across sectors of productivity growth *per se*, and some of the papers discussed shifts in the 'functional' income distribution across sectors and recipient classes. Tables 12.2–12.4 give overviews of the main country findings regarding growth, employment, productivity, inequality, sources of effective demand and overall macroeconomic performance. Their periodization is based on the policy 'episodes' identified by the country authors in their papers.

8.1   Growth and macro performance

Apart from years of overt crisis, most countries achieved moderate growth rates of Gross domestic product (GDP) in the 1990s. As already observed, Russia and not quite so disastrously Jamaica, Paraguay and Zimbabwe were the main losers. Except in Argentina before 1997–98, Chile, the Dominican Republic, India and Korea prior to its crisis, rates of growth of household per capita income were negative or modestly positive. Toward the end of the decade, growth had tapered off in many countries due to emerging domestic financial crises (Paraguay, Colombia, Ecuador) or external events. Adverse foreign shocks included the impacts of the Asian crisis on capital flows to Russia and Brazil (with spillover effects on Argentina), and falling export earnings for most primary exporting economies due to plummeting commodity prices.

Capital inflows increased substantially to most countries (in some cases, only prior to their respective crises). As discussed above, incoming foreign capital tended to be associated with increases in international reserves, domestic credit expansion and real appreciation. Stronger exchange rates were generally associated with higher interest rates and increasing interest spreads. Capital inflows, credit creation and real appreciation together stimulated aggregate demand to increase more rapidly than GDP, with consequent widening of the current account deficit.

8.2   Income inequality

Inequality of primary incomes increased in most countries. Virtually without exception, wage differentials between skilled and unskilled workers

Table 12.2 Growth, employment and inequality

	Periods	Characterization	Growth	RER	Employment rate	Real wages	Income inequality		Employment structure	
							Overall primary incomes (labour force)	Skilled/unskilled	Traded/non-traded	Formal/informal
1 Argentina	1991–94	Plan Conv, Expansion 1	8.9	+	+	++	+	+		
	1995	Tequila effect	−4.6	+	−	−	+	+		
	1996–97	Expansion II	6.5	+	−	+	+	+		
2 Bolivia	1980–85	Destabilization	−1.6	+	−	−				
	1986–89	Stabilization	1.6	−	−	+	+	+		
	1990–97	Post-liberalization	4.2	−	+	+/−	+	+	0/−	+
3 Brazil	1982–86	Pre-reform period	4.4	+	+	+	0	−	−	+
	1987–91	Liberalization	−0.3	−	0	−	0	0	+	+
	1992–94	Post-liberalization I	5.4	−	−	+	0	+	+	−
	1994–97	Post-liberalization II	3.2	+	−	+	0	−	−	0
4 Chile	1970–74	Demand expansion, hyperinfl.	1.0	+	+	−	−	−	+	
	1976–81	Liberalization	9.4	+	+	++	+	+	−	
	1985–89	Readjustment	8.4	−	++	++	+	+	−	
	1990–97	Free trade agreements	9.4	+	+	++	+	−	−	
5 Colombia	1992–95	Liberalization and boom	5.2	+	+	++	+	+	−	+
	1995–98	Stagnation	1.4	+	−	+	+	+	−	−

Table 12.2 (cont.)

	Periods	Characterization	Growth	RER	Employment rate	Real wages	Income inequality		Employent sturcture	
							Overall primary incomes (labour force)	Skilled/ unskilled	Traded/ non-traded	Formal/ informal
6 Costa Rica	1985–91	Trade lib. (CA)	3.7	+	+	–		+	–	+
	1992–98	Further opening	4.3	0	+	+		+	–	+
7 Cuba	1989–93	Opening forex market	–8.5	++	+/0	–	+		+	–
	1994–98	Fiscal adj, flexib own-account	4.4	–/+	–/0	+	–		–	–
8 Dominican Republic	1991–98	Post-liberalization	6.1	++	+	+	+	+	–	+
9 Ecuador	1988–91	Pre-reform	2.6	–	+/–	–	+	+	–	–
	1992–98	Stab. and liberalization	2.7	++	–/+	+	+	+	0	–
10 El Salvador	1980–82	BoP Crisis	–9.5	+	––	–	–	+		
	1983–89	War economy	1.3	++	–	–	+			
	1990–95	BoP and financial liberalization	6.0	++	+	0/–	+	–		
	1996–98	Demand contraction	3.0	+	0/–	0/–	0/+	–		
11 Guatemala	1987–92	BoP liberalization	3.9	–		–			+	–
	1992–97	BoP cum dom. fin. lib.	4.0	+		+			+	–

	Period		Growth							
12 Jamaica	1980–89	Pre-liberalization	1.6	+				+		+
	1990–92	Financial liberalization	1.2	+				+	–	+
	1993–98	Trade liberalization	–0.7	+			–	+	–	+
13 Mexico	1988–94	Trade and financial liberalization	3.9	++	+/–	+	+	+	+	
	1994–95	Peso crisis and NAFTA	–6.2	+		+	+	+	+	
	1996–98	Post-crisis	5.8	+			–	+		
14 Paraguay	1988–91	Trade and exchange rate reform	3.8	+/0	+	+	+	+	+	+
	1992–94	MERCOSUR	3.6	–	0		+	+	+	–
	1995–98	Financial reform	2.0	+	–	+/0	+	–		+
15 Peru	1986–90	Hyperinflation	–1.1	++		–		–		–
	1991–98	BoP liberalization	4.9	+/0	+	++	–/0	+	+/0	+
16 Uruguay	1986–90	Pre-MERCOSUR	2.5	–		+	0/–		0/–	0
	1990–97	MERCOSUR	4.1	+		+/–	+/0	+	+/0	0/–
17 India	1986–91	Pre-reform period	5.9	+		+		–		–
	1992–96	Liberalization	5.3	–/+		–		+		+
18 Korea	1980–88	Lib., depreciation, boom	9.4	+/–/–/+	+	++(6.0)	++	–	++	+
	1988–93	Appreciation, slowing growth	7.2	–	0	++(9.4)	+	0/–	+	+
	1993–97	Capital account liberalization	7.5	+/–	+/0	++(5.4)	0	0	+/–	+
	1997–98	Financial crisis	–5.8	–		(–9.3)	–	++		–
19 Russia	1990–92	Declining growth	–9.8	–				–	0/–	0
	1992–94	Lib. of current account	–10.7	++	+/–	+/–		+		–
	1994–97	Convertibility, capital acct. lib.	–2.2	++		–/+	–/+	+	–/+	–
	1998	Crisis	–4.6	–		–		–	0/–	0
20 Turkey	1980–88	Exp. promotion and trade lib.	5.4	–	++		–	+	+	
	1989–93	Unregulated fin. liberalization	4.8	++	+/0	++	++	++	++	–
	1994	Financial crisis	–5.5	–		–	+	+	+	
	1995–97	Post-crisis adjustment	7.2	+/0	+	+/0	+/0	++	+/0	–

Table 12.2 (cont.)

Periods	Characterization	Growth	RER	Employment rate	Real wages	Income inequality		Employment structure	
						Overall primary incomes (labour force)	Skilled/ unskilled	Traded/ non-traded	Formal/ informal
21 Zimbabwe 1986–90	Pre-liberalization period	5.2	–	+	+	+	+	+/0	+/0
1991–92	Transition and drought	–1.8	+	0/–	–	–	+	–	–
1993–97	Post-liberalization period	3.6	–	0	–	–	+	–	–

Key to variables:
++ = strong increase; + = increase; +/0 = slight increase, almost stable; 0 = no change
0/– = slight decrease, almost stable; – = decrease; – – = strong decrease
+/–/+ = fluctuating trend (stop–go)
Growth = annual rate of GDP
RER = real exchange rate (+ = real appreciation)
Employment rate = change in employed as share of EAP (+ = rise in employment or decrease in unemployment)
Real wages = change in average wage rate
Inequality = refers to per worker primary income (wages, other) (+ = rising inequality)
change in ratio earnings of skilled and unskilled workers
Source: Author's compilation from Ganuza et al. (2000) and Taylor (2000).

rose with liberalization, reflecting employment reallocation as suggested in Figure 12.1. Relative to the economically active population (following the standard definition), the unemployment rate was stable or tended to rise, again consistent with Figure 12.1. Excess labour was absorbed in the non-traded, informal trade and services sectors (Bolivia, Colombia, Ecuador, India, Peru, Russia) or where traditional agriculture served as a sponge for the labour market (Costa Rica, Guatemala, Mexico).

Primary income inequality seemed to increase for several reasons. In Argentina, productivity increases in the traded goods sector affected all skill levels. With greater wage rigidity for unskilled workers, there was a reduction in earnings inequality in the sector. Increasing overall inequality was due to rising income concentration in the non-traded sector along with greater skill intensity of new investment and to the rise of unemployment in traded goods. In contrast, in Mexico reorganization of manufacturing production was found to be a major source of greater skill demand in manufacturing, pushing up wage inequality in the traded goods sector with many of the displaced workers absorbed by agriculture (at least until 1994). As already indicated, in other cases productivity growth in traded goods pushed up skill differentials in that sector along with the gap between formal and informal sector workers.

In Colombia, primary inequality increased as people with low skill levels lost jobs and suffered real wage reductions – labour demand appeared insensitive to the wage cuts. In India, poverty and inequality both went up, in part because of policy-induced increases in food prices and cutbacks in public expenditure. These initiatives were subsequently reversed, as policy responded to the political reaction that followed. Tracing the distributional effects of two decades of liberalization in Korea is not easy. Through the 1980s, unemployment decreased, the wage share increased, wage inequality (Gini coefficient and the ratio of average wages in the top and bottom deciles) declined, skill premiums fell, and the wage differential between large and small enterprises went down. Rising wage and falling profit shares put distributional pressure on the traditional growth model, which had been led by investment demand supported by high corporate and household saving rates and a fiscal surplus. A transition toward growth led by consumption from wage income is as yet incomplete.

The favourable distributional trends petered out in the early 1990s, in part because of increased subcontracting by the chaebol (conglomerate firms) to domestic suppliers with lower wage and productivity levels, in Korea's version of the shifts depicted in Figure 12.1. When the crisis hit, the International Monetary Fund imposed an outlandishly intense austerity package that lasted through mid-1998. The unemployment rate rose by five percentage points and the real wage fell by 9 per cent. Excepting the top

Table 12.3   Aggregate demand decomposition

		Demand decomposition	
	Periods	Characterization	Aggregate demand
1 Argentina	1990–94	Private consumption boom	9.6
	1995–96	Private demand contraction	0.5
	1996–97	Private demand (C, I) recovery	10.1
2 Bolivia	1980–85	Private consumption and govt. led	−1.5
	1986–89	Export led	2.1
	1990–97	Export led	4.8
3 Brazil	1982–86	Govt. and export led	−0.9
	1987–91	Govt. led	3.0
	1992–94	Private cons. and govt. led	0.9
	1994–97	Private investment and consumption	5.2
4 Chile	1970–74	Private and gov. cons.	1.0
	1976–81	Cons. squeeze, exports	9.4
	1985–89	Investment, exports	8.4
	1990–97	Investment, exports	9.4
5 Colombia	1990–92	Export and govt. led	2.2
	1992–95	Private consumption boom	9.6
	1995–98	Private exp. contraction	1.5
6 Costa Rica	1985–91	Export led	5.7
	1992–98	Export led	6.5
7 Cuba	1989–93	Private demand squeeze	−13.7
	1994–98	Publ. exp and export recovery	7.0
8 Dominican Rep.	1991–97	Private demand and export led	8.8
9 Ecuador	1988–91	Private demand	4.4
	1992–98	Export led	2.9
10 El Salvador	1990–95	Investment and export	41.7
	1996–97	Export	6.7
11 Guatemala	1986–91	Consumption led	3.4
	1991–98	Consumption led	5.0
12 Jamaica	1980–89	Private consumption led	2.0
	1990–92	Export led	8.1
	1993–98	Private dem. and export contraction	−3.1

	Direct multiplier effects			Effect of leakages		Private spending ('investment'–savings')	Government spending ('government'–'tax')	External demand ('exports'–'imports')
I/s	G/t	E/m	s	t	m			
+	n.a.	—	+/−	n.a.	—			
−	n.a.	+	+	n.a.	+			
+	+/0	−	0	−	−			
+	—	+/−	++	0	+/−	+	−/+	+
−/+	0	+	−	0	0	−	−/+	−/+
+	+	+	−	0	−	−/+	0	−/+
)	+	+	−	0	+			
−	+	−	−	−	−			
+	+	−	0	−	−			
+	—	−	+	0	−			
—	+	−	—	0/−	+/0	0.2	2.7	−1.9
)	+	−	0/−	−	+	7.4	1.6	0.4
++	+/0	++	+/0	+/0	+	5.8	0.2	2.4
++	+/0	++	−	+/0	+	6.5	0.2	2.7
−	++	+	−	0	−	−9.2	3.9	5.3
−	+	+	++	−	−	4.6	1.7	0.5
—	+/−	+	0	0	−	−2.0	3.6	1.0
−	+	++	−	++	−	1.7	0.7	3.3
+	+	++	+/0	+	−	0.4	0.7	5.4
—	—	++	—	+	—	−61.6	6.9	13.4
−+	++	+	++	−	−	52.8	−41.1	6.4
−	+	+	−	0	−	4.7	1.2	2.9
−	0/−	−	+	−	0			
−	0	++	−	0	0			
−+	—	+	+	—	—			
—	++	++	—	+	−			
−	+/0	0	+/0	0/−	−	2.8	0.8	−0.3
−/0	+/−/+	+	+	−	−	3.0	0.8	1.1
−	—	0	++	−	0			
−	—	+	−	+	−			
−/−/+	+	−	+	+	+			

Table 12.3 (cont.)

		Demand decomposition	
	Periods	Characterization	Aggregate demand
13 Mexico	1988–94	Consumption boom	5.5
	1994–95	Crisis and cons. squeeze	−7.8
	1996–98	Investment recovery	8.3
14 Paraguay	1988–91	Private demand expansion	6.7
	1992–94	Private demand expansion	10.8
	1995–98	Private dem. and export contraction	−0.6
15 Peru	1986–90	Collapse private demand	−1.9
	1991–97	Private demand recovery	5.6
16 Uruguay	1986–90	Export led. priv. demand squeeze	2.9
	1990–94	Private demand expansion	8.4
	1994–97	Private demand and exports	4.4
17 India	1986–91	Pre-reform period	5.4
	1992–96	Liberalization	7.5
18 Korea	1980–88	Lib., depreciation, boom	8.3
	1988–93	Appreciation, slowing growth	6.9
	1993–97	Capital account liberalization	9.6
19 Russia	1990–92	Declining growth	2.4
	1992–94	Lib. of current account	−19.2
	1994–97	Convertibility, capital acct. lib.	−3.0
20 Turkey	1980–88	Exp. promotion and trade lib.	6.2
	1989–93	Unregulated fin. liberalization	5.2
	1994	Financial crisis	−4.9
	1995–97	Post-crisis adjustment	10.1
21 Zimbabwe	1986–90	Pre-liberalization period	5.5
	1993–97	Post-liberalization period	4.6

Key to variables:
+ + = strong increase; + = increase; +/0 = slight increase, almost stable; 0 = no change
0/− = slight decrease, almost stable; − = decrease; — = strong decrease
+/−/+ = fluctuating trend (stop–go).
Aggregate demand = GDP + imports (numbers refer to annual rates of growth).
Source: Author's compilation from Ganuza et al. (2000) and Taylor (2000).

						Decomposition of effective sources of change in aggregate demand (see terms at bottom of table)		
						Private spending ('investment'– savings')	Government spending ('government'– 'tax')	External demand ('exports'– 'imports')
Direct multiplier effects			Effect of leakages					
I/s	G/t	E/m	s	t	m			
++	+/0	−	++	0	—			
—	0	++	−	+	+			
+	+/0	0	−	0	—			
+	+	0/−	−/+	0	−			
+	−	0/−	++	0	−			
+	+	−	+	0/−	+			
++	+	−	+	+	+	2.7	−1.3	−3.4
++	+	−/0	−	−	−	5.1	1.1	−0.6
−	−/+/−	+	0	0	0	0.7	0.6	2.7
++	+/0	−	++	−/+	—	8.2	1.0	−1.0
−/+	−	+	+/0	0/−	−	2.5	0.0	1.7
	++	−	−	+	−			
−	+	−	−	+/−	—			
+/0	−	+	−	0/−	+			
−	0	0	−	0/−	0			
++	0	0/−	+	+/0	—			
—	++	+/0	n.a.	+	—			
—	+	−	+	++	—			
—	+	−	+	++	—			
−	—	−	+/−	−	—			
−	++	−	+	+/0	—			
−	−	−	−	—	+			
−	+/0	—	+	+/0	—			
−	+	+	+	−	−			
−	−	++	+	0	−			

Table 12.4 Productivity and employment

	Periods	Characterization	Productivity growth Overall	T	NT	Sector reallocation effects Employment	Labour supply decomposition Participation rate	Unemployment rate	Employment rate
1 Argentina	1991–94	Plan Conv., Expansion 1	7.8	n.a.	n.a.	negative	+	++	—
	1995–96	Tequila effect	2.7	n.a.	n.a.	negative	+	++	0/–
	1996–97	Expansion II	1.2	n.a.	n.a.	small	+	–	+/0
2 Bolivia	1980–92	Destabilization/stabilization	-3.0	-3.2	-3.2				
	1992–97	Post-liberalization	1.0	1.0	0.8				
3 Brazil	1982–86	Pre-reform period	0.7	2.0	-0.4		+	–	+
	1987–91	Liberalization	-4.0	-2.4	-5.1		0	0	0
	1992–94	Post-liberalization I	4.4	2.4	4.6		+	+	–
	1994–97	Post-liberalization II	0.9	4.4	-1.2		0	+	–
4 Chile	1970–74	Demand expansion, hyperinfl.	0.8	0.1	1.3	small	–	+	+/0
	1976–81	Liberalization	2.6	3.7	1.9	small (–)	+	–	+
	1985–89	Readjustment	0.1	-1.2	0.9	small (–)	+	–	+
	1990–97	Free trade agreements	3.9	4.8	3.5	small (–)	+/0	–	+/0
5 Colombia	1992–95	Liberalization and boom	2.6	2.7	2.9	small			
	1995–98	Stagnation	2.0	2.8	1.9	small			
6 Costa Rica	1987–91	Trade lib.	1.5	2.3	0.9	small	–	-/0	-/0
	1992–98	Further opening	0.6	3.0	-1.0	small	+	-/0	+
7 Cuba	1989–93	Opening forex market	-8.3	-13.7	-5.0	0	–	+	+/0
	1994–98	Fiscal adj, flexib. own-account act.	4.1	11.1	0.1	0	–	–	-/0
8 Dominican Rep.	1991–96	Post-liberalization	3.5	5.7	2.3	small	–	–	+
9 Ecuador	1982–97	Pre-reform	0.1	1.3	-0.9	large (away from NT)	0	–	+

# Country	Period	Description						
10 El Salvador	1991–95	BoP and financial liberalization	14.3	−0.6	31.3	large		+
	1995–96	Demand contract	9.6	4.4	14.0	small	0	+
11 Guatemala	1987–92	BoP liberalization	0.4	−0.4	1.1	large	0/−	−
	1992–97	BoP cum dom. fin. lib.	0.3	−1.3	0.8	large	0	
12 Jamaica	1980–89	Pre-liberalization	3.2	1.7	0.9	small	0	−
	1990–92	Financial liberalization	3.7	1.2	2.1	small		−
	1993–98	Trade liberalization	−1.0	0.5	−1.6	small	+	+
13 Mexico	1988–93	Financial liberalization	0.6	6.0	−0.5	small		−
	1994–97	Peso crisis, NAFTA, adjustm.	−0.8	−0.2	−2.1	small		
14 Paraguay	1982–92	Trade and exchange rate reform	−0.4	1.2	−2.5	large (away from T)	+	+/−
	1992–97	MERCOSUR and fin. liberalization	−5.7	−2.1	−8.7	large (away from T)	+	−/0
15 Peru	1986–90	High inflation period	0.7	1.1	0.6		−	+
	1991–98	BoP liberalization	0.6	1.1	0.5		+	−
16 Uruguay	1986–90	Pre-MERCOSUR	0.4	−0.7	0.6		+	−
	1990–94	MERCOSUR (I)	3.8	0.0	2.2		+	−/0
	1994–97	MERCOSUR (II)	2.7	6.5	2.4		+	+
17 India	1986–91	Pre-reform period	3.8	n.a.	n.a.	none	+	−
	1992–96	Liberalization	2.5	n.a.	n.a.	negative	++	+/0
18 Korea	1980–88	Lib., depreciation, boom	6.4	n.a.	n.a.	large	++	0/−
	1988–93	Appreciation, slowing growth	4.8	n.a.	n.a.	large	++	0
	1993–97	Capital account liberalization	5.3	n.a.	n.a.	small	+	0/−
	1997–98	Financial crisis	n.a.	n.a.	n.a.	negative	−	−
19 Russia	1990–92	Declining growth	−7.5	−9.5	−5.5	negative	+/0	++
	1992–94	Lib. of current account	−8.5	−11.0	−6.0	negative	−	++
	1994–97	Convertibility, capital acct. lib.	−1.0	9.0	−5.5	none	−	++
	1998	Crisis	−3.0	−3.0	−4.0	negative	0	+

Table 12.4 (cont.)

	Periods	Characterization	Productivity growth			Sector realloaction effects	Labour supply decomposition		
			Overall	T	NT	Employment	Participation rate	Unemployment rate	Employment rate
20 Turkey	1980–88	Exp. promotion and trade lib.	2.6	−2.1	8.3	small	+	–	++
	1989–93	Unregulated fin. liberalization	1.7	1.2	2.3	none	+	–	+
	1994	Financial crisis	−7.5	−13.1	−0.6	negative	0	0/–	+/0
	1995–97	Post-crisis adjustment	3.5	3.2	3.9	none	+	–	+
21 Zimbabwe	1986–90	Pre-liberalization period	1.5	1.2	1.6	none	+/0	–	+
	1991–92	Transition and drought	−3.0	−6.8	−0.2	negative	0	+	0/–
	1993–97	Post-liberalization period	0.9	−1.0	2.4	negative	+/0	0	0

Key to variables:
Productivity growth = annual rate of change of productivity (Q/L).
T = traded goods sectors.
NT = non-traded sectors.
Reallocation effects: see decomposition methodology in Taylor et al. (1998).
Source: Author's compilation from Ganuza et al. (2000) and Taylor (2000).

decile which benefited from higher interest rates on its assets, average household incomes fell across the board, with the greatest reductions (of the order of 20 per cent) in the bottom deciles. Government spending on social support was increased in 1998, and following relaxation of the IMF's demand restraints there was strong output growth (partly led by domestic demand) in 1999. Whether the crisis will provoke a long-term trend toward increasing inequality in Korea remains to be seen.

One last example of distributional deterioration is in Russia. Prior to its demise, the Soviet system had two main proto-classes, the *nomenklatura* in charge of the party/state governing apparatus and the rest of the population. The *nomenklatura* were the clear gainers from the transition, as in connection with the criminal 'mafia' they seized control of the major productive assets in a blatantly rigged privatization process and engaged in massive capital flight. The capital outflow largely offset any current account improvement from higher world prices or volumes of energy exports, leaving the economy in a difficult external position.

Employment increased in relatively successfully adjusting sectors such as energy, FIRE and public administration, and was held fairly stable elsewhere. As in Cuba after its external shock, job protection combined with falling output and real wage reduction due to forced saving led to negative apparent productivity growth in virtually all sectors. The only Russians (the so-called 'new Russians') whose real earnings rose were people in upper income strata who benefited from forced saving and the rapid, corrupt privatization. In less than a decade, the Gini coefficient literally doubled, from around 0.3 to 0.6. Around four-fifths of the population are now poor or very poor according to the official poverty lines.

Only in a handful of economies is the distributional picture not mostly gloomy. In El Salvador and Costa Rica, rapid employment growth of unskilled workers, particularly in export sectors, offset widening between group (skill) differentials. In Chile, overall labour market tightening probably was the main factor behind a reduction in wage differentials in the 1990s.[5] In Brazil, elimination of hyperinflation and labour demand shifts towards the unskilled have been factors underlying the dampening of primary income differentials. Earnings trends have also been influenced by minimum wage policies, such as in Ecuador where upward adjustments in the minimum wage allowed for a temporary decline in wage inequality (1992–95), despite an overall rising trend (1990–98).

8.3 Sources of effective demand

As noted in connection with Figure 12.1, real exchange rate appreciation has been a central characteristic of the post-liberalization period in most countries. Trade expansion and diversification stimulated growth only where depreciation occurred or the currency was kept weak (Bolivia, Chile, Colombia 1990–92, Korea and Russia post-1998, Mexico post-1995, Uruguay 1986–90). Similar observations hold for small Latin-American countries with credible incentive systems for non-traditional exports (Dominican Republic, Chile, Costa Rica, El Salvador and Uruguay via MERCOSUR).

These observations are of interest because one of the principal justifications for external liberalization was its anticipated effect on trade performance. Due to efficiency gains induced by freer trade, 'export-led' growth was supposed to be an immediate consequence. It did not happen, at least in terms of effective demand generation in most of the countries in Table 12.3. As the detailed studies demonstrate, exports did tend to rise with liberalization but import leakages went up as well, especially when the local currency appreciated in real terms. Trade therefore held back or added weakly to effective demand. Growth stimulus from trade was present, but much less strongly than originally supposed by advocates of liberalization.[6]

The public sector's contribution to demand varied across countries. It was positive in Chile and Costa Rica, in Columbia due to increases in social spending, in Cuba as it recovered from external shocks in 1994–98, in India where the consolidated government deficit has supported demand for many years, and in Russia as plummeting demand was at least slowed by the fact that government spending did not decrease quite so rapidly as receipts from a failing taxation system. Elsewhere, government's impact on demand was broadly neutral. Positive or 'stop–go' public sector demand effects are a surprising outcome, given the rhetoric about downsizing the state that accompanied the drive toward liberalization.

Without strong contributions from the foreign and public sectors, private sector demand growth emerged as the major driving force in several countries. In particular, import-led consumption booms following trade and financial liberalization were the rule rather than the exception. They were triggered by both cheapening of imported traded goods (import liberalization and real exchange rate appreciation) and expansion of domestic credit supply (fomented by the surge in capital flows and domestic financial liberalization). Private savings rates fell in consequence. Fewer cases were observed in which domestic demand was driven by expanding private investment, but it did occur in Argentina, Chile and Korea in the 1990s. The rapid reduction in demand in Russia was provoked by an investment collapse in an economy that had historically been driven by high rates of accumulation. In Mexico, late in the decade, higher private capital formation could give hope for a brighter future were it not for a setback due to global instability in 1998–99.

8.4 Productivity and employment growth

With Korea prior to its crisis as a notable exception, only modest aggregate productivity increases were observed. Where data are available, they are broadly consistent with greater observed productivity growth in traded than non-traded sectors. As observed above, the change in aggregate productivity is a result of the sum of productivity changes by sectors (weighted by sectoral output shares) plus a positive reallocation effect if labour moves from low- to high-productivity sectors. Findings from the country studies indicate that within-sector productivity shifts and output growth rates largely determined the aggregate outcomes. However, in some cases there was a negative reallocation effect as workers moved toward low productivity non-traded goods sectors. In Guatemala, Mexico and Ecuador these sectors served as important 'employers of last resort'.

With Cuba and Russia as exceptions, the share of the economically active population (or the 'participation rate') increased under liberalization. With the exception of Turkey, the unemployed as a proportion of the economically active went up as well, especially after crises and/or later in the decade. Given the modest growth of GDP noted previously, a lacklustre employment performance under liberalization is scarcely surprising.

9.   RESULTS OF SOCIAL POLICY

The macroeconomic conditions emerging from external liberalization were scarcely favourable for an often outdated traded goods sector making the transition to a free trade environment. Productivity increased, yet output gains were usually not strong enough to offset employment and wage losses via other sectors of the economy. The result has been a loss of relatively high-paying jobs, replaced by underemployment and lower wages in the service sector, often in the informal economy. Such labour market adjustments contributed to greater inequality in almost all countries.

Social policy is a tool that can in principle be used by governments to cushion the adverse effects of external liberalization. Authors of the nine studies in Taylor (2000) paid special attention to this issue. Their findings show that the countries can broadly be divided into three groups in terms of their social spending during liberalization: those that did increase spending, those that couldn't and those that chose not to.

Colombia, Cuba and Korea introduced programmes to offset some of the negative consequences of liberalization. Colombia broadened its tax base, allowing expanded social security coverage as well as improved school attendance rates, access to drinking water, and housing. Cuba, during its external shock of 1989–93, suffered output, productivity and real-wage contraction. Needing to generate foreign exchange, the government restructured the economy toward exports. One consequence was rising inequality between people working in export sectors and the rest of the population. To lessen this divide, the government stepped up programmes compensating workers not employed in exports. In Korea, the economic crisis provided the impetus for expanding social services, an area historically neglected in favour of growth. Government outlays for social expenditures increased from 5 per cent of GDP in the 1980s to 7.8 per cent in 1997.

Russia, Turkey and Zimbabwe faced fiscal resource constraints and cut back on social programmes. Russia is the most acute example. Privatization of its energy industries coupled with a lack of capital controls led to external capital flight. This resource loss meant that the government did not have resources to compensate workers who lost their jobs because of liberalization. Funding of health, education and other services deteriorated severely.

In Turkey and Zimbabwe, an unwillingness to raise taxes forced reductions in social programmes. During the 1980s, Turkey expanded public spending on social interventions via deficit finance. By 1993, this effort was no longer sustainable, leading to cutbacks. In Zimbabwe, external liberalization has been accompanied by a tightening of government spending in an attempt to control inflation. Programmes instituted during the 1980s in an attempt to lessen inequality between racial groups have been retrenched.

In Argentina, India and Mexico, external liberalization has not been accompanied by increased social spending. Argentina responded to the increase in unemployment caused by liberalization by making the labour market more flexible, leading to more underemployment and lower wages. However, a state-subsidized employment programme in health and education enabled some, mostly female, workers to get jobs. With the removal of tariffs, India lost an important source of government revenue, forcing reductions in spending on rural development, health, education and housing. In Mexico, the government has not instituted social programmes to help those hurt by the transition. Instead, it dismantled long-standing support for peasant agriculture to the detriment of rural incomes.

10. POLICY ALTERNATIVES

The usual caveats about policy prescriptions apply. Given the diversity of country experiences just reported, it is risky to generalize about lessons and conclusions. Of course, diversity of outcomes is a result in itself. It negates general sweeping statements about whether the reforms have been exclusively beneficial or exclusively costly in terms of growth, employment and equity. If one is to sing a sad song, however, the evidence certainly shows that, in the post-liberalization era, few if any of the countries considered seem to have found a sustainable growth path. Employment growth has generally been slow to dismal, and rising primary income disparity (in some cases over and above already high levels of inequality) has been the rule.

Better performances such as those in Mexico and Korea after their financial crises (as of the year 2000, three years of sustained growth in Mexico and one in Korea) were associated with avoiding the macro price mixture of a strong real exchange rate and high domestic interest rates. Post-crisis effective demand was led by the foreign sector in Mexico and by private consumption and investment spending in Korea, suggesting that each recovering country may have its own particular demand path. Similar conclusions apply to the handful of Latin-American economies that combined adequate growth with improvement or stability of indexes of inequality. Their better performances were associated with a policy mix that combined: (a) avoiding a macro price mixture of real exchange rate appreciation and high domestic interest rates; (b) maintaining a system of well-directed export incentives, whether put in place at the national level or as part of regional integration agreements; and (c) having a system of capital controls and prudential financial regulation able to contain the negative consequences of capital surges. In some cases, cross-border financial flows were extremely important, for example emigrant remittances in El Salvador are more than 10 per cent of GDP.

For the other countries, the news is less good. Turkey and Argentina continue to wander in a slow growth, falling employment and increasing inequality wilderness. India's growth and equity performance has not improved with liberalization, and despite a strong effort on the social policy front, Colombia's is worse. In part because of an explicit effort to cushion the liberalization shock, Cuba's growth and equity performances are mediocre. Jamaica's, Zimbabwe's and especially Russia's are disasters.

Of the three views regarding liberalization mentioned at the outset, the first 'market friendly' narrative is hard to discern in the countries analysed here. In line with the second view, some might argue that their distributional deterioration was *not* the result of liberalization and globalization, but they would have to strain to make the case. For most of the countries, it is difficult to refute the third view that liberalization and deteriorating growth and equity performances can easily go hand in hand.

Finally, fundamental questions arise regarding social coherence and social policy. The mainstream view of liberalization emphasizes its likely positive effects on economic performance. Adverse transitional impacts can in principle be smoothed by social policies, and in any case after some time 'a rising tide lifts all boats' (except for, is as sometimes added, the ones that sink). The much more disquieting possibility is that liberalization can unleash dynamic forces leading not only to an unimpressive aggregate economic performance but also to long-term slow employment expansion and increasing income concentration. In principle, governments could put countervailing social policies into place. In practice, they probably lack the capacity to do so because of their own fiscal and administrative limitations.

Such constraints on social policy and burden-sharing can be reduced by investment in the capability of the state, as experience in now industrialized countries demonstrated in the nineteenth century and again after World War II in the construction of welfare states (Polanyi, 1944). But an explicit political decision would be needed before such investments could be undertaken. It would be comparable in scope to the one that led to the worldwide spread of liberalization in the first place. Nevertheless, for the countries considered here, the initial outcomes of liberalization suggest that a 'double movement' à la Polanyi, first toward and then away from an extreme liberal policy stance, could be forthcoming in the not so distant future. Inadequate social performance of any economic policy line leads ultimately to its reversal as society organizes to protect its own.

NOTES

1. The research was supported by the Division for Social Policy and Development of the United Nations, the United Nations Development Programme, and the John D. and Catherine T. MacArthur Foundation.
2. See Taylor (1991) for an algebraic treatment of linkages like those described in the text in models closely related to the one illustrated in Figure 12.1.
3. Scaling the expected change in the exchange rate by its current level puts the quantity e/e – the expected rate of return from capital gains on foreign securities – on a comparable footing with the two interest rates.
4. For the analytical details, see Janine Berg and Lance Taylor, 'External Liberalization, Economic Performance, and Social Policy' in Taylor (2000), available on the website www.newschool.edu/cepa.
5. It should be recalled that liberalization began in Chile in the 1970s and inequality increased considerably up to the end of the 1980s.
6. By way of clarification, *effects* of changes in saving, tax and import parameters are reported with positive signs in the tables. For example, the saving rate dropped sharply in Mexico in 1988–94, strongly stimulating aggregate demand.

REFERENCES

Amadeo, Edward J. and Valeria Pero (2000) 'Adjustment, Stabilization, and the Structure of Employment in Brazil', *Journal of Development Studies*, **36** (4) 120–48.
Ganuza, Enrique, Lance Taylor and Rob Vos (eds) (2000), *External Liberalization*

and Economic Performance in Latin America and the Caribbean, New York: United Nations Development Programme.

Hicks, John R. (1965), *Capital and Growth*, Oxford: Clarendon Press.

Kindleberger, Charles P. (1996), *Manias, Panics and Crashes* (3rd edn), New York: John Wiley and Sons.

Krugman, Paul and Lance Taylor (1978), 'Contractionary Effects of Devaluation', *Journal of International Economics*, **8** (3) 445–56.

Londoño, Juan Luis and Miguel Székely (1998), 'Sorpresas Distributivas después de una Década de Reformas', *Pensamiento Iberoamericano-Revista de Económica Política* (Special Issue).

Ocampo, José Antonio and Lance Taylor (1998), 'Trade Liberalization in Developing Economies: Modest Benefits but Problems with Productivity Growth, Macro Prices and Income Distribution', *Economic Journal*, **108** (450),1523–46.

Polanyi, Karl (1944), *The Great Transformation*, New York: Rinehart.

Ros, Jaime (1999), 'La Liberalization de la Balanza de Pagos en Mexico: Efectos en el Crecimiento, el Empleo y la Desigualdad Salarial', Paper presented at UNDP–CEPAL–IDB conference on the *Effects of Balance of Payments Liberalization on Employment, Distribution, Poverty and Growth*, Rio de Janeiro, February.

Sen, Amartya (1999), *Development as Freedom*, New York: Alfred A. Knopf.

Stolper, Wolfgang F. and Paul A. Samuelson (1941), 'Protection and Real Wages', *Review of Economic Studies*, **9**, 58–73.

Taylor, Lance (1991), *Income Distribution, Inflation, and Growth*, Cambridge, Mass: MIT Press.

Taylor, Lance (2000), 'Exchange Rate Determination in the Portfolio Balances, Mundell Fleming, and (Perhaps) More Plausible Models', Working Paper 8, Centre for Economic Policy Analysis, New School for Social Research, New York.

Taylor, Lance (ed.) (2000), *External Liberalization, Economic Performance and Social Policy*, New York: Oxford University Press.

Vos, Rob (1995), 'Financial Liberalization, Growth and Adjustment: Some Lessons from Developing Countries', in Stephany Griffith-Jones and Zdenek Drábek (eds), *Financial Reform in Central and Eastern Europe*, London: Macmillan, pp. 179–220.

Wood, Adrian (1997), 'Openness and Wage Inequality in Developing Countries: the Latin American Challenge to East Asian Conventional Wisdom', *World Bank Economic Review*, **11** (1), 33–57.

13. Opening up India's agriculture: Close versus strategic integration

Servaas Storm*

1. INTRODUCTION

How open in agricultural trade should a developing country be to the world economy? Is there a case for complete agricultural trade liberalization? If not, how much liberalization should a country attempt? The answers to these strategic questions depend on the implications of agricultural trade liberalization for both growth and income distribution (Levy and van Wijnbergen, 1995; Storm, 2000). While the size of the efficiency gains and growth stimulus due to trade reform is disputed (Ocampo and Taylor, 1998), it is generally accepted that trade liberalization entails significant, and generally regressive, shifts in income distribution (Bourguignon et al., 1992; Rodrik, 1995; Rattsø and Taylor, 1999). Distributional concerns are in fact the single most important factor explaining developing countries' reluctance to liberalize their agricultural trade. This raises new questions. Who benefits and who loses from the change in policies? Is it possible to identify alternative or supplementary policies that can be put in place to alleviate possible negative distributional shifts? And how is food price stability to be maintained in a liberalized open economy? These questions are addressed in this chapter for the Indian economy. The analysis, however, is of wider interest than the Indian reform process itself, because agriculture has often been a major stumbling block in trade reform negotiations in other (developing) countries as well.

This chapter relies on counterfactual simulations performed with the help of the multiperiod computable general equilibrium (CGE) model developed in Storm (1997). The focus of the model at hand is on the growth effects of policy reform, unlike other CGE studies, notably Subramanian (1993) and Panda and Quizon (1998), which are comparatively static in

* The author acknowledges financial support from The Netherlands Foundation for the Advancement of Tropical Research (WOTRO).

nature, with no attention being paid to transition dynamics. Moreover, these static models, along with the available multiperiod models by Parikh et al. (1997) and Chadha et al. (1998), are all Say's Law models, assuming full employment and supposedly focusing on long-run resource allocation. The implication is, as noted by Subramanian (1996) and Rattsø and Taylor (1999), that these models cannot address questions of macro adjustment and instability, because the aggregate (investment) demand effects implicit in the trade liberalization are nullified by the assumption of full employment. In contrast, in the model used in this chapter, Say's Law is rejected and the focus is explicitly on macroeconomic adjustments, involving variations in the utilization rate of resources and in income distribution to generate the savings needed to finance investment demand.

The chapter is organized as follows. Section 2 provides background on India's agriculture, reviewing its major structural features and recent changes in the country's agricultural trade policies. Section 3 sketches the model (model structure, data and calibration are discussed in Storm, 1997). Section 4 assesses the growth effects and distributional implications for India of opening up its agricultural sector. Section 5 studies the medium-run effects of combined (agricultural) trade and domestic policy reforms and analyses the economy's vulnerability to external shocks under varying degrees of trade openness. Section 6 presents two alternative scenarios in which Indian agriculture is strategically (rather than closely) integrated with world markets. Section 7 concludes.

2.   BACKGROUND

To appreciate the significance of the implications of (agricultural) trade liberalization for India's growth and income distribution, it is necessary to have some understanding of key characteristics of its (rural) economy as well as of recent changes in its trade policy regime.

2.1   Structural features

Notwithstanding the fact that, over time, agriculture's share in gross domestic product (GDP) has come down to less than 30 per cent (see Table 13.1), 65 per cent of India's labour force is still engaged in agriculture, which is increasingly lagging behind the industrial sector in terms of labour productivity. Agriculture is also an important source of exports, contributing roughly 20 per cent to India's export earnings. India's poor are overwhelmingly concentrated in rural areas and their incomes largely derive from own-farm production, wages earned as casual agricultural labourers, and

Table 13.1   Structural features of India's agriculture

	1983	1987–88	1993–94
Share of agriculture in GDP at factor cost	36.2	31.4	29.5
Agricultural labour productivity[a]	27.2	26.5	23.1
Rural population (millions)	546.7	593.4	657.3
Percentage share of rural in total population	76.1	75.1	73.4
Percentage share of agriculture in labour force	68.6	65.0	64.7
Share of casual workers in rural labour force	31.5	32.9	35.6
Share of agriculture in exports (per cent)	27.8	21.6	18.7
Chemical fertilizer (kg/ha)	37.1	51.5	66.7
Gross irrigated/gross cropped area (per cent)	30.0	32.8	
Rural poverty (headcount measure)	45.3	39.6	38.7
Share of food in private consumption (per cent)	52.0	49.8	47.5
Distribution of operational holdings: numbers (area)[b]			
Marginal (<1 ha) farms (per cent)	57.1 (12.7)	58.4 (14.2)	
Small (1 to 2 ha) farms (per cent)	18.3 (14.9)	18.7 (16.4)	
Medium (2 to 10 ha) farms (per cent)	22.4 (50.8)	21.1 (50.6)	
Large (>10 ha) farms (per cent)	2.2 (21.6)	1.8 (18.8)	
Marginal budget share of cereals			
Very poor rural (urban) income earners	0.50 (0.36)		
Moderately poor rural (urban) income earners	0.31 (0.15)		
Income elasticity of cereals			
Very poor rural (urban) income earners	0.87 (0.70)		
Moderately poor rural (urban) income earners	0.51 (0.28)		

Notes:
[a] Per cent of industrial labour productivity.
[b] Figures in parentheses indicate the distribution of *area* across holding categories.
Sources: (1) *National Accounts Statistics*, various years; (2) Visaria (1998); (3) FAI (1997); (4) Sen (1997); (5) Radhakrishna and Ravi (1992); and (6) *Economic Survey*, various issues.

incomes earned in rural industries. The number of rural poor was a staggering 254 million persons in 1993–94 or 28 per cent of India's population. At the very low income levels that characterize nearly half of India's population, income elasticities for food are relatively high (Table 13.1). As a result, measures to increase nominal rural wages will be self-defeating if there is no accompanying rise in agricultural output (Storm, 2000). This is because the resulting (agriculture-induced) inflation will erode nominal income gains, given that the adjustment of nominal rural wages to inflation is rather slow: past work (for example, Ravallion and Datt, 1995; Sen, 1998) suggests an adjustment period of at least three to five years before real wages are restored following a one-shot inflationary episode.

Raising agricultural growth is therefore an obvious route to reducing (rural) poverty in a broad-based and self-sustaining manner, because by increasing the rural demand for labour, it will increase employment and wages for the poor, who are mostly agricultural workers. The crucial question is how to induce this necessary agricultural output increase. One common answer is that getting prices right for farmers is the key to sustained growth of agricultural productivity, output and incomes. The major way of doing so is by means of a thorough liberalization of the foreign trade regime (Bhagwati and Srinivasan, 1993): reducing the tariff and quota protection of industry, eliminating the real exchange rate misalignment via depreciation, and removing the anti-export bias in agriculture. However, the trade reforms, which are expected to raise agricultural prices, will have two conflicting effects on income distribution and poverty. The first effect is positive: higher prices will raise agricultural output and employment, which – depending on rural labour market slack – may result in increased nominal wages. The crucial issue here is by how much agricultural output will increase, given that the price responsiveness of aggregate agricultural supply is low. This is so because of the presence of structural rigidities, constraining farmers' choices and decision making in production and investment, which originate from a combination of two sources (Rao and Storm, 1998): the inadequate availability of rural infrastructure (including irrigation, electricity, transport and education),[1] and the large inequalities in land ownership (see Table 13.1) and access to capital. The second effect of the increase in agricultural prices is negative: a real wage fall for most of India's poor (and even some of the non-poor), who are net purchasers of food and whose incomes are not indexed to inflation (Sen, 1998). It follows that the trade reforms incur the risk of both transitional and permanent reductions in real wages, a deterioration of income distribution and increases in poverty. Because there is more at stake than (possible) efficiency gains, this chapter's focus is on the longer-term distributional implications of liberalizing India's external trade.

2.2 Trade liberalization

It has long been implicitly understood in India that the stabilization of foodgrain prices is the most important form of social safety net there is; it also is, as argued by Dutt and Rao (1999), the closest thing to an incomes policy that a poor country can wield. Not surprisingly, therefore, over the past three decades, domestic price stabilization has been the main concern of India's trade policy regime for agriculture, which regulated the volume of exports and imports through quantitative restrictions (QRs) or canalization through state trading organizations (Nayyar and Sen, 1994). This concern about domestic prices has been particularly important for exportables and importables which are wage goods, or inputs into wage goods production, because – as discussed above – the majority of India's poor do not have incomes that are index-linked. Jha and Srinivasan (1997) show that India's food price stabilization policy has been successful: foodgrain prices were not only higher, but also fluctuated much more in the years before the mid-1970s than in the 1980s and 1990s.

However, as part of the post-1991 reforms, India's agricultural trade policy regime has been subjected to a fundamental change, which reflects the new perceptions articulated by the government that, over time, the domestic prices of inputs used and outputs produced by Indian agriculture will have to move closer to world prices (Bhagwati and Srinivasan, 1993; Nayyar and Sen, 1994). While the domestic policy reforms were limited (only some fertilizers' prices were decontrolled), the changes in agricultural trade policy – summarized in Table 13.2 – have been significant. First, the canalization of agricultural trade flows has been almost abandoned and most import duties have been brought down. Second, many of the QRs on agricultural imports have been dismantled. Third, the export of rice has been fully liberalized and exports of other crops have been allowed freely within prespecified quantitative ceilings. As a result, the openness of India's agricultural sector has considerably increased (Storm, 2000). The trade liberalization is likely to be continued because India wants to continue to be part of the multilateral trading system. To do so, India has to satisfy the following World Trade Organization (WTO) conditions. First, in future, India's imports (that is, market access) can be restricted only for special reasons such as balance of payments considerations and not for the general protection of domestic agriculture. Second, such restrictions must be price-based alone, which means that all non-tariff measures (including QRs) have to be converted into their tariff equivalents; these tariffs, in turn, have to be reduced by an average of 24 per cent (with a 15 per cent minimum cut per tariff line) over the period 1994–2004. Third, India must provide a guaranteed minimum market access to imports of at least 3.33

Table 13.2 India: Recent agricultural trade policy reforms

Trade Status	Exportables		Importables	
	Imports	Exports	Imports	Exports
Prior to June 1991	NTBs for 96 per cent of agricultural production (rice, wheat, cotton).	QRs for most commodities (rice, wheat, cotton). Free for established exports (for example, tea, coffee, oilseeds, spices, fish, fruits and vegetables).	NTBs for 96 per cent of agricultural production (coarse cereals, sugar, edible oils, dairy and livestock). Free for pulses, raw wool.	QRs for most commodities.
Significant policy changes	Cotton: 0 per cent tariff (1994).	Exports of rice, durum wheat and wheat flower liberalized (1994).	Sugar: 0 per cent tariff (1994); edible oils: 30 per cent tariff (1995), 20 per cent tariff (1996); pulses: tariff reduced from 10 to 5 per cent (1995).	Export of rapeseed and sunflower liberalized (1995).
Status as of July 1997	NTBs for 77 per cent of agricultural production.	QRs for most commodities, except rice and established exports.	NTBs for 77 per cent of agricultural production.	QRs for most commodities except rice and established exports.

Sources: World Bank (1996) and Acharya (1997).

per cent of domestic consumption. Fourth, its domestic support to agriculture, which includes the direct budgetary support in the form of expenditure disbursed, the indirect support in the form of revenue foregone, and the support implicit in any divergence between domestic and world prices of inputs purchased and outputs sold by agriculture, is subject to a maximum of 10 per cent of the value of output in each product and in the aggregate.

3.   THE MODEL IN OUTLINE

To evaluate the growth and distributional implications of foodgrain price stabilization in an open-economy context, an extended version of the multi-period CGE model described in Storm (1997) is used. The model divides the economy into an urban and a rural sector. The urban sector produces three tradeable industrial goods (fertilizers, capital goods and consumer goods) and a non-tradeable services good. For each of these goods, production is determined by (domestic and foreign) demand. The rural sector produces four tradeable goods and one non-tradeable. Tradeables include rice, wheat, commercial crops and other agricultural products. Traditional food crops including millets and barley are non-traded. Each of these goods is produced with fixed intermediate inputs and sector-specific capital. The model distinguishes between irrigated and rain-fed land, because yields and yield responses to fertilizers differ between types of land.

The model reflects the structural asymmetries between agriculture and non-agriculture, characteristic of the Indian economy (and other low-income economies). Let S_1 and S_2 denote index sets over agricultural (supply-constrained) and non-agricultural (demand-constrained) sectors respectively, and let $S = S_1 \cup S_2$. Prices adjust to clear markets in each sector $i \in S_1$, while in each industry $i \in S_2$ demand supply equilibrium is brought about by output adjustments, assuming that production operates under conditions of excess capacity (Srinivasan, 1992). Except for exogenous growth of labour productivity in the non-agricultural sectors, technology is constant. Non-agricultural prices are based on mark-up rules and nominal wages are indexed to the consumer price index (CPI). Nominal wage rates in agriculture are exogenous, reflecting the empirical fact that rural wages are not indexed to inflation in the short to medium run (Ravallion and Datt, 1995; Sen, 1998).

Production generates incomes: rural and urban wages, rents to irrigated and rain-fed land and livestock farming, and rents to capital in non-agriculture. Factor incomes are mapped into household incomes using a matrix of fixed ownership shares. There are seven household classes, classified by ownership of factors of production. Four are in the rural sector:

landless rural workers, whose only asset is labour; and small, medium-sized and large farmers. The other three are urban: urban workers; urban marginals, being the poorest 82 per cent of the urban self-employed; and urban capitalists, the richest 18 per cent of the urban self-employed. Rural households receive government transfers in kind through rural employment programmes, while urban households receive subsidized food (through the public distribution system). Households save a constant proportion of their disposable income; the savings rates are fixed and class-specific. Each group has different preferences, given by a linear expenditure system (LES). In this LES, the proportion of fixed consumption of rural goods is higher for rural landless workers, small farmers and urban marginals than for large farmers and urban capitalists, so food price changes have a larger impact on the first three groups. Also, own-price elasticities of foodgrain demand are low for all social classes, while the corresponding cross-price elasticities are high, particularly for landless rural and urban workers.

Crop production is determined in two steps. First, cropwise area allocation is determined and, next, the yield level per unit of land is established. The area allocation across crops itself is preceded by the determination of total gross cropped area, as a function of agricultural (irrigation) investment. The allocation of land across crops is based on Nerlovian adaptive response equations, the driving variable being the expected price of a crop relative to the weighted average price of the other crops; price expectations are based on past prices. Per hectare yield depends on fertilizer use, which is a ratio of the fertilizer and crop price. For rice and wheat, the (price) elasticities of fertilizer response and demand functions are higher in irrigated than in non-irrigated agriculture (Table 13.3). The short-run crop supply response to a price increase typically is low (and operates through fertilizer use and yields), while the medium-term response, which includes the effects of intertemporal area reallocations and of productivity-raising investments, is much stronger.

Trade restrictions are modelled as fix-price rationing, assuming that imports and domestic goods are imperfect substitutes:

$$\mu_i^* = (p_i/p_{mi})^{\sigma_i}(\phi_i/(1-\phi_i))^{\sigma_i} \quad i \in T \tag{1}$$

where μ_i^* is the desired ratio of imports m_i to domestic sales d_i, p_i is the domestic price, p_{mi} is the exogenous import price, ϕ_i is the CES distribution parameter and σ_i is the substitution elasticity. T is the index set of goods for which external trade is endogenously determined.

Because of import restrictions, actual imports are only a fraction i of the desired level:

Table 13.3   Values of agricultural model parameters

Price elasticity of gross cropped area	Irrigated	Non-irrigated
Rice	0.05	0.18
Wheat	0.79	0.50
Other food crops	0.29	0.05
Commercial crops	0.35	0.29
Price elasticity of fertilizer demand	Irrigated	Non-irrigated
Rice	−0.56	−0.30
Wheat	−0.65	−0.23
Other food crops	−0.15	−0.15
Commercial crops	−0.33	−0.33
Elasticity of yield wrt fertilizer price (implicit)	Aggregate	
Rice	−0.13	
Wheat	−0.24	
Other food crops	−0.05	
Commercial crops	−0.10	
Elasticity of private agricultural investment wrt		
Lagged public agricultural investment	0.67	
Lagged terms of trade	1.44	

Source: Storm (1997).

$$m_i = \gamma_{mi} \mu_i^* d_i \quad i \in T. \tag{2}$$

Similarly, export demands are given by (3):

$$e_i = \gamma_{ei} \varepsilon_i (p_{wi}/p_{ei})^{\eta_i} \quad i \in T, \tag{3}$$

where i is the price elasticity of export demand, p_{wi} is the given world price and p_{ei} is the Indian export price. Export restrictions exist only for the traded agricultural goods, while import restrictions prevail only in the traded industrial sectors. Table 13.4 presents the rationing factors and the substitution elasticities used in the experiments.

At each moment, aggregate domestic demand z_{di} for good i is:

$$z_{di} = \sum_j \alpha_{ij} x_i^s + c_i + \chi_i + i_i \quad i \in S, \tag{4}$$

where $\Sigma_j \alpha_{ij} x_i^s$ is the demand for intermediate inputs, c_i is private consumption, χ_i public consumption and i_i is investment demand. Domestic absorption d_i equals:

$$d_i = \delta_i z_{di} \quad i \in S, \tag{5}$$

Table 13.4 Structure of India's trade (base year)

	Trade ratios*		Import tariff	Import substitution elasticity	Rationing factor	
	Imports	Exports			Imports	Exports
Rice	0.04	1.64	–	5.0	1.00	0.32
Wheat	0.23	1.36	–	5.0	1.00	0.32
Commercial crops	2.04	1.26	0.02	1.5	1.00	0.36
Capital goods	2.77	3.64	0.50	2.0	0.92	1.00
Consumer goods	3.55	5.80	0.25	2.0	0.92	1.00

Note: * Percentage share of imports in absorption and share of exports in production, respectively.
Source: Storm (1997).

where $\delta_i = (\phi_i(\mu_i)^{-\rho_i} + 1)^{(-1/\rho_i)}$, $i \in T$ and $\delta_i = (z_{di} - m_i)/z_{di}$ $i \in N$. N is the index set of goods for external trade is exogenous; note that $S = N \cup T$. Total demand for domestic goods equals:

$$x_i^d = d_i + e_i \quad i \in S. \tag{6}$$

The equilibrium conditions are commodity market clearing:

$$x_i^d - x_i^s = f(p_i) = 0 \quad i \in S_1 \tag{7}$$

$$x_i^d - x_i^s = f(x_i^s) = 0 \quad i \in S_2 \tag{8}$$

and balance of payments equilibrium:

$$\sum_i rp_{mi}m_i + \sum_i \alpha_{mi}p_{mi}x_i^s - \sum_i rp_{ei}e_i - rF = H, \tag{9}$$

where $\sum_i \alpha_{mi}p_{mi}x_i^s$ are intermediate imports, rF are remittances and H is the exogenously given level of foreign capital inflow. The model thus determines, via these excess demand functions, commodity prices and outputs as well as the nominal exchange rate r.

The model includes the following intertemporal adjustment mechanisms in agriculture. First, crop procurement prices, which are revised annually, are updated on the basis of market prices and the intersectoral terms of trade. Second, public and private investment in agriculture results in the expansion of irrigated area with a one-year lag. Private investment J_p depends on the one-period lagged domestic terms of trade TT and one-period lagged public investment J_g in agriculture:

$$J_{p,t} = q(TT_{t-1}, J_{g,t-1}) \quad q'_{TT} > 0, q'_{Jg} > 0. \tag{10}$$

Public investment crowds in private investment, reflecting the fact that agricultural growth in India, as in many other developing economies, can only be based on land-augmenting investment, much of which is done by the government or is dependent on publicly supplied infrastructure (Rao, 1993). The values of the investment elasticities are given in Table 13.3. Finally, farmers decide about next period's crop allocation on the basis of a Nerlovian partial adjustment model; the price elasticities of cropped area are also given in Table 13.3.

4. GROWTH AND DISTRIBUTION UNDER FREE TRADE

This section compares the model's base run with unchanged (trade) policies with an alternative policy in which India's foreign trade in agriculture and non-agriculture is freed up. The base run is documented in Table 13.5. Trade liberalization here implies the gradual removal of all tariffs and restrictions (import quotas, export bans, licensing requirements and so on) on foreign trade over a period of four years, so that in the fifth year trade is fully liberalized; in terms of the model equations it is assumed that all tariffs equal zero and the rationing factors γ_{mi} and γ_{ei} equal unity in year 5. Furthermore, in this experiment (as in the other simulations) the following conditions are imposed: (i) the BoP's current account deficit is kept fixed, preventing any expansion of the economy fuelled by foreign borrowing, and the nominal exchange rate adjusts so as to maintain a predetermined level of foreign capital inflow; and (ii) to offset the decrease in tariff revenues and maintain fiscal neutrality, indirect taxes on non-agricultural commodities are changed so as to keep the government revenue deficit constant. Key features of the trade reform experiment are summarized in column 2 of Table 13.5.

It can be seen that gradual reform leads to a sizeable decline in GDP growth by one percentage point on average per annum, despite a significant step-up in export growth. The contraction is due to a decline in private consumption and in aggregate investment. Private consumption falls in real terms because, with higher post-reform crop prices and given (i) that food demand is relatively price-inelastic, and (ii) that cross-price effects due to crop price changes are significant and negative, consumers are forced to spend less on non-agricultural and more on agricultural goods. As a result, non-agricultural output and income growth decline, negatively affecting private non-agricultural investment. The improved domestic terms of trade for agriculture raise private investment in irrigation, which raises agriculture's cropping intensity over time and thereby contributes to more rapid crop output growth. However, the increase in agricultural income growth is not large enough to offset the decline in non-agricultural growth. This result is robust: Storm (1997) shows that, employing far larger, but still empirically plausible, investment and price response elasticities in this experiment, the improvement in farmers' incentives due to the trade liberalization does not raise agricultural growth enough to offset the non-agricultural contraction.

Gradual trade reform is also inflationary: measured by the CPI, the average annual inflation increases to 13.7 per cent. First, rising crop prices raise intermediate input costs in non-agriculture, which are passed on to

Table 13.5 Results of the (agricultural) trade liberalization experiments

	Base run (1)	Gradual trade reform (2)	Gradual 'close' integration (3)	'Strategic' integration (4)	Gradual trade reform + investment (5)
National accounts					
GDP at market prices	6.3	5.3	5.2	7.0	6.5
Private consumption	5.0	3.5	3.7	5.7	5.1
Gross investment	5.4	4.8	4.9	6.4	6.1
Exports	8.0	14.7	12.1	8.2	14.6
Imports	7.0	11.9	11.2	7.3	12.9
Income distribution					
Landless labourers	4.4	0.5	3.3	5.1	4.9
Small farmers	5.0	2.9	3.4	6.3	5.7
Medium farmers	5.8	5.1	4.7	6.9	6.4
Large farmers	6.8	6.5	5.8	7.6	7.2
Urban workers	6.5	4.0	5.6	6.9	6.0
Urban marginals	7.1	5.4	4.6	7.7	6.4
Urban capitalists	7.4	5.0	4.4	7.7	6.0
Prices					
CPI	7.7	13.7	6.9	8.1	7.9
GDP deflator	7.9	13.8	6.9	8.2	8.0
Exchange rate*	4.8	12.3	4.1	3.7	5.4

Note: * Nominal.
Source: Storm (2000, 2001).

312

higher prices; rising crop prices are further met by demands for higher non-agricultural money wages, which augment the rise in non-agricultural production costs and prices. Second, because (agricultural) exports rise less than (industrial) imports, the exchange rate depreciates to maintain the predetermined level of foreign capital inflow. The depreciation itself is inflationary, because it raises non-agricultural mark-up prices through its impact on intermediate import costs. The strong inflation has serious distributional implications: while the growth rates of real incomes of all income classes decline (compared with the base run), some groups suffer more than others. In particular, large farmers, benefiting from the crop price increases and crop output growth, are able to remain almost insulated from the contractionary effects of the trade reform. In contrast, landless rural labourers and small farmers, who are net buyers of food, suffer dramatic real income declines. These simulation results underscore the conclusion of much of the literature on India's structural reforms that the severest distributional effect of agricultural trade reform will come from a relative rise in foodgrain prices (Subramanian, 1993; Nayyar and Sen, 1994). A key issue is thus what can be done to generate a more equitable sharing of the costs of introducing free trade in agriculture.[2]

5. TRADE AND DOMESTIC REFORMS

Proponents of agricultural trade policy reform, for example World Bank (1996), argue that the benefits from opening up will materialize only when the liberalization is combined with drastic domestic policy reforms. Their suggested agenda for agricultural reform thus revolves on the close integration of Indian agriculture with the world economy by setting the prices right by means of the withdrawal of subsidies on inputs (mainly fertilizers) and the liberalization of trade in agricultural commodities. The essence of the proposed reform package is to move agriculture from the prevailing low input–low output price regime to a regime of high input–high output prices, and aligning the inter-crop price ratios in the domestic market with world market ratios.

5.1 Close integration with the world economy

The third column of Table 13.5 shows the impact of the close integration of Indian agriculture with the world markets, where protection and domestic agricultural input subsidies are reduced over four years, so that in the fifth year the economy is closely integrated with the world economy. Compared with the base run, the trade and domestic reforms turn out both contractionary and deflationary. Annual real GDP growth declines to 5.2 per cent, while the consumer price inflation falls to 6.9 per cent per annum. This price decline stands in sharp contrast to the significant inflation, when the gradual trade reform is not accompanied by domestic reforms (column 2). The difference in inflationary impact is due to the fact that (aggregate) agricultural income declines as a result of the close integration but increases in response to the gradual trade reform. In the latter case, the opening up of India's agriculture substantially improves relative prices for farmers, who respond by raising their investments and the use of modern inputs; this leads to a step-up in agricultural growth, though not large enough to prevent a continued rise in agricultural prices. The result is inflation and non-agricultural contraction, both augmented by a nominal exchange rate depreciation. In contrast, under close integration, the incentive structure for farmers deteriorates, because the gain from higher output prices (due to the opening up) is more than offset by the rise in input costs, caused by the removal of input subsidies. The outcome is lower agricultural output growth at lower prices. The fall in agricultural prices leads to an economy-wide deflation of wages and (mark-up) prices, which mitigates the loss of India's international competitiveness in non-agricultural tradeables during the trade liberalization. In effect, non-agricultural imports are lower, and there is much less pressure on the balance of payments; the exchange depreciation with close integration turns out to be less than that in the base run, which by itself has a deflationary effect.

However, the move to a regime of high input–high output prices remains contractionary, since both agricultural and non-agricultural growth decline. Distributionally, the urban self-employed are hit worst: average annual real income growth declines by 41 per cent for urban capitalists and by 35 per cent for urban marginals. Helped by the deflation, urban workers suffer a relatively modest income growth decline of 14 per cent. Within the rural sector, in contrast, the trade and domestic reforms are distributionally regressive: the relative income growth declines of rural labourers (− 25 per cent) and small farmers (− 32 per cent) are significantly larger than those of medium (− 19 per cent) and large (− 15 per cent) farmers. In effect, close integration results in a deteriorated growth performance as well as income distribution.

5.2   Open-economy foodgrain price stabilization

The opening up of India's agriculture is likely to reduce the effectiveness of conventional instruments of food price stabilization, which depend critically on the public regulation of agricultural exports and imports (Nayyar and Sen, 1994). Given that the volatility of world food prices is higher than domestic price volatility, this raises a crucial issue: how food price stability is to be maintained in a liberalized context. Of the instruments available,[3] the option of imposing variable levies on otherwise free agricultural exports and imports has been argued to be both administratively feasible and relatively efficient (Storm, 1999). This section assesses the general equilibrium effects of imposing such variable levies on agricultural external trade in response to an external shock. The variable levies p_i are set to keep domestic crop prices p_i within a price band using the following policy reaction function:

$$\tau_i = (p_i^*/p_i)^2 - 1 \quad |p_i^* - p_i| > \xi \quad i = 1,2,4, \tag{11}$$

where p_i^* is the target price of crop i. If the difference (in absolute terms) between the target price and the actual price exceeds a prespecified level ($\xi = 0.03$), a variable levy τ_i will be imposed on either the crop's exports or imports in an attempt to stabilize domestic prices. The reaction function is quadratic. This system of variable trade levies is introduced in response to a 20 per cent rise in the world price of rice, which is imposed in years 2, 3, 4 and 5 of the close integration experiment to assess the economy's vulnerability under varying degrees of trade openness. The base run prices of rice, wheat and commercial crops are set as the target prices p_i^*. Table 13.6 compares the macroeconomic effects of these shocks with and without variable levies.[4]

The world market price increase for rice leads to a step-up in rice exports. Domestic rice supply being inelastic, the consequence is a decline in domestic availability of rice, as a result of which the domestic rice price increases. This raises the CPI, which contributes – via nominal non-agricultural wages – to mark-up price inflation. There is a notable rise in the inflationary impact when the economy becomes more open: the same external shock raises the CPI by 2.3 per cent in year 5 (when the liberalization is complete), but only by 1.4 per cent in year 2 (the second year of the reform process). The inflation has only a small impact on aggregate real GDP. The reason is that the rise in aggregate agricultural income (due to the output expansion and price rise) is offset by a fall in non-agricultural income (caused by the agricultural price increase). These small effects at the aggregate level do hide considerable changes in the distribution of incomes. Rural landless labourers and all urban income classes suffer significant real income losses, while the other rural groups enjoy real income growth. Importantly, these real income changes become larger (in absolute terms) as the economy's openness to trade increases. Table 13.6 shows, for example, that the real income fall for rural workers increases from 0.6 per cent in year 2 to 1.1 per cent in year 5. Hence, as the trade openness increases, positive terms of

Table 13.6 *Macroeconomic effects of an exogenous external shock without (A) and with (B) variable trade levies (in per cent deviations from the gradual 'close' integration experiment)*

| | A 20 per cent rise in the world price of rice in: | | | | | | | |
| | Year 2 | | Year 3 | | Year 4 | | Year 5 | |
	(A)	(B)	(A)	(B)	(A)	(B)	(A)	(B)
Inflation (CPI)	1.35	0.76	1.43	0.80	1.55	0.83	2.25	1.03
GDP market prices	−0.03	0.04	0.01	0.09	−0.03	0.06	−0.06	0.15
Agricultural income	1.24	0.79	1.36	0.89	1.48	0.92	2.05	1.23
Real income of:								
Landless labourers:	−0.64	−0.31	−0.66	−0.28	−0.71	−0.30	−1.08	−0.31
− Employment	−7.97		−10.69		−7.20		−5.11	
− Real wage	94.60		106.71		95.45		91.45	
− Non-wage income	6.60		−1.12		9.31		11.53	
− Transfers	6.76		5.10		2.44		2.14	
Small farmers	0.40	0.31	0.55	0.43	0.50	0.38	0.72	0.58
Medium farmers	0.92	0.59	1.03	0.68	1.02	0.65	1.45	0.90
Large farmers	0.52	0.38	0.56	0.43	0.53	0.40	0.68	0.56
Urban workers	−0.93	−0.44	−0.99	−0.42	−1.05	−0.43	−1.57	−0.43
Urban marginals	−0.42	−0.17	−0.39	−0.11	−0.46	−0.15	−0.75	−0.13
Urban capitalists	−0.59	−0.29	−0.65	−0.31	−0.70	−0.32	−1.09	−0.37
Export share*	4.40	3.53	6.28	5.02	6.12	4.91	9.66	8.03
Rice export levy (%)		7.32		7.52		7.76		9.37

Note: * Per cent of rice output.
Source: Storm (1999).

316

trade shocks, which raise domestic crop prices, will have more significant regressive distributional effects. Storm (1999) decomposes the changes in classwise real income into four sources, that is, the real income change due to a change in employment, a real wage change, a change in real non-wage income and a change in real transfer income. Table 13.6 lists the results for landless rural labourers. It can be seen that the real wage decline is the major source (-97 per cent on average) of the real income change of rural workers; this decline is only partly offset by the real income gain ($+8$ per cent on average) from increased employment, consistent with crop output growth.

However, the negative macroeconomic effects of the positive external price shock can be significantly reduced by imposing a variable levy on rice exports. In year 2, due to a levy of 7.3 per cent, the share of exports in rice output is only 3.5 per cent (as compared with 4.4 per cent in the no-levy case). The levy thus discourages exports and encourages domestic sales of rice, as a result of which the rice price is lower than in the no-levy case. This helps reduce economy-wide inflationary pressures: the CPI increase in response to the shock is 0.8 per cent as compared with 1.4 per cent without the levy. Distributionally, the containment of the food inflation is to the benefit of rural landless labourers, mainly because it substantially reduces the fall in real rural wages (by more than 50 per cent), which is the major source of their real income loss. It also helps to significantly reduce the real income loss of the urban income groups, partly because of the real wage effect (for urban workers) and partly because of the fact that the non-agricultural demand and output contraction is smaller due to the smaller rise in crop prices. The rural land-owning classes are the main losers of the levy, again because of the smaller rise in crop prices. It thus seems possible to offset at least partially the distributionally regressive effects of an external shock by the imposition of a variable trade levy. These results also hold when the shock occurs in one of the later years, when the country's trade openness has further increased. In the fully liberalized system in year 5, a levy on rice exports of 9.4 per cent is used to stabilize domestic prices and reduce the real income losses of the vulnerable classes. It is further noteworthy that, in all years, the size of the levy would be consistent with WTO regulations (Storm, 1999).

6. STRATEGIC INTEGRATION OF INDIA'S AGRICULTURE WITH WORLD MARKETS

The growth effects of close integration are disappointing: because existing structural rigidities in agriculture inhibit its supply response, the reforms have a larger impact on (relative) agricultural prices than on crop outputs. While the relative price improvement for agriculture does raise private farm investment and agricultural growth, it also erodes nominal wages and non-agricultural profits, thereby depressing non-agricultural consumption and investment. As a result, the increase in agricultural growth is more than offset by a fall in non-agricultural growth, and real GDP contracts. With respect to equity, it is clear that, besides changing the relative price structure, close integration has an absolute price implication which follows from the fact that nominal wages in the unorganized sectors of the Indian economy have a very low degree of price indexation. The price rise due to the reforms is therefore distributionally regressive and brings with it a rise in poverty as well. Taken together, the substantial and unevenly distributed costs of a strategy of close integration argue for more selective engagement of Indian agriculture with the world economy. What then is the desirable degree of openness of India's agricultural sector? The last two columns of Table 13.5 show the medium-term impact of two attempts at strategically integrating Indian agriculture with the world markets. However, unlike the close integration approach, there is no universal definition of strategic integration, because the desirable nature and degree of government intervention (in trade) may vary across commodities and over time. The experiments reported here thus represent only two possibilities out of many.

In the first experiment (column 4), strategic integration is operationalized as follows. First, the markets of rice, wheat and commercial crops are guided by government intervention: the domestic market prices are kept at their base-run level by active public procurement; the minimum support or procurement prices are raised to the level of the market prices in each year of the five-year period; a wedge is maintained between domestic and world prices. Second, any public procurement of rice, wheat and commercial crops over and above their base-run procurement levels is sold by the government in the international markets; any procurement shortfall is met by additional imports; public stocks consequently remain at their base-run levels. There is no free trade in these three crops: the level of net exports of rice, wheat and commercial crops is regulated by the government. As discussed in Storm (2001), the government may do so by imposing quantitative restrictions on exports and imports under the Special Treatment clause of the GATT accord, or alternatively by regulating trade flows using variable export and import duties (as in section 5.2), which – within certain bounds – is also consistent with WTO obligations.[5] Finally, to weaken the structural rigidities in agriculture, which inhibit its supply response, public investment in agriculture is raised by 50 per cent (and public investment in non-agriculture is reduced by an equivalent amount).

Table 13.5 shows that this form of strategic integration is significantly expansionary: the average annual growth rate of real GDP at market prices increases from 6.3 per cent in the base run to 7 per cent. This expansionary impact is primarily made possible by the rise in irrigation coverage and hence in cropping intensity, triggered by the increased public agricultural investment.[6] The consequent increase in crop outputs at constant prices results in higher agricultural incomes. It also leads to higher crop exports which – given the unchanged (protectionist) industrial trade policy regime – reduces BoP pressures and results in a lower currency depreciation (of 3.7 per cent on average per annum) as compared with the base run. This lower rate of currency depreciation has three effects. First, it reduces imported intermediate input costs and consequently reduces non-agricultural prices. Second, with constant crop prices, this implies an improvement in the agricultural terms of trade, higher private investment by farmers and faster crop output growth. Third, the decline in the cost of imported fertilizers stimulates fertilizer use, crop yield growth and crop output growth. In other words, strategic integration raises agricultural growth directly (through expanded irrigation) and indirectly (via an agricultural terms-of-trade improvement effected by the lower currency depreciation). This form of economic openness is inflationary though, raising the CPI inflation from 7.7 to 8.1 per cent on average per year.[7] It is also a distributionally progressive option: rural landless labourers and small farmers benefit most in relative terms, which indicates that the higher agricultural output and employment growth more than compensate for the increase in inflation. Urban income earners also benefit from the reform, because the strong agricultural output and income growth spills over into higher non-agricultural outputs via intermediate and final demand. All this is achieved without a similar step-up in crop exports as in the first two experiments.

The final simulation in Table 13.5 explores the consequences of gradual trade liberalization in combination with a programme of public investments in land improvements. This option looks promising because private investment is known to be 'crowded-in' by public investment (Chakravarty, 1987) and, as a consequence, the return on it is likely to be high.[8] In the simulation, public investment in irrigation is raised by 75 per cent per annum and the fertilizer subsidy rate is increased from 26.3 to 50 per cent for the whole five-year period. It should be emphasized that the public revenue deficit is kept fixed at its base-run level by means of indirect tax rate changes (as in the earlier experiments). The gradual trade reform 'cum agriculture first' strategy is expansionary; there is a cumulative gain in real GDP of around Rs. 257 billion at constant prices compared with the base run or 7.7 per cent of real base-run GDP in the final year. By raising the irrigation coverage for all crops, the rise in public agricultural investment enables farmers to increase cropping intensity and raise crop outputs. This results in lower crop prices, which – by improving agriculture's export competitiveness – contribute to higher agricultural export growth, reduced BoP pressures and a lower currency depreciation. Importantly, the extent of the currency depreciation is contained further by the gradual nature of the trade reform, which reduces its immediate negative BoP impact while buying time for agriculture to let the additional investment substantially expand its productive base and exports (Storm, 2000). The lower currency depreciation, in turn, helps reduce domestic inflation, which explains why the strategy is distributionally progressive for the rural sector. Rural landless labourers benefit in real terms: their cumulative real income gain is Rs. 26 billion or about 4 per cent of their cumulative base-run income. Urban income earners continue to suffer a real income decline, though the income contraction is less than in the first two experiments. As a result, private consumption and investment are higher and, consequently, real GDP growth is higher.

7. CONCLUSIONS

This paper demonstrates, in a realistic analysis of the consequences of including agriculture in India's current trade reforms, that the costs of liberalizing India's external trade in agricultural products are large and also unequally distributed. The main reason for this result is the difference between the speeds of adjustment of crop supply and demand. In isolation, trade liberalization immediately raises (previously constrained) export demand, while structural rigidities in agriculture inhibit its supply response. Given that the consumption demand for foodgrains is relatively price-inelastic, a small excess demand for foodgrains leads to relatively large price increases. The agricultural price increases stimulate private farm investment and hence raise productivity and crop outputs, but the additional supply growth is not large enough to meet the growth in (export) demand. The inflation is augmented and sustained by a large currency depreciation, required to maintain balance of payments equilibrium. The end result is a combination of higher crop outputs and exports, higher crop prices and lower domestic foodgrain consumption. In the absence of supplementary measures, only the large farmers benefit from the trade policy reform, while the lower income groups, particularly rural landless labourers and small farmers, bear a disproportionate share of the costs. When combined with domestic reforms, trade liberalization remains contractionary, but is no longer inflationary. The outcome is a slowdown of agricultural and non-agricultural growth and lower prices. While all groups suffer real income losses, the poorer ones are hit hardest. These negative effects on rural income distribution are certainly a factor in the resistance by (small) farmers and rural labourers against the trade reforms and thus help explain why it is proving so hard to open up Indian agriculture.

It is therefore important to identify alternative policies of strategic integration. One approach proposed in this chapter would be to retain a wedge between domestic and world market prices of agricultural commodities, thereby creating room for vigorous market-guiding price and investment policies in Indian agriculture. This wedge could take the form of variable levies on agricultural trade of a magnitude well within WTO rules. Growth can then be stimulated by public investment growth in irrigation and other rural infrastructure (rather than by removing the price bias against agriculture) and prices be maintained at levels commensurate with average income levels, while providing an incentive to farmers to invest and use modern inputs. The second approach highlighted in this chapter consists of introducing supplementary adjustment measures to generate a more equitable sharing of the costs (and possible gains) of the transition. By raising land productivity, the adjustment measures, that is, additional public investment in agriculture combined with increased fertilizer subsidization, make it possible for the rural poor to have a higher real income along the adjustment path than on the base-run path of sustained protection; at the same time, 'gradualism cum agriculture-first' leads to aggregate income gains. The results of both experiments in which India's agriculture is strategically integrated with the world markets do show that achieving rapid and equitable agricultural growth requires more, not less, intervention by the government, which should not treat liberalization as an excuse for abandoning its strategic role in agricultural development.

NOTES

1. India's irrigation coverage is only 33 per cent, restricting the scope for multiple cropping and constraining the speed of adoption of higher-yielding seed varieties and the intensification of 'modern' inputs.
2. The adverse impact on the poor underscores the need for targeted, cost-effective safety-net programmes to protect the poor from the cost of agricultural trade liberalization. The option of supplementing the trade reform by a social safety-net programme is not considered here, partly because it would require more funding of (rural and urban) employment programmes, which is not available because of fiscal constraints, partly because it remains an 'unproductive' welfare scheme. Instead the option of providing the poor, in the transition period, with additional rural infrastructure and price incentives is investigated in section 6.
3. There are other alternatives such as commodity options and future contracts, which are administratively more difficult to implement and are likely to involve subsidies. On this, see Jha and Srinivasan (1997) and references therein.
4. In contrast to the other experiments, it is assumed in the simulations reported here that the nominal exchange rate is fixed and foreign savings are endogenous.
5. It is possible to calculate the implicit tariff and/or subsidy rates which would have been

required to regulate the exports and imports of rice, wheat and commercial crops in such a manner as to keep their domestic prices at base-run levels. In the 'strategic' integration experiment that follows, in any given year, the maximum rate of export subsidy would have been 7.4 per cent on rice, 13.6 per cent on wheat and 36.7 per cent on commercial crops. Likewise, in any given year, the maximum import duty would have been 15.1 per cent on rice, 31.3 per cent on wheat and 10.2 per cent on commercial crops. Excluding the maximum import tariff on wheat, these rates would have been WTO consistent.

6. And by higher private agricultural investment which is 'crowded-in' by the increase in public investment in rural infrastructure.
7. The increase in inflation is caused by the increases in prices of other food crops (section 3) and other agricultural products (section 5). These prices increase because the growth of real incomes (and demand) is faster than the growth in their supplies.
8. This 'crowding-in' effect is incorporated in the model via q'_{Jg}.

REFERENCES

Acharya, S.S. (1997), 'Agricultural price policy and development: Some facts and emerging issues', *Indian Journal of Agricultural Economics*, **52**(1), 1–47.

Behrman, J. and T. Srinivasan (eds) (1995), *Handbook of Development Economics: Volume 3B*, Amsterdam: North-Holland.

Bhagwati, J. and T. Srinivasan (1993), *India's Economic Reforms*, Report submitted to the Government of India, Delhi: Ministry of Finance.

Bourguignon, F., C. Morrisson and A. Suwa (1992), *Adjustment and the Rural Sector: A Counterfactual Analysis of Morocco*, in I. Goldin and A. Winters (1992).

Byres, T.J. (ed.) (1988), *The Indian Economy: Major Debates since Independence*, Delhi: Oxford University Press.

Central Statistical Organization (various years), *National Accounts Statistics*, New Delhi.

Chadha, G. and A.N. Sharma (eds) (1997), *Growth, Employment and Poverty: Change and Continuity in rural India*, Delhi: Vikas.

Chadha, R., S. Pohit, A. Deardorff and R. Stern (1998), 'Analysis of India's policy reforms', *The World Economy*, **21**(2), 235–60.

Chakravarty, S. (1987), *Development Planning: The Indian Experience*, Oxford: Clarendon Press.

Dutt, A.K. and J.M. Rao (1999), 'Globalization and its social discontents: The case of India', Paper prepared for the CEPA–Wider conference on *Globalization and the Social Sector*, 29–31 January, New York: New School for Social Research.

Fertilizer Association of India (1997), *Fertiliser Statistics, 1996–1997*, New Delhi: Fertilizer Association of India.

Goldin, I. and L.A. Winters (eds) (1992), *Open Economies: Structural Adjustment and Agriculture*, Cambridge: Cambridge University Press.

Jha, S. and P.V. Srinivasan (1997), 'Grain price stabilization in India', Report prepared for the World Bank, Indira Gandhi Institute of Development Research (IGIDR), Mumbai.

Levy, S. and S. van Wijnbergen (1995), 'Transition problems in economic reform: Agriculture in the North-American Free Trade Arrangement', *American Economic Review*, **85**(4), 738–54.

Ministry of Finance (various years), *Economic Survey*, New Delhi.

Nayyar, D. and A. Sen (1994), 'International trade and the agricultural sector in India', *Economic and Political Weekly*, **29**(20), 1187–1203.

Ocampo, J.A. and L. Taylor (1998), 'Trade liberalization in developing countries: Modest benefits but problems with productivity growth, macro prices and income distribution', *The Economic Journal*, **108**, 1523–46.

Panda, M. and J. Quizon (1998), 'Growth and distribution under trade liberalization in India', *mimeo*, Indira Gandhi Institute of Development Research (IGIDR), Mumbai.

Parikh, K.S., N. Narayana, M. Panda and A. Kumar (1997), 'Agricultural trade liberalization: Growth, welfare and large country effects', *Agricultural Economics*, **17**(1), 1–20.

Radhakrishna, R. and C. Ravi (1992), 'Effects of growth, relative prices and preferences on food and nutrition', *Indian Economic Review*, **27**, 303–24.

Radhakrishna, R. and A.N. Sharma (eds) (1998), *Empowering Rural Labour in India: Market, State and Mobilisation*, Delhi: Institute for Human Development.

Rao, J.M. (1993), 'Distribution and growth with an infrastructure constraint', *Cambridge Journal of Economics*, **17**(4), 369–89.

Rao, J.M. and S. Storm (1998), *Distribution and growth in Indian agriculture*, in T.J. Byres (1998), pp. 193–248.

Rattsø, J. and L. Taylor (1999), 'CGE modelling of trade liberalization in Sub-Saharan Africa: An evaluation', *The World Bank Economic Review*, forthcoming.

Ravallion, M. and G. Datt (1995), 'Growth, wages and poverty: Time-series evidence from rural India', *mimeo*, Washington, D.C.: The World Bank.

Rodrik, D. (1995), *Trade and industrial policy reform*, in J. Behrman and T. Srinivasan (1995).

Sahn, D.E. (ed.) (1996), *Economic Reform and the Poor in Africa*, Oxford: Clarendon Press.

Sen, A. (1997), *Structural adjustment and rural poverty*, in G. Chadha and A.N. Sharma (1997).

Sen, A. (1998), *Rural labour markets and poverty*, in R. Radharkrishna and A.N. Sharma (1998).

Srinivasan, P. (1992), 'Excess capacities in Indian industries: Supply or demand determined?', *Economic and Political Weekly*, **27**, 2437–41.

Storm, S. (1997), 'The unfinished agenda: Indian agriculture under the structural reforms', *The Journal of International Trade and Economic Development*, **6**(2), 249–86.

Storm, S. (1999), 'Foodgrain price stabilisation in an open economy: A CGE analysis of variable trade levies for India', *The Journal of Development Studies*, **36**(2), 136–59.

Storm, S. (2000), 'Transition problems in policy reform: Agricultural trade liberalization in India', *mimeo*, Rotterdam: Erasmus University Rotterdam.

Storm, S. (2001), 'The desirable form of openness for Indian agriculture', *Cambridge Journal of Economics*, **25**(2), 185–207.

Subramanian, S. (1993), *Agricultural Trade Liberalization and India*, Paris: OECD.

Subramanian, S. (1996), *Vulnerability to price shocks under alternative policies in Cameroon*, in D.E. Sahn (1996).

Visaria, P. (1998), 'Employment and workforce in India: Implications for national income estimates', *mimeo*, Delhi: Institute of Economic Growth.

World Bank (1996), *Five Years of Stabilization and Reform and the Challenges Ahead*, Washington, D.C.: World Bank.

14. Biological stress signals in the context of poverty studies: India 1970–95

Lalita Chakravarty*

1. INTRODUCTION

This is an attempt to align two sets of data. One set refers to the field of poverty studies. The other refers to biological 'stress signals' as indicated by mortality and fertility indicators. It is accepted as a convention in current discussions on poverty and destitution to leave the field of mortality studies as irrelevant for the study of poverty (Dasgupta, 1993). Biological stress signals of heightened mortality in particular have been relegated to either the field of epidemiology or, in special cases, the study of famines. It will be argued below that this neat separation of the two fields of study – mortality and poverty – is unwarranted in the present state of development.

   The geographical area chosen for our present purpose is the millet zone of India, that is, the four states of Gujarat, Karnataka, Maharashtra and Rajasthan, though an all-India picture is presented at the outset. The all-India data set is used for two purposes, that is, to explain the methodology used in this paper and to align poverty and mortality data at the all-India level. The time period chosen is 1970 to 1995. Within this period, three sub-

* The author is deeply grateful to Professor K.L. Krishna of the Delhi School of Economics and has benefited from comments made by Jean Drèze and Suresh D. Tendulkar of the same institute. She would like to thank: Prof. Ram Ramaswamy of the Center for Physical Sciences, JNU, for his help in getting the meteorological data on droughts in India from Dr D.R. Sikka; Dr S. Ghose of Vidya Sagar University, West Bengal; and the editors, both of whom gave invaluable help. A fellowship from Nehru Memorial Museum and Library, New Delhi (1994–97) greatly helped to finish this study. Discussions with C.W.M. Naastepad of Delft University of Technology and Utrecht University and Servaas Storm of Erasmus University Rotterdam and their help with the econometric analysis make me feel confident to present biological stress signals as 'facts' not to be overlooked in the context of poverty studies. Yet faults may remain which are my own responsibility.

periods can be distinguished, namely the 1970s, the 1980s and the first half of the 1990s. It will be shown with the help of data that are useful for the study of famines that the first half of the 1970s was a continuation of a long history – starting in the colonial period of the late nineteenth century – of major and minor famines induced by drought-related shortfalls in the local production of foodgrains (Maharatna, 1996a).

The classic picture of famine registered a qualitative change in the 1980s. Despite shortfalls in production in the years 1982–87, 'slump famines', characteristic of the first part of the 1970s, disappeared from the scene. An exception is 1988, which will be discussed in detail while discussing causal factors later in the chapter.

The stress signal of heightened mortality reappeared in 1991–92. This mortality crisis, that started in 1991 in Karnataka and Maharashtra and spread to Gujarat and Rajasthan in 1992 (as well as to other populous states of UP, MP, AP, and Orissa that are not in the millet zone), was a reflection of increases in poverty. All three Foster, Greer and Thorbecke (FGT)[1] poverty indices rose at the all-India level on a short-term basis in 1992 – which was first admitted in 1995 (Tendulkar and Jain, 1995). Yet this time there was hardly any exogenous shock of drought-induced failure of foodgrain production. Something else was happening as the causative factor which could not be captured by price and wage signals. Signals from fertility indicators were also suggesting that the nature of biological crisis of the 1990s was (at least partly) different from the earlier ones, though mortality signals were strong and complete (Rajasthan was the only exception). We propose that the mortality crises of 1991–92 be labelled as one of little 'boom-famines' (Drèze et al., 1995), induced by structural adjustment processes initiated in 1990–91.

This chapter is organized as follows. Section 2 borrows from two different fields of research – historical demography and economics – to offer a possible explanation for the occurrence of biological stress. Problems of measurement of biological stress are discussed in section 3. This is followed by a presentation of mortality and fertility data and an attempt at identification of biological stress for India and the millet zone in sections 4 and 5 respectively. We then explore in section 6 the role of three possible causes of short-term peaks in mortality, that is, natural calamities like the infamous droughts of the millet zone, socio-economic calamities like 'entitlement failure' due to, for instance, inflation, and finally a failure of institutional support for the poor in 'deep poverty'. Next, the short-term behaviour of fertility indicators together with mortality signals are discussed to isolate the causal factors. The third causal factor, that is, institutional arrangements to support the floor of wages, is suggested by a significant change in the linkage between the two sets of signals, mortality and fertility. The whole of section

6 is an attempt to see if mortality and fertility signals corroborate entitlement failure primarily due to natural catastrophes like droughts, partial or total, or whether other factors also play a role. Final remarks on the 'alignment' of poverty and mortality come in the concluding section 7.

2.   THEORETICAL BACKGROUND

In this section, we borrow from two different fields of research, namely historical demography and economics, to firstly identify biological stress, and secondly, to offer an explanation for the occurrence of biological stress.

We borrow from historical demography the definition of biological crisis as the synchronic rise in mortality rates and fall in fertility rates (adjusted for conception lead). The second basic presupposition borrowed from historical demography is that biological crises may originate not in epidemics but in short-term food shortage. For the sake of brevity we shall refer to such crises as 'little famines'. An implication of this study of 'little famines' is that the study of biological stress signals as defined above and for the period specified can be done without specific reference to epidemiological data or, for that matter, without expecting much illumination from data on causes of death.[2] This is so for two reasons. Firstly, it is not the point here that neither national nor international codes on 'causes of death' include any entry like starvation death and that is why an analysis of 'little famines' must ignore such data. The point here refers to the nature of the mortality transition that is under way.[3] The rapidity and robustness of the mortality decline in India can be traced back to the 1920s, although the process gained momentum after the Second World War. This is evident from rising trends in the life expectancy at birth, $e(0)$ (both for men and women), since the early years, as well as in the rise of $e(5)$ since the 1950s. The causative factors behind this periodized trend are generally put into two groups: the control of major known epidemics in the third world countries; and rising levels of per capita income in almost all politically stable regions. The period under study, 1970–95, starts after known major epidemics are totally controlled, while some are even eradicated, notwithstanding the stubborn prevalence of endemic tuberculosis or of waterborne enteric ailments, of pulmonary diseases or the old culprit malaria. This is also the period that has not witnessed any large-scale breakdown of public health due to rampages of new killer diseases (even when we take into account short outbreaks of plague, dengue or hepatitis B).

The second reason for ignoring the epidemiological angle while analysing mortality data for 1970–95 is more controversial. Can increases in per capita income, as an indication of an improved diet – that is, per capita intake of calories, protein and other nutrients – be taken as the causative factor behind falling adult mortality, or a rising trend of *e* (5)? This is still debated, partly because there are some 'outlier' countries across the world. However,

> It should come as no surprise that poor people are in worse health than others. [. . .] because the poor are less likely to be educated and must often use shared sources of water and surface water (lakes, streams, ponds) without adequate sanitation facilities, they are dangerously exposed to illness and premature death. [. . .] Bad health and premature death are, arguably, the most tragic manifestations of poverty. [. . .] The research carried out for this report found that the poor face a disproportionately higher risk than the rich of falling sick, particularly from infectious diseases [. . .] the poor suffer disproportionally more from communicable and vector (pest) borne diseases, which is also borne out by other analyses. Tuberculosis, malaria and leprose, as well as the mortality rate of children under two (which is dominated by diarrhea and respiratory ailments), are all examples of such diseases. [. . .] Poor members of scheduled casts run even higher risks of premature death. [. . .] This pattern of greater correlation between income and communicable diseases has been noted in other countries. (World Bank, 1998, p. 28)

For the purpose of this study we assume that the long chain of causative factors that worked behind the European escape from high-level mortality, that is, food–nutrition–water–shelter–sanitation, has been broken up into two bits. These two bits are working simultaneously in a country like India, with the exception of the state of Kerala which is an outlier in the Indian as well as the international context. One bit of the chain is food and nutrition; the other bit is the rest of the long chain. We here refer to the first bit. Per capita intake of cereals or other complementary basic food items may not be on a continuously rising trend, but there are fewer and fewer periods of 'gap' (that is, periods of starvation or semi-starvation) in food–nutrition intake, compared with the frequency of 'gap' periods in the past. When there are fewer 'gaps' there is better utilization of 'stored energy' (stored either as lipids or as glycogen or as protein) and this may explain a downward time trend in mortality, even when infectious diseases together with mass poverty prevail. In the case of women, a fall in the fertility rates of a high birth rate regime will further enhance the process of 'better utilization' of a low-calorie diet, particularly in the reproductive age span. In other words, we can study the downward time trends and fluctuations around that trend of mortality in India for the last three decades of this century without bringing in epidemiology (Zurbrigg, 1994; Fogel, 1992, 1994; McKeown, 1978; Murray et al., 1992).

The presupposition borrowed from historical demography (of food shortage rather than epidemics as a cause of biological stress) leads up to a possible explanation for the occurrence of biological stress. The major assumption is that there is 'inequality in death', as demographer Pressant put it in the context of the mortality transition in Western Europe. The well-known theory of entitlement failure has already pointed to two different ways in which food shortage may arise. One is the loss of employment. The other is a fall in real purchasing power due to price increases. Slump famines refer to the first, while boom famines refer to the second. The point is that food shortages do not affect the entire population equally. Starting from an already low level of food intake, losses in employment or in real purchasing power will hurt the poor more than the non-poor. Within the poor, those who are very poor and have one fatal weakness, that is, their survival is crucially dependent on the availability of supports to their consumption needs when the period of stress is prolonged (because they do not have tradable assets), will be biologically more vulnerable. The biological stress of a short-term drastic fall in an already low level of basic caloric intake (the latter being defined by the 'absolute poverty line') will show up in a synchronic rise in mortality rates and a fall in fertility indicators. This assumption of 'inequality in death' holds true today for modern India. This pattern of 'stress signals' of short-term duration by definition (Maharatna, 1996a) may be superimposed on falling time trends, and be isolated from random fluctuations (see section 4).[4]

To this we want to add the following. Firstly, we want to offer a modified entitlement theory. A short-term entitlement failure due to an agricultural failure can be contained, or even prevented, by appropriate institutional support for the poor which keeps up their real purchasing power in times of stress. Public 'food for work' programmes, public distribution systems or other relief measures are important examples of targeted institutional support providing a floor to the real purchasing power of the poor. It can even be argued, as is done by Sen (1997), that any step up in public spending during a stress period does help to contain the imminent entitlement failure. By implication, the occurrence of severe biological stress suggests that institutional support for the poor has been inadequate.

Secondly, we want to explain the continuation of biological stress with reference to an effort intensification process. Entitlement failure, irrespective of its causes, can only explain a short-term rise in biological stress. The reasons for longer duration are several. In response to the entitlement failure, the poor migrate to other regions or states, intensifying their search for additional employment. Migration and intensified search, although providing workers with an escape route in times of economic stress, are both dimensions of an effort intensification process, which involves increased labour mobility accompanied by a growing casualization of the mass of workers at the bottom of the economy (see, for instance, Breman

(1996)). There is, moreover, a possibility of a multiplication of 'jobs' on a piece-rate basis, done serially in a given period of time. This will show up as a higher level of man-days worked on a daily or weekly basis instead of the usual status basis (Gupta, 1996a). This dimension of the effort intensification process will not show up as a drop in the time rate of wages, even if money wages are adjusted for price rises. It will show up as increased biological stress (a hint of this process is in Dasgupta (1993)). This effort intensification process at the very low levels of purchasing power, unless compensated, has a significant negative impact on workers' health, eventually resulting in higher mortality rates. Hence, the effort intensification process set in motion by the entitlement failure may explain why mortality rates remain relatively high for a longer period following a short-term peak.

3. PROBLEMS OF METHOD AND MEASUREMENT

When trying to assess the relation between mortality and poverty, three methodological issues arise, namely: (i) the unit of measurement; (ii) the separation of biological stress-related fluctuations in mortality rates from random fluctuations and from an overall time trend; and (iii) the question of alignment of mortality and poverty data. The third point will be taken up in section 6, which discusses old and new causes of biological stress. Section 4 deals with the second point. In this section we will take up the first point.

The notion of a typical microeconomic unit that can either succumb or can go through the process of 'little famines' and is the object of the labour intensification regime in the Structural Adjustment Programme (SAP) period is essential for this research project. This brings in three basic assumptions regarding micro units on whom statistical data of poverty and mortality are mapped, and some data on fertility are of course required to complete the evidence of a full-scale biological shock. What are the basic characteristics of this micro unit?

The first assumption regarding micro units is that entitlement failure is reflected in mortality rates of men in the working age groups (15–60+). Mortality rates of adult women give a complex picture. The intra-household distribution within the reciprocity system, as well as biological reproductive tasks, are two aspects of her life that make her mortality response more complex than that of men.[5] The second assumption regarding the micro units under study is that their consumption expenditures are below the mean value of the overall expenditure of the 'poor'. Our focus here is on a group of relatively very poor, as contrasted to the poor near the poverty line.[6] This means that unless institutional arrangements are made, an entitlement failure occurs to a geographically fixed group of 'very poor' people and households, and they do send up mortality signals approximately three months after the onset of the biological shock. It is significant to notice here that the fluctuations in the head-count ratio of poverty are less important in the context of isolating short-term peaks in 'mass poverty' than the other two FGT indices, that is, the depth of poverty and the skewness of poverty measures.

It will be apparent from the discussion up to this point that the central focus is on mortality crisis. The fertility behaviour under stress and for short duration is studied more for corroborative evidence of biological crisis than for its linkage with 'poverty' measures. It is important to keep this in mind before we bring in the data set. A consistent pattern of 'peaked short-term mortality and dipped short-term fertility' may not be present towards the end of a stretch of 26 years, during which many other factors (such as family planning and fertility targeting) have influenced fertility. We shall mention various aspects of changing fertility behaviour in section 5, but shall not go into more detailed statistical analysis.

4. TRENDS, RANDOMNESS AND STRESS SIGNALS IN ALL-INDIA MORTALITY DATA

It is not necessary to repeat our comments regarding our unit of analysis (see section 3), but it is important to specify the purpose for which this data set of estimates of Age-Specific Mortality Rates (ASMRs) will be used. Our purpose is to separate out randomness in the fluctuations in mortality rates from a 'pattern of stress signals' given out by heightened values of some of these rates in particular calendar years. Our data source is the bulletins of the Sample Registration Survey (SRS) Division of the Office of the Registrar General of India, Vital Statistics Department.[7]

Let us discuss the recognition of a pattern as distinct from random fluctuations. This we will do with the help of the ASMRs for males presented in Table 14.1. Two methods have been applied. Each of the methods consists of two steps, namely the identification of peaks and the application of a test for randomness. The test used is the 'sign test for qualitative data', and this step is common to both methods.

The first method is as follows. If we read along any particular column in Table 14.1, for instance $m(30–34)$, and mark any reading that is higher than the reading preceding it as a peak, then we get a certain number of peaks. This is called the chain-base method of identifying peaks. We then read the number of peaks across a row. A certain number of peaks out of 14 readings in a row indicates that a particular year is a qualitatively different

Table 14.1 Adult mortality and signs of higher stress mortality^{a,b,c}

Year	10–14	15–19	20–24	25–29	30–34	35–39	40–44	45–49	50–54	55–59	60–64	65–69	70+	All[d]	M 15a	F 15b	16a	16b	16c	16d
	1	2	3	4	5	6	7	8	9	10	11	12	13	14	15a	15b	16a	16b	16c	16d
1970	2.0	*2.5	2.9	*3.3	4.0	4.7	8.0	11.9	17.9	25.5	42.7	53.6	*117.1	15.8	3	3	—	—	—	—
1971	2.1	1.9	*3.0	3.0	3.9	5.5	7.4	10.5	*19.0	24.6	37.0	53.8	110.3	14.7	2	3	5	—	—	—
*1972	1.9	*2.4	*2.9	*3.4	*4.1	5.4	*8.6	*12.2	*19.1	*27.5	*43.3	*61.9	*128.8	*16.3	12	14	11	—	—	—
1973	*2.3	2.2	*2.9	2.9	*4.5	5.3	7.6	*12.0	17.2	26.0	*42.6	55.8	112.4	*15.1	6	12	2	2	—	—
1974	1.8	*2.3	2.7	2.8	3.5	*5.7	7.2	*11.9	16.9	*27.2	37.7	*57.2	106.0	14.3	5	4	4	1	—	—
*1975	*2.0	2.1	2.6	*3.1	*4.1	*6.8	*8.2	*13.3	15.0	*28.7	39.6	*59.0	*120.3	*15.5	10	13	11	4	—	—
1976	*2.4	*2.5	2.7	*3.1	*4.2	4.5	*9.5	12.1	*19.5	*28.6	*48.4	*57.6	*114.6	*14.7	12	5	7	7	—	—
1977	1.8	*2.3	*3.1	2.5	3.6	*5.5	*8.2	*11.6	*18.5	*26.6	*39.4	*55.1	104.4	*14.0	10	10	2	2	—	—
1978	*2.0	2.1	*2.7	*3.4	*3.8	*5.2	*7.4	*11.4	*17.5	*26.9	*42.7	*56.5	*110.2	*13.8	13	8	7	1	—	—
1979	1.6	1.7	2.5	2.4	3.6	*5.1	6.7	9.0	14.8	24.2	35.3	46.2	93.6	12.6	1	2	1	0	0	—
1980	1.7	2.0	2.3	2.3	3.4	4.7	*7.2	9.6	14.6	21.5	35.0	*59.0	98.5	12.4	2	1	6	0	6	—
1981	*1.8	1.9	2.4	2.5	*3.7	4.6	6.5	9.5	15.3	*23.8	36.3	51.7	102.6	12.4	3	5	8	0	9	—
1982	1.6	1.8	2.3	*2.8	3.4	4.3	6.3	9.3	14.4	20.7	33.4	48.3	95.5	11.9	3	1	1	0	5	—
1983	1.5	*2.0	2.5	2.6	*3.6	4.6	6.2	9.0	15.0	21.5	35.7	*52.0	*103.6	12.0	4	0	10	0	6	—
1984	1.6	1.6	*2.8	*2.8	3.2	4.4	*6.6	*10.0	*15.6	21.0	*36.1	*50.6	*110.8	*12.4	10	11	9	0	8	—
1985	*1.8	1.9	*2.6	*2.8	*3.4	4.2	*6.8	*9.7	*15.0	*22.7	*36.8	48.6	*104.8	*11.8	11	10	5	0	10	—
1986	1.5	*2.0	2.4	2.6	3.0	*4.7	6.1	*9.6	*15.0	20.5	*35.0	47.6	95.6	11.0	5	4	2	0	6	—
1987	1.5	*1.9	2.3	2.2	3.1	3.9	*6.2	8.7	13.5	20.3	*35.0	47.1	94.2	10.9	3	1	2	0	3	—
1988	1.4	1.8	2.3	2.4	2.9	*4.5	*6.4	9.0	*14.0	20.7	33.2	*50.5	*100.9	*11.0	6	9	9	0	3	—
1989	*1.5	1.7	2.3	*2.6	3.1	4.0	5.8	*9.0	13.2	20.1	*33.0	*48.2	94.7	10.4	5	3	3	0	3	—
1990	1.4	1.7	*2.4	2.5	3.1	3.9	5.7	*9.0	13.2	*20.9	28.9	*47.3	91.4	9.7	4	5	2	0	2	—
*1991	*1.4	*1.8	*2.5	*2.9	*3.3	*4.2	5.1	*9.1	*13.4	*21.2	*33.0	45.9	*96.5	10.0	11	6	11	0	4	11
1992	1.3	*1.9	*2.3	2.4	3.2	3.9	*5.6	*9.3	*13.1	*20.1	*32.4	*47.4	*95.7	*10.0	11	14	4	0	4	7
1993	1.2	1.6	2.1	2.3	2.9	*4.0	5.1	8.0	*13.2	*20.6	30.7	46.2	*94.5	*9.5	6	8	3	0	1	3
1994	1.2	1.6	2.1	*2.7	*3.2	3.7	*5.5	*8.5	*12.9	*19.6	*31.2	*45.1	*94.2	*9.6	10	10	6	0	2	4

Number of mortality peaks:[e] — Indexation method (columns 15a M, 15b F, 16a, 16b, 16c, 16d)

331

Table 14.1   (cont.)

Year	10-14	15-19	20-24	25-29	30-34	35-39	40-44	45-49	50-54	55-59	60-64	65-69	70+	All^d	Number of mortality peaks:^e					
															M	F	Indexation method			
	1	2	3	4	5	6	7	8	9	10	11	12	13	14	15a	15b	16a	16b	16c	16d
11995	*1.3	*1.7	2.1	*2.6	*3.1	*3.7	*5.5	*8.1	12.0	17.5	28.0	41.6	*91.4	*9.3	9	9	2	0	1	1
α	−0.04	−0.03	−0.03	−0.03	−0.05	−0.08	−0.13	−0.16	−0.25	−0.36	−0.52	−0.57	−1.03	−0.28						
t	−9.1	−6.3	−7.2	−3.7	−7.8	−6.5	−8.5	−7.7	−9.3	−8.4	−7.2	−7.3	−6.4	−20.8						
R^2	0.78	0.62	0.69	0.37	0.72	0.64	0.76	0.71	0.78	0.75	0.69	0.69	0.63	0.95						

Notes:

^a Columns 1–14 give all-India *male* ASMR (rural and urban) by five-year age group (per 00).

^b Columns 15 and 16 give the number of peaks in, respectively, adult male and adult female ASMR (all-India). The method of counting peaks is explained in the text.

^c Stars in this table mark deviations from an overall (downward) trend in mortality rates. The bottom three rows of this table present the estimation results for the trend function (described in chapter note 9). In the second row from the bottom, *t* stands for the *t*-value.

^d All ages, including age group *m*(0–10).

^e Columns 15(a)–(b) give the number of peaks in respectively, male and female mortality as derived from de-trended ASMR data. Columns 16(a)–(d) give the numbers of peaks in male mortality according to the indexation method. Column 16(a) gives the results of the chain-base method. Columns 16(b)–(d) give the results of the fixed-base method for base years 1972, 1979 and 1990 respectively.

Source: Bulletins of the SRS Division of the Office of the Registrar General of India, Vital Statistics Department.

sample from the preceding year.[8] To separate out randomness from stress-induced mortality we apply the sign test for qualitative data. The cut-off point at a 10 per cent level of significance is 10 out of 14 by the 'sign test' (a test that is commonly applied to qualitative data).

This pattern of stressful years as yet is of limited value since the comparison has been made between two successive years without paying attention to a possible trend in mortality data. A trend factor can be taken into account in two different ways, that is, either by indexing the annual data to a fixed base and shifting this base over time, or by fitting a mathematical trend and focusing only on the residuals for recognition of stress signals.

The fixed-base method will be useful, and may complement the chain-base method, if the fixed base is chosen carefully to represent a normal year. A 'normal' year will mean that it has a 'normal' number of peaks as compared with the years preceding and following it. What is equally important is that this base year is periodically shifted downwards in time. Given the length of the period, we will use three alternative years as a base, namely 1972, 1979 and 1990. This method of indexing has some advantages over the chain base. It helps to identify prolonged biological stress in the data by picking up signals that come out as weak in the chain-base method. Let us notice the characteristics of this indexing method in Table 14.1. Column 16a gives the number of peaks by the simple chain method, when the base shifts every year. If we fix the base at 1972, as in column 16b, the effect of choosing a bad year as a base year becomes evident. All peaks vanish after 1978. This vanishing of peaks is also due to the presence of a downward trend in the data, producing lower values for almost all years after 1972, especially years that are more distant in time. We therefore shift the base downwards to later years, firstly to 1979 which was a good year. Then 1985 emerges as a crisis year. If we finally shift the base to 1990, which was another good year, we find that 1991 emerges as another crisis year, while 1992 emerges as a rather enigmatic year (if seven peaks can be taken as a warning signal).

The second method starts by examining whether the time series data exhibit a trend. This we do with the help of a regression analysis for each age group separately (columns 1–13) as well as for all ages taken together (column 14).[9] This trend analysis reveals a significant downward linear trend in mortality for all age groups (as well as for all ages taken together). The regression results are given at the bottom of Table 14.1. The next step then is to de-trend the ASMR data. This is done by calculating annual deviations from the trend for each age group. This results in a number of positive deviations from the trend for each age group (in each column). The positive deviations will be called peaks. They are marked with stars in columns 1–14 of Table 14.1. We then follow the same procedure as above, that is, we count the number of peaks (marked by stars) across rows (the result for any particular calendar year is given in column 15a) and subject the number of stars in a row to the sign test. Column 15b of Table 14.1 gives the all-India mortality peaks for women, calculated by the same method. Years that come up with clear signals of 10 or more peaks for men as well as women are heavily underlined.

What is the overall picture of mortality signals at the all-India level? Crisis mortality years that come out immediately as common to both methods are 1972, 1975, 1985 and 1991. We also notice that there is some correspondence between the two methods as far as the enigmatic years 1992 and 1994 are concerned. The year 1992 comes out as a year of strong and complete mortality signal from the de-trending method. It seems that the last half of the 1980s is free of male mortality signals. We will come back to this in section 6, when we discuss periodization in mortality data.

We had stated in the beginning of section 3 that besides problems of (a) mapping mortality and poverty on micro units, and (b) separation of signals from other disturbances, we have to align measured poverty with the broad picture of mortality. It is for this purpose that three FGT indices are given in Table 14.2. As far as the overall trends are concerned, poverty and mortality data align very well. Both show a downward trend up to 1989, while both rise above the trend level in 1991 and 1992. The year 1972 also comes up as a year of heightened mortality as well as poverty.

Before proceeding with our analysis, there are two more points to be noted. Firstly, we bring in the notion of simultaneity. Nine peaks is surely not strong enough to cross the sign test at a 10 per cent level of significance, yet it is a weak signal of stress not to be ignored. This is especially so if it occurs simultaneously with strong signals for other groups. These weak signals will be utilized when constructing state-level mortality signals in section 5. Biological crisis increases attrition rates in males, females, infants and children, irrespective of what group is primarily responsible for entitlement in the labour market mode of operation. Therefore, to have a complete picture of crisis mortality, all four groups must give a stress signal separately and simultaneously. This will be referred to as the simultaneity criterion. If a signal for a group is missing, or weak, then it will be called an incomplete signal.

Secondly, we bring in the notion of a 'dip' in the data. It is advisable to keep these dips in the picture for the following reasons. As crisis management improves – through activities of the state machinery, or extending market operations of micro units, or due to activities of other agencies – a peaked mortality, say in age group $m(x+4)$ in period t, is sometimes followed by a sharp dip d in the mortality rate of the same age group in the next period $(t+1)$. This dip d in the data is important to keep in mind

Table 14.2 Poverty indices, all-India 1970–94[a,b]

NSS round	Survey period	Headcount index			Poverty gap index			Squared poverty gap		
		R	U	N	R	U	N	R	U	N
25	1970/71	54.84	44.98	52.88	16.545	13.347	15.910	6.798	5.349	6.510
27	1972/73	55.36	45.67	53.37	17.348	13.459	16.548	7.328	5.262	6.903
28	1973/74	55.72	47.96	54.10	17.175	13.602	16.430	7.128	5.219	6.730
32	1977/78	50.60	40.50	48.36	15.025	11.687	14.284	6.057	4.526	5.717
38	1983	45.31	35.65	43.00	12.649	9.517	11.901	4.841	3.557	4.534
42	1986/87	38.81	34.29	37.69	10.013	9.100	9.787	3.700	3.395	3.625
43	1987/88	39.23	36.20	38.47	9.275	9.121	9.237	2.982	3.056	3.000
44	1988/89	39.06	36.60	38.44	9.504	9.537	9.512	3.291	3.293	3.292
45	1989/90	34.30	33.40	34.07	7.799	8.505	7.979	2.575	3.038	2.693
46	1990/91	36.43	32.76	35.49	8.644	8.509	8.609	2.926	3.121	2.976
47	1991	37.42	33.23	36.34	8.288	8.244	8.277	2.680	2.902	2.737
48	1992	43.47	33.73	40.93	10.881	8.824	10.345	3.810	3.191	3.649
50	1993/94	36.66	30.51	35.04	8.387	7.405	8.128	2.792	2.417	2.693
Trend 1951–94[c]		−0.86	−0.75	−0.88	−1.84	−1.43	−1.79	−2.65	−2.05	−2.56

Notes:
[a] With correction for CPIAL. Poverty line = Rs. 49 per capita per month at Oct 73–Jun. 74 rural prices.
[b] Explanation of symbols: R = rural, U = urban, N = national. NSS = National Sample Survey of consumer expenditure.
[c] Trend rate of growth during 1951–94 (per cent).
Source: Datt (1997).

because the mortality rate of $m(x+4)$ may peak in $(t+2)$ as soon as an extraordinary effort to combat the crisis is removed from the scene. The dip is also due to the 'cohort effect' after a crisis year, when new entrants with a different health status or material status combine with some of the older members.

We may now compare this all-India pattern of heightened mortality and poverty with indications of stress signals in the four states of the millet zone. The pattern at the state level may (partly) differ from the overall pattern since the states in the millet zone do not have a large enough weightage in terms of population to push up all-India ASMRs. The state-level data may then reveal important information about specific state-level conditions.

5. STRESS SIGNALS IN THE MILLET ZONE

Although a mortality crisis is the main feature of a biological crisis, corroborative evidence of a sharp dip in fertility is necessary to capture the phenomenon of biological stress. We therefore bring in fertility indicators to complete the picture of biological stress. A year of biological stress will be identified with the help of what we will refer to as the simultaneity criterion. The simultaneity criterion will be satisfied if mortality signals (that is, 10 peaks or more) for adult males, adult females, infants and children, as well as fertility signals come together in a particular year. In this case we will speak of a complete signal. If, out of the five symbols, some fail to appear as stress-signalled, then that will be taken as an incomplete signal.

We have used three indices of fertility, the crude birth rate for the rural areas, CBR(R), the total fertility rate for urban and rural areas combined, TFR(U+R), and the total fertility rate for the rural areas only, TFR(R). Being based on three indices, a fertility signal itself can be complete or incomplete. Notes to Tables 14.3 and 14.4 indicate when there is a complete distress signal in fertility, and when there is an incomplete signal.

We repeat here that as far as the historical evolution of mortality signals is concerned, it is important to consider not only complete, strong signals, but also other combinations of 'strength' and 'completeness'.[10] Thus we have two aspects of 'simultaneity criteria', that is, completeness and strength of mortality signals. In our analysis of the millet zone, completeness and strength will be given due weight in order to build up an event evolving over time.

Tables 14.3 and 14.4 present evidence on mortality and fertility signals side by side. Mortality signals are given for adult males (M), adult females (F), infants (I) and children (C) (the full picture of male and female mortality peaks at the all-India and state level, from which the signals have been derived, is presented in the Appendix).[11] Table 14.3 presents mortality and fertility signals derived from de-trended ASMR and fertility data (as explained in section 4 and in the notes to Table 14.3) while Table 14.4 presents mortality and fertility signals derived according to the indexation method (explained in section 4).

Two more questions need to be addressed while using FI together with ASMR data. The first is the question of the nine-month lead in the conception index so as to get the onset of the crisis fixed in a calendar year. The ASMR and FI may get linked in different calendar years. Take the case of a natural cause such as a failure of sowing generally referred to as 'drought', or a failure of harvesting, or both combined, which happens when the major kharif crop fails. Such a natural disaster may cause mortality and the conception index to fall in calendar year t while fertility falls only nine months later, that is, either in year t or in year $(t+1)$. Secondly, with respect to ASMRs, it should be noted that stress mortality signals may appear with a lag when various micro units (persons as well as households) have different durations of sustaining power against a fall in basic caloric consumption.

Let us now look at Tables 14.3 and 14.4 and see if we can discern a pattern of stress signals. From Tables 14.3 and 14.4 we find that: (i) complete signals of dipped fertility and heightened mortality show up in a number of years in the 1970s, particularly in 1973 and around 1977/78 – for Gujarat the whole period 1975–78 looks enigmatic; (ii) such complete stress signals (of heightened mortality combined with lowered fertility) disappeared in the 1980s except for 1988 (when they did appear in the two Northern states Gujarat and Rajasthan, which had been going through full-scale 'droughts' in the two previous years); and (iii) full-scale mortality and fertility signals reappear in Karnataka and Maharashtra in 1991 and 1992.[12]

How does this picture of mortality align with measured poverty? Poverty indices for the four states of the millet zone are given in Table 14.5. We will comment only on the years for which poverty indices are available. Interestingly, for Gujarat (incomplete) stress signals for the years 1973 and 1977 do not go hand in hand with an increase in the HC, but they are accompanied (in 1972/73 and 1977/78) by a rise in PG and SPG indicators, which measure the depth of poverty. The increase in all three poverty indices in 1986/87 did not get reflected in increased biological stress in the calendar years 1986 and 1987. Increased biological stress in 1988 was preceded by increased poverty in 1987/88 by the HC index only. The year 1992 comes up with a clear signal of biological stress as well as increased poverty by all measures. For Karnataka, increased poverty in 1972/73 and 1973/74

Table 14.3 Biological stress signals in the millet zone – de-trending method[a,b,c]

Year	Gujarat					Karnataka					Maharashtra					Rajasthan				
	M	F	I	C	FI	M	F	I	C	FI	M	F	I	C	FI	M	F	I	C	FI
1970				x		–									?	–	–			?
1971					z?		11	x								–	–			
1972				x			11	x			10		x				10		x	
1973		9	x	x	z		11	x	x	z	9	12	x	x	z					z?
1974										z	9									z
1975	11		x		?	9				z?	9				?			x		z
1976	10		x	x					x	z				x	z				x	z
1977	10		x	x	z?				x	z?	13	11	x	x	z			x	x	z
1978	10					11	10	x	x	?					z			x	x	z
1979				x	z			x		z			x		z					z
1980					z?				x	z					z?				x	
1981					?					z		9	x		?	11	9	x		?
1982					?					z?										
1983						9		x					x							
1984				x	z?			x					x	x			10	x	x	
1985			x	x	z?											9	10	x	x	
1986			x	x	z?								x							

Year	M	F	I	C	FI	M	F	I	C	FI	M	F	I	C	FI	M	F	I	C	FI
1987								x												
1988	<u>12</u>	11	x	x	z	9				x						<u>12</u>	12	x	x	z
1989		<u>11</u>	x	x	?							9						x	x	z
1990			x		z					x				x				x	x	z
1991				x		<u>12</u>	11	x	x	?	13	11	x	x	z			x	x	z?
1992	<u>10</u>	9	x	x			<u>11</u>	x	z	<u>10</u>	11	x	x	z					z
1993	<u>11</u>								x	x				x	x	z				
1994			x		z	<u>9</u>	10	x	x	<u>12</u>	10	x	x	z		9	x	x	z	
1995			x	x		<u>9</u>		x	x	?	9	13	x	x	z			x	x	z

Notes:

[a] M, F, I and C stand for mortality rates for males, females, female infants and female children respectively. The M and F columns give the number of mortality peaks for males and females respectively if the number of mortality peaks equals 9 (a weak signal) or more (a strong signal). Empty cells indicate 8 or fewer mortality peaks. An 'x' in the I and C columns indicates a positive deviation from the overall downward trend in, respectively, infant and child mortality rates.

[b] FI stands for the fertility signal. The three fertility indicators are the crude birth rate in rural areas, CBR(R), the total fertility rate in rural areas, TFR(R), and the total fertility rate in rural and urban areas combined, TFR(R + U). The TFR as well as the CBR here refer to estimated fertility rates for 1971–75, Sample Registration Survey (SRS) data. A 'z' indicates a strong signal, that is, a drop below the overall declining trend in all three fertility indicators simultaneously. A 'z?' indicates a moderate signal, that is, a fall from trend in two out of three fertility indicators. A '?' indicates a weak signal, that is, a drop below trend in only one out of the three fertility signals. See Tables 14.6 to 14.9 for data.

[c] Underlined are years in which four or all out of the five indices simultaneously show stress signals. For Maharashtra, the years 1991 and 1992, though showing only three out of five signals, are also underlined because of the strength of these mortality and fertility signals.

Source: Author's estimates.

339

Table 14.4   Biological stress signals in the millet zone – indexation method[a,b,c,d,e]

	Gujarat					Karnataka					Maharashtra					Rajasthan				
	M	F	I	C	FI	M	F	I	C	FI	M	F	I	C	FI	M	F	I	C	FI
1970																–	–			
1971																–	–			
1972	x		x	x		9		x	x	@	x	x		x	@	x	x	x	x	
1973	9	x	x	x	@		x		x	@	d	d	x	x	@	x	x	x	x	@
1974	d9	d								@						d	d			@
1975	x	9	x		@	x	x	x	x								9	x	x	
1976	x			x		d	d9	x	x		x	x	x	x	?	9	x	d	x	@
1977	d9			x	@	x					d	d	x					x	d	
1978	d9				@		?			@					@		9	x	x	
1979																				
1980																			x	
1981		d9			@											x	9	x		@
1982					?	9			x							d9	9			
1983	x	x	x	d	?	d9	x	x								d9	x			
1984	d	d	d	d	@		x	x			9	9	x			9	9	x	x	@
1985		d9								?	d9	d		x	@					?
1986			x		@					@										@
1987				x	@										@					@

340

	M	F	I	C	FI	M	F	I	C	FI	M	F	I	C	FI
1988	x	x			@		x	x		@		x	x	x	@
1989	d9	x			@			x		@		d	d	d	?
1990			x	x	?										
1991	x	x			@	x	x	x		@	9	9	x	d	@
1992	9	x	x	?		9	9			@	d	9	x	x	?
1993			x		?			x		?			x		?
1994	x	x			?								x		
1995			x		@		x					x	x		@

Notes:

a M, F, I and C stand for mortality rates for males, females, female infants and female children respectively.

b The M and F columns give the number of mortality peaks for males and females respectively. Here, an 'x' indicates a peak in mortality rates for at least 10 out of 14 age groups according to the chain-base and/or fixed-base method. A '9' indicates 9 peaks which is a weak signal. A 'd' indicates the occurrence of a dip with an unusually low value judged by the trend in mortality data. A 'd9' indicates 9 peaks plus at least one 'd' value, suggesting the presence of either relief measures or a healthier cohort due to higher attrition in the previous year.

c An 'x' in the I and C columns indicates a significant rise in, respectively, female infant and female child mortality rates.

d FI stands for the fertility signal. See the relevant note to Table 14.3 for an explanation of its components (CBR(R), TFR(R) and TFR(R + U)). An '@' indicates a drop in fertility by the three indices simultaneously. When the drop in TFR is slight, or only two out of the three fertility indicators show a decline, a question mark is put against FI. See Tables 14.6 to 14.9 for data.

e Crisis years (complete signals) are underlined.

Source: Author's estimates.

Table 14.5 *Poverty indices, millet zone – 1970–94[a,b]*

NSS round	Survey period	Gujarat			Karnataka			Maharashtra			Rajasthan		
		HC	PG	SPG	HC	PG	SPG	HC	PG	SPG	HC	PG	SPG
25	1970/71	61.38	18.816	7.673	58.00	17.440	7.063	61.96	18.584	7.541	65.28	24.459	12.006
27	1972/73	61.60	19.140	7.851	56.57	17.153	7.222	81.13	30.340	9.999	63.42	21.949	9.891
28	1973/74	58.07	15.529	5.740	60.97	18.799	7.660	64.61	20.317	8.506	59.26	18.460	7.634
32	1977/78	55.27	17.717	7.447	54.22	17.661	7.725	78.78	21.958	7.709	53.52	14.611	5.575
38	1983	39.23	8.735	2.721	44.68	12.978	5.157	54.56	15.789	6.073	48.99	15.586	6.654
42	1986/87	42.63	12.206	4.958	46.15	13.815	5.618	53.92	16.027	6.392	45.65	13.168	5.238
43	1987/88	42.93	9.741	3.074	43.49	11.272	4.000	52.32	14.023	5.163	50.35	14.888	5.967
45	1989/90	36.98	7.813	2.396	54.43	15.246	5.720	45.53	11.652	4.149	40.49	12.194	5.190
46	1990/91	43.13	8.006	2.148	42.73	13.304	5.587	43.05	11.951	4.498	38.96	12.097	5.045
48	1992	46.78	13.528	5.745	56.94	15.759	6.023	60.63	18.071	7.073	50.90	13.761	5.249
50	1993/94	35.39	7.371	2.316	40.97	9.745	3.345	47.81	13.160	5.089	47.52	11.762	4.118

Notes:
[a] Explanation of symbols: HC stands for the head count index, PG for the poverty gap index and SPG for the squared poverty gap index. Data given concern indices for rural area.
[b] Underlined are all values representing an increase over the year preceding it.
Source: Datt (1997).

was reflected in (incomplete) stress signals in 1972 and 1973. A complete stress signal in 1978 was preceded by an increase in the SPG, the index most sensitive to the depth of poverty. Increased poverty, by all three poverty indices, in 1989/90 has not led to clear signs of increased biological stress (although, in comparison with the 1980s in general, male mortality is relatively high). The calendar year 1992 again shows clear signals of increased poverty (by all three indices) as well as biological stress. For Maharastra, the stress years 1972, 1973 and 1977 align well with the rise in all three poverty indices in the National Sample Survey (NSS) round 1972/73 and with two out of the three indices in 1977/78. Like in Gujarat in 1986/87 and in Karnataka in 1989/90, the year 1986/87 comes out as a year of increased poverty which is not reflected in a clear stress signal. Increased poverty in the NSS rounds 1990/91 and 1992 however was reflected in significant stress signals in 1991 and 1992. In Rajasthan, (incomplete) stress signals show up in 1972 and 1973 without accompanying registered increases in poverty. Vice versa, increased poverty in 1983 was not reflected in a clear stress signal in 1983, although female mortality peaked in 1984 and 1985. The year 1988 comes up as a year of increased poverty as well as complete biological stress, while 1992 shows increased poverty and an incomplete signal of biological stress.

The basic questions calling for an answer are: (i) what caused the emergence of stress signals in the 1970s; (ii) why did mortality signals disappear from the scene in the 1980s; and (iii) what caused stress signals to reappear in the 1990s? For this purpose we turn to Tables 14.6 to 14.9, which refer to the four states of the millet zone in alphabetical order, that is, Gujarat, Karnataka, Maharashtra and Rajasthan. The first column in each of these tables gives the calendar year. Columns 1 and 2 give the number of mortality peaks in the de-trended ASMR data for males and females respectively. An asterisk put against a calendar year (in column 3) indicates that this year has come out as a year of stress according to the indexation method. The last three columns of each table give the fertility data, while the fourth column from the left gives the fertility signals derived from the de-trended fertility data (in the manner explained in the relevant note to Table 14.3).

The remaining columns report on two factors qualifying as possible proximate causes of increased stress signals. These are, first of all, droughts and secondly, inflationary pressure as indicated by either an increase in the Consumer Price Index for Agricultural Labourers (CPIAL) or a decline in real wages. Droughts are either total or partial.[13] If all the agro-climatic zones of a particular state suffer, then it is a total drought. If only some suffer then it is a partial drought. Column 5 gives year-to-year variations in the CPIAL based on the agricultural year, that is, July $(t-1)$ to June (t). An analysis of the data presented in Tables 14.3 to 14.9 points to a change in

Table 14.6 Drought and the fertility index: Gujarat

	Peaks[a]		Stress[b]	Real[c] wage	CPIAL[d]	Drought	Fertility indicators		
	M	F					CBR (R)	TFR (R)	TFR (R+U)
Year	1	2	3	4	5	6	7	8a	8b	8c
1970	7	6		1.57	1.70	6.1		43.2	6.1	5.8
1971	4	6		1.78	1.73	1.4	Partial	41.5	5.9	5.6
1972	8	6		1.86	1.83	6.1	Total	41.8	6.0	5.6
1973	7	9	W*	1.45	2.25	22.9		37.1	5.3	4.9
1974	5	6		1.41	2.46	9.4	Total	40.0	5.7	5.4
1975	11	11	WA*	1.17	3.19	29.6		38.9	5.5	5.1
1976	10	10		1.62	2.91	−9.0		39.0	5.5	5.2
1977	10	8		2.20	2.66	8.6	?	37.8	5.2	4.8
1978	10	5		2.02	2.85	7.3	?	37.4	5.2	4.8
1979	6	5		2.15	2.87	0.6	?	36.0	4.9	4.6
1980	6	3		1.98	3.22	12.2		37.1	5.0	4.7
1981	6	8		1.90	3.56	10.5	?	36.1	4.6	4.3
1982	4	6		1.84	3.97	11.7	Total	35.6	4.6	4.2
1983	8	7		2.12	4.07	2.5		35.2	4.5	4.2
1984	6	5		2.29	4.51	11.0	Partial	34.6	4.2	4.0
1985	6	8		2.69	4.68	3.8	Partial	33.8	4.2	3.9
1986	5	3		2.53	5.18	10.6	Total	32.9	4.0	3.8
1987	2	4		2.57	5.30	2.4	Total	31.6	3.8	3.6
1988	12	11	A*	2.19	5.97	12.6	?	30.1	3.6	3.4
1989	5	11		2.47	6.15	3.1		29.6	3.9	3.6
1990	7	6		2.40	6.63	7.8		30.2	3.5	3.4
1991	7	4		2.38	7.42	11.8	?	28.2	3.2	3.1
1992	10	9	WA*	2.28	9.22	24.3	?	29.5	3.4	3.2
1993	11	7		2.46	9.94	7.8		29.1	3.3	3.2
1994	8	8		2.53	10.46	5.3		28.5	3.3	3.1
1995	4	1		2.54				27.9	3.4	3.2

Notes:

[a] Number of positive deviations from mortality trend across age groups 1–14 – male and female.

[b] Stars are put against years that show up as signals of biological stress according to the indexing methods of calculating mortality and fertility peaks. An asterisk * indicates a complete signal. An asterisk together with a 'W' indicates a weak signal while an 'A' indicates an incomplete signal.

[c] *Source:* Özler, Datt and Ravallion (1996), updated by Abhijit Sen. Real wages are given for the agricultural year (July–June) for base year 1960–61. Since mortality will come (if at all) *after* declines in purchasing power, the real wage for the agricultural year 1969/70 is given in the row for 1970 in this table, and so on.

[d] Consumer price index for agricultural labourers, base year 1960/61. Column 4 gives the CPIAL for the agricultural year July $t-1$–June t against calendar year t. Column 5 gives the per cent change in the CPIAL over the previous year.

Table 14.7 Drought and the fertility index: Karnataka[a]

							Fertility indicators		
	Peaks		Real				CBR	TFR	TFR
	M	F	Stress	wage	CPIAL	Drought	(R)	(R)	(R + U)
Year	1	2	3	4	5	6	7	8a	8b	8c
1970	–	–		1.32	1.77	−2.8				
1971	6	2		1.31	1.88	6.2		34.6	4.8	4.4
1972	7	11	W*	1.35	1.92	2.5	Partial	32.8	4.5	4.3
1973	8	11		1.21	2.18	13.4		30.1	4.2	3.9
1974	6	3		1.18	2.75	26.3	?	29.5	4.0	3.7
1975	9	7	A*	0.99	3.44	25.0		29.7	4.1	3.7
1976	7	8	WA*	1.23	3.21	−6.7	Partial	31.1	4.0	3.8
1977	8	6		1.51	3.09	−3.8		27.2	3.8	3.6
1978	11	10		1.67	3.08	−0.3		30.2	4.1	3.8
1979	7	3		1.70	2.93	−5.0	?	29.0	3.9	3.6
1980	3	6		1.59	3.35	14.5	?	28.9	3.8	3.5
1981	2	5		1.42	3.98	18.9		29.2	3.8	3.6
1982	4	4		1.17	4.65	16.7	Partial	28.8	3.8	3.6
1983	7	1		1.41	4.55	−2.2		30.2	4.0	3.7
1984	9	6		1.37	5.25	15.4		30.9	4.0	3.8
1985	3	5		1.35	5.41	3.1	Partial	30.9	3.9	3.6
1986	3	5		1.76	5.50	1.7	Partial	29.9	3.7	3.5
1987	2	3		1.66	5.57	1.3		29.9	3.7	3.4
1988	4	5		1.61	6.18	11.1		30.1	3.7	3.4
1989	8	4		1.85	7.39	19.5	?	29.1	3.5	3.3
1990	3	5		2.01	7.59	2.7	Partial	29.0	3.5	3.2
1991	13	11	A*	1.95	8.07	6.4	?	27.9	3.3	3.1
1992	10	11	A*	1.69	10.10	25.2	?	27.4	3.1	2.9
1993	5	8		1.45	11.44	13.2	?	26.7	3.1	2.9
1994	11	10		2.05	11.05	−3.4		26.0	3.1	2.8
1995	7	13		1.81				25.1	2.9	2.7

Note: [a] See notes to Table 14.6.
Source: Author's estimates.

Equity, employment and environment

Table 14.8   Drought and the fertility index: Maharashtra[a]

| | Peaks | | | Real | | | | Fertility indicators | | |
	M	F	Stress	wage	CPIAL		Drought	CBR (R)	TFR (R)	TFR (R+U)
Year	1	2	3	4	5	6	7	8a	8b	8c
1970	6	4		1.55	1.83	3.6		32.1	4.5	4.4
1971	4	3		1.48	1.92	4.8	Partial	33.7	4.9	4.6
1972	10	8	A*	1.43	2.07	7.8	Partial	33.5	4.8	4.5
1973	9	12	W*	1.19	2.44	17.6		28.9	4.2	3.9
1974	9	7		1.14	2.77	13.4	Partial	29.1	4.1	4.1
1975	8	7		0.95	3.65	31.8		29.9	4.3	4.3
1976	8	4		0.98	3.48	4.6		30.1	4.2	3.9
1977	13	11	A*	1.10	3.10	−11.0	Partial	26.8	3.5	3.4
1978	6	7		1.15	3.20	3.5		27.6	3.7	3.5
1979	8	5		1.31	3.16	−1.5		28.3	3.8	3.5
1980	5	7		1.27	3.62	14.6		30.9	4.0	3.7
1981	4	9		1.16	4.05	11.9	Partial	30.4	4.0	3.6
1982	2	1		1.13	4.59	13.4		31.3	4.1	3.8
1983	3	3		1.36	4.56	−0.7		31.4	4.2	3.7
1984	7	5	WA*	1.58	5.17	13.5	Partial	32.1	4.1	3.8
1985	6	1		1.82	5.21	0.7	Partial	29.8	3.8	3.5
1986	9	4		1.86	5.43	4.3	Partial	31.7	4.0	3.6
1987	4	5		1.68	5.81	6.9	Partial	30.2	3.7	3.5
1988	9	6		1.68	6.33	9.0		31.4	3.9	3.5
1989	5	2		1.69	7.06	11.5	?	30.6	3.6	3.4
1990	4	4		2.09	7.48	6.0	?	29.5	3.6	3.2
1991	12	11	*	2.23	8.01	7.1	?	28.0	3.4	3.0
1992	6	11	WA*	1.90	10.68	33.3	?	27.4	3.3	2.9
1993	4	7		1.19	11.06	3.5	?	27.1	3.2	2.9
1994	10	10		2.40	10.67	−3.5		26.9	3.2	2.9
1995	9	8		2.37				26.0	3.3	2.9

Note: [a] See notes to Table 14.6.
Source: Author's estimates.

Table 14.9 Drought and the fertility index: Rajasthan[a]

	Peaks			Real wage	CPIAL	Drought	Fertility indicators		
	M	F	Stress				CBR (R)	TFR (R)	TFR (R + U)
Year	1	2	3	4	5	6	7	8a	8b	8c
1970	–	–		2.08	1.96	7.3				
1971	–	–		2.13	1.73	−11.4				
1972	7	10	A*	2.21	1.76	1.4	Total	43.5	6.4	6.3
1973	6	8	*	1.88	2.28	29.4		39.4	5.8	5.6
1974	5	3		1.87	2.84	24.9	Partial	37.8	5.6	5.4
1975	7	7		1.52	3.69	30.0		38.1	5.6	5.4
1976	6	5	W*	1.93	2.92	−21.1	?	34.7	5.1	4.9
1977	7	7		2.52	2.78	−4.7		35.0	5.2	5.0
1978	6	7		2.43	3.27	17.5		36.7	5.3	5.1
1979	4	5		2.39	3.17	−3.0	Total	36.0	5.3	5.2
1980	4	5		2.27	3.61	14.2		39.7	5.8	5.6
1981	11	9	WA*	2.24	4.25	17.6	?	38.3	5.5	5.2
1982	6	3		2.49	4.60	8.1	Total	39.3	5.6	5.3
1983	8	8		2.54	4.47	−2.7	Total!	41.5	6.2	5.9
1984	7	10	W*	2.61	4.73	5.7	?	40.8	6.0	5.7
1985	9	10		2.41	5.25	11.1	?	41.1	5.8	5.5
1986	5	4		2.05	5.97	13.7	Total	37.9	5.3	5.0
1987	7	6		2.50	5.65	−5.3	Total	36.3	5.0	4.8
1988	12	12	*	2.97	6.64	17.5		34.4	4.8	4.5
1989	3	9		2.53	7.37	11.0		35.4	5.0	4.7
1990	5	3		2.40	7.77	5.4	?	34.7	4.8	4.5
1991	4	8	W*	2.41	8.85	14.0		36.0	4.9	4.6
1992	5	8	WA*	2.55	10.30	16.3	?	36.4	4.8	4.5
1993	6	4		2.46	10.57	2.6	?	35.5	4.7	4.5
1994	9	5		2.27	12.35	16.8		35.2	4.8	4.5
1995	6	6		2.30				34.8	4.7	4.4

Note: [a] See notes to Table 14.6.
Source: Author's estimates.

the nature of the causes leading to biological stress. For this we turn to the next section.

6. OLD AND NEW CAUSES OF BIOLOGICAL STRESS

In the first half of the 1970s, stress signals clearly correlate with droughts (see Tables 14.6 to 14.9). In Gujarat, years of stress signals (1973 and 1975) followed years of total drought (1972 and 1974). In Karnataka, complete and incomplete signals of biological stress showed up in two years (1972 and 1973) following a partial drought in 1972. In Maharashtra, stress signals appeared in 1972 and 1973 after partial droughts in 1971 and 1972. A complete and strong signal appeared in 1977 as well – again a year of partial drought. In Rajasthan, a year of total drought (1972) gives stress signals in 1972 and 1973 (see Tables 14.3 to 14.4).

Remarkably, the absence of stress signals in the 1980s goes hand in hand with both droughts and inflationary years (see Tables 14.6 to 14.9). Droughts show up in three out of the four states (in different combinations) in the years 1982–87 while 1986 was a drought year for all states. Yet, only Rajasthan gives signals in 1984 and 1985 – and these are incomplete, too. The explanation for the absence of complete stress signals may lie in the relief works which were mounted in these states in response to the drought. This is the period, which started in 1974, during which temporary relief works and, later, the 'target group' approach to poverty eradication, gave a *de facto* floor to agricultural wages.[14] This explains the absence of mortality signals in this period. Due to a *de facto* floor to entitlement, life-risk was averted, although, judging from fertility signals and heightened infant and child mortality in some years, hardships persisted. The phase of 'slump famines' of the early 1970s induced by natural causes like droughts gave way to a new phase marked by FI signals unaccompanied by adult male and female ASMR signals. This *de facto* floor to entitlement was, however, very fragile. As soon as state governments curtailed expenditure under the SAPs in 1991, the floor caved in (Roy, 1997; Sen, 1996), and the mortality signal reappeared. It came first in Maharashtra and Karnataka which had a temporary shortfall in the production of millet; then it appeared in Gujarat and Rajasthan.

For the 1990s, a basic question demanding an answer is whether stress signals have remained related to droughts, which was the classic pattern of 'slump famines' in the early 1970s (as well as in the earlier decades of the century), or whether there are other causative factors. State-level millet production figures do indicate dips in output and acreage in 1991/92. However, meteorological data indicate that a 'natural cause' for this decline, such as inadequate rains or a move into sub-marginal land of low productivity, was surely absent in those years. It may then be concluded that a slump in overall agricultural activity was not the primal feature of the 1991/92 stress condition. We therefore have to look for other explanatory factors.

It may be added in this context that apart from the four states under consideration in this chapter, populous states like Uttar Pradesh, Madhya Pradesh and Andhra Pradesh gave mortality signals in 1992 as well. FGT poverty indices rose also in two states of the rice zone: Tamil Nadu and Kerala. Although 'pockets' and tracts of semi-arid land are surely present in these states, none of the five states mentioned experienced severe droughts in the 1990s. This suggests that more pervasive forces, other than slumps in agricultural production, were at work. We would like to point out that three factors may be operating: (1) a reallocation of agricultural activity away from millets, which are the staple food of the poor; (2) inflationary pressure; and (3) effort intensification.

It is to be noted that the 1990s were marked by an overall decline in coarse cereal production in the millet zone. Table 14.10 shows that coarse cereal output growth has been negative in Gujarat, Maharashtra and Rajasthan in the 1990s. The main cause of this has been the fall in area under coarse cereals. Only in Karnataka has coarse cereal output growth been positive, despite a fall in acreage. This fall in acreage under coarse cereals does not represent an overall decline in agricultural production but rather a shift in production away from coarse cereals since, as Table 14.10 shows, gross cropped area registered a modest increase in the 1990s in Gujarat, Karnataka and Rajasthan, while being stagnant in Maharashtra. This decline in the local availability of the staple food of the poor may have been one of the factors behind the mortality and fertility stress signals in the years 1991, 1992, 1994 and 1995. In other words, 'boom famines' may have to be brought in as an explanatory factor (Thamarajakshi, 1997). The change in the cropping pattern in the 1990s coincides with drastic changes in the agricultural policy regime (including international trade policy) which improved incentives for commercial (exportable) crops. We may add here that exports of millet rose very sharply in this time period, with Haryana emerging as one of the main exporting states (Gupta, 1996b). This raises the question of whether the policy changes under the structural adjustment programme could have been (at least in part) responsible for the cropping pattern changes recorded in Table 14.10.

To what extent 'boom famines' are related to inflationary pressure is still an open question. Tables 14.6 to 14.9 present data on the CPIAL as well as real wages. However, a clear relation between these factors, as indicators of the purchasing power of the poor, and mortality does not emerge from our

Table 14.10 Foodgrain production in the millet zone – 1970–71 to 1997–98[a,b,c]

	Gujarat					Karnataka				
			Coarse cereals					Coarse cereals		
	GCA	FGA	A	Y	P	GCA	FGA	A	Y	P
1972/73–1980/81	0.7	−0.1	−2.7	4.4	1.6	0.3	0.7	0.2	1.5	1.7
1980/81–1990/91	−0.2	−0.3	−1.0	0.1	−0.9	0.9	0.0	−0.2	0.9	0.6
1990/91–1995/96	0.7	−2.1	−4.6	2.7	−2.0	0.2	−0.6	−1.5	4.8	3.2

	Maharashtra					Rajasthan				
			Coarse cereals					Coarse cereals		
	GCA	FGA	A	Y	P	GCA	FGA	A	Y	P
1972/73–1980/81	0.8	1.4	2.1	6.4	8.5	0.7	−0.2	−0.9	−2.0	−2.8
1980/81–1990/91	0.7	0.0	0.2	2.0	1.8	0.7	−0.2	0.2	4.8	5.0
1990/91–1995/96	0.0	−0.7	−1.3	1.1	−0.2	0.8	0.6	−2.1	−1.4	−3.4

Notes:
[a] Explanation of symbols: GCA stands for gross cropped area; FGA is gross cropped area under foodgrains; A is area; Y is yield per hectare; P is production (P = A*Y).
[b] Figures in the table are average annual growth rates between year t_0 and t_1 where t_0 and t_1 are five-year averages with, respectively, t_0 and t_1 as the middle observation.
[c] The high yield and production growth rates recorded in Maharashtra in the period 1972/73–1980/81 is due to the low base levels in the period 1970/71–1974/75, caused by drought conditions.

Source: Area and Production of Principal Crops in India (various issues), Directorate of Economics and Statistics, Ministry of Agriculture, Government of India, New Delhi.

data. Regression of mortality data on real wages and a time trend do reveal a negative relation between the two, at least for the three states of Gujarat, Karnataka and Maharashtra, but the relation is not significant. It would be too early to conclude, on the basis of these tentative regressions based on relatively aggregative data, that the familiar relationship between price-cum-wage fluctuations on the one hand and short-term mortality fluctuations on the other has disappeared. Even if it has disappeared, this would call for an explanation. A delinking of wage–price–mortality would be understandable for the 1980s from our description of the floor to real wages provided by the target approach to poverty. For the 1990s it would still require explanation.

Finally, with the onset and continuation of the so-called 'structural adjustment programme' launched in 1991, we are witnessing a process of effort intensification. We see that labour networks expand in response to regional conditions of stress, and circulatory migration increases. In addition, we witness an increased casualization of labour. This means that the costs of search for labour, in terms of money and time as well as extra calories spent, have increased tremendously (Sen, 1996; Roy, 1997; Gupta, 1996a). On the other hand, given the low wages obtained by migratory workers within India, and in contrast to international migration such as in the case of Kerala, this migratory labour does not bring in great financial relief. Casualized and migratory labour thus bear the cost of decreased local employment opportunities and households dependent on them will also undergo the stress.

7. CONCLUSION

Biological stress signals, that is, the simultaneous occurrence of heightened mortality and lowered fertility rates, are traditionally relegated to the field of epidemiology, and not considered relevant for the study of poverty. This chapter argues that biological stress can be relevant for the study of poverty, particularly so in the current phase of India's development, which represents a break in the nature of the causes of poverty.

The pattern of stress signals derived from data on male and female mortality and fertility rates for the period 1970–95 points to a change in the causes of biological stress. In the 1970s, we observe a close alignment of biological stress signals and increased poverty. Biological stress in the 1970s correlates with droughts which, by causing price rises and thereby real wage losses, led to entitlement failure and short-term mortality peaks. This relationship between price-cum-wage fluctuations on the one hand and short-term mortality fluctuations on the other disappeared in the 1980s. We propose that the absence of biological stress signals in most of the 1980s, despite the occurrence of droughts, is due to effective public intervention in the form of either relief works or the target group approach to poverty. These measures succeeded in providing a *de facto* floor to food consumption. Poverty (which is measured in terms of monetary expenditure) does go up but biological stress is contained. In the 1990s, biological stress is difficult to explain in terms of droughts (which were absent) or a real wage fall. Two other possible causes of biological stress are highlighted, that is, the reallocation of agricultural activity away from millets, and effort intensification. Both may be related to India's new economic policies which started in 1991. The change in agricultural cropping pattern may show up in increased poverty as well as biological stress. Effort intensification, however, which need not lead to lower employment or wages but does result in increased costs in terms of money, effort and extra calories spent, is likely to show up in biological stress but need not show up in increased poverty. It is yet to be explored what kind of biological indices are capable of adequately reflecting both the poverty and the physical stress of the labouring masses working under the currently evolving institutional arrangements, though pioneering research work has started (Drèze and Sen, 1989, pp. 177–8).

NOTES

1. The squared poverty gap index developed by Foster, Greer and Thorbecke (1984) is defined as:

$$[P_\lambda = (1/N)\Sigma_i^n[(y^* - y_i)/y^*]^\lambda; \quad y_i < y^*, \lambda \geq 0,]$$

where y^* is the poverty line, N is the total population of which n persons are poor, and y_i is per capita income. The λ can be viewed as a measure of poverty aversion: the higher λ, the greater the weight given to the poorest person. When $\lambda = 0$, P_0 becomes the headcount ratio, that is, n/N. When $\lambda = 1$, P_1 becomes the poverty gap measure, that is, $(1/N)\Sigma_i^n[(y^* - y_i)/y^*]$. And when $\lambda = 2$, P_2 is the distributionally sensitive squared poverty gap measure. If the distance $(y^* - y^{**})$, where y^{**} is the mean of the income distribution of the poor, does not remain constant over time, then the three FGT indices give different sorts of information and the choice between them becomes a problem. Focusing either on the trend of $(y^* - y^{**})$ or on the trend of the distribution of the poor around y^* as indicated by second or higher order moments, P_2 and so on becomes a politically sensitive issue (Ravallion, 1998; Sen, 1997).

2. We may quote Murray et al. (1992) in this connection to emphasize that the role of communicable diseases comes out as twice as important as other causes for rural men in India and China in 1988. Maternal diseases come as the second killer for women. The Chinese rural pattern and the Indian Sample Registration Survey (rural cum urban) pattern correspond well in this respect; old health hazards still dominate the mortality scene. It is thus safe to assume that the 'food–nutrition–endemic-ill-health' syndrome, which comes under the rubric of 'problems of poverty in the health sector', is most important in the context of our analysis. Dyson (1991a,b) emphasized the role of the malaria epidemic as the most immediate cause for the Berar famine mortality in the late nineteenth century. He has thus underplayed the role of starvation, that is, 'gaps' in regular caloric

intake, as the cause of heightened mortality. Zurbrigg (1992, 1994) argues that the history of malaria in the Punjab (1868–1940) cannot be understood without reference to 'gaps' in periods of starvation preceding the onset of the epidemic disease.

3. I here refer to the transition in adult mortality rates – targeted variables like infant and child mortality demand a separate explanatory model.

4. This paper discusses situations of short-term entitlement failure, which occur despite opposing trend factors. Notably: (a) there is a slowly rising trend in per capita food crop production in almost all major states of India; (b) there is a matching rising trend in the real wages of agricultural casual labour; (c) in spite of the 'labour-sink' phenomenon in the agricultural sector, there is rural diversification of employment; and (d) there is increased availability of food through private trade as well as through the public distribution system, although there is risk aversion and thus price bias in grain trade (Barrett, 1996).

5. It can be shown with the help of National Sample Survey data that, to date, men and women of this subcontinent are differentially 'responsible' for two different reproduction schemes. Men are entitled to rewards for being responsible for 'work' and thus keeping the material reproduction scheme going. Women are responsible for keeping the biological reproduction scheme going and thus are not 'primary workers'. If we analyse a set of three dualities, that is, the duality of primary versus secondary worker, the duality of labour market exchange versus household (reciprocity mode) work and the duality of ownership rights to the material means of production versus usufruct rights only, then we can see that the first claim of higher entitlement as a primary worker, busy in the labour market, and free to own, are men and men only. Agarwal (1994) may be cited. This note summarizes earlier work by the present author (Chakravarty, 1991). Stephan Klasen (1996) has shown that even in sub-Saharan Africa, where an anti-female bias did not show up in anthropometric measures of children, first surveyed by Svedberg (1990), the oppressive nature of the three dualities is now showing up in higher mortality rates for females as compared with those for males. Klasen mentions six explanatory factors, which can easily be fitted into the scheme of dualities discussed above.

6. The very poor need a consumption loan or grant if the period of stress extends beyond three months. Since the traditional 'lean season' in Indian agriculture does not extend beyond a couple of months in the monsoon-dependent agroclimatic tracts, we may take three months as the traditionally institutionalized period of consumption loans. If the period of biological stress extends beyond this, then there are mortality signals (Dev and Ranade, 1998).

7. Bhat and Preston (1984) accept the reliability of mortality data as generated by the SRS. The coverage of the sample for males (all-India) was found to be 93 per cent as against the census data for 1971–81. For females, however, the use of ASMR data may be questioned because age reporting in India is known to be particularly faulty for females. Therefore, female mortality data will be used only to supplement male mortality data.

8. We have been careful in scrutinizing the data and have used the 'cohort effect of grouped data' only as an extra explanatory factor, that is, not the main factor. For example, an age cohort $(x+4)$ in period t may suffer and lose some members due to stress in this period and carry forward other members, some of whom are morbid and also near the upper end of the age limit. Thus, a heightened mortality at t in age group 25–29 may get carried forward to $(t+1)$ in age group 30–34. The degree of correlation between heightened values of mortality in two adjacent groups is high in the middle age group for the millet zone. The time taken to adjust to lower values of mortality, that is, the adjustment lag, may be interpreted in one of the following two ways. One works through the inner composition of the age cohort $(x+4)$, as far as the health status of new entrants is concerned, the other works through changing weights of sub-samples of the poor and the non-poor within the age group.

9. The trend is estimated as the linear function $E_{it} = c_i + \alpha_i * T$ where E_{it} is the estimated trend value of mortality of age group i in year t, c_i is a constant, α_i stands for the regression coefficient and T is a time variable. The regression results for each age group are reported in the bottom three rows of Table 14.1.

10. We explained in section 4 why it is important to keep incomplete signals of stress in the picture. The data of Rajasthan, for the three consecutive years of 1986, 1987 and 1988, are cases in point, the first two years being years of total drought when stress signals did not appear but came in full force in 1988 (see the figures on Rajasthan, Table 14.4).
11. We have considered only female infants and female children since they have been found to be more vulnerable to crisis mortality when there is food shortage. This has been the historical pattern (Maharatna, 1996b).
12. During 1991–95 the FI signal remained linked to the mortality signal if de-trended data are used; if we use the indexation method the link is less clear.
13. Original meteorological data were supplied by the director of the Meteorological Division, Dr S.R. Sikka. Dr Sikka's article on Rajasthan is separately mentioned in the bibliography (Sikka, 1997).
14. There is exhaustive official literature on various 'public works' programmes. For unofficial, but exhaustive research work, one may consult Dev (1996), Dev et al. (1994) and Dev and Ranade (1998).

REFERENCES

Agarwal, D. (1994), *A field of one's own: Gender and land rights in South Asia*, Delhi: Oxford University Press.
Barrett, C.B. (1996), 'Urban bias in price risk: The geography of food price distributions in low-income economies', *Journal of Development Studies*, **32**(6), 830–49.
Bhat, P.M. and S.H. Preston (1984), 'New evidence on fertility and mortality trends in India', *Population and Development Review*, **10**(3), 481–503.
Breman, J. (1996), *Footloose labour: Working in India's informal economy*, Cambridge: Cambridge University Press.
Chakravarty, L. (1991), 'Agrarian economics and demographic regimes in India, 1951–81, in J. Breman and S. Mundle (eds), *Rural Transformation in Asia*, Delhi: Oxford University Press, pp. 338–401.
Dasgupta, P.S. (1993), *An inquiry into well-Being and destitution*, Oxford: Clarendon Press.
Datt, G. (1997), 'Poverty in India and Indian states: An update', *mimeo*, Washington D.C.: International Food Policy Institute.
Dev, S.M. (1996), 'Food security: PDS versus EGS, a tale of states', *Economic and Political Weekly*, **31**(27).
Dev, S.M., K.S. Parikh and M. Suryanarayana (1994), *India*, in M. Quibria.
Dev, S.M. and A. Ranade (1998), 'Rising food prices and rural poverty', *Economic and Political Weekly*, **33**(39).
Drèze, J. and A. Sen (1989), *Hunger and public action*, Oxford: Clarendon Press.
Drèze, J., A. Sen and A. Hussain (eds) (1995), *The political economy of hunger: Selected essays*, Oxford: Clarendon Press.
Dyson, T. (1991a), 'On the demography of South-Asian famines, Part I', *Population Studies*, **45**(1).
Dyson, T. (1991b), 'On the demography of South-Asian famines, Part II', *Population Studies*, **45**(2).
Fogel, R.W. (1992), *Second thoughts on the European escape from hunger: Famines, chronic malnutrition and mortality rates*, Oxford: Clarendon Press.
Fogel, R.W. (1994), *The relevance of Malthus for the study of mortality today: Long-run influences on health, mortality, labour force participation and population*

growth, Oxford: Oxford University Press.

Foster, J., J. Greer and E. Thorbecke (1984), 'A class of decomposable poverty measures', *Econometrica*, **52**(3), 761–6.

Gupta, S.P. (1996a), *Recent economic reforms in India and their impact on the poor and vulnerable sections of society*, Delhi: Sage.

Gupta, V.N. (1996b), 'A raw deal for coarse cereals', *The Economic Times*, 20 April.

Klasen, S. (1996), 'Nutrition, health and mortality in Sub-Saharan Africa – Is there a gender bias?', *Journal of Development Studies*, **32**(6), 913–32.

Maharatna, A. (1996a), *The demography of famines: An Indian historical perspective*, Delhi: Oxford University Press.

Maharatna, A. (1996b), 'Infant and child mortality during famines in late 19th and early 20th century India', *Economic and Political Weekly*, **31**(27), 1774–83.

McKeown, T. (1978), 'Fertility, mortality and cause of death: An examination of issues related to the modern rise of population', *Population Studies*, **33**.

Murray, C., J.G. Yang and X. Qiao (1992), *Adult mortality: Levels, patterns and causes*, Oxford: Oxford University Press.

Özler, B., G. Datt and M. Ravallion (1996), 'Database on poverty and growth in India', *mimeo*, Policy Research Department, World Bank, Washington, D.C.

Quibria, M. (ed.) (1994), *Rural poverty in developing Asia, vol. I*, Manilla: Asian Development Bank.

Ravallion, M. (1998), 'Reform, food prices and poverty in India', *Economic and Political Weekly*, **33**(1), 29–36.

Roy, S. (1997), 'Globalisation, structural change and poverty: conceptual and policy issues', *Economic and Political Weekly*, **32**(33–34).

Sen, A. (1996), 'Economic reforms, employment and poverty – Trends and options', *Economic and Political Weekly*, **31**(35–37), 2459–77.

Sen, A. (1997), *Structural adjustment and rural poverty: Variables that really matter*, Delhi: Vikas Publishing House, pp. 78–109.

Sikka, D. (1997), 'Desert climate and its dynamics', *Current Science*, **72**(1).

Svedberg, P. (1990), 'Undernutrition in Sub-Saharan Africa: Is there a gender bias?', *Journal of Development Studies*, **26**(3), 469–86.

Tendulkar, S.D. and L. Jain (1995), 'Economic reforms and poverty', *Economic and Political Weekly*, **30**(23).

Thamarajakshi, R. (1997), 'Economic reforms and state intervention in foodgrain markets', *Economic and Political Weekly*, **32**(30).

World Bank (1998), *Reducing poverty in India – Options for more effective public services*, Country Study, World Bank, Washington D.C.

Zurbrigg, S. (1992), 'Hunger and epidemic malaria in Punjab (1868–1940)', *Economic and Political Weekly*, **27**(4).

Zurbrigg, S. (1994), 'Recent insights into the role of hunger in the history of health', *mimeo*, presented at the Centre for Health Studies, York University, Toronto on 29 March.

APPENDIX

Table 14A1.1   Adult male mortality peaks – all-India and millet zone[a]

Year	All-India		Gujarat		Karnataka		Maharashtra		Rajasthan	
	1a	1b (2.7)	2a	2b (6.4)	3a	3b (6.3)	4a	4b (6.6)	5a	5b (7.0)
1970	3	1.2	7	6.5	–	–	6	6.3	–	–
1971	2	0.6	4	1.4	6	7.9	4	4.1	–	–
1972	12	5.3	8	5.6	7	5.7	10	10.9	7	8.0
1973	6	2.7	7	5.2	8	10.2	9	9.6	6	4.2
1974	5	1.6	5	5.8	6	5.2	9	8.4	5	6.4
1975	10	7.3	11	8.5	9	11.4	9	4.6	7	7.9
1976	12	11.1	10	8.1	7	8.4	8	7.2	6	13.0
1977	10	4.8	10	5.7	8	13.1	13	14.4	7	12.5
1978	13	5.5	10	10.1	11	13.7	6	10.2	6	2.9
1979	1	0.3	6	6.9	7	3.4	8	6.3	4	3.8
1980	2	1.0	6	7.4	3	1.9	5	2.8	4	7.7
1981	3	0.6	6	8.0	2	0.3	4	3.1	11	14.5
1982	1	0.1	4	2.2	4	2.1	2	0.9	6	1.7
1983	4	0.6	8	6.2	7	6.1	3	2.1	8	3.9
1984	9	3.1	6	9.4	9	4.9	8	5.4	7	6.9
1985	11	3.2	6	4.5	2	2.2	6	7.0	9	7.3
1986	5	1.5	5	2.2	3	1.8	8	6.2	5	5.9
1987	3	0.5	2	0.7	2	1.6	4	2.5	7	5.1
1988	6	1.6	12	19.5	4	1.3	9	9.7	12	17.8
1989	5	0.6	5	4.1	8	7.4	5	3.9	3	3.3
1990	4	0.7	7	6.2	4	1.4	4	6.3	5	4.0
1991	12	4.5	7	3.6	13	10.1	12	9.9	4	5.2
1992	11	3.3	10	7.0	10	9.4	6	5.0	5	7.1
1993	6	1.4	11	13.1	5	6.0	4	1.7	6	5.6
1994	10	3.5	8	7.5	12	11.9	9	7.2	9	6.3
1995	9	3.0	4	1.9	9	9.4	9	16.4	6	6.3

Note:
[a] Entries in columns (a) give the number of mortality peaks for the year concerned. Entries in columns (b) report on the annual amplitude of the mortality peaks or the average per cent deviation from trend in the year concerned, computed as $\Sigma_1^{14}[100*((V_i - T_i)/T_i/14]$ where V stands for the entry in column (b), T for the estimated trend value and the subscript i indicates the age group. The average deviation from trend for each column (that is, the average of each (b) column) is given at the top of the (b) column concerned.

Table 14A1.2   Adult female mortality peaks – all-India and millet zone[a]

Year	All-India		Gujarat		Karnataka		Maharashtra		Rajasthan	
	1a	1b (3.1)	2a	2b (6.7)	3a	3b (7.4)	4a	4b (7.5)	5a	5b (8.1)
1970	3	0.6	6	7.4	–	–	4	4.5	–	–
1971	3	0.5	6	5.4	2	0.8	3	3.3	–	–
1972	14	13.9	6	2.8	11	17.8	8	9.8	10	13.9
1973	12	3.7	9	13.5	11	13.8	12	18.5	8	12.9
1974	4	2.0	6	3.6	3	3.4	7	9.1	3	1.6
1975	13	10.3	11	11.3	7	10.5	7	8.7	7	7.9
1976	5	2.5	10	12.4	8	10.7	4	2.2	5	7.4
1977	10	6.7	8	9.8	6	8.8	11	17.5	7	5.0
1978	8	3.6	5	5.1	10	14.8	7	13.8	7	7.0
1979	2	0.2	5	5.2	3	4.7	5	7.2	5	5.0
1980	1	0.1	3	3.3	6	3.5	7	7.7	5	6.0
1981	5	0.7	8	5.3	5	6.5	9	9.8	9	11.6
1982	0	0.0	6	7.2	4	2.2	1	0.3	3	3.3
1983	1	0.0	7	5.2	1	0.2	3	2.3	8	8.6
1984	11	4.7	5	2.5	6	2.8	5	6.2	10	11.2
1985	10	2.8	8	7.1	5	4.4	1	0.1	10	12.8
1986	4	0.6	3	2.5	5	6.1	4	2.6	4	3.6
1987	1	0.1	4	1.4	3	1.0	5	3.2	6	2.1
1988	9	2.7	11	13.8	6	4.4	6	2.4	12	17.0
1989	3	0.5	11	8.3	4	3.1	2	1.9	9	8.7
1990	5	1.0	6	5.6	5	3.2	4	4.4	3	2.0
1991	6	3.0	4	3.9	11	12.7	11	12.2	8	7.0
1992	14	9.2	9	14.9	11	14.3	11	20.1	8	14.2
1993	8	2.9	7	9.2	8	12.3	7	7.8	4	4.4
1994	10	4.9	8	8.8	10	10.0	10	8.8	5	17.2
1995	9	2.8	1	0.0	13	11.8	8	11.7	6	3.8

Note:
[a] Entries in columns (a) give the number of mortality peaks for the year concerned. Entries in columns (b) report on the annual amplitude of the mortality peaks or the average per cent deviation from trend in the year concerned, computed as $\Sigma_1^{14}[100*((V_i - T_i)/14]$ where V stands for the entry in column (b), T for the estimated trend value and the subscript i indicates the age group. The average deviation from trend for each column (that is, the average of each (b) column) is given at the top of the (b) column concerned.

15. Small is big, but is it still beautiful? Small-scale industries: An India–China dialogue
Ashwani Saith

1. SMALL-SCALE INDUSTRIES: A GOOD PRESS

There are many virtues, imagined or real, ascribed to small-scale industrialization. Some of these are admitted by default on the assumption that small enterprises would inherently be different and have characteristics opposite to large-scale enterprises. Chernobyl, the Bhopal gas tragedy and the giant oil-spills all tend to affirm such a reading. Small has thus been conflated with being employment-friendly, environment-friendly and hinterland-friendly, or simply people-friendly. Small is big, but is small still beautiful? There are indications, in the case of small-scale industries in Asia, that small has grown to be strong, and not so pretty. The small-scale sector has been a major contributor to Asian economic growth, and nowhere more so than in China, where township and village enterprises (TVEs) have posted the highest sectoral growth rates ever since the reforms initiated in 1978, and probably even before then. While macroeconomic performance in India has lagged behind China by far, here as well the small-scale sector has generally outstripped the large-scale organized formal manufacturing sector in the matter of growth, employment and exports. This chapter offers a comparative assessment of the factors underlying the contrasting performances of the two emerging Asian economic giants, and highlights key outstanding policy issues that are likely to occupy the foreground. The main focus is on the Indian case, with the Chinese experience introduced selectively for comparison.

2. STARTING TOGETHER

China and India shared broadly similar structural terrain at the outset of their modern development phase; initial orientations in the early plans had similar aspirations; but while the Chinese route to the market went through two decades of dramatic systemic transformation, the Indian one has displayed greater institutional continuities usually acting as constraints. Both economies had significant problems of mass poverty and acute regional disparities at the start. Both launched programmes of accelerated industrialization favouring large-scale heavy industries, but both had inserted special programmes for rural industrialization into the national strategy in view of the limited employment capacity of this driver, and also to take the burden of producing consumer goods for the masses off the agenda of the modern sector. Thus small-scale industrialization had a corrective orientation towards employment, and distributional and regional disparities from the outset. Both have had market-friendly reforms introduced around the same time, though in the Chinese case the break with the past was more definitive and unfolded in a controlled sequence. Both had managed to develop their human capital base and social infrastructure; while India performed well with regard to higher education levels, however, it lagged behind on other scores. And both share a challenging global economic environment combining challenges, opportunities and threats, in negotiating which both have involved their overseas, non-resident communities.

But there are major differences to register as well: Chinese growth has been much faster, more sustained, more egalitarian. Part of the reasons underlying this is the fact that the two economies were cast in contrasting institutional frameworks: while China leveraged fast growth through a combination of a strong state and collectivist institutions, in India inegalitarian institutional structures and slower fitful growth were set off against the intrinsic merits that reside in democratic polity. From the point of view of small-scale industrialization, these factors had an important role to play, since simultaneous agricultural growth within an egalitarian environment was highly conducive to laying a broad base for this sector. The rural collectivist framework allowed, indeed required, the conversion of traditional rural crafts and domestic industries into cooperatives, and this laid the basis for their subsequent modernization. It is worth noting that the small-scale industrial sector was far more homogenous and that subsequent growth did not have the effect of displacing the so-called inferior-goods industries through competitive processes. In the Indian case, modern industrialization has had the side-effect of displacing a less competitive part of the small-scale, rural or household sectors.

3. THE INDIAN POLICY CONJUNCTURE

In terms of political economy, Indian economic policy towards the small-scale industrial sector has had to negotiate a path between four influences.

The Gandhian undercurrent is still perceptible and can be invoked expeditiously in favour of protecting the village and khadi industries sector. This is evident when attempts are made to overturn the framework installed by the second influence, namely that of the Nehru–Mahalanobis strategy in which the cottage industries sector was made the beneficiary of market reservation in order to augment the employment generating capacity of the national plans that tended to favour the capital-intensive large industrial sector. The third takes the form of the current free market-oriented approach which has to contend with these two influences. But even as their potency wanes, governments, seeking re-election by popular mandate, find it difficult to ride roughshod over populist demands for government support and protection. In this regard, China presents a diagonal opposite, in that economic as well as institutional policies do not have to meet this often debilitating criterion.

The Nehru–Mahalanobis era of planning has yielded in discrete stages to that of economic reforms. But just as the first was far from being a fully planned centrally controlled system, the latter isn't quite a fully market-led set-up either. There are several shifts to note. First, the overall orientation is much more export-friendly. But the same positive stance to the open economy also opens the doors to competitive imports, including those in a significant range of items produced previously by the small-scale sector under a protective shelter. It is worth noting that the timing of the change in the macroeconomic policy environment coincides with new global tendencies towards the relative deindustrialization (in terms of manufacturing) of the traditional industrial bases in the North and West, and a relative reindustrialization of parts of the third-world periphery. The reverse trend – compared with that observable in the mainstream industrialization process – undoubtedly opens up opportunities and spaces for some developing economies to exploit.

Second, there is a clear policy in favour of increased de-reservation and removing quotas, and this also exposes India's small-scale sector to competition from domestic sources. At the same time, the lifting or raising of restrictive ceilings could allow some small-scale industry of the units to grow rapidly. This is a significant first step on a long road. The policy of reservation in favour of the small-scale or rural industrial sector has been operational since April 1967. The first notification covered 47 items for reservation for exclusive manufacture in the small-scale sector; within a decade, the number of items had risen to 836 (in April 1978), where it has since stabilized. (*Small-Scale Industry Expert Committee Report*, 1997, p. A–3, Table 1). These items covered 25 per cent of the output of the small-scale industries sector in the First SIDO Census of 1972, and 28 per cent in the Second Census of 1987–88. The *Vijayraghavan Advisory Committee*

Report on Reservation (1996) recommended that 95 products should be de-reserved, and that the status of another 63 be amended. Prominent among the reasons cited are the facts that these items could not be produced within the specified investment ceiling of Rs 6 million; that higher investments were necessary to take advantage of technical innovations; on grounds of safety and hygiene; 'in order to meet the changed demand of consumers for quality goods'; and to exploit the potential for exports. Put together, these reasons suggest that one element in the reservation for the small-scale industrial sector was the 'ghettoization' of that sector. Following the *Abid Hussain Report*, another 15 items were de-reserved in April 1997 (*Economic Survey*, 1997–98, p. 109); and the ceilings for investment were raised five-fold from Rs 6 million to Rs 30 million. Apart from the need to ease these constraints on scale of operations, the *SSEEC Report* (1997) makes two pertinent observations: first, that 'the fundamental difficulty with reservation as an instrument of policy is that it does not discriminate between production units on the basis of their efficiency – current or potential' (II–7); and second, that 'state policy for small-scale industry stressed protection of fledgling enterprises against predatory competition from large companies. There was excessive emphasis on small-enterprises being in competition with the large; . . . new policies being designed to support small scale enterprises must encourage . . . inter-dependence' (VI–1).

Third, corrections to factor price distortions should in principle favour the labour-intensive sector by removing subsidization of capital. On the other hand, this would also make capital and credit that much more expensive for the small-scale sector. Fourth, there is a strong intention to encourage public–private partnerships, say through using public seed capital funds to encourage private investments in small-scale enterprises. On available information it is difficult to assess to what extent this 'new' element goes beyond the linguistic, since there have always been such 'partnerships' in one form or another. Likewise, the policy package of supply-side interventions in support of the small-scale industrial sector, while making several adjustments, largely retains a familiar look, with emphasis on access to capital, technical support and marketing being prioritized. The institutional framework within which support is delivered takes the form of a plethora of official organizations and agencies, many charged with overlapping functions, reporting variously to several ministries that might only loosely coordinate action between them. It is arguable that the maze of bureaucracy that has developed around the state-supported and protected programme might well have now become a burden, rather than a benefit to the ultimate objectives of the strategy; there could be the potential for some severe rationalization of administrative structures in this area. Some initiatives announced recently within the context of the new National Programme for Rural Industrialization (NPRI) are discussed later.

The overall strategy also has components that are targeted on specific constituencies such as the rural poor. In the context of rural industries, two such elements are significant. The first is the support given to rural non-farm activities as conduits for reaching the poor; and second, the use made of the broader instrument of targeting backward regions, where the densities of poverty are noticeably higher. The former primarily takes three forms: the employment schemes for the rural poor; training and skill creation programmes for youth (such as TRYSEM); and Integrated Rural Development Programme schemes which provide credit for asset creation for the rural poor. None of these programmes focuses on directly rural industry as such, but rather on the constituencies of the rural population that rural industrialization strategies are intended to assist; they constitute alternative forms of support. The difficulty with such a linkage to poverty alleviation is that it can undermine the commercial viability of the investments that come to be viewed as socially legitimized transfer payments. These and other effects add up to a complex whole, and the overall outcome of the new policy impulses will need to be monitored and continually assessed.

4.   THE TIRUPUR TEXTILES CLUSTER: A MICROCOSMIC ENCAPSULATION OF SUCCESS AND FAILURE

Some key preoccupations and blind spots, and the aspirations and constraints, of current policies can be better comprehended and assessed through tracking the evolution of one such dynamic cluster – the Tirupur small-scale industrial cluster specializing in textile products largely for the export market.

Tirupur, in Tamil Nadu, provides a spectacular illustration of an export-oriented growth centre constituted as an industrial cluster. It has a long history, with the first ginning mill starting up in 1911. By 1951, there were 35 knitting mills, 12 ginning mills and another 23 units dyeing, bleaching or printing cloth; two decades later, these numbers had multiplied to 415, 38 and 87 respectively; by 1991, these had galloped to 2800, 77 and 575 units. Thus Tirupur, with a population of approximately half a million persons, has developed into a major textiles-related production cluster. Growth has been maintained since: thus the number of dyeing and bleaching units – a source of environmental concern – had risen from 450 in 1991 to 866 in March 1997, most of these being in the small-scale and cottage industries sector. This remarkable expansion has been export-driven: between 1990–91 and 1995–96, exports of textile fabrics and manufactures including ready-made garments grew annually at about 31 per cent per annum in dollar terms. Over this period, Tirupur's share of all Indian exports of cotton hosiery rose from an astonishing 40 per cent to about 50 per cent in volume or value terms.

This success story has a multi-faceted policy significance. First, however reluctantly, it has to be acknowledged that an enabling base or space for success was provided and protected by the market and demand reservation measures that were the hallmark of the Indian policy regime with respect to the small-scale sector; while many large-scale units in the industry contracted assorted forms of industrial sickness under this regime, the small sector benefited. It will therefore be revealing to monitor future progress under open market, competitive conditions as such reservationist measures begin to be dismantled. Second, the case provides a prime example in support of the policy-thinking favouring clustering as a desirable, prototypical organizational form for small-scale industrial development. The proximate reasons cited for the success would be the local availability of raw materials, of cheap and skilled labour, of good road and rail connections to major towns and markets, and favourable climate and water 'that gives lustre to the clothes' (as reported by the Tirupur Exporters' Association (Shankar et al.,1998b, p. 8)). Underlying the success are more complex factors which fall under the new label of 'collective efficiency', which denotes a set of interweaving conditions and circumstances which enhance the dynamic growth capability of the cluster as a whole through simultaneously encouraging intra-cluster competitive and cooperative interactions, focusing especially on information sharing, cost-reduction and market-oriented innovation. Third, it has been emphasized, rightly, that this is an organic and spontaneously evolving process, and that the successful outcome on view in Tirupur is highly path-dependent. This is especially relevant in the current policy context in favour of small-scale industrial clusters. The question arises whether such successes can be created and assembled from scratch through policy intervention, that is, whether it is possible to distil a formula of supply-side interventions which could replicate such dynamic industrial forms. Not surprisingly, there are differences of opinion in this regard. For instance, a significant feature has been the matching evolution of an enabling institutional environment which provides a creative interface between local entrepreneurs, government agencies, clients and other parties. Over time, the emergence and joint performance of various collective players has been vital; this includes the Tirupur Dyers' Association, Tirupur Exporters' Association, Apparel Promotion Council, South India Textile Research Association and Tamil

Nadu Industrial Development Corporation, and other banking and financial agencies. Fourth, the recent spurt in its growth rates has been interpreted by some as confirmation of the importance of the macroeconomic policy environment as a key input in influencing the success of such clusters, balancing the view that the necessary and sufficient factors explaining success were embedded in the internal constitution and behaviour of the cluster itself.

4.1 Success for some, but not for all: the untold environmental story

However, no success is without its underside. Clusters concentrate and intensify the visibility of effects. The success of Tirupur is set in sharp relief, but so is the extent of the environmental damage it has caused, the cost and consequences of which it has passed on, until quite recently, to the local population. The evidence on the scale of the impact is sobering. The Tirupur area has no provision for the collection, treatment or disposal of the sewage and other municipal effluents, and the usual practice is that these are deposited into water bodies or on the land mass. Two pollution indicators were estimated for 1997–98: the per capita contribution of bio-chemical oxygen demand (BOD) from sewage was estimated at 45 grams per day; and that for per capita chlorine contribution was 6 grams per day. Comparing these with the effluent flows generated by the bleaching and dyeing units in Tirupur, the study found that these units produced an impact which was equivalent to that produced by 80 per cent of the Tirupur population for BOD factor, and equivalent to a staggering 70 times the Tirupur population with respect to the chlorine factor. Local groups contended that the untreated effluents endangered aquatic life and were carcinogenic; that the water in the two local rivers and nearby wells had been rendered undrinkable; and that the slurries discharged from the units were deposited in the local dam, which had effectively become a storage tank for such effluents, making the water unsuitable even for irrigation (Shankar et. al., 1998b, p. 68). An investigation of electrical conductivity values in a sample of 60 borewells in municipal areas of Tirupur town revealed that the level (in us/cm) was below the tolerance limit of 2250 for irrigation in only one sample; and below the 'injurious' level of 3000 in only another 3 cases. In 23 borewells, it was in the 3000–6000 range, in 15 between 6000 and 10000, and in 20 cases the value was above 10000. For another sample of 30 borewells in the industrial areas, again the value was below the permissible limit in just 1, with 20 cases showing levels in excess of 10000. There is also evidence that the quality of well water deteriorated over the 1990–95 period.

4.2   Do problems induce solutions? Public action and institutional change

Paradoxically, this disastrous negative externality, usually not explicitly factored into the narrative of Tirupur's success, also provides further evidence of dynamism of a different kind. It provides an important example of the public and legal interaction between the narrow economic process and its profit-seeking players, and the wider group of social actors and stakeholders who suffer the negative external environmental effects. The Tamil Nadu Pollution Control Board specifies identical source-specific standards for pollution for dyeing and bleaching units regardless of their scale of operation. The smaller ones usually had no effluent treatment facilities for lack of land, finance and professional expertise. But there was also little pressure to internalize the costs of this externality, since until the acceleration of growth in the 1980s the cumulative effects were not acutely visible. The relevant tolerance limits for pollutants were thus only laid down in 1984, and then not implemented for lack of political interest. The argument underlying this inaction was that 'these units have made significant contributions to production, exports, employment and income generation in the Tirupur area. In fact, the hosiery industry in Tirupur was applauded as a model of export-oriented industrial development based largely on private initiative. Hence government agencies and industrial circles felt that rigorous enforcement of the standards might cripple the growth of the industry' (Shankar et al., 1998b, p. 71). However, pressure from public action, in the form of public interest litigation and legal actions leading to directions from the Green Bench of the Madras High Court, altered the balance of opinion and prioritization. Units which were not served by an individual or a common effluent treatment plant were ordered to be closed down, and 114 units out of a total of 866 actually went out of operation. Effective pressure also came in the form of the real threat the non-compliance with environmental standards was beginning to pose to the export success itself, as various trading partners begin to place restrictions on such imports that do not meet their stringent requirements. Thus Germany does not permit the import of fabric using azo dyes, and textile exports are confronted with the need to attain levels necessary for ISO 14001 certification and other appropriate forms of eco-labelling. Governmental initiatives have supported this environmental transitional process through technical back-up, facilitation and through substantial capital subsidies on the setting up of common effluent treatment plants (CETPs).

Such a transition can also be lauded as a welcome sign of successful public action – ranging from the international to the local – to pressurize industry and government to factor in the costs of pollution. Indeed, analysts have treated this as a basis for arguing that the organizational form of the industrial cluster strongly exhibits the very desirable characteristic of 'collective efficiency' (Schmitz and Nadvi, 1998). To the other network-ing and intra-cluster advantages of inter-unit learning and interdepen-dence is added the ability to exploit the economies of scale in the matter of shared effluent treatment plants. A few qualifications might be appro-priate. For one, while it is true that 8 CETPs covered as many as 288 units, as many as 464 units had individual plants, suggesting that collective action wasn't critical in the majority of the members of the cluster anyway. And such collective efficiency was demonstrated only under acute pres-sure, which would question its conflation with a sense of social awareness and responsibility. Further, there is no information on whether the envi-ronmental norms are actually being maintained in the operation of these facilities, since all evidence has thus far focused on the installation of the treatment plants.

From a public or social perspective, the bottom line to the environmen-tal story is a particularly dismaying one. Detailed analysis reveals that for the CETPs, the pollution abatement cost is as little as 0.5 per cent of sales revenue for the largest sharing units, and no more than 1.3 per cent of sales for the smallest units. For the IETPs, the corresponding range is 0.4 and 0.9 per cent of sales. This is a remarkably low figure and suggests that these costs are readily bearable by large and small units without any perceptible economic dislocation. When viewed against the massive cumulative envi-ronmental damage caused by the earlier policy of indifference, these figures provide the dimensions of the implications of market failure, especially when coupled with state failure.

5. STRENGTH AS WEAKNESS: THE QUALITY OF EMPLOYMENT

To some, the source of the competitive strength of the small-scale indus-trial sector is also its Achilles' heel. This sector usually falls outside the purview of labour laws and codes of practice. It can therefore compete effectively in labour-intensive products, and indeed large-scale enterprises often enter into sub-contracting relationships precisely to exploit this advantage, or in simpler terms, to exploit its labour. The small-scale indus-trial sector is not a good employer, and arguments in its favour that rest on its capacity to generate employment need to be tempered with legitimate concerns over the quality of such work. Policy debates over the latter have focused on the link, for instance, between child labour and education, but the fact that child labour is overwhelmingly located in this sector has somehow not been highlighted. In general, there are five types of problems here; most of these are blatantly visible in the Indian scenario, and are beginning to emerge in the Chinese one:

1. The terms of employment are sub-standard: low wages, often below legal minimum levels; irregular pay; arbitrary deductions; long hours of work; little, if any, and usually unpaid, holiday time; no benefits in terms of pensions or other provident funds; no sickness leave; no maternity leave; no unemployment insurance; no skill development programmes other than learning on the job; virtually no job security; no written formal contracts.
2. Extremely rudimentary working conditions involving serious health hazards, risk of injury, and discomfort; crowded unhygienic work premises, exposure to various forms of pollution.
3. More than any other part of the economy, this sector is characterized by a high incidence of vulnerable categories of labour, for example female and child labour.
4. Workers suffer from non-representation in the matter of rights and their enforcement, and have little access to legal redress.
5. There are serious long-term hidden costs which are being passed on to the workers: the shortening of the span of a healthy working life; the loss of earning capabilities on account of accidents and injury and so on; and the shutting off of more rewarding life opportunities for children who are excluded from the schooling and education process.

In some industries, this quality dimension has been made very visible through the new orientation of the international trade regime, and also by the rights-driven non-governmental organizations (NGOs) which have made this cause their own, as in the case of child labour in the carpet export industry. The problem, however, is extremely widespread and questions the foundational premises of the small-and-beautiful paradigm. Thus, Burra (1995) and Anker et al. (1998) provide evidence of the incidence of child labour and the specific hazards children are exposed to in several major small-scale industrial clusters, namely the glass industry in Firozabad, lock-making in Aligarh (see Box 15.1), gem-polishing in Jaipur, the Khurja potteries, and the brassware industry of Moradabad. Other major cases include: diamond-cutting, slate-making, powerloom textiles, cotton hosiery, carpet-weaving, match-making, silk and silk products, brocade and *zari*, brick kilns, handicrafts, *beedi* and very many others; all this excludes the domestic and services sector where the incidence of child work is also high. The case of Tirupur, a dynamic export-oriented small-scale industrial cluster increasingly cited as a success story was considered in the previous section, highlighting the untold story of environmental disaster.

Box 15.1   Locked in: Child labour in a traditional lock-making small-scale industrial cluster

There is unmistakable evidence that the jobs of polishing on buffing machines, electroplating and spray painting are injurious to the health of workers, whether adults or children. Polishers inhale emery powder and metal dust and they work in such crammed spaces that workers frequently get injured because pieces of metal hit them. Working in electroplating units for children means that they have to keep their hands in solutions of dangerous chemicals like potassium cyanide for long periods, and die when the universal curiosity of children to taste anything new, in this case these foul liquids, seizes them. Children in spray painting units inhale unacceptably large doses of paint and paint thinners leading to severe chest disorders. Breathlessness, fever, tuberculosis, bronchitis, asthma and pneumoconiosis are some of the symptoms and diseases that affect the children of the lock industry. Malnutrition and poverty combine to exacerbate the ill-effects of their working conditions and considerably shorten their lives. The most telling evidence of the hazards involved in polishing, electroplating and spray painting is found in the fact that no unit employer employs his own children in any of these processes. The other processes of the lock industry do not seem to be hazardous in themselves for the health of children. But children working on hand-presses do lose the tips of their fingers when fatigue blunts their senses.

(Burra, 1995, pp. 77–8)

It needs also to be recorded that Tirupur has been estimated to have one-third of its work force drawn from the ranks of children.

There are several rights-related issues here. The first concerns the conditions and terms of work; the other more fundamental one concerns the child's right to education; the third is whether child labour should exist at all, this arising from a perceived conflict between child labour and the child's right to some notion of childhood; and the question of learning to listen to the voices of children. There is an increasing acceptance of the idea that the elimination of child labour should be viewed within a non-negotiable rights-led perspective on development. The counter-issue has always been posed in the form of the likely impact on the incomes of the poor household using child labour, and also at a national level on the loss of industrial competitiveness and opportunities. The former issue has been addressed in precept and at the level of a successful prototypical (but now much replicated) NGO intervention (Sinha, 2000; Wazir, 2000). Relatedly,

Anker et al. (1998, p. 13) argue that the elimination of child labour would only cause a small increase in the cost of production – usually no more than 5 per cent. This is hardly astronomical, and would appear to be quite capable of being absorbed within the system without undue loss of competitiveness. However, if such cost increases could not be passed on, they could eat significantly into the profits of the loom owner in the carpet industry, thereby invoking his opposition to any such intervention. In contrast, the cost increase for the foreign consumer is no more than 2 per cent, and hence a very comfortable price to pay for opposing child labour. While the situation differs considerably across different industries, and while the eventual outcome can only be estimated as a counterfactual via a simplified model, these estimates do provide a political-economy basis for expecting such issues to remain contentious and difficult to resolve over the foreseeable future. Over the same period, it should be expected that pressures for the elimination of child labour are likely to intensify. This situation will concern India significantly, and China virtually not at all. In China, children are increasingly dropping out of school and entering the labour force, mostly within the household economy in order to release an adult to migrate or to take on some external economic activity. But such rates are still low, and outright child labour on a hired, waged basis is virtually absent. India stands at the other end of this scale, with small-scale industries, very often the ones heavily engaged in export-oriented production, strongly implicated in this unsavoury dimension of the labour market.

6.   A NEW INDIAN POLICY INITIATIVE: CLUSTER DEVELOPMENT

It is arguable that the arrival of coalition politics in India is likely to undermine confidence in the willingness or ability of successive governments with different hues to maintain a straight course with regard to economic reforms and other economic policies. However, on a positive note, the recent pronouncements of the last government suggest that there might be a strong area of implicit agreement in policy orientation across a broad section of the current political spectrum. The budget speech of the last Finance Minister included a bold policy statement on rural industrialization (see Box 15.2). Indeed, it went beyond the usual litanous platitudes uttered periodically by politicians in their mandatory public avowals of adherence to Gandhian precepts. It remains to be seen if the new government will pick up and run with this initiative, or whether it will find it a misfit in its own economic policy package.

The new, or revised, policy regime declares itself strongly in favour of

---

Box 15.2   National Programme for Rural Industrialization (NPRI)

Rural Industrialization is important for creating employment opportunities, raising rural incomes and strengthening agriculture–industry linkages. Thus far it has been pursued by a multiplicity of government agencies. However, the impact of these programmes at the grass-roots level has remained modest. We must integrate the efforts of the various government agencies and ensure active community participation. Accordingly, I propose a National Programme for Rural Industrialization (NPRI) with the mission to set up 100 rural clusters every year to give a boost to rural industrialization. This is being done for the benefit of rural artisans and unemployed youth. In the long run, it will reduce rural–urban disparities. The Small Industry Development Organization will coordinate this programme. The Khadi and Village Industries Commission (KVIC) will play an important role in this. The marketing infrastructure available with KVIC would be put to optimum use in this effort. It will go a long way in the marketing of rural industrial products if KVIC could develop its own brand name for the purpose. The proposed rural clusters will spread throughout the country, with a reasonable balance between high potential and backward rural areas.

Extract from speech of Shri Yashwant Sinha, Finance Minister,
Government of India, 27 February 1999

---

using the industrial clusters as an effective means for promoting small-scale industrialization. If only there could be enough Tirupurs! One recent report inventorizes 138 industrial clusters in the country as a whole. The fresh policy announcement regarding the new NPRI calls for a hundred *new* clusters to be set up annually. There is a guarded indication that the inherent weakness of traditional village industries is recognized, that the focus is to shift from protecting these to promoting the new dynamic forms within a policy of decentralized industrial production systems based on the operative principle of flexible specialization, exploiting economies of scale and generating collective efficiency within an unprotected open market environment.

However, that small-scale industrialization was still being viewed, at least partially, as an instrument for meeting social developmental objectives directly, is signalled by the central importance given to the role of the proposed NPRI in the strategy for employment creation. The Khadi Village Industries Commission (KVIC) has launched a rural employment generation programme (REGP) with a target of creating 2 million jobs by the terminal year of the Ninth Plan.[1] The emphasis in the REGP is for the setting up of 'viable industries based on bankable projects', and the intention is to achieve through this the other target set by the Union Finance Minister for initiating 100 rural clusters every year under the NPRI. The total expenditure envisaged for the NPRI is about Rs 10 billion, to be spent on infrastructure and programmes.

Thus, one can elicit three targets: 2 million new, sustainable jobs; 100 rural industrial clusters per year adding up to 500 over the plan period; and Rs 10 billion of total governmental expenditure. This implies an expenditure of Rs 20 million per cluster; and the generation of 4000 jobs per cluster; involving a governmental outlay of Rs 5000 per job created. On average, this also implies something like one rural industrial cluster per district. On available information, it is not possible to sketch the form or shape of these clusters. Even assuming that the idea of setting up rural industries under KVIC translates into units which are small in scale, the average number of units within a cluster could vary widely. Using the average for the entire non-factory sector, the average unit is seen to employ 2.07 workers; for the Directory of Manufacturing Establishments (DME) non-factory enterprises, the average is 10.31 workers; for the non-DME non-factory enterprises, the average is 1.56 workers; and for the own-account establishments, the average number of workers per unit is 1.78. For small-scale industry in the factory sector, the average employment per unit is 32.01 workers; for the factory sector in all enterprises, the average is 75.40.[2] On this basis, assuming alternatives of 2 or 5 workers per establishment, the number of units per cluster would, on average, be 2000 or 800. Such a cluster, if spatially concentrated and demarcated, is clearly a very large entity. Even if the parameters are adjusted considerably, the planned clusters are likely to comprise several hundred units each.

One synthetic vision of the organizational and institutional framework within which the NPRI could, would or should be embedded can be constructed from the pronouncements of different stakeholders. The Finance Minister noted in his speech that 'thus far it [that is, rural industrialization] has been pursued by a multiplicity of government agencies. However, the impact of these programmes at the grass-roots level has remained modest. We must integrate the efforts of the various government agencies and ensure active community participation.' The Union Minister for industries followed up to call for the simultaneous involvement of the district industrial centres (DICs), NGOs, self-help groups, regional rural banks and state finance corporations in the implementation of the REGP (which could be viewed as another incarnation of the NPRI). Taking this further, the chairman of KVIC has argued that 'if the funds available for rural industry programmes with the central agencies like KVIC, Central Social Welfare

Board, CAPART, DST, SIDBI, NABARD and other departments are only clubbed together as a well-coordinated and integrated programme at an appropriate level, the net impact could be much more than it is today.' Not surprisingly, he calls for KVIC to be made the nucleus of the programme; alternatively a National Commission for Rural Industrialization could be created. A National Institute for Rural Industrialization could also be set up in Wardha and its regional centres located in the various Institutes of Technology and the Institutes of Management across the country.[3] More specifically, to ensure higher levels of productivity and quality of rural industrial products, a National Coordinated Project on Scientific and Technological Inputs for Rural Industrialization Programme should be initiated involving DST, CSIR, AICTE, CAPART and KVIC. Further, KVIC itself would set up a new national rural industries marketing corporation to introduce branding and quality control.[4] It would appear that whether or not a single speech has the power eventually to launch a thousand clusters, it might in the meantime provide the basis of setting up half a dozen new official agencies, bodies, institutes, commissions or programmes. This is paradoxical, if not quixotic, in the face of the Finance Minister's argument in relation to the unproductive impact in the past of 'a multiplicity of government agencies'. It might also be a sobering exercise to tot up the unproductive recurrent expenditures involved in the running of these suggested bodies, let alone the outlays for creating the infrastructure in which they and their functionaries would need to be ensconced. Clearly bureaucracy is alive and well, and up to its usual expansionary games.

There are two important respects in which the programme opens new trajectories. The first of these is institutional and pertains to the integration of the diverse official and semi-official bodies with a functional role in rural industrialization under one umbrella or label. Such a development could be considered at both macro and micro levels. At the latter, the need would be to create an integrated one-window service to cater to the needs of rural industries at the district level and below. This initiative was taken in the late 1970s in the form of the DIC, and hence what might be necessary could be to revitalize these Centres and make them dynamic, proactive and responsive to problem solving in the local domain. Part of this function would also be for the DICs to act as the critical point on the interface, or as a conduit between higher level specialized agencies involved in various aspects of rural industrialization programmes, and the ultimate intended beneficiaries or targets of these services and resources, namely the rural industrial producers and units. It is here that the macro-level institutional aspect kicks in. This concerns the announced intention of integrating the diverse national-level bodies into a unified national rural industrial industrialization programme. To the extent that this could provide an effective one-stop integrated umbrella service organization, one might envisage gains in administrative and operational efficiency. However, there remains the possibility that the proposed reform might simply add yet another layer of bureaucracy without rationalizing the structure. In the best outcome, a leaner and more focused national organization could provide the backstopping point for DICs.

The second point of departure concerns the introduction of the device of industrial clusters in the context of rural industrialization. This could be potentially significant in substantive terms. The crucial question here is how the policy instrument of clustering is conceptualized, designed and implemented. Would each cluster be specialized in terms of skills and product lines, and comprise rural industrial units exclusively? Or would the clusters include multi-sized units with some degree of vertical integration? This option would be precluded if entry was limited only to rural units. Is it feasible to think of entire clusters each with a single specialization? The notion of clustering has arisen from such regional concentrations of units – linked or integrated through sub-contracting or cooperative systems on a horizontal or vertical basis – all specializing in a similar range of processes and product lines, usually involving specific skills and inputs. To the extent that the idea of specialization is abandoned, 'clusters' will begin to resemble the earlier organizational form of industrial estates, distinguished now by the fact that they happen to be rural in location. An intermediate position, which might in the end be the one dictated simply by feasibility considerations, would have several specialized clusters all sharing a rural industrial space. (See Box 15.3.)

Box 15.3   Indian rural industrial estates

The industrial estates developed by the government have been plagued by under-utilization due to wrong location. A striking evidence of this can be found in NCAER's survey of rural estates; the share of functioning units was 46 per cent of sheds and plots in Maharashtra; 60 per cent in Karnataka; 47 per cent in Andhra Pradesh; 50 per cent in Tripura and a dismal 22 per cent in Bihar. By contrast, the rate of utilization of urban estates was much better but not entirely satisfactory: 81 per cent in Karnataka, 74 per cent in Haryana, 71 per cent in Andhra Pradesh and 62 per cent in Maharashtra and a depressing 35 per cent in Bihar. Industrial estates developed by the government suffer the consequences of ignoring the overriding importance of agglomeration economies in inducing investment by small- and medium-scale enterprises.

Extracted from *Report of the Expert Committee on Small Enterprises* (draft), 27 January 1997, New Delhi

There remains the question as to whether the clusters are intended to be locational entities or simply networks operating over a broader space, connecting units of specific specializations through a nodal point. Such a cluster would be virtual in nature, in that it would comprise a net of units which would continue to operate *in situ* in their prior, scattered locations. The new element would be the creation of a network, and thus a specialized cluster. In this manner, there could again be multiple clusters in any given geographical space, say a district, all coordinated by the central focal agency, located say in the DIC. This option would not constitute a very radical departure from the existing situation, though it would be assertive to state that DICs operate networks of similarly specialized units functioning within district boundaries.

6.1   Industrial clusters as new institutional space

It is clear that industrial clusters are coming to be viewed as the crucial dynamic form within which to encourage small-scale industrialization. These concentrations are expected to incorporate all things desirable: collective efficiency, flexible specialization, agglomeration economies and optimal forms of horizontal competition as well as cooperation and vertical integration. As argued above, there are justifiable doubts as to whether these clusters can be created by policy fiat, or whether their emergence is the outcome of a long period of organic evolution involving mutations and adaptations in response to opportunities and threats posed by the local and wider environment. However, in one regard, industrial clustering would open up institutional possibilities for addressing the two key issues of the quality of employment and of environmental outcomes. Clusters make such effects concentrated, and also visible. This in turn could both induce and enable countervailing action whether in the form of local public action, through governmental intervention, or some combination of these forces. It also reduces the transaction costs of implementing and monitoring changes to the labour and environmental regimes. Such initiatives are but at a nascent stage in both countries, but the potential for reform is enormous, and it is possible that a few successful cases will set the tone, agenda and pace of such overdue changes.

7.   GROWING APART?

7.1   China

The Chinese TVE sector has experienced explosive growth in the period since the reforms, building creatively on the strong base inherited from the

Table 15.1   The growth of TVE exports in China, 1988–97

Year	1988	1991	1993	1995	1997
TVE exports (US$ billion)	8.02	14.8	38.1	64.5	84.6
TVE % share in total exports	16.9	20.6	41.5	43.3	46.3
Average exchange rate (yuan/$)	3.718	5.327	5.761	8.369	8.270

Note:
TVE exports include direct and indirect exports, including those through sub-contracting with SOEs and foreign companies, and charges on processing for foreign firms.
Source: Perotti et al., (1999), p. 161, Table 2.

previous economic regime. TVEs account for a highly significant proportion of the expansion of industrial output, but an even higher one of employment and exports (see Table 15.1). While growth has been concentrated in the south coastal provinces, there have been considerable spin-offs for the populations of other provinces through the labour market. While this sector grew rapidly under conditions of market protection and inward-oriented development in the collectivist era, it has continued to grow (even accelerated) in the post-reform period when the orientation has been radically shifted in favour of exports.

7.2   Why are NRIs not like OCs?

In explaining China's growth performance, there are five inter-related features that need emphasis. The first is the importance of the TVE sector which has posted a remarkable pace of sustained expansion over the past two decades. The second is the concentration of this growth in the coastal provinces of the country, especially in the south. Third is the very heavy inflow of foreign direct investments, at a rate several times that into India. Fourth is the substantial involvement of the overseas Chinese (OC) business community, especially as sources for this FDI flow. Finally, the fifth feature is the very high growth rate of exports, visible perhaps in sharpest relief with regard to the TVE sector. These factors are all interconnected and underscore the role of the OC community in providing the foreign capital, the entrepreneurial and trading expertise, and also the market outlets for the TVE sector. This raises the question: why hasn't the non-resident Indian community played the same dynamic and catalytic role as the OC community has in the Chinese context?

There are several related factors that could be cited. The overseas Indian communities are dominated relatively more by professionals. They tend to be more oriented towards indirectly made portfolio or secondary market investments, or investments in real estate than in direct involvement. The overseas business community, strong as it is, is embedded in distant systems which lack a wide and vibrant economic interface with the Indian economy. This community is also largely country specific, and operates within such constraints, whereas the OC community in Asia could legitimately be regarded as a cross-border regional network. Further, the OC network is lodged in a region which has itself experienced rapid growth, partly on account of its own contributions. There is also a much higher degree of receptivity on the part of the host country, that is, China, with regard to the initiatives of the OC community. And significantly, FDI in China by OCs enters an economic space that is not already densely populated with competitors, where local rules of the game tend to create moral hazard and risks in the manner that seems to characterize the Indian case. These differences are important in view of the significant linkage between such overseas connections and the possibilities of stimulating modern small-scale industrialization on a revamped policy basis.

8.   TWO SHARED FAILURES

8.1   Persisting regional disparities

The other objective explicitly mentioned in the plan announcement relates to the use of these programmes as a means to reduce regional disparities. The experience of industrial estates is quite unequivocal: strong gravitational pulls exerted by the more advanced regions are likely to account disproportionately for the location of such clusters. Certainly, this would be the outcome should the question of location be resolved by market forces. There is a wide range of evidence of the repeated failure of such locational policies – as agents of reducing regional spreads – across several decades and countries, and there are few grounds to feel optimistic that the present context will prove to be an exception to this robust general finding. Should location be left to spontaneous market forces, there is every reason to believe that such clusters would be found in the developed regions which boast high levels of infrastructural and market development, of high population densities at high levels of per capita income, of high levels of prior industrial and/or agricultural development. A recent study of industrial clusters in India tends to underwrite such a conclusion. Of the 138 industrial clusters identified in India, Andhra Pradesh, Assam, Bihar, Madhya Pradesh and Orissa together accounted for just 7 in all; at the other end, Gujarat, Haryana, Maharashtra and Punjab had as many as 71.[5] It is also useful to note that of the 138 clusters, only 12 were classified as having been induced by policy interventions; and of these 12 only one was located in a rural area. Further, of these 12, 11 were modern small-scale industrial clusters rather than traditional, or artisanal, rural industrial units. The twin implications of this pattern are: first, that left to themselves, rural, artisanal, poorer areas tend to be shunned in terms of location; and second, that even when such clusters are induced by interventions, they tend to follow rather the same profile. It would thus be somewhat unrealistic to expect the new programme to buck this well-established pattern; at least, this must remain arguable until more detailed and specific plans are set out to enable these objectives to be fulfilled.

The Chinese experience of rural industrialization, generally successful as it has been in both pre- and post-reform periods, also confirms this particular failure in an unqualified fashion: in both phases, despite the operation of supportive policies and the existence of a sympathetic policy regime, regional disparities widened alongside rural industrialization. Indeed, the 'walking on two legs' policy of the high collectivist era provided a powerful stimulus for a bootstraps type of local development everywhere. But it soon became evident that the potential for such rural industrial development was itself determined by the level of development of agriculture and modern industry in the region, and for a specific collective its distance from major urban settlements. The rural-industrial sector thus became a source of exacerbating, rather than reducing, regional disparities. The logic has remained unchanged in the post-reform period; only the pace of divergence has accelerated.

8.2 Environment unfriendliness

The second obvious failure is with regard to the environment, and here the greater pace and success of the Chinese TVE sector could only have imposed a higher cost on society. Unfortunately, there are no systematic environmental audits to rely on. It is worth noting that the early successes of the rural industrial sector under the collective system also encountered some serious environmental effects from the promotion of chemical plants at local level. However, there was an institutional response, and such effects that were widespread and could be easily recognized were countered. In the contemporary scene, the two countries are following rather similar trajectories with regard to environmental monitoring and controls though the system is weak and evolving in both. In China, the response of the state is perhaps more direct and forceful, while in India local action and the channels of public interest litigation are more pronounced. Both countries face urgent and arduous tasks in this sphere.

9. CONCLUSION

The small-scale industrial sector might well have had a similar start in life in the Indian and the Chinese economies. But it has grown up very differently, and the specificities of the development and institutional paths of the two countries have provided space and dynamism in the Chinese case which have proven elusive in the Indian economy, despite similar protective attitudes towards this sector in its infancy. But in China it is perhaps now the large-scale sector which is losing out to the small-scale one. The Chinese TVE sector, especially in the coastal belt, has come of age and developed all-round production, innovation, managerial and entrepreneurial capabilities. In India, the passage to maturity is far from complete. New policies will assist this process, but this dynamism is unlikely to be created by policy fiat. Much will depend on the performance of the two major sectors of the economy, since the small-scale industrial sector, at the end of the day, lives partially in a dependency relationship with its bigger siblings.

NOTES

1. It must be assumed that the target applies to a total rate of two million additional jobs on a sustainable basis.
2. The data used here are taken from Table A–1, Chapter IV–28, of the *Report of the Expert Committee on Small Enterprises* (draft), 27 January 1997, New Delhi.
3. The symbolic ideological obeisance appears nominal, but could have had its polemical appeal to a coalition leader wanting to locate his party visibly in Gandhian space. The intention appears to be to (window-)dress the new programme in Gandhian garb.
4. 'Khadi panel unveils rural employment generation plan', *Financial Express*, 8 April 1999.
5. There is very strong positive correlation between the per capita income of the state and the number of clusters in each state normalized by its population. The data for this are derived from Gulati (1996) as reported in the *Report of the Expert Committee on Small Enterprises*, 1997 (A64–A68).

REFERENCES

Anker, R. (1998), 'Overview and Introduction', in R. Anker et al. (eds), *Economics of Child Labour in Hazardous Industries of India*, Baroda: Centre for Operations Research and Training.

Breman, J., P. Kloos and A. Saith (eds) (1997), *The Village in Asia Revisited*, Delhi: Oxford University Press.

Burra, Neera (1995), *Born to Work: Child Labour in India*, Delhi: Oxford University Press.

Cadene, Phillipe and Mark Holmstrom (1998), *Decentralized Production in India: Industrial Districts, Flexible Specialization and Employment*, New Delhi: Sage.

Chadha, G.K. (1996), 'The Industrialization Strategy and Growth of Rural

Industry in India', *SAAT Working Papers*, South Asia Multidisciplinary Advisory Team, June, New Delhi: ILO.

Financial Express (1999), 'Khadi Panel Unveils Rural Employment Generation Plan', 8 April, New Delhi.

Government of India (1996), *Report of the Expert Committee on Small-Scale Sector Reservation* (Vijayraghavan Committee Report), New Delhi: Government of India.

Government of India (1997), *Report of the Expert Committee on Small Enterprises* (Abid Hussain Committee Report), New Delhi: Government of India.

Government of India (1997), *Report of the Expert Committee on Small Enterprises*, draft, 27 January, New Delhi: Government of India.

Gulati, Mukesh (1996), 'Restructuring and Modernization of SME Clusters in India', November, Vienna: UNIDO.

Knorringa, Peter (1998), 'Barriers to Flexible Specialisation in Agra's Footwear Industry', in P. Cadene and M. Holmstrom, 1998.

Perotti, E., Laixiang Sun and Liang Zou (1999), 'State-Owned versus Township and Village Enterprises in China', *Comparative Economic Studies*, **XLI** (2–3), pp. 151–79.

Schmitz, H. and K. Nadvi (eds) (2000), 'Industrial Clusters in Developing Countries', Special Issue, *World Development*, **27** (9).

Shankar et al./MSE/UNDP (1998b), *Economic Analysis of Environmental Problems in Bleaching and Dyeing Units and Suggestions for Policy Action*, draft, New Delhi: Madras School of Economics, Madras and UNDP.

Sinha, Shanta (2000), 'Child Labour and Education', in R. Wazir (ed.), 2000.

SRUTI (1995), *India's Artisans: A Status Report*, Delhi: SRUTI (Society for Rural, Urban and Tribal Initiative).

Wazir, Rekha (ed.) (2000), *The Gender Gap in Basic Education: NGOs as Change Agents*, New Delhi: Sage.

16. The state of development and the environment: Challenges for the new century

Gopal K. Kadekodi

1. INTRODUCTION

In a comprehensive survey of the state of development economics during the past 50 years, Jean Waelbroeck (1998) draws the following important starter for this chapter:

> Development economics has made remarkable progress in the past 50 years. There is greater dominance than formerly by one school of thought, but the range of that school's research has become much broader. ... Gone is the idea that development means industrialization and that the main policy problem is to manage the interface between country and city *(spatial duality?)*. Today development is viewed as an integrated transformation, of which urbanization and industrialization are but two components. ... blind imitation of northern institutions may be counterproductive. ... Gone are the days when policy advice was directed primarily at planners. Policy makers are utility maximizers, too; ... The new thinking is sometimes challenged by criticisms that highlight the somewhat vague concept of governance, according to which the task of economists is to help design a system of interacting state and private institutions that, led by the state, cooperate in achieving social goals. Whether solid theory will come out of this line of thinking remains to be seen. (Waelbroeck (1998), pp. 347–8. Expressions in italics have been added by the author.)

Just as much as Waelbroeck has voiced his concern about the state of development economics, a large number of social and natural scientists have looked at the past and reflected upon it (Drèze and Sen, 1995; Nabli and Nugent, 1989; Daly and Cobb, 1989; Boulding, 1966; Hardin, 1968; Bardhan, 1996; Sen, 1989; Malinvaud, 1992; Wellisz, 1992). In his over 30 years of research on the problems of developing economies, Prof. George Waardenburg persistently noted that the indigenous technology and skills of the local population should set the boundaries of production and consumption and be the guiding principles for the setting up of developmental strategies (Waardenburg,1988; Waardenburg and Lavakave, 1989; and Waardenburg, Adriaansen and Storm, 1989). Many of his views about the present day contradictions and directions for the future of the developing societies prompted me to address this problem from the environmental perspective of the coming century.

Since much has been written about the evolution of the theory of development economics, followed by empirical evidences and justifications (see Chenery and Srinivasan, 1989; Lal, 1992 for a more comprehensive set of papers covering various themes and topics; Kuznets, 1955; Yotopoulos and Nugent, 1976, for instance on empirical evidences), I do not venture to repeat the main conclusions from this literature. Instead I pose the following unstated and not well recognized problem, except among the few, perhaps in the writings of Daly and Cobb (1989), Boulding (1966) and a survey article by Dasgupta and Maler (1989).

If only the classical economists had spelled out that on by 'land' is meant 'environment and natural resource' that has a value and price which is not a gift of nature and which is not boundless, the state of economic theory as well as economic development would have been different.[1] The world would have voiced unitedly to use, develop and preserve all the natural resources in the most sustainable way to enter into the next century. Long ago the Theory of Development Economics would have been called the Theory of Sustainable Economics.

An attempt is made in this chapter to develop this hypothesis. The chapter's organization is as follows. In section 2, a brief review of selected development paradigms and the theories that dealt with them is made. Section 3 goes into the shape of development economics with added dimensions of environmental and natural resources as exclusive precursors. The concept of sustainable development is elaborated here. The last section proposes the future of sustainable economics, both in theory and practice.

2. DEVELOPMENT PARADIGMS

As much as the history of the world, the concept of development is not new. Sen (1989) summarily states it as 'enhancing living conditions'. There is nothing special about developing countries or economies going through a process of development. What makes development economics a subject for discussion is the manner in which the process of development is designed for different countries, including developed ones. Accordingly, the evolution of development economics is always time and space (or location) specific. For instance, Adam Smith's concern was development through free trade and colonization. He was then talking about pre-industrialized developed countries only. More specifically he had England and its colonies in mind. The economic instruments he had advocated were the international division of labour and specialization, vent for surplus, the propagation of a *laisser-faire* economy and colonization outside. Clearly, he did not develop his theory with keeping poverty and income inequality in mind, and he was certainly not worried at all about the depletion of natural resources (all of which were of a concern of the developing countries or colonies). Smith had not visualized the development problems of the world beyond the functioning of the 'market'. This is very clear from his writings quoted below:

> As every individual, therefore, endeavours as much as he can both to employ his capital in the support of domestic industry, and so to direct that industry that its produce may be of the greatest value; every individual necessarily labours to render the annual revenue of the society as great as he can. He generally, indeed, neither intends to promote the public interest, nor knows how much he is promoting it. By preferring the support of domestic to that of foreign industry he intends only his own security; and by directing that industry in such a manner as its produce may be of the greatest value, he intends only his own gain, and he is in this, as in many other cases, led by an invisible hand to promote an end which was no part of his intention. Nor is it always the worse for the society that it was no part of it. By pursuing his own interest he frequently promotes that of the society more effectively than when he really intends to promote it. (Adam Smith (1981 edition) Book IV, Chapter 2, p. 456)

The last sentence of the above quote is very important at this juncture of the beginning of the new century. Certainly, Smith's model of development in today's context does not hold much water for the reason that the externality benefit of individual gain does not automatically add up to the greatest social gain, at least for two reasons. First, not all externality gains or costs are internalized in a market-oriented system (Pigou, 1952 edition). Second, such a social welfare function itself may not exist (Arrow, 1963 edition). However, in the context of development, as argued by Sen (1983), it is not a matter of having a social welfare function under strict dictatorship, but arriving at conscientious decisions on social justice, social harmony, and social security through an economic institution of collective action and majority voting among the communities.[2]

Rather the Physiocrats much before Adam Smith were more concerned about the natural resources of Europe when they concentrated on (sustainable) agriculture rather than industry or manufacturing as the avenue for development. Their prescription is much more relevant for countries such as India and China, a thought to which I will return later on. But it was John Stuart Mill (in 1848) who, in my opinion, first provided a definition on development in a more systematic way. It is useful to read what he wrote then.

> In the leading countries of the world, and in all others as they come within the influence of those leading countries, there is at least one progressive movement which continues with little interruption from year to year and from generation to generation; a progress in wealth; an advancement of what is called material prosperity. ... It will, therefore, be our first object to examine the nature and consequences of this progressive change; the elements which constitute it, and the effects it produces on the various economical facts of which we have been tracing the laws, and especially on wages, profits, rents, values, and prices. (John Stuart Mill (1985 edition), p. 56)

Note that Mill used the expression 'progressive change' for material prosperity instead of accumulation of wealth. Like Smith, Mill was referring to the industrializing European countries in framing his thoughts on development. But, after going through an enquiry of changing economic entities and indicators as mentioned in the quote above, J.S. Mill recognized the limitations to accumulation of wealth due to scarcity of natural resources. That is when he warned the economies about the 'unavoidable stationary state'.

Ricardo (Sraffa, 1951), much before J.S. Mill, was equally concerned about the process of unlimited growth of wealth. He had recognized, in a simplistic way, that the scope for national progress or development is limited due to diminishing returns of land (as a form of natural resource). But Ricardo did not develop a theory of valuing natural resources, as he had relied upon the labour theory of value for determining all values. To quote him:

> The value of a commodity, or the quantity of any other commodity for which it will exchange, depends on the relative quantity of labour which is necessary for its production, and not on the greater or less compensation which is paid for that labour. (David Ricardo, reproduced in Sraffa (1951) p. 11)

Rather, Ricardo only dealt with natural resources as part of his theory of rent to the extent that he emphasized their original and indestructible power (quality of the soil). Where Ricardo misled the world was in his understanding of the boundless nature of natural resources such as air, water and wind being gifts of nature not commanding a price.[3]

With the readings of Adam Smith, the Physiocrats, the Mercantilists, J.S. Mill, Ricardo and many others, one can now twine the logic of development as a process, around country-specific space and time that were referred to by them. However, some of the important doctrines of development should be analysed in more detail. I wish to take up only three of them. They are the theory of the dual economy and development, free trade and development, and income distribution and the growth process.[4]

Take the case of income distribution and growth. Starting from the classical to the neo-classical models of growth, the growth mechanism never ensured a justifiable income distribution.[5] The classical theory of a 'natural price' of labour only ensured that the labour class can subsist and perpetuate itself, without either increase or diminution. The neo-classical models of distribution on the other hand, via the marginal productivity theory of wage determination, did not ensure anything in terms of a just income distribution. In the context of development, an argument is generally made on the lines of the 'trickle-down' theory of growth that can provide betterment in income distribution.[6] But three critical points must be mentioned here. First, there exists a circularity in the argument of the 'trickle-down theory'. To induce growth in such a situation, investment in capital-intensive industrialization is necessary. But increasing capital intensity (say a higher K–L ratio) will lead to greater diversion of income in the form of rent and profits, rather than wages – and hence greater income inequality. This precisely is the criticism on growth models of Solow (1974, 1978) and Kaldor (1963) among others. Second, capital accumulation is possible, according to neo-classical economists, only through a lower interest rate. If the lower discount rate is relevant to induce both growth and a better income distribution, why was the same not applied for maintaining the natural capital intact? This is a point to which I will return later on. Third, there is not sufficient empirical evidence for the view that in the initial phase of economic development it is logical to have a worsening income distribution, which would get corrected by itself in the later phase of development (Kuznets, 1955; Yotopoulous and Nugent, 1976; Scruggs, 1998).[7] As shown in Tables 16.1 to 16.3, most recent cross-section data from India and OECD countries do not suggest anything on the lines of the Kuznets hypothesis. But interestingly enough, recently a similar argument has been put forward relating economic development and the state of environmental degradation (or depletion).[8]

Next consider the theory of development through trade. Purely from the theory of comparative advantage, one should appreciate the strength of this approach to development. I say 'purely', because it is too abstract to apply in reality. There are a number of studies to show the disadvantage in which small developing countries have landed, attributed to the so-called Centre–Periphery or dependency hypothesis (Bardhan, 1966). Secondly, there is also evidence that trade immiserizes growth and income distribution by widening the income disparity between developed and developing countries (Prebisch, 1951; Singer, 1950; and Waelbroeck, 1998). Third, it is now recognized that the assumptions concerning the nature and availability of natural resources underlying conventional trade theory are fallacious. Ricardo had recognized the importance of natural resources in manufacturing, but hastened to say that 'In them nature does nothing, man does

Table 16.1 Poverty, inequality and their linkage with ecology in India

State	Per capita income, 1987–88 (rupees)	Rural poverty (%), 1986–87	Gini inequality index (%)	Theil index (%)	Deforestation between 1972–75 and 1980–82 (%)	Total wasteland as % of area in 1980–82
Orissa	498	56.7	27.3	12.4	18.6	7.41
Bihar	472	53.3	25.0	9.9	11.4	5.80
West Bengal	898	50.8	24.3	11.6	21.7	6.42
Madhya Pradesh	633	49.3	31.4	16.8	16.9	6.58
Maharashtra	1 159	46.5	29.9	15.3	25.3	9.69
Tamil Nadu	915	44.8	30.3	15.2	21.0	7.77
Assam	655	42.3	21.5	7.6	6.2	2.43
Karnataka	776	39.5	28.8	13.6	12.9	8.51
Kerala	607	38.6	30.7	15.3	18.9	14.67
Uttar Pradesh	639	35.0	34.7	20.5	13.9	5.82
Gujarat	853	32.2	30.6	18.9	46.3	16.89
Rajasthan	583	31.7	30.3	15.0	46.9	37.81
Andhra Pradesh	758	27.1	31.0	18.0	17.5	8.91
Jammu and Kashmir	684	27.0	28.1	13.3	35.4	41.48
Haryana	1 233	22.6	29.3	14.0	50.0	7.54
Punjab	1 755	15.3	30.2	15.1	54.5	7.00

Notes:
1. Wasteland is defined as salt affected land + gullied or ravinous land + water logged or marshy land + culturable undulating land with or without scrub + forest blanks + sandy areas + non-culturable wasteland.
2. Gini and Theil indices are on per capita consumption for 1986–87.
Sources: Centre for Monitoring the Indian Economy; Kakwani and Subbarao (1992); and the National Remote Sensing Agency of India.

385

Table 16.2 Income and inequality in OECD countries

Country	Income (US $)	Gini-index	CO_2 (per capita)
Austria	10509	31.4	7.8
Belgium	11109	28.3	12.9
Canada	14133	31.0	18.1
Denmark	11342	31.0	5.3
Finland	10851	30.9	9.0
France	11756	34.9	10.5
Germany	11920	30.6	6.6
Ireland	6823	35.7	7.9
Italy	10323	34.3	6.7
Japan	10072	33.4	7.9
The Netherlands	11284	28.1	11.2
Norway	12141	31.2	7.6
Spain	7390	26.8	12.3
Sweden	12456	32.4	8.8
Switzerland	14301	33.8	12.3
UK	10167	24.9	12.8
USA	15294	35.2	20.9

Sources: World Bank (1992), *World Development Report 1992*; and OECD (1995), *Environmental Data Compendium.*

all'. He treated most of the natural resources as a free gift of nature (and for that matter Marx thought that minerals have no *in situ* value, but have value only to the extent that labour is involved, and otherwise not). Moreover, the effect of exhaustible resources upon the production processes was not understood until Jevons (1965 edition) and Marshall (1949 edition) talked about it much later. The endowments of natural capital are different between the trading countries. In economic theory and practice, there is no agreement on the valuation of them.[9] Unless a unique system of intrinsic valuation for natural resources on a global basis (and not on a location and time-specific scarcity basis) is established, it is difficult to apply any theory of trade to arrive at the optimal use of natural resources. Moreover, the much talked about Heckscher–Ohlin theory of trade, if applied in the context of differing natural resource endowments across countries, implies the immiserization of natural resource-rich countries and various trade-related externality effects in them.[10]

Finally, let me touch upon the theory of dualism and development (Ranis, 1989; Sen, 1966). Considered to be one of the greatest contributions of development economics to the design of industrialization, this theory is

Table 16.3 Correlation coefficients between indicators of sustainability (world scenario)

	Top 35 countries	Middle 35 countries	Bottom 35 countries	All countries	Expected sign	Top 35 countries	Middle 35 countries	Bottom 35 countries	All countries
Per cent change in forest and woodland (1975–77 and 1985–87)	0	0.29	0.01	0.29	+	NA	−0.18	0.03	−0.17
Population density per 1000 ha in 1989	−0.28	−0.23	−0.43	−0.09	+	NA	−0.23	−0.36	−0.21
All forests lost so far (per cent of total area) up to 1990	NA	−0.38	0.04	−0.45	+	NA	−0.03	−0.30	0.06
Per capita consumption of commercial energy (gigajoules) 1987	−0.52	0.79	0.62	0.97	+	NA	−0.42	−0.43	−0.29
Commercial energy consumption per 1980 US $ (kilojoules) 1987	−0.03	0.27	−0.74	0.19	+	NA	−0.43	−0.74	0.03
CO_2 emission per capita (metric tonnes)	0.43	−0.09	0.08	0.37	+	NA	0.18	0.18	0.03
Methane emission per capita (metric tonnes)	0.04	0.12	−0.13	0.54	+	NA	−0.40	−0.37	−0.03
CFC kg, per capita	−0.05	0.71	0.55	0.77	+	NA	−0.20	0.31	−0.26

Notes:
1. The classification from top, middle and bottom countries coincides with the World Bank classification of less, middle and highly developed countries.
2. NA means not obtainable or not relevant.
Source: Calculated from *World Resource 1990*, World Resources.

based on several assumptions. The crucial ones concern the dichotomization of the economy into two productive sectors, such as agriculture and non-agriculture, which have an asymmetry in their production structures (land and labour as inputs in agriculture, capital and labour as inputs in non-agricultural sector); savings coming from the agriculture (as a fuel for growth) but being invested only in the modern non-agricultural sector; and surplus labour in the agricultural sector to be moved to the non-agricultural modern sector without any friction. As much as Sen (1966) has countered the theory, questioning the assumptions (particularly on the definition of surplus labour), the assumption concerning the flow of savings from agriculture to non-agriculture is questionable. But more pertinent is the issue of natural resources, being the necessary complementary input in both agriculture and non-agriculture, which was not dealt with in this dual economy model. There are ecological and other studies to show that the rise in the natural resource use in the modern sector (for example, minerals and fossil fuel), producing such capital goods as tractors, pesticides, inorganic chemicals and so on, goes hand in hand with an increase in use of natural resources by the agricultural sector (for example, extension and intensification of agriculture, marine fishing, aquaculture and so on). One can see the wedge between the two sectors vanishing as soon as the assumption of non-substitutability and non-comparability between the two sectors is removed, the cost of labour relocation in the urban modern sector is accounted for, and natural resources are introduced in the production processes of both the sectors.

3. SUSTAINABLE DEVELOPMENT REPLACING ECONOMIC DEVELOPMENT

If development is concerned with enhancement of living conditions, sustainable development goes beyond that, to ensure no reduction in living conditions for the future generations to come (WCED, 1987). The approaches so far developed to attain such a state of the economy, however, are different, following different schools of thought. Some of the major ones are mentioned here.

Just as growth is said to be possible by replacement or accumulation of capital (Solow, 1974), one school of thought (Pearce and Turner, 1990) argues that sustainable development is possible by *maintaining the natural capital intact*. Clearly then, the choice of technology, flow of capital and social options on population will be different from those under an expanding capital growth-oriented economic development. On the other hand, followers of the neo-classical school argue that both man-made capital and 'controllable resources of services' are to be treated as capital and, applying the standard substitution approach, the use of natural resources can be optimally derived (Herfindahl and Kneese, 1974). Yet another school of thought, the thermo-dynamic school of natural capital, argues that 'to the extent irreversible waste generation in the process of use of natural resources is involved, the increasing entropy should be kept in mind in allocating the natural resources' (Georgescu-Roegen, 1971; Daly, 1977; Boulding, 1966; Perrings, 1987).[11]

There are certain specific reasons to talk about sustainable development, distinct from development. First, already in the twentieth century, a realization has come that development is more than any individual nation's concern. It is a matter of maximizing the gains from inter-dependency between nations and factors of production. But this is not to jump to the conclusion that free trade is the right economic instrument to maximize individual country gains. This interdependency is due to the fact that – at the global level – natural resources are scarce and need to be shared over time and space. The inter-dependency arises not only because countries need to share the same natural resources, but also because the use of natural resources and man-made capital is to a large extent complementary. Given this complementarity, pure capital growth-oriented and free trade-based models of development may not hold much in store for the new century. Second, the existing economic doctrines (whichever school of thought they are drawn from) have not found a solution to the dilemma of growth with inequity (both internally and globally). Some recent writings on this are Sen and Drèze (1991), Boyce (1994) and Bardhan (1984) among others, which suggest concentrating on social, institutional and political equality rather than on economic equality. Examples of this are equality and rights in educational and health status, in gender and democratic frameworks, in social caste order structures, and better capability building and recognition of rights. But a precondition of the achievement of global and national level equality in these dimensions with growth is equality in rights in the use of the natural and environmental resources. There is a need to think on the lines of global commons (Daly and Cobb, 1989; WCED, 1987).

In the entire evolution of economic instruments for development, nowhere has a prima-facie case been made about the role of environmental and natural resources as an exclusive and inevitable fundamental resource for development. One can make some counter-arguments with citations from Jevons, Ricardo, Malthus, Marx or Pigou. It must be reckoned that in almost all the development paradigms, natural and environmental resources have been either treated under externality or as a free gift of nature and hence are valueless or have substitutions with no repercussions on growth and development.

There are a number of theoretical and empirical studies on sustainable economics, which need not be reviewed in this short chapter (Daly and Cobb, 1989; Daly, 1977; Pearce and Turner, 1989; Perrings, 1987; Chopra and Kadekodi, 1999). But some distinct features of developing such theories may be summarized. First, while a neo-classical model of development argues for a non-zero discount rate, a theory of optimal sustainable development will ask for zero discount rate (Koopmans, 1973; Pearce and Turner, 1989). On a realistic basis, if not a zero discount rate, a low rate of discount for natural resources has been argued. Second, to the extent that waste assimilation is not free (as assumed in neo-classical models), the allocation of resources for waste management will change the allocative efficiency conditions.[12] Third, the use of natural resources directly as consumption (for example, preservation benefits) will also alter the allocative efficiency of natural resources over time and space. This is the basic debate on the use of natural and environmental resources for development versus preservation (Krutilla and Fisher, 1985). Fourth, depletion of natural resources in the absence of substitutes will amount to a very high shadow price for them, making the world think totally differently.[13] Finally, sustainable development asks for a whole new institutional approach to manage the process. Among many alternatives are collective action, participatory approaches, linking private and property resources, etc (Chopra and Kadekodi, 1999).

4. MODELS OF SUSTAINABLE DEVELOPMENT FOR THE NEW CENTURY

A question can be asked at this stage: what is in store by way of theory or approaches on sustainable development for the twenty-first century? Among many possibilities, I prefer to offer some, by way of answering the question Waelbroek (1998) has raised in his survey paper. I propose the following three major propositions: (i) extending the neo-classical and/or Keynesian approach to include natural resources as a stock variable; (ii) linking the new institutional economics with a theory of sustainable development; and (iii) stretching the thermodynamic school of thought on sustainable development.

In the neo-classical tradition, what is missing are the methods and approaches to value natural resources on a global basis. As argued earlier, unless environmental and natural resources are valued on a global basis, it is not possible to develop theories of production and trade.[14] The theory of value will have to be revisited! In any case some progress has been made to date (Pearce, 1993; Howarth and Norgaard, 1992; Daly and Townsend,

*Table 16.4   Private and common property resources in India (1990–92,
'000 hectares)*

State	Operational holdings	Current fallow	Private property resources	Common property resources	Wasteland
	(1)	(2)	(1)+(2)	(3)	(4)
Andhra Pradesh	14460	2485	16945	6286	5949
Assam	3160	88	3248	1984	1592
Bihar	10900	1765	12665	5348	2582
Gujarat	10290	1039	11329	3386	4580
Haryana	3710	169	3879	187	374
Himachal Pradesh	1020	45	1065	5019	3060
Jammu & Kashmir	1010	97	1107	525	7061
Karnataka	12320	1290	13610	3661	2712
Kerala	1800	44	1844	124	165
Madhya Pradesh	22110	762	22872	14109	9186
Maharashtra	20930	869	21799	7196	7931
Meghalaya	300	59	359	732	973
Nagaland	970	118	1088	871	1032
Orissa	5300	119	5419	4547	2072
Punjab	4030	82	4112	359	378
Rajasthan	20970	1814	22784	14196	11017
Tamil Nadu	7470	1264	8734	2399	2298
Tripura	310	1	311	311	236
Uttar Pradesh	17990	1084	19074	2687	6557
West Bengal	5660	395	6055	646	505
Total	164710	13589	178299	73927	70260

Source: Centre for Monitoring the Indian Economy (1993), Statistical Abstract,
Hyderabad.

1993). It was Weitzman (1976) and subsequently several others (Hartwick,
1990) who extended the neo-classical models of resource allocation for the
maximization of welfare. In substance, their approaches amount to restat-
ing income, as an indicator of sustainable welfare or development, as:

$$Y = C + p_i \times I + p_n \times \delta N$$

where Y=income; C=consumption; I=investment on man-made capital;
N=natural resources; p_i and p_n are the shadow prices of investment and
natural resources, and δ stands for change. In other words, both man-made

capital and changes in natural capital are to be accounted for equally with appropriate shadow prices. The net welfare can be less if the change in environmental and natural resources is negative. Using the usual Harrod–Domar model of growth it can then be shown that the rate of growth of the economy (call it that of 'well-being' if you like) can be expressed as:

$$Y'/Y = [s \times Y - k_n \times N'] / [k_i \times Y]$$

where k_i and k_n are the potential incremental-capital output ratios of investment and on natural capital (preservation or regeneration) and s is the marginal propensity to save. Clearly, this growth rate is smaller than the standard Harrod–Domar growth rate. Pearce and Atkinson (1993) use a similar model to show that, in several countries of the world, the strong condition for sustainability implies negative growth rates. Their estimates, with necessary explanations, are reproduced in Table 16.5.

Alternatively, in a simplistic manner, if $D =$ an indicator of development (as a rate), $s =$ marginal propensity to save, $p =$ productivity of new investment, $n =$ rate of growth of population, and $d =$ rate of depletion (or degradation) of natural capital, then the development indicator can be expressed as:

$$D = s \times p - n - d.$$

It will not be too difficult to see the possibilities of negative development performance. All these, in brief, amount to developing a stronger theory of integrating environmental and natural resources within an economic framework. The challenges for the twenty-first century will be the valuation of natural resources, integrating these values with income accounting and deriving paths of sustainable development.

Next is the issue of the institutional framework. By now it is fairly well stated that as far as managing natural resources is concerned, the emergence of new institutional economics is extremely relevant (Ostrom, 1990; Bromley, 1991; Kadekodi, 1998b; Nabli and Nugent, 1989; Dasgupta and Maler, 1995; Berkes, 1989; Wiesbrod, 1987; Olson, 1965). The world has witnessed, to a great extent, the collapse of institutions such as the 'market' or the 'control and command-based planned system' to manage the natural resources in a sustainable way. The evolution of community-managed common property resources seems to be one answer to this problem. There are two reasons for this argument. First, a considerable amount of complementarity link exists between private and common property resources (Kadekodi, 1998b). See Table 16.4 to illustrate this in the Indian context.

Table 16.5 Sustainability indicator (%) of selected national economies

	S/Y	δ_M/Y	δ_N	Z
Sustainable economies				
Brazil	20	7	10	+3
Costa Rica	26	3	8	+15
Czechoslovakia	30	10	7	+13
Finland	28	15	2	+11
Germany (West)	26	12	4	+10
Hungary	26	10	5	+11
Japan	33	14	2	+17
The Netherlands	25	10	1	+14
Poland	30	11	3	+16
USA	18	12	4	+2
Zimbabwe	24	10	5	+9
Marginally sustainable				
Mexico	24	12	12	0
The Philippines	15	11	4	0
Unsustainable				
Burkina Faso	2	1	10	−9
Ethiopia	3	1	9	−7
Indonesia	20	5	17	−2
Madagascar	8	1	16	−9
Malawi	8	7	4	−3
Mali	−4	4	6	−14
Nigeria	15	3	17	−5
Papua New Guinea	15	9	7	−1

Notes:
S = national saving; Y = national income; δ_M = the depreciation rate on man-made capital; δ_N = the depreciation rate on and damage to natural resources and the environment; Z = sustainability indicator. These indicators, however, do not take into account the complementarity between natural resources and man-made capital. While S/Y represents the standard economic indicator of sustainability, Z represents the net effect of environmental degradation.
Source: Reprinted from *Ecological Economics*, **8**, D.W. Pearce and G.D. Atkinson, 'Capital Theory and the Measurement of Sustainable Development: An Indicator of Weak Sustainability', 103–108, 1993, with permission from Elsevier Science.

Second, following Sen (1989) among many alternatives, collective choice on a participatory basis is more stable.

But the theory of collective action requires some thinking on the deployment of labour and the presence of private property resources (as a motivation for managing common property resources). Since collective labour is not the same as wage labour, there is a need to have a model of wage determination for labour deployed for managing private property resources as well as rewards for collective labour. Consider the following type of specification:

$$Y = F[\,P \times f(L_r),\, R,\, L_p\,]$$

where Y = output, P = private property resource, R = common property resource, and L_p and L_r are the labour employment on private property resources and on common property resources, respectively. The community labour plays the role of technical efficiency in using private resources more effectively. Following Uzawa-type models of technical change, it will be possible to arrive at the optimal levels of community participation (or the optimal size of the collective group), and the rewards in the form of royalty or surplus value. Some issues of this new institutional option are not available to be addressed by social scientists. First, there is a question of size of the collective group. Should it be a function of demographic pressure (say, level of poverty) or driven by resource constraints, or by CPR–PPR linkages? Olson (1965), Ostrom (1990) and Kadekodi (1998b) are attempts to arrive at some clues. Second, there is a question of finding a good (non-dictatorial) leadership. The role of leadership within the collective group, however, can not be easily valued, but it is a must. This aspect of collective action is much less studied, but is certainly of great research interest for the coming century. Third, in order to sustain such an institution over generations (unlike the market), the interest in common property resources must persist within the group over generations.

Finally, I raise the issue of treating environmental and natural resources within a bio-energy (or bio-economic) system. Superimposing the laws of physics (for example, thermodynamics, gravitation, expression for energy, input–output system, velocity or relativity) and biology (for example, mutation, evolution) is nothing new in economics. While many such physical laws have found some roots in the development of basic economic theories, recognition of natural and environmental resources as complementary to all other factors of production is not fully understood by economists. Standard economic models of production are based on the theory of substitution only. This characterization of a production process has run into several problems. Some of the notable ones are the treatment of resources as scarce (and hence commanding a price) rather than non-renewable or non-replaceable; resource use leading to generation of waste (whose free disposal is not easy); and the use of natural resources in the production of man-made capital (such as use of iron ore to make steel and subsequently a tractor) demanding more natural resources such as water and soil (an act of indirect complementarity). Therefore, instead of setting production as value added by the factors of production, it should be treated as transformation of resources into useful products and waste products. Because of this joint nature of the production process, waste generation can not be set aside as an externality problem. Furthermore, the waste assimilation capacity should enter along with man-made capital and natural capital as another factor of input.

$$Y = F \text{ [man-made capital, natural capital, waste assimilation capacity or capital, labour].}$$

Natural capital resources are complementary to man-made capital. Waste assimilation capacity is complementary to labour as well as man-made capital. Daly (1997) draws the attention to a puzzle for economists with such a production specification in mind. How to define marginal productivities of man-made capital or labour in the presence of such complementarities, wherein natural capital or waste assimilation capacities are assumed to be constants (as givens, which is an incorrect assumption)? Some answer to this has emerged from the works of Pearce (1988). According to his results, it is possible to derive the marginal costs of production as well as of waste generation starting from the production levels at which the waste assimilation is set at a floor level. There will be a contour of cost curves corresponding to different and changing levels of waste assimilation capacities. Pearce then suggests using the total marginal costs along with the marginal revenue of the production processes to derive the optimal levels of production. The foregoing discussion is meant to suggest that the problem of non-substitutability between man-made and natural capital should be taken much more seriously. Also the fact that waste generation is an inevitable result of any production and consumption processes should be taken as a warning for human societies to have indicators of balancing between these two, for better allocation and use of natural resources.

Rethinking development as sustainable development is the challenge for the coming years.

NOTES

1. One can also add here that the neo-classical models based on scarcity and economic instruments of 'market and substitution possibilities' are also not well placed in dealing with natural resources. I will not take up this hypothesis in any substantial way in this chapter, but reserve it for another paper. But some comments on these lines are made in sections 2 and 3 of this paper.

2. In the framework of community participation and collective action most of the instruments Sen suggested are possible. See Kadekodi (1998a,b).
3. While quoting J.B. Say, he was quite aware of nature as having the unique productive power, which is not paid for. To quote Say: 'The earth, as we have already seen, is not the only agent of nature which has a productive power; but it is the only one, or nearly so, that one set of men take to themselves, to the exclusion of others; and of which, consequently, they can appropriate the benefits. The waters of rivers, and of the sea, by the power which they have of giving movement to our machines, carrying our boats, nourishing our fish, have also a productive power; the wind which turns our mills, and even the heat of the sun, work for us; but happily no one has yet been able to say, the wind and the sun are mine, and the service which they render must be paid for.' (J.B. Say: *Traite d'Economie politique*, vol. III, p. 124.)
4. Other notable paradigms are the Schumpeterian model of development with technological evolution, the Keynesian model of public intervention, Preobrazhensky's (1926) model for Russia, Mahalanobis's model of a planned economy, the structuralist approach to economic development (Syrquin, 1989) and so on.
5. The Marxist solution to this problem is an institutional approach through class power and class alliances, which is outside of typical economic theory. I will return to the institutional approaches later in this chapter.
6. For a discussion on this in the Indian context, see Chakravarty (1987).
7. Being a much discussed topic in the literature, further elaboration on this is not made here.
8. An inverted U-shaped relationship between them is proposed, on which not much empirical evidence is available. I will return to this issue later in this chapter.
9. See the models of Hotelling (1931) in competitive and monopoly market situations, El Serafy (1989) for depletable resources and a comprehensive theoretical book by Dasgupta and Heal (1979). Under the Climate Change Convention, no specific agreement has taken place on the valuation of natural resources on a global basis.
10. There are three observations to be made here. First, even to apply Heckscher–Ohlin theory, the factor price of natural resources will have to be the same between trading countries, which is not the case in the real world. Second, the depletion and degradation of natural and environmental resources amounts to an inter-generational loss of equity, uncompensated. Third, many natural resources even today are priceless! See Anderson and Blackhurst (1992).
11. Even recycling as an option is going to be much more energy and natural resource intensive. Therefore, only a long-term view on the use of natural resources can reduce the entropy.
12. Even defensive expenses against pollution will reduce resources for legitimate private consumption expenditure.
13. See Dasgupta and Heal (1979). This is the kind of problem that has come up in development debate regarding climate change (due to ozone depletion).
14. There is a school of thought which makes a case for environmental and natural resources to be valued on a local, regional, national and global basis. This argument can be useful for designing production processes at the project level. But, for developing a comprehensive theory for trade being a factor of production, it is necessary to have a unique set of global prices.

REFERENCES

Anderson, K. and R. Blackhurst (1992), *The Greening of World Trade*, Ann Arbor: University of Michigan Press.

Arrow, K. (1963), *Social Choice and Individual Values*, 2nd edition, New York: Wiley.

Bardhan, Pranab (1984), *The Political Economy of Development in India*, Oxford: Blackwell Press.

Bardhan, Pranab (1996), 'Alternative Approaches to Development Economics', in H. Chenery and T.N. Srinivasan (eds), *Handbook of Development Economics*, Amsterdam: Elsevier Science, pp. 39–72.

Berkes, Fikret (ed.) (1989), *Common Property Resources: Ecology and Community Based Sustainable Development*, London: Belhaven Press.

Boulding, Kenneth E. (1966), 'The Economics of the Coming Spaceship Earth', in Henry Jarret (ed.), *Environmental Quality in a Growing Economy*, Baltimore: Johns Hopkins Press.

Boyce, R. (1994), 'Inequality as a Cause of Environmental Degradation', *Ecological Economics,* **11** (2), 169–78.

Bromley, D.W. (1991), *Environment and Economy: Property Rights and Public Policy*, Cambridge, MA: Basil Blackwell.

Centre for Monitoring the Indian Economy (various years), *Statistical Abstract*, Hyderabad.

Chakravarty, S. (1987), *Development Planning: The Indian Experience*, Oxford: Clarendon Press.

Chenery, H. and T.N. Srinivasan (eds) (1989), *Handbook of Development Economics*, Amsterdam: Elsevier Science.

Chopra, K. and Gopal K. Kadekodi (1999), *Operationalizing Sustainable Development*, New Delhi: Sage.

Daly, Herman (1977), *Steady State Economics*, San Francisco, CA: Freeman Press.

Daly, H.E. (1997), 'Georgescu-Roegen versus Solow/Stiglitz', *Ecological Economics*, **22** (2), 261–6.

Daly, Herman and J.B. Cobb (1989), *For the Common Good: Redirecting the Economy toward Community, the Environment, and a Sustainable Future*, Boston: Beacon Press.

Daly, H.E. and K.N. Townsend (1993), *Valuing the Earth: Economics, Ecology, Ethics*, Cambridge, MA: MIT Press.

Dasgupta, P. and J.M. Heal (1979), *Economic Theory and Exhaustible Resources*, Cambridge: Cambridge University Press.

Dasgupta, P. and Karl-Goran Maler (1995), 'Poverty, Institutions, and Environmental Resource Base', in J. Berham and T.N. Srinivasan (eds), *Handbook of Development Economics,* Vol. 3A, Amsterdam: Elsevier Science, pp. 2371–463.

Drèze, J. and Amartya Sen (1995), *India: Economic Development and Social Opportunity*, New Delhi: Oxford University Press.

El Serafy, Salah (1989), 'The Proper Calculation of Income from Depletable Natural Resources', in Y.J. Ahmed, S. El Serafy and E. Lutz (eds), *Environmental Accounting for Sustainable Development: A UNDP–World Bank Symposium*, Washington, D.C.: The World Bank.

Georgescu-Roegen, N. (1971), *The Entropy Law and the Economic Process*, Cambridge, MA: Harvard University Press.

Hardin, G. (1968), 'The Tragedy of the Commons', *Science*, **162**, 1243–8.

Hartwick, J.M. (1990), 'Natural Resources, National Accounting and Economic Depreciation', *Journal of Public Economics*, **43** (3), 291–304.

Herfindahl, O. and A.V. Kneese (1974), *Natural Theory of Natural Resources*, Columbus: Charles E. Merill.

Hotelling, Harold (1931), 'The Economics of Exhaustible Resources', *Journal of Political Economy*, **39**, 137–75.

Howarth, B. and Norgaard, R. (1992), 'Environmental Valuation Under Sustainable Development', *American Economic Review*, **82** (2), 473–7.

Jevons, H.S. (1965 edition), *The Coal Question*, 3rd ed., Augustus M. Kelley Publications.

Kadekodi, Gopal K. (1998a), 'Participatory Development in the Midst of Economic Reform Process', in M.M. Agarwal, A. Barua, S.K. Das and M. Pant (eds), *Indian Economy in Transition: Environmental and Developmental Issues*, New Delhi: Har-Anand Publishers, pp. 39–55.

Kadekodi, Gopal K. (1998b), 'Common Pool Resources: An Institutional Movement from Open Access to Common Property Resources', *Energy Resources*, **20** (2), pp.317–32.

Kakwani, N. and K. Subba Rao (1992), 'Rural Poverty in India, 1973–86', in G. K. Kadekodi and G.V.S.N. Murty (eds), *Poverty in India: Data Base Issues*, New Delhi: Vikas Publishing House, pp. 273–345.

Kaldor, N. and J.A. Mirrlees (1962), 'A New Model of Economic Growth', *Review of Economic Studies*, **XXIX**, 174–92.

Koopmans, T.C. (1973), 'Some Observations on Optimal Economic Growth and Exhaustible Resources', in H. Bos, C. Linnemann and P. de Wolff (eds), *Economic Structure and Development*, Amsterdam: North Holland Publications.

Krutilla, J.V. and A.C. Fisher (1985), *The Economics of Natural Resources*, Baltimore: Johns Hopkins University Press.

Kuznets, S. (1955), 'Economic Growth and Income Inequality', *American Economic Review*, **49** (1), 1–28.

Lal, D. (ed.) (1992), *Development Economics Volume 4*, Aldershot: Edward Elgar.

Malinvaud, A. (1992), 'The Future of Economic Planning', *The Indian Economic Review*, **XXVII**, special issue, 15–24.

Marshall, Alfred (1949 edition), *Principles of Economics*, 8th ed., London: Macmillan.

Mill, J.S. (1985 edition), *Principles of Political Economy*, London: Penguin Classics.

Nabli, M.K. and Jeffrey Nugent (1989), 'The New Institutional Economics and its Application to Development', *World Development*, **17** (9), 1333–47.

OECD (1995), *Environmental Data Compendium*, Paris: Organisation for Economic Cooperation and Development.

Olson, M. (1965), *The Logic of Collective Action: Public Goods and the Theory of Groups*, Cambridge, MA: Harvard University Press.

Ostrom, E. (1990), *Governing the Commons: The Evolution of Institutions for Collective Action*, New York: Cambridge University Press.

Pearce, David (1988), 'Optimal Price for Sustainable Development', in D. Collard, D. Pearce and D. Ulph (eds), *Economics, Growth and Sustainable Development*, London: Macmillan.

Pearce, D.W. (1993), *Economic Values and Natural World*, Cambridge, MA: MIT Press.

Pearce, D.W. and G.D. Atkinson (1993), 'Capital Theory and the Measurement of Sustainable Development: An Indicator of Weak Sustainability', *Ecological Economics*, **8** (1), 103–8.

Pearce, D. and R.K. Turner (1990), *Economics of Natural Resources and the Environment*, London: Harvester-Wheatsheaf.

Perrings, Charles (1987), *Economy and Environment: A Theoretical Essay on the Interdependence of Economic and Environmental Systems*, Cambridge: Cambridge University Press.

Pigou, A.C. (1952 edition), *The Economics of Welfare*, London: Macmillan.

Prebisch, Ralph (1951), *The Economic Development of Latin America and Its Principal Problems*, New York: United Nations for ECLA.

Preobrazhensky, E. (1965 edition), *The New Economics*, English translation, Cambridge, MA: Clarendon Press.

Ranis, G. (1989), 'Analytics of Development: Dualism', in H. Chenery and T.N. Srinivasan (eds), *Handbook of Development Economics*, Amsterdam: Elsevier Science Publication, pp. 74–91.

Say, J.B. (1841), *Traité d'Economie politique*, Paris: Guillaumin.

Scruggs, L.A. (1998), 'Political and Economic Inequality and the Environment', *Ecological Economics*, **26** (3), 259–75.

Sen, A.K. (1966), 'Peasant and Dualism with or without Surplus Labour', *Journal of Political Economy*, **74**, 425–50.

Sen, A.K. (1983), *Choice, Welfare and Measurement*, Delhi: Oxford University Press.

Sen, Amartya (1989), 'The Concept of Development', in H. Chenery and T.N. Srinivasan (eds), *Handbook of Development Economics*, Volume 1, Book 1, Amsterdam: Elsevier Science, pp. 9–26.

Sen, A. and Jean Drèze (eds) (1991), *The Political Economy of Hunger*, three books, Oxford: Clarendon Press.

Singer, H.W. (1950), 'The Distribution Gains between Investing and Borrowing Countries', *American Economic Review*, **40**, 473–85.

Smith, Adam (1981 edition), *An Inquiry into the Nature and Causes of the Wealth of Nations*, Indianapolis: Liberty Classics.

Solow, Robert (1974), 'The Economics of Resources or the Resources of Economics', *American Economic Review*, **66** (1), 1–14.

Solow, Robert (1978), 'Resources and Economic Growth', *American Economic Review*, **70** (2), 511.

Sraffa, Piero (1951), *David Ricardo: On the Principles of Political Economy and Taxation*, Volume 1, Cambridge: Cambridge University Press.

Syrquin, M. (1989), 'Patterns of Structural Change', in H. Chenery and T.N. Srinivasan (eds), *Handbook of Development Economics*, Volume 1, pp. 205–48.

Waardenburg, J.G. (1988), 'Small-Scale Leather Shoe Manufacturing in Agra: A Case Study in Small-Scale Industry in India's Development', in K.B. Suri (ed.), *Small Scale Enterprises in Industrial Development: The Indian Experience*, New Delhi: Sage Publications, pp.131–56.

Waardenburg, J.G. and P.J. Lavakare (eds) (1989), *Science Policies in International Perspective*, London: Pinter Publishers.

Waardenburg, J.G., W.L.M. Adriaansen and S.T.H. Storm (1989), 'Forty Years of Experience in Development Theory and Practice', in W.L.M. Adriaansen and J.G. Waardenburg (eds), *A Dual World Economy*, Wolters-Noordhof, Groningen: and New Delhi: Oxford University Press, pp. 7–57.

Waelbroek, J. (1998), 'Half a Century of Development Economics: A Review Based on the Handbook of Development Economics', *The World Bank Economic Review*, **12** (2), 323–52.

Weitzman, M. (1976), 'On the Welfare Significance of National Product in a Dynamic Economy', *Quarterly Journal of Economics*, **90** (1), 156–62.

Wellisz, S. (1992), 'Twenty Years of Planning in Developing Countries', in D. Lal (ed.), *Development Economics*, Volume 4, Aldershot: Edward Elgar, pp. 464–78.

Wiesbrod, B.A. (1987), 'The Management of Common Property Resources:

Collective Action as an Alternative to Privatization or State Regulation', *Cambridge Journal of Economics*, **11**, 20–34.

The World Commission on Environment and Development (WCED) (1987), *Our Common Future*, Delhi: Oxford University Press.

World Bank (1992), *World Development Report: 1992*, Oxford: Oxford University Press.

World Resources Institute (1990), *World Resources Report*, Washington, DC.

Yotopoulos, P.A. and J.B. Nugent (1976), *Economics of Development: Empirical Investigations*, New York: Harper and Row.

Index